First World War
and Army of Occupation
War Diary
France, Belgium and Germany

51 DIVISION
152 Infantry Brigade
Gordon Highlanders
6th Battalion
1 June 1916 - 30 September 1918

WO95/2868/1

The Naval & Military Press Ltd
www.nmarchive.com
Published in association with The National Archives

Published by

The Naval & Military Press Ltd

Unit 10 Ridgewood Industrial Park,

Uckfield, East Sussex,

TN22 5QE England

Tel: +44 (0) 1825 749494

www.naval-military-press.com

www.nmarchive.com

This diary has been reprinted in facsimile from the original. Any imperfections are inevitably reproduced and the quality may fall short of modern type and cartographic standards.

© Crown Copyright
Images reproduced by permission of The National Archives, London, England, 2015.

Contents

Document type	Place/Title	Date From	Date To
Heading	WO95/2868-1 6 Battalion Gordon Highlanders June 1916-Sept 1918		
Heading	51 Division 152 Brigade 1/6 Bn Gordons Highlanders 1916 June 1918 Sept From 7 Div-20 Bde		
Heading	War Diary Of 1/6 Bn. Gordon Highlanders From 1st June 1916 To 30th June 1916		
War Diary		02/06/1916	23/06/1916
Miscellaneous	152nd Infantry Brigade	01/07/1918	01/07/1918
Operation(al) Order(s)	Operation Orders No.36 by Captain W.B. Welsh Commanding 6th Gordon Highlanders. Bray.	05/06/1916	05/06/1916
Miscellaneous	Operation Order By Lieut Colonel J. Dawson D.S.O. Commanding 6th Gordon Highlanders in the Field 12th June 1916	12/06/1916	12/06/1916
Miscellaneous	Operation Orders by Lieut Colonel J. Dawson D.S.O. Commanding Snipe in the Field 17th June 1916	17/06/1916	17/06/1916
Miscellaneous	Operation Orders by Lieut Colonel J. Dawson D.S.O. Commanding 6th Gordon Highlanders in the Field 23rd June 1916	23/06/1916	23/06/1916
Miscellaneous	Operation Orders By Lieut Colonel J. Dawson D.S.O. Commanding 6th Gordon Highlanders Bray 28th June 1916	28/06/1916	28/06/1916
Heading	152nd Brigade 51st Division 1/6th Battalion The Gordon Highlanders July 1916		
Heading	War Diary Of 1/6th Bn. Gordon Highrs July 1916		
War Diary	In The Field	01/06/1916	31/06/1916
Miscellaneous	Operation Orders By Lieut Colonel J. Dawson D.S.O. Commanding 6th Gordon Highlanders Bois Des Alleux 11th July 1916	11/07/1916	11/07/1916
Miscellaneous	Operation Orders By Lieut Colonel J. Dawson D.S.O. Commanding 6th Gordon Highlanders Longuevilette 20th July 1916	20/07/1916	20/07/1916
Miscellaneous	Table A		
Miscellaneous	Table B		
Miscellaneous	O/C Company Lewis Gun Officer Transport Officer	12/07/1916	12/07/1916
Miscellaneous	Operation Orders By Lieut Colonel J. Dawson D.S.O. Commanding 6th Gordon Highlanders in the Field 14th July 1916	14/07/1916	14/07/1916
Miscellaneous	Operation Orders By Lieut Colonel J. Dawson D.S.O. Commanding 6th Gordon Highlanders ACQ 15th July 1916	15/07/1916	15/07/1916
Miscellaneous	Copy Of Letter Received by Lieut/Colonel J. Dawson D.S.O. from Brig General W.C. Ross, lately Commanding 152nd Brigade.	14/07/1916	14/07/1916
Heading	152nd Brigade 51st Division 1/6th Battalion Gordon Highlanders August 1916		
War Diary	In The Field	01/08/1916	31/08/1916
Miscellaneous	152nd Infantry Brigade	05/09/1916	05/09/1916
Miscellaneous	Patrol Report	05/08/1916	05/08/1916

Operation(al) Order(s)	Operation Order No. 52 By Lieut Colonel J. Dawson D.S.O. Commanding 6th Gordon Highlanders Betaincourt 10th August 1916	10/08/1916	10/08/1916
Operation(al) Order(s)	Operation Order No. 53 By Lieut Colonel J. Dawson D.S.O. Commanding 6th Gordon Highlanders Blaringhem 17th August 1916	17/08/1916	17/08/1916
Operation(al) Order(s)	Operation Order No. 54 By Lieut Colonel J. Dawson D.S.O. Commanding 6th Gordon Highlanders In The Field 25th August 1916	25/08/1916	25/08/1916
Heading	War Diary Of 1/6th Battn. Gordon Highlanders From 1st September 1916 To 30th September 1916		
War Diary	Near Armentieres	01/09/1916	19/09/1916
War Diary	Near Bailleul	20/09/1916	30/09/1916
War Diary	Near Armentieres	15/09/1916	23/09/1916
War Diary	Near Bailleul	25/09/1916	30/09/1916
Miscellaneous	Memorandum	30/09/1916	30/09/1916
Operation(al) Order(s)	Operation Orders No.55 by Lieut/Colonel J. Dawson, D.S.O. Commanding 6th Gordon Highlanders In-the-Field, 4th Septr 1916	04/09/1916	04/09/1916
Operation(al) Order(s)	Operation Orders No.56 by Lieut. Colonel J. Dawson, D.S.O. Commanding Snipe, In-the-Field, 14th September 1916	14/09/1916	14/09/1916
Map	Map		
Heading	War Diary Of 1/6th Battn. The Gordon Highlanders From 1st October 1916 To 31st October 1916		
War Diary	In The Field	01/10/1916	31/10/1916
Operation(al) Order(s)	Operation Orders No.60 by Lieut/Colonel J. Dawson, D.S.O. Commdg 6th Gordon Highlanders. Bailleul. 29th Septr 1916	29/09/1916	29/09/1916
Operation(al) Order(s)	Operation Order No. 61 By Lieut Colonel J. Dawson D.S.O. Commanding 6th Gordon Highlanders Longuevillette 1st October 1916	01/10/1916	01/10/1916
Operation(al) Order(s)	Operation Order No. 62 By Lieut Colonel J. Dawson D.S.O. Commanding 6th Gordon Highlanders in the Field 4th October 1916	04/10/1916	04/10/1916
Operation(al) Order(s)	Operation Order No. 63 By Lieut Colonel J. Dawson D.S.O. Commanding 6th Gordon Highlanders Louvencourt 11th October 1916	11/10/1916	11/10/1916
Operation(al) Order(s)	Operation Order No. 64 By Lieut Colonel J. Dawson D.S.O. Commanding 6th Gordon Highlanders Bus Des Artois 16th October 1916	16/10/1916	16/10/1916
Miscellaneous	Operation Orders By Lieut Colonel J. Dawson D.S.O. Commanding 6th Gordon Highlanders Forceville 21st October 1916	21/10/1916	21/10/1916
Operation(al) Order(s)	Operation Orders No.66 by Lieut. Colonel J. Dawson, D.S.O. Commanding 6th Gordon Highlanders Forceville 29th Octr 1916	29/10/1916	29/10/1916
Operation(al) Order(s)	Operation Orders No.67 by Lieut. Colonel J. Dawson, D.S.O. Commanding 1/6th Bn. Gordon Highlanders Forceville 30th Octr 1916	30/10/1916	30/10/1916
Heading	War Diary Of 1/6th Battn. The Gordon Highlanders November 1916		
War Diary	In The Field	01/11/1916	30/11/1916
Operation(al) Order(s)	Operation Order No. 68 By Lieut Colonel J. Dawson D.S.O. Commanding 6th Gordon Highlanders Forceville 9th November 1916	09/11/1916	09/11/1916

Operation(al) Order(s)	Operation Order No. 69 By Lieut Colonel J. Dawson D.S.O. Commanding 6th Gordon Highlanders In the Field 11th November 1916	11/11/1916	11/11/1916
Operation(al) Order(s)	Operation Order No. 70 By Lieut Colonel J. Dawson D.S.O. Commanding 6th Gordon Highlanders Mailly Wood 18th November 1916	18/11/1916	18/11/1916
Operation(al) Order(s)	Operation Order No. 71 By Lieut Colonel J. Dawson D.S.O. Commanding PUFF in the Field 22nd Nov 1916	22/11/1916	22/11/1916
Operation(al) Order(s)	Operation Order No. 72 By Lieut Colonel J. Dawson D.S.O. Commanding 6th Gordon Highlanders Forceville 26th Novr 1916	26/11/1916	26/11/1916
Heading	War Diary Of 1/6th Battn. The Gordon Highlanders From 1st December 1916 To 31st December 1916		
War Diary	Bouzincourt	01/12/1916	03/12/1916
War Diary	Near Aveluy	03/12/1916	09/12/1916
War Diary	Courcelette	09/12/1916	16/12/1916
War Diary	Near Ovillers	16/12/1916	16/12/1916
War Diary	Bouzincourt	16/12/1916	21/12/1916
War Diary	Near Aveluy	21/12/1916	31/12/1916
Operation(al) Order(s)	Operation Orders No.73 By Major J.W. Adams. Commanding 6th Gordon Highlanders. Bouzincourt. 2nd December 1916	02/12/1916	02/12/1916
Operation(al) Order(s)	Operation Orders No.74 by Major J.W. Adams. Commanding 6th Gordon Highlanders. near Aveluy. 8th Decr 1916	08/12/1916	08/12/1916
Miscellaneous	Table Of Reliefs Issued With Operation Orders No.76		
Miscellaneous	Warning Order by Major J.W. Adams Comdg 6th Gordon Highlanders near Aveluy 7th Decr 1916	07/12/1916	07/12/1916
Operation(al) Order(s)	Operation Orders No.75 by Major J.W. Adams. Commanding 6th Gordon Highlanders. Bouzincourt. 20th December 1916	20/12/1916	20/12/1916
Operation(al) Order(s)	Operation Orders No.76 by Major J.W. Adams. Commanding 6th Gordon Highlanders. In-the-Field. 26th December 1916	26/12/1916	26/12/1916
Operation(al) Order(s)	Operation Orders No.77 by Major J.W. Adams. Commanding 6th Gordon Highlanders. In-the-Field. 31st December 1916	31/12/1916	31/12/1916
Heading	War Diary Of 1/6th Bn. The Gordon Highlanders From 1st January 1917 To 31st January 1917		
War Diary	Front Line	01/01/1917	02/01/1917
War Diary	Ovillers Huts	02/01/1917	03/01/1917
War Diary	Bouzincourt	03/01/1917	07/01/1917
War Diary	Bruce Huts	08/01/1917	12/01/1917
War Diary	Bouzincourt	12/01/1917	13/01/1917
War Diary	Raincheval	13/01/1917	14/01/1917
War Diary	Bois Bergues	14/01/1917	15/01/1917
War Diary	Yvrench	15/01/1917	16/01/1917
War Diary	Hautvillers	16/01/1917	31/01/1917
Miscellaneous	A Form Messages And Signals.		
Heading	War Diary Of 1/6th Bn. Gordon Highlanders From 1st February 1917 To 28th February 1917		
War Diary	Hautvillers	01/02/1917	05/02/1917
War Diary	Gapennes	05/02/1917	06/02/1917
War Diary	Buire Au Bois	06/02/1917	07/02/1917
War Diary	Framecourt	07/02/1917	08/02/1917
War Diary	Grlencourt	08/02/1917	09/02/1917

War Diary	Hermin	09/02/1917	10/02/1917
War Diary	Ecoivres	10/02/1917	11/02/1917
War Diary	Maroeuil	11/02/1917	27/02/1917
War Diary	ACQ	27/02/1917	28/02/1917
Miscellaneous	Operation Orders And Instructions	02/02/1917	02/02/1917
Operation(al) Order(s)	Operation Orders No.86 by Lieut Colonel J. Dawson, D.S.O. Commanding 6th Gordon Highlanders. Hautvillers. 4th February 1917	04/02/1917	04/02/1917
Operation(al) Order(s)	Operation Orders No.87 by Lieut. Col. J. Dawson, D.S.O. Commanding 6th Gordon Highlanders. Gapennes. 5th February 1917	05/02/1917	05/02/1917
Operation(al) Order(s)	Operation Orders No.88 by Lieut. Colonel J. Dawson, D.S.O. Commanding 6th Gordon Highlanders. Buire-Au-Bois. 6th February 1917	06/02/1917	06/02/1917
Operation(al) Order(s)	Operation Orders No.89 by Lieut Colonel J. Dawson, D.S.O. Commanding 6th Gordon Highlanders.		
Miscellaneous	6th Gordon Highrs	06/02/1917	06/02/1917
Operation(al) Order(s)	Operation Orders No.90 by Lieut Colonel J. Dawson, D.S.O. Commanding 6th Gordon Highlanders. Orlencourt 8th February 1917	08/02/1917	08/02/1917
Operation(al) Order(s)	Operation Orders No.91 by Lieut Colonel J. Dawson, D.S.O. Commanding 6th Gordon Highlanders. Hermin 9th February 1917	09/02/1917	09/02/1917
Operation(al) Order(s)	Operation Orders No.92 by Lieut Colonel J. Dawson, D.S.O. Commanding 6th Gordon Highlanders. Ecoivres 10th February 1917	10/02/1917	10/02/1917
Operation(al) Order(s)	Operation Orders No.93 by Lieut Colonel J. Dawson, D.S.O. Commanding 6th Gordon Highlanders. Maroeuil 14th February 1917	14/02/1917	14/02/1917
Operation(al) Order(s)	Operation Orders No.94 by Lieut Colonel J. Dawson, D.S.O. Commanding 6th Gordon Highlanders. Maroeuil 16th February 1917	16/02/1917	16/02/1917
Operation(al) Order(s)	Operation Orders No.95 by Lieut Colonel J. Dawson, D.S.O. Commanding 6th Gordon Highlanders. Roclincourt trenches 19th Feb 1917	19/02/1917	19/02/1917
Operation(al) Order(s)	Operation Orders No.96 by Lieut Colonel J. Dawson, D.S.O. Commanding 6th Gordon Highlanders. Roclincourt Trenches 22nd Feb 1917	22/02/1917	22/02/1917
Miscellaneous	Special Operation Orders By Lieut Colonel J.Dawson D.S.O. Commanding 6th Gordon Highlanders ACQ 27th February 1917	27/02/1917	27/02/1917
Heading	War Diary Of 1/6th Bn. Gordon Highlanders From 1st March 1917 To 31st March 1917		
War Diary	ACQ	01/03/1917	14/03/1917
War Diary	Roclincourt	14/03/1917	17/03/1917
War Diary	Bois De Maroeuil	17/03/1917	18/03/1917
War Diary	Agnieres & Caucourt	18/03/1917	18/03/1917
War Diary	Ecoivres	22/03/1917	31/03/1917
Miscellaneous	152nd Infantry Brigade-Special Order	06/03/1917	06/03/1917
Miscellaneous	Battalion Orders by Lieut. Colonel J. Dawson, D.S.O. Commanding 6th. Gordon Highlanders. ACQ, 1st. March 1917.	01/03/1917	01/03/1917
Miscellaneous	Battalion Orders by Lieut. Colonel J. Dawson, D.S.O. Commanding 6th. Gordon Highlanders. ACQ, 2nd. March 1917	02/03/1917	02/03/1917

Miscellaneous	Battalion Orders by Lieut. Colonel J. Dawson, D.S.O. Commanding 6th. Gordon Highlanders. ACQ, 3rd. March 1917	03/03/1917	03/03/1917
Miscellaneous	Battalion Orders by Lieut. Colonel J. Dawson, D.S.O. Commanding 6th. Gordon Highlanders. ACQ, 4th. March 1917	04/03/1917	04/03/1917
Miscellaneous	Notes	04/03/1917	04/03/1917
Miscellaneous	Appendix A		
Map	Map		
Miscellaneous	Group Equipment		
Operation(al) Order(s)	Operation Orders No.98 by Lieut Colonel J. Dawson, D.S.O. Commanding 6th Gordon Highlanders. ACQ 14th March 1917	14/03/1917	14/03/1917
Operation(al) Order(s)	Operation Orders No.98 by Lieut Colonel J. Dawson, D.S.O. Roclincourt 16th March 1917	16/03/1917	16/03/1917
Operation(al) Order(s)	Operation Orders No.99 by Lieut Colonel J. Dawson, D.S.O. Commanding 6th Gordon Highlanders. Bois De Maroeuil 17th March 1917	17/03/1917	17/03/1917
Operation(al) Order(s)	Operation Orders No.100 by Lieut Colonel J. Dawson, D.S.O. Commanding 6th Gordon Highlanders. Agnieres 21st March 1917	21/03/1917	21/03/1917
Miscellaneous	Instructions For Attack Practice		
Heading	War Diary Of 1/6th Bn. Gordon Highlanders For April 1917		
War Diary	Ecoivres	01/04/1917	01/04/1917
War Diary	Bois De Maroeuil	02/04/1917	07/04/1917
War Diary	Roclincourt	08/04/1917	11/04/1917
War Diary	Ecoivres	12/04/1917	12/04/1917
War Diary	Penin	13/04/1917	16/04/1917
War Diary	Arras	16/04/1917	18/04/1917
War Diary	Trenches	17/04/1917	18/04/1917
War Diary	Arras	19/04/1917	22/04/1917
War Diary	In The Field	22/04/1917	24/04/1917
War Diary	St. Nicholas	24/04/1917	26/04/1917
War Diary	Capelle Fermont	26/04/1917	28/04/1917
War Diary	Gouy En Ternois	28/04/1917	30/04/1917
Map	Map		
Operation(al) Order(s)	Operation Order No. 101 by Lieut Colonel J. Dawson, D.S.O. Commanding 6th Gordon Highlanders. Ecoivres April 1st 1917	01/04/1917	01/04/1917
Operation(al) Order(s)	Operation Order No. 102 by Lieut Colonel J. Dawson, D.S.O. Commanding 6th Gordon Highlanders. Bois De Maroeuil 6th April 1917	06/04/1917	06/04/1917
Operation(al) Order(s)	Operation Orders No.102 by Lieut Colonel J. Dawson, D.S.O. Commanding 6th Gordon Highlanders. Bois De Maroeuil 6th April 1917	06/04/1917	06/04/1917
Miscellaneous	Assembly Orders	07/04/1917	07/04/1917
Operation(al) Order(s)	Operation Orders No.103 by Lieut Colonel J. Dawson, D.S.O. Commanding 6th Gordon Highlanders. Ecoivres, 13th April 1917	13/04/1917	13/04/1917
Miscellaneous	Trench Routine		
Miscellaneous	Trench Equipment		
Miscellaneous	List Of Battle Casualties		
Operation(al) Order(s)	Operation Orders No.105 by Lieut Colonel J. Dawson, D.S.O. Commanding 6th Gordon Highlanders. Arras 18th April 1917	18/04/1917	18/04/1917

Operation(al) Order(s)	6th Gordon Highlanders. Operation Orders No.106	22/04/1917	22/04/1917
Miscellaneous	List Of Battle Casualties	23/04/1917	23/04/1917
Operation(al) Order(s)	6th Gordon Highlanders. Operation Orders No.107	28/04/1917	28/04/1917
Miscellaneous	Instructions For Offensive Operations		
Miscellaneous	Instructions For Offensive Operations	05/04/1917	05/04/1917
Miscellaneous	Report On Recent Engagement	14/04/1917	14/04/1917
Miscellaneous	6th Battalion Highlanders	22/04/1917	22/04/1917
Miscellaneous	Instructions For Offensive Operations		
Miscellaneous	Addenda To Instructions For Offensive Operations		
Miscellaneous	Report On The 6th Gordon Highlanders	23/04/1917	23/04/1917
Map	Map		
Diagram etc	Diagram		
Heading	War Diary Of 1/6th Bn. The Gordon Highlanders May 1917		
War Diary	Gouy-En-Ternois	01/05/1917	10/05/1917
War Diary	Arras	10/05/1917	11/05/1917
War Diary	Bivouac	12/05/1917	12/05/1917
War Diary	Trenches	13/05/1917	15/05/1917
War Diary	Arras	17/05/1917	30/05/1917
War Diary	Foufflin Ricametz	30/05/1917	31/05/1917
Miscellaneous	Report On Operations Of 6th Gordon Highlanders	15/05/1917	15/05/1917
Map	Map		
Miscellaneous	Divisional H.Q.	18/05/1917	18/05/1917
Miscellaneous	Special Orders	19/05/1917	19/05/1917
Miscellaneous	152nd Infantry Brigade	28/04/1917	28/04/1917
Miscellaneous	Divisional H.Q.	18/05/1917	18/05/1917
Miscellaneous	Special Order	19/05/1917	19/05/1917
Heading	War Diary Of 1/6th Bn. The Gordon Highlanders June 1917		
War Diary	Foufflin Ricametz	01/06/1917	03/06/1917
War Diary	Heuchin	04/06/1917	04/06/1917
War Diary	Delette & Coyecque	05/06/1917	07/06/1917
War Diary	Arques	08/06/1917	08/06/1917
War Diary	Ganspette Bleu Maison	09/06/1917	21/06/1917
War Diary	Booneghem	22/06/1917	02/07/1917
War Diary	Camp "D" at A.30.Central	03/07/1917	07/07/1917
War Diary	In The Line	07/07/1917	08/07/1917
War Diary	Lederzeele	11/07/1917	23/07/1917
War Diary	St. Janster Biezen	23/07/1917	29/07/1917
War Diary	Camp "E" At A.30 Central	29/07/1917	30/07/1917
War Diary	In The Line	30/07/1917	01/08/1917
Miscellaneous	Instructions For Offensive Operations		
Miscellaneous	Appendix "A". Time Table Of Advance.		
Miscellaneous	Appendix "B". Points Of Liaison (a) On Right Flank. (b) On Left Flank.		
Miscellaneous	Appendix "C". Action Of Tanks.		
Miscellaneous	Appendix "D" Medical Arrangements.		
Miscellaneous	Appendix "E". Location And Contents Of Dumps.		
Miscellaneous	Appendix "F". Information Required.		
Miscellaneous	Appendix "G". Position Of Battalion Headquarters on "Z" Day.		
Miscellaneous	Appendix "H". Communication.		
Miscellaneous	Appendix "I". Chain Of Responsibility.		
Miscellaneous	Appendix "J"		
Miscellaneous	Instructions For Offensive Operations		
Miscellaneous	Instructions For Offensive Operations	14/07/1917	14/07/1917

Miscellaneous	Instructions For Offensive Operations	24/07/1917	24/07/1917
Miscellaneous	Instructions For Offensive Operations	17/07/1917	17/07/1917
Miscellaneous	Instructions For Offensive Operations	24/07/1917	24/07/1917
Miscellaneous	Instructions For Offensive Operations	18/07/1917	18/07/1917
Miscellaneous	Instructions For Offensive Operations		
War Diary	In The Line	01/08/1917	01/08/1917
War Diary	A.30.Central	02/08/1917	04/08/1917
War Diary	Siege Camp	05/08/1917	08/08/1917
War Diary	St. Janster Biezen	09/08/1917	29/08/1917
War Diary	In The Line	29/08/1917	31/08/1917
Miscellaneous	Past Operations Copy	07/08/1917	07/08/1917
War Diary	In The Line	01/09/1917	02/09/1917
War Diary	Canal Bank	03/09/1917	06/09/1917
War Diary	Dirty Bucket Camp	07/09/1917	20/09/1917
War Diary	Canal Bank	21/09/1917	21/09/1917
War Diary	In The Line	21/09/1917	25/09/1917
War Diary	Siege Camp	26/09/1917	29/09/1917
Miscellaneous	6th Gordon Highlanders	30/09/1917	30/09/1917
Miscellaneous	6th Gordon Highlanders	15/09/1917	15/09/1917
Heading	War Diary October 1917 6th Bn Gordon Hrs		
War Diary	In The Field	01/10/1917	01/10/1917
War Diary	Achiet-Le-Petit	02/10/1917	06/10/1917
War Diary	Durham Lines	07/10/1917	16/10/1917
War Diary	In The Trenches	17/10/1917	30/10/1917
War Diary	Dainville	31/10/1917	31/10/1917
Operation(al) Order(s)	6th Gordon Highlanders. Operation Orders No.139	27/09/1917	27/09/1917
Operation(al) Order(s)	6th Gordon Highlanders. Operation Orders No.140	05/10/1917	05/10/1917
Operation(al) Order(s)	Nasal Operation Orders No.142	18/10/1917	18/10/1917
Operation(al) Order(s)	6th Gordon Highlanders Operation Orders No.143	21/10/1917	21/10/1917
Miscellaneous	Table A		
Operation(al) Order(s)	6th Gordon Highlanders. Operation Orders No.144	30/10/1917	30/10/1917
Heading	152nd Brigade 51st Division 1/6th Battalion Gordon Highlanders November 1917		
War Diary	Dainville	01/11/1917	17/11/1917
War Diary	Rocquigny	18/11/1917	18/11/1917
War Diary	Metz	19/11/1917	20/11/1917
War Diary	British Front Line	20/11/1917	24/11/1917
War Diary	Ytres	24/11/1917	25/11/1917
War Diary	Millencourt	25/11/1917	30/11/1917
Miscellaneous	Report On Operations Carried Out By 6th Battalion The Gordon Highlanders	20/11/1917	20/11/1917
Miscellaneous	Report On The Operation Carried Out By The 6th Battalion The Gordon Highlanders	23/11/1917	23/11/1917
Miscellaneous	6th Gordon Highlanders	23/11/1917	23/11/1917
Miscellaneous	List Of Officers	20/11/1917	20/11/1917
Miscellaneous	Appendix A		
Operation(al) Order(s)	6th Gordon Highlanders. Operation Orders No.145	16/11/1917	16/11/1917
Operation(al) Order(s)	6th Gordon Highlanders. Operation Orders No.146	16/11/1917	16/11/1917
Miscellaneous	Appendix I		
Miscellaneous	Appendix II. Subject-Intelligence Arrangements.		
Miscellaneous	Appendix III. Subject-Contact Patrol and Flares.		
Miscellaneous	Appendix IV.		
Miscellaneous	Table		
Miscellaneous	Appendix V		
Miscellaneous	Appendix VI		
Operation(al) Order(s)	6th Gordon Highlanders. Operation Orders No.148	17/11/1917	17/11/1917

Miscellaneous	Appendix VII		
Operation(al) Order(s)	6th Gordon Highlanders. Operation Orders No.147	18/11/1917	18/11/1917
Operation(al) Order(s)	6th Gordon Highlanders. Operation Orders No.149	23/11/1917	23/11/1917
Operation(al) Order(s)	6th Gordon Highlanders. Operation Orders No.150	24/11/1917	24/11/1917
Miscellaneous	Supplementary Orders For Demonstration Attack	13/10/1917	13/10/1917
Miscellaneous	Orders For Demonstration Attack		
Diagram etc	Diagram		
War Diary	Millencourt	30/11/1917	30/11/1917
War Diary	Barastre	01/12/1917	01/12/1917
War Diary	Fremicourt	02/12/1917	04/12/1917
War Diary	In Trenches	04/12/1917	10/12/1917
War Diary	Fremicourt	11/12/1917	22/12/1917
War Diary	In Trenches	22/12/1917	30/12/1917
War Diary	Fremicourt	31/12/1917	31/12/1917
Heading	War Diary Of 1/6th Bn. Gordon Highrs From 1st To 31st Jan 1918		
War Diary	Fremicourt	01/01/1918	06/01/1918
War Diary	Lebucquiere	07/01/1918	17/01/1918
War Diary	Achiet-Le-Petit	18/01/1918	11/02/1918
War Diary	Lebucquiere	12/02/1918	12/02/1918
War Diary	In Trenches	12/02/1918	20/02/1918
War Diary	Fremicourt	21/02/1918	28/02/1918
Heading	51st Division 152nd Infantry Brigade 1/6th Battalion Gordon Highlanders March 1918		
Heading	War Diary Of 1/6th Gordon Highrs March 1918		
War Diary	Fremicourt	01/03/1918	01/03/1918
War Diary	In Trenches	02/03/1918	07/03/1918
War Diary	O'Shea Camp	08/03/1918	18/03/1918
War Diary	In Trenches	19/03/1918	26/03/1918
War Diary	Neuvillette	27/03/1918	29/03/1918
War Diary	Labeuvriere	29/03/1918	31/03/1918
Miscellaneous	1/6th Gordon Diary March 1918		
Miscellaneous	Account Of Operation Commencing Near Boursies	26/03/1918	26/03/1918
Heading	51st Division 152nd Infantry Brigade 1/6th Battalion The Gordon Highlanders April 1918		
Heading	War Diary Of 1/6th Battn Gordon Highlanders From 1st April 1918 To 30th April 1918		
War Diary	Labeuvriere	01/04/1918	02/04/1918
War Diary	Oblinghem	03/04/1918	03/04/1918
War Diary	Lapugnoy	04/04/1918	05/04/1918
War Diary	Ham-En Artois	06/04/1918	09/04/1918
War Diary	Busnes	14/04/1918	15/04/1918
War Diary	Witternesse	16/04/1918	30/04/1918
Miscellaneous	Strength	30/04/1918	30/04/1918
Miscellaneous	Appendix No.I. Account of Operations near Zelobes commencing on 9th April 1918 and lasting to 13th April 1918.	13/04/1918	13/04/1918
Miscellaneous	Notes on Operations near Zelobes commencing on 9th April 1918 and lasting till 13th April 1918. Appendix II.	13/04/1918	13/04/1918
Miscellaneous	Notes On Operations near Zelobes commencing on 9th April 1918 and lasting to 15th April 1918. Appendix No.III	15/04/1918	15/04/1918
Miscellaneous	6th Gordon Highlanders. Appendix No.IV	13/04/1918	13/04/1918
Miscellaneous	Appendix No.V	18/04/1918	18/04/1918
Miscellaneous	Extracts From Report On Vielle Chapelle	14/04/1917	14/04/1917

Miscellaneous	6th Gordon Highlanders. Casualties Sustained 9th-13th April 1918. Appendix No.VI	13/04/1918	13/04/1918
Operation(al) Order(s)	6th Gordon Highlanders. Operation Orders No.181	27/04/1918	27/04/1918
Operation(al) Order(s)	6th Gordon Highlanders. Operation Orders No.180	26/04/1918	26/04/1918
Operation(al) Order(s)	6th Gordon Highlanders. Operation Orders No.179	20/04/1918	20/04/1918
Operation(al) Order(s)	6th Gordon Highlanders. Operation Orders No.178	09/04/1918	09/04/1918
Operation(al) Order(s)	6th Gordon Highlanders. Operation Orders No.177	05/04/1918	05/04/1918
Operation(al) Order(s)	6th Gordon Highlanders. Operation Orders No.176	04/04/1918	04/04/1918
Operation(al) Order(s)	6th Gordon Highlanders. Operation Orders No.175	02/04/1918	02/04/1918
Heading	War Diary 1/6th Bn Gordon Highrs For May 1918		
War Diary	Witternesse	01/05/1918	05/05/1918
War Diary	Neuville St Vaast	06/05/1918	06/05/1918
War Diary	In The Line	07/05/1918	31/05/1918
Miscellaneous	Nominal Roll Of Officers		
War Diary	In The Line	01/06/1918	04/06/1918
War Diary	Ecurie Wood Camp	05/06/1918	10/06/1918
War Diary	In The Line	11/06/1918	21/06/1918
War Diary	Ecurie Wood Camp	22/06/1918	27/06/1918
War Diary	In The Line	28/06/1918	30/06/1918
Heading	152nd Brigade 51st (Highland) Division 1/6th Battn. Gordon Highlanders July 1918		
Miscellaneous	Herewith War Diary For Month Of July	13/08/1918	13/08/1918
War Diary	Trenches	01/07/1918	09/07/1918
War Diary	Trenches & Ecurie Wood Camp	10/07/1918	10/07/1918
War Diary	Ecurie Wood Camp & St. Michel	11/07/1918	13/07/1918
War Diary	St Michel	13/07/1918	13/07/1918
War Diary	On Train	14/07/1918	15/07/1918
War Diary	Romilly Sur-Seine	16/07/1918	17/07/1918
War Diary	Gionges	17/07/1918	17/07/1918
War Diary	Champillon Sur Marne	17/07/1918	17/07/1918
War Diary	In The Field	20/07/1918	31/07/1918
Miscellaneous	Account Of Operations	31/07/1918	31/07/1918
Miscellaneous	Notes On Operations	27/07/1918	27/07/1918
Heading	War Diary Of 6th Battalion The Gordon Highlanders For Period 1st August 1918 Volume 46 31st August 1918		
War Diary	Nanteuil Oiry	01/08/1918	02/08/1918
War Diary	Avize	03/08/1918	03/08/1918
War Diary	Caucourt	04/08/1918	17/08/1918
War Diary	Caucourt In The Line	18/08/1918	18/08/1918
War Diary	In The Line	19/08/1918	28/08/1918
War Diary	Balmoral Flanders Camps	29/08/1918	31/08/1918
Operation(al) Order(s)	6th Gordon Highlanders. Operation Orders No.202	02/08/1918	02/08/1918
Miscellaneous	Administrative Instructions	02/08/1918	02/08/1918
Operation(al) Order(s)	6th Gordon Highlanders Operations Orders No.203	14/08/1918	14/08/1918
Miscellaneous	Administrative Instructions	19/08/1918	19/08/1918
Miscellaneous	Operation Order for attack by Two Companies.	20/08/1918	20/08/1918
Miscellaneous	Administrative Arrangements For O.O No.204	20/08/1918	20/08/1918
Miscellaneous	Addendum To O.O. No.206	26/08/1918	26/08/1918
Operation(al) Order(s)	6th Gordon Highlanders Operation Order No. 206	25/08/1918	25/08/1918
Miscellaneous	Administrative Instructions	25/08/1918	25/08/1918
Miscellaneous	Nominal Roll Of Officers	30/08/1918	30/08/1918
Heading	War Diary Of 6th Battn. The Gordon Highlanders For Period 1/9/18 To 30/9/18 (Volume 47)		
Operation(al) Order(s)	6th Gordon Highlanders. Operation Orders No.208	08/09/1918	08/09/1918
War Diary	Duff Camp	01/09/1918	02/09/1918

War Diary	Trenches	03/09/1918	12/09/1918
War Diary	Chateau De La Haie	13/09/1918	22/09/1918
War Diary	Duff Camp	23/09/1918	28/09/1918
War Diary	Railway Embankment	29/09/1918	30/09/1918
Operation(al) Order(s)	Operation Order No. 207	02/09/1918	02/09/1918
Miscellaneous	Administrative Instructions	02/09/1918	02/09/1918
Miscellaneous	Corrigendum To Operation Orders No. 207	03/09/1918	03/09/1918
Operation(al) Order(s)	6th Gordon Highlanders. Operation Orders No.210	22/09/1918	22/09/1918
Miscellaneous	Administrative Instructions	22/09/1918	22/09/1918
Miscellaneous	Amendment To Operation Order No. 211	20/09/1918	20/09/1918
Operation(al) Order(s)	6th Gordon Highlanders. Operation Orders No.211	28/09/1918	28/09/1918
Miscellaneous	Administrative Instructions	28/09/1918	28/09/1918

① WO 95/2868

6 Battalion Gordon Highlanders
June 1916 – Sept 1918

51 DIVISION

152 BRIGADE

1/6 BN GORDONS HIGHLANDERS

1916 JUNE – 1918 SEPT

FROM 7 DIV – 20 BDE

1/6 & 1/7 BNS AMALGAMATED AND FROM 1918 OCT KNOWN AS 6/7 BN 152 BDE

152nd Inf. B'de.
SECRET   134

WAR DIARY.

of

1/6th Bn. GORDON HIGHLANDERS.

From 1st June, 1916.

to

30th June 1916.

CONFIDENTIAL.

Army Form C. 2118

WAR DIARY
INTELLIGENCE SUMMARY
(Erase heading not required.)

Instructions regarding War Diaries and Intelligence Summaries are contained in F. S. Regs., Part II. and the Staff Manual respectively. Title Pages will be prepared in manuscript.

Place	Date	Hour	Summary of Events and Information	Remarks and references to Appendices
			1/6th Bn. The Gordon Highlanders. (T.F.)	
	June 1.		Left GRAND RULLECOURT and marched to BRAY.	
	" 2-5.		In Billets at BRAY.	
	" 6-11.		Occupied Trenches E. of Neuville St. Vaast -[Sector Left One - 0.62 -P.73 Trench Maps ROCLINCOURT A,4,c,90,85 to GIVENCHY S,28,o,4,10.] 1/5th Gordon Highrs. on our Right and 1/8th Argyle & Sutherland Highrs. on Left - took over from 1/5th Seaforth Highrs.	
	" 12-17.		In Brigade Reserve occupying Dug-outs near Neuville St. Vaast - relieved by 1/5th Seaforth Highlanders.	
	" 18-23.		Re-occupied Trenches held from 6th-11th - took over from 1/5th Seaforth Highrs.	
	" 24-27.) " 28-30.)		In Divisional Reserve) Billets at BRAY. ") " ST ELOY.	
	17		During the month 7 Officers joined the Battalion from the United Kingdom	
	23		Draft of 60 Other Ranks joined Battalion from U.K.	
			" " 104 " " " " "	

In-the-Field,
30th June 1916.

Joe Dawson Lieut. Colonel,
Commanding 1/6th Gordon Highlanders.

152nd Inf. Bde. SECRET No. 134.

Headquarters,

152nd Infantry Brigade.

I send herewith War Diary for June, 1916, for Battalion under my Command.

J.A.Dawson Lieut. Colonel,

Comdg. 1/6 th Batt̃n. Gordon Highrs

1st July, 1916.

SECRET
Copy No......

Operation Orders No 36.
by
Captain W. B. Welch,
Commanding 6th Gordon Highlanders.
BRAY, 5th June, 1916.

Map Reference 1/40.000 Sheet 51 B
Trench Map 1/10.000 36 b S.E. 4, 36 c S.W. 3.

1. OPERATION:
   On the night of the 6th/7th June, the 6th Battalion Gordon Highlanders will relieve the 5th Battalion Seaforth Highlanders in the trenches in the right sub-sector.
   O/C Companies will move to LA TARGETTE cross roads A 8 a 65 independently.

2. STARTING POINT:
   Os/C Companies will arrange to pass the Starting Point, in this case the Alarm Post, at the times stated below.
   Companies will move by Platoons at intervals of not less than 200 yards
   "A" Company   1st platoon to pass Starting Point at 8.15 p.m
   "B" Company   do.   8.30 p.m
   "C" Company   do.   8.45 p.m
   "D" Company   do.   9 p.m.
   Battalion Headquarters will accompany the 1st Platoon.

3. GUIDES:
   Platoon guides will be at LA TARGETTE cross roads at 9 p.m.

4. MACHINE GUNS:
   Machine Gunners will move into the trenches during the afternoon under arrangements made by M.G. Officer.

5. SIGNALLERS:
   Signallers will parade at 2.15 p.m. Guides will be at LA TARGETTE cross roads at 3 p.m.

6. EQUIPMENT:
   Each man will carry 120 rounds S.A.A., 1 day's rations in addition to the iron ration, and a full waterbottle.

7. REPORTS:
   Completion of all reliefs will be immediately reported to Battalion Headquarters.

8. TRANSPORT:
   Transport and Quartermaster Store will not move from BRAY.

Mathieson Capt. & Adj.
6th Gordon Highlanders.

Copy No 1. Adjutant
       2. O/C "A"
       3. " "B"
       4. " "C"
       5. " "D"
       6. M.G. Officer
       7. Grenade Officer
       8. Transport Officer and Quartermaster
       9. R.S.M. for Details
      10. O/C 5th Seaforth Highlanders.

Operation Orders by Lieut Colonel J Dawson, DSO
Commanding 6th Gordon Highlanders
In the Field, 12th June 1916.

1. The Battalion will be relieved to-night by 5th Seaforth Highlanders and proceed to Brigade Reserve.
    (a) Headquarters, "A" Coy & Lewis Gunners NEUVILLE ST VAAST
    (b) "B" Coy near present Battalion Headquarters in POND STREET
    (c) "C" Coy near BIRMINGHAM DUMP.
    (d) "D" Coy in the PYLONES.

2. "C" & "D" Companies will be at the disposal of OC left sub-sector.
    "B" Company will be at disposal of OC right sub-sector.
    OsC these Companies will report on arrival to these OC sub-sectors and receive instructions.

3. When each platoon is relieved it will be led by its guide to its new quarters.

4. Duplicate inventories of Trench Stores are to be now prepared.

5. Note of work contemplated or at present in hand to be given to relieving officers.

6. Steel Helmets, Vigilant & Lifeguard periscopes, telescopic rifles, camp kettles are to be taken out by the Companies.

7. Headquarters, "A" & "B" Companies, & Lewis Gunners' rations will be dumped at the usual place.
    "C" & "D" Companies' at BIRMINGHAM DUMP.
    Companies will provide their own ration parties.

8. In future, dinners will be cooked near Company quarters.

9. When reliefs are completed intimation will be sent to present Battalion Headquarters, & when new positions are occupied, reports to this effect are to be sent to Sub-sector Headquarters, and to Battalion Headquarters in NEUVILLE ST VAAST.

Atkinson Capt & Adj
6th Gordon Highlanders.

Copy No. 1

Operation Orders by Lieut. Colonel J. Dawson. DSO
Commanding 6n/6
In the Field. 17th June 1916

1. Operations:

The Companies will take over from 5th Seaforth Highlanders on 18.6.16, the same sections of the line as they previously held.

2. Routes:

All reliefs will take place by platoons.

(a) "C" Company moving by GOODMAN TRENCH will have its first platoon in the lines at 5.30 p.m.

(b) "D" Company will follow the last platoon of "C".

(c) "B" Company moving by POND STREET will have its first platoon in the lines at 5.30 p.m.

(d) "A" Company moving by LA FOURCHE will have its first platoon in the lines at 5.30 p.m.

3. Guides:

One man per platoon will be told off to guide back the relieved platoon. As "A" & "B" Companies 5th Seaforths are returning to billets of "B" & "A" Companies 6th Gordons, the guides of our "B" Company will attach themselves to platoons of "A" Company, and vice versa, before the Companies move off.

4. Dispositions:

O's/C or Seconds in Command B, C, & D Companies will report at 2 p.m. to 5th Seaforths B, C, & D Company Headquarters and learn new dispositions, visiting the fronts affected.

5. Lewis Guns & Grenade

Lewis Gun and Grenade Officers will get in touch with corresponding Seaforth Officers, ascertain present situation, and arrange time of relief.

6. Work Programme

Strict attention must be paid to programme of work handed over, and men must be detailed to carry on at once.

J. Henshaw Capt & Adj
6th Gordon Highlanders.

Copy No. 1

Operation Orders by Lieut Colonel J. Dawson, DSO.
Commanding 6th Gordon Highlanders
In the Field. 23rd June 1916.

Map Reference - France 51 B & C 1/40.000.

1. <u>Operations</u>.

The 1/6th Gordon Highlanders will be relieved in the trenches by the 1/5th Seaforth Highlanders on the evening of the 24th instant. The first platoons 5th Seaforths will reach their positions by 5.30 p.m. On relief the following moves will take place.

(a) The Battalion will move by platoons into Brigade Reserve about NEUVILLE ST VAAST, being distributed as follows:-

Headquarters and A Company in NEUVILLE ST VAAST

B Company near Battalion Headquarters left one subsector.

C Company near L 2 Battalion Headquarters at BIRMINGHAM DUMP.

D Company PYLONES.

(b) On the arrival of the first platoon of the Companies of the 8th Argyle & Sutherland Highlanders at the above mentioned places Companies will move off by platoons to BRAY.

2. <u>Routes</u>:

On relief by 1/5th Seaforths Companies will move to their new positions by the following routes :-

A Company :- DE LA FOURCHE Trench and PARALLEL VIII

B Company :- POND STREET.

C and D Companies GOODMAN TRENCH.

3. <u>Lewis Guns</u>.

Lewis Guns will be relieved under arrangements to be made by the respective Lewis Gun Officers.

II.

4. **Periscopes &c.**

All periscopes, Very Pistols, and Telescopic Rifles, which are Battalion property, are to be taken out.

5. **Transport:**

Machine Gun limbers and one other limber will be at the Cookhouse at 11 p.m.

6. **Ration Party:**

O/C B Company will detail a party to carry up the rations of the 5th. Seaforth Highlanders. These rations will be up at the usual time.

7. **Battalion Headquarters:**

On completion of relief by the 5th Seaforths, Battalion Headquarters will move to the PORTIQUE in NEUVILLE St VAAST

8. **Reports.**

Os/C Companies will report their relief in the front line and their arrivals in billets at BRAY.

9. **Billets**

The Quartermaster will arrange for billets in BRAY.

Atkinson — Capt & Adj.
6th Gordon Highlanders.

Copy No 1   Adjutant
     2   O/C A
     3   " B
     4   " C
     5   " D
     6   Lewis Gun Officer
     7   O/C 5th. Seaforths
     8   " 8th. A & S.H.
     9   Quartermaster & Transport Officer
    10   R.S.M.

Operation Orders by Lieut/Colonel J. Dawson, D.S.O.
Commanding 6th Gordon Highlanders
BRAY, 28th June, 1916.

----

1. **MOVE:**

    The Battalion will move to new billets in the BOIS DES ALLEUX to-day by Companies.   Companies will move off at the following times:-

    "D" Company   12 noon (Dinners before starting)
    "B" Company   2.30 p.m.
    "C" Company   3 p.m.
    "A" Company   3.30 p.m.
    Headquarters)
    Lewis Gunners) 4 p.m.

2. **BILLETS:**

    All billets and surroundings are to be left scrupulously clean.   A certificate to this effect will be handed in to Orderly Room before Companies move off.

3. **BAGGAGE:**

    Officers' kits and baggage will be ready for loading by 2 p.m.

                                                      Capt. & Adj.
                                      6th Gordon Highlanders.

Copy No 1   Adjutant
       2   O/C "A"
       3   " "B"
       4   " "C"
       5   " "D"
       6   L.M.G. Officer
       7   Quartermaster & Tpt. Officer
       8   R.S.M.

152nd Brigade.

51st Division.

1/6th BATTALION

THE GORDON HIGHLANDERS.

JULY 1916

Battalion Operation Orders attached.

Vol 21

152nd Brigade SECRET
No. 134.

WAR DIARY
of
1/6th Bn. Gordon Highrs.

JULY, 1916.

1/6 GORDON HIGHS.

Army Form C. 2118

WAR DIARY
or
INTELLIGENCE SUMMARY

(Erase heading not required.)

Instructions regarding War Diaries and Intelligence Summaries are contained in F. S. Regs., Part II. and the Staff Manual respectively. Title Pages will be prepared in manuscript.

Place	Date	Hour	Summary of Events and Information	Remarks and references to Appendices
In the field	1–6		In trenches E. of NEUVILLE ST VAAST (Sectn LEFT I) (5th GORDON HRS RIGHT ; 8th ARGYLL & SUTHERLAND HRS LEFT)	
	7–12		In billets at ST ELOY and BOIS DES ALLEUX.	
	13–14		NEUVILLE ST VAAST between marching & fatigues.	
	15		In billets at SUS ST LEGER	
	16–19		" " LONGUEVILLETTE	
	20		" " BUIRE	
	21–22		Bivouac " BOTTOM COPSE, E. of FRICOURT	
	22–23		" " W. of FRICOURT	
	23–24		" " MÉCORDEL – BECOURT	
	25		" at CATERPILLAR WOOD	
	26–31		" " MAMETZ WOOD.	

Graham Will
1/6 Gordon High[rs]

Copy No. 1

Operation Orders by Lieut/Colonel J. Dawson, D.S.O.
Commanding 6th Gordon Highlanders,
BOIS DES ALLEUX, 11th July, 1916.

- - - - - oOo - - - - -

Map Reference 1/40,000 Sheets 51 B. and C.

1. **OPERATION:**
    The 6th Battalion Gordon Highlanders will take over the Mining Fatigues in left section from 2/15th London Regiment on night 12/13th July.

2. **BILLETS:**
    "B" and "C" Companies, together with 60 men from "A" Company will be billeted in NEUVILLE ST VAAST.
    "A" Company less 60 men and "D" Company will be billeted at AUX REITZ.

3. **FATIGUES:**
    Fatigues will be found by Companies in accordance with the attached Tables A. and B. They will be found by Companies as from the evening 12th July.

4. **SPECIALISTS:**
    All Specialists, with the exception of Signallers, Cycle orderlies, and S.Bs. will rejoin their Companies.
    The Lewis Gunners of "B" Company will be kept separate, and remain under the command of the L.G.O.

5. **NEUVILLE DEFENCES:**
    While the Battalion is employed in Mining Fatigues it is allotted to the Neuville defences. Os/C "B" and "C" Companies, together with their platoon commanders and C.S.Ms., and Lewis Gun Officer will report at Headquarters 2/15th London Regiment by 5 p.m. 12th instant to recconoitre the defences and to inspect their billets.
    Os/C "A" and "D" Companies will send one Officer to inspect their billets at AUX REITZ.

6. **MOVES:**
    (1) Men required for the first relief will parade at 5 p.m under a supernumerary officer to be detailed by each Company. They will move to AUX REITZ and NEUVILLE by TERRITORIAL TRENCH. Officers who have gone on in advance will meet their platoons at AUX REITZ corner and guide them to their billets.
    (2) Remainder of Battalion will parade at 9.45 p.m. and move by platoons to AUX REITZ corner where platoons will be met by platoon officers.

7. **OFFICERS' KITS AND BAGGAGE:**
    All Officers' kits and baggage will be ready for loading by 8 p.m.

8. **BATTALION HEADQUARTERS:**
    Battalion Headquarters in NEUVILLE will be at WINCHESTER HOUSE in DENIS LE ROCK TRENCH.

9. **HUTS:**
    All Huts and their surroundings will be left scrupulously clean. The usual certificates will be required.

10. **OFFICERS:**
    Five officers per Company will be taken up by Companies. Names of officers proceeding to be reported to Orderly Room to-morrow morning.

Page 2.

11. <u>N.C.Os</u>. Two N.C.Os. per Company will be left behind. These N.C.Os. will be responsible for their Company huts until they are occupied.

12. <u>LEWIS GUNS</u>: Four Lewis Guns will be taken up.

13. <u>RATIONS</u>: One day's rations will be carried on the man.

                                                                Capt. & Adj.
                                            6th Gordon Highlanders.

Copy No 1   Adjutant
         2   O/C "A"
         3   " "B"
         4   " "C"
         5   " "D"
         6   L.G.O.
         7   Q.M. and Transport Officer
         8   O/C 2/15th London Regiment
         9   R.S.M.
        10   Grenade Officer.

Operation Orders by Lieut. Colonel J. Dawson D.S.O.
Commanding 1/6th Gordon Highlanders;
Longuevilette, 20th July 1916.

---

1. Battalion will move to MERICOURT by train today, entraining at CANDAS.

2. PARADE.

   Battalion will parade at 3.40 p.m. on the road opposite the Church ready to move off in the order - Head Quarters, D, A, B, C, Lewis Gunners.

   Train leaves CANDAS at 5 p.m.

3. TEAS.

   Teas will be at 2.45 p.m.

4. All Billets must be left scrupulously clean. The usual Certificates as to their cleanliness will be required.

                                                    Capt. & Adj.
                                              1/6th Gordon Highlanders.

Copy No. 1   Adjutant.
        2-5 O.C. Companies.
        6   Lewis Gun Officer.
        7   Grenade Officer.
        8   R. S. M.

Table A.

Fatigues found by Coys billeted in bivouac.

No.	Coy.	No of men	Rendez vous	Kontinue Hours	Reporting to
1	B	25	Junction of Quarrie & Cross Street.	9.30 p.m. – 5.30 a.m.	142nd Coy. R.E.
2	B	25	Do.	Do.	Do.
3	B	25	Do.	Do.	Do.
4	B	24	Do.	Do.	Do.
5	B	24	Cross Street.	Do.	182nd Coy. R.E.
6 hour Guards of B Coy	Do.	20	Town Major's Office.	9 p.m. – 3 a.m.	Town Major.
7	Do.	5	Do.	9.30 p.m. – 2.30 a.m.	Do.
1	C	25	Junction of Quarrie & Cross Street.	5.30 a.m. – 1.30 p.m.	142nd Coy. R.E.
2	C	25	Do.	Do.	Do.
3	C	25	Do.	Do.	Do.
4	C	24	Do.	Do.	Do.
8	A	12	Cross Street.	Do.	182nd Coy. R.E.
1	A	25	Junction of Quarrie & Cross Street.	1.30 p.m. – 9.30 p.m.	142nd Coy. R.E.
2	C	25	Do.	Do.	Do.
3	B	25	Do.	Do.	Do.
4	½ A ½ B	10	Do.	Do.	Do.
		217			
9	A	12	Hd Qrs 182nd Coy. R.E.	Do.	182nd Coy. R.E.

Table B

Fatigues found by Coy. Clerks at Aux. Ritz

	Coy.	No. of men	Rendez-vous	Working Hours	Reporting to
1st Relief {	1	A	25	Aux Ritz	10 pm – 6 am	110th Coy. R.E.
	2	A	20	Margate	Do.	Do.
	3	A	20	Do.	Do.	Do.
	4	A	1	Do.	Do.	Do.
2nd Relief {	1	A	25	Aux Ritz	6:30 am – 2:30 pm	Do.
	2	A	20	Margate	Do.	Do.
	3	A	20	Do.	Do.	Do.
	4	A	1	Do.	Do.	Do.
3rd Relief {	1	A	25	Aux Ritz	2:30 pm – 10:30 pm	Do.
	2	A	20	Margate	Do.	Do.
	3	A	20	Do.	Do.	Do.
	4	A	1	Do.	Do.	Do.

O/C " " Company,

Lewis Gun Officer,

Transport Officer.

With reference to Operation Orders of yesterday's date the following further instructions are issued:-

1. An Officer will inspect each fatigue party before it moves off, and see that it is complete.

2. Cooking will be done under Company arrangements. These arrangements must be carefully studied in order to ensure regularity.

3. Men carrying sandbags etc. will wear an empty sandbag on their shoulders to avoid damaging their tunics. This sandbag will be kept in position by means of 2 safety pins which are being issued to-day to each man.
These safety pins are to enable the gas helmet to be carried in the position of readiness, and care must therefore be taken to prevent their loss. They will be carried pinned to the inside of the satchel.

4. Guides will be provided by the 2/15th London Regiment for the first relief, but steps must be taken to ensure that the 2nd and 3rd reliefs arrive in time at their rendezvous.

5. A rough sketch map of TERRITORIAL TRENCH and the communication trenches leading to Company billets is enclosed.

Capt. & Adj.
6th Gordon Highlanders.

12.7.1916.

Copy No......

Operation Orders by Lieut/Colonel J. Dawson, D.S.O.
Commanding 6th Gordon Highlanders
In-the-Field, 14th July, 1916.

Map Reference   Sheets 1/40.000 51 B and 51 C

1. **OPERATIONS:-**
   The Battalion will move out of NEUVILLE and proceed to billets in ECOIVRES to-night.

2. **FATIGUES:-**
   The fatigues furnished by the Battalion will be taken over by the   London Regiment.

3. **MOVES:-**
   Lewis Guns will move out as soon as their limbers arrive.
   Companies will move off as follows by platoons:-
   "B" Company   11.30 p.m.
   "C"   11.45 p.m.
   "A" Detachment
      in NEUVILLE   12 midnight
   "A" Company   12.15 a.m.
   "D"   12.30 a.m.

4. **TRANSPORT:-**
   1 Limber, Lewis Gun limbers, and Mess Cart will be at the Cookhouse and AUX REITZ.

5. **GENERAL:-**   has
   If Any fatigue party not returned before the Company moves off, one officer will be left behind to bring the party on.

6.

(signed) [illegible] Capt & Adj.
6th Gordon Highlanders.

Copy No 1   Adjutant
       2   O/C "A"
       3   "   "B"
       4   "   "C"
       5   "   "D"
       6   L.G.O.
       7   R.S.M.
       8   O/C London Regiment

Copy No. 1....

Operation Orders by Lieut/Colonel J. Dawson, D.S.O.
Commanding 6th Gordon Highlanders,
ACQ, 15th July, 1916.

----

1. **OPERATIONS**

    The Battalion will move by bus to-day to new area about SUS - ST-LEGER and BEAUDRICOURT.

2. **PARADE**

    The Battalion will parade ready to move off at 11.45 a.m. Companies will reach the outskirts of ACQ from the direction of ECOIVRES not later than 11.30 a.m. where they will be met by guides and shown the parade ground.

3. **DRESS**

    Kilt aprons will not be worn, but will be carried in the pack.

4. **REFILLING POINT**

    Refilling point on the 16th instant will be on the road between LUCHEUX and GROUCHES at 9 a.m.

                                    [signature] Capt & Adj.
                                    6th Gordon Highlanders.

Copy No 1   Adjutant
       2   O/C "A"
       3   " "B"
       4   " "C"
       5   " "D"
       6   L.G.O.
       7   Quartermaster and Transport Officer
       8   R.S.M.

Copy of letter received by Lieut/Colonel J. Dawson, D.S.O.
from
Brig. General W.C.Ross, lately Commanding 152nd Brigade.

- - - - - - - - - - -

Dear Colonel Dawson,
                I regret very much that it has suddenly become necessary for me to go home, and it is not possible for me to go and say goodbye to the 6th Gordons.

                It has been unfortunate for me that circumstances have precluded my seeing the Battalion as a whole on parade during the short time I have had the honour of having the Battalion under my command. But I have seen enough of the officers and other ranks in the trenches, their manner of doing their various duties and their steadiness under fire, to convince me that the 6th Gordons of to-day are as good a Battalion in all respects as any wearing His Majesty's uniform. I am satisfied that they will always maintain under all circumstances the good repute they have already earned, and I shall always feel proud of having been associated with them even for a short time on Active Service

                I wish you and all officers and other ranks in the Battalion every possible luck, and I shall be deeply gratified if you will convey this to them.

                Yours very truly,

                    (signed) W. C. Ross, Brig. General.

14th July, 1916.

152nd Brigade.
51st Division.

1/6th BATTALION

GORDON HIGHLANDERS

AUGUST 1 9 1 6::::

SECRET
DHQ
3rd Echelon

Army Form C. 2118

WAR DIARY
INTELLIGENCE SUMMARY
(Erase heading not required.)

Instructions regarding War Diaries and Intelligence Summaries are contained in F. S. Regs., Part II. and the Staff Manual respectively. Title Pages will be prepared in manuscript.

Place	Date	Hour	Summary of Events and Information	Remarks and references to Appendices
In the field.	Aug 1916			
	1-5		Holding HIGH WOOD (K.R.R., 34th Division on left, 1/5th Seaforth Highrs on right) Enemy's positions reconnoitred and fixed; saps pushed forward and Heads connected across Wood; front wired. In the British Official Communique of 6th it stated:- "A little further progress was made by us in HIGH WOOD"	MAP FRANCE 36 NW
	6		Bivouac SOUTH side of FRICOURT WOOD. Total casualties in SOMME operations:- 23 Killed, 137 Wounded.	
	7-8		Bivouac NORTH of BUIRE	
	9		Entrain for LONGPRE, and billeted at BETTENCOURT.	
	10-11		Billeted at BETTENCOURT.	
	12-17		Billeted near BLARINGHEM	
	18-25		In Divisional Reserve at ARMENTIERES.	
	26-31		Holding Subsidiary Line of Trenches S.E. of ARMENTIERES from LEITH WALK (I.9.c.6.5.) to BUTERNE FARM (C.28.c.7.2.) (6th Black Watch on left, and 22nd Northumberland Fusiliers - Tyneside Scottish - on right.)	

31.8.1916

J. Duncan
Lieut/Colonel,
Commanding 6th Gordon Highlanders.

Headquarters,

152nd Infantry Brigade.

I send herewith War Diary for August, 1916, for Battalion under my Command.

[signature] Lieut. Col.
Comdg. 1/6th Bn. Gordon Hrs.

5. 9. 16.

PATROL REPORT - 1/6th GORDON HIGHLANDERS.   5th August, 1916.

1. At 10.30 am Patrol went out from about 30 yards along new Front Trench and one man crawled about 30 yards forward parallel to edge of wood. He was within 5 yards of barbed wire interlaced from cut saplings. The trench was 15 yards behind the wire and from 20 to 30 yards behind this another trench was seen. No wire apparent but difficult to see. Three men with steel helmets (flat on top and not sloping like ours) walked along trench. The men's heads were above parapet.

At 10 am

2. An Officer and 2 men left sap 3 behind the German Field Gun pit next our lines and went forward to another pit directly in front. About 30 yards away a sap running along the right front was seen. No wire apparent. Unfortunately a German (wearing British helmet) saw the party and moved down sap. He pretended not to have seen the men but knowing they were "spotted" the men began to crawl back. Before they had gone far about half a dozen shots were fired at them from the sap

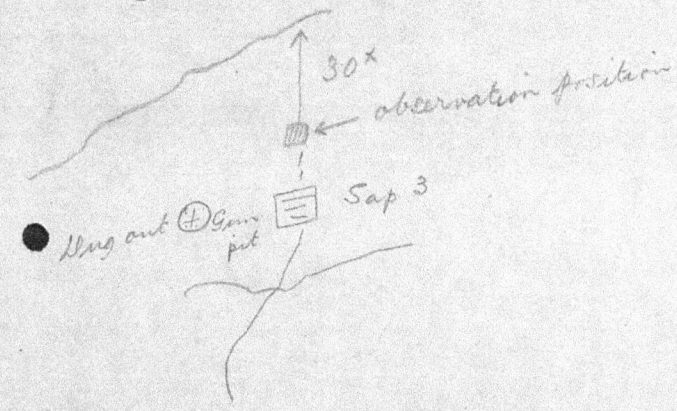

3. Observation of ground between DELVILLE WOOD and FLERS and of WOOD Lane. (Haze rendered distant observation very difficult)
The FLERS - LONGUEVAL ROAD was kept under observation for an hour and half but no movement was seen.

In WOOD LANE TRENCH there is a considerable amount of fresh earth thrown up. Near the WOOD there is no attempt at wiring but parapet is sand-bagged. No movement was noticeable in this trench except a sniper. No appearance of Sentries, judging from the snipers movements, the trench would be about 4½ feet deep in most places. During the bombardment Sentries seem to have been moved into the trench and appeared to be on the alert.
(Copies of all Patrol Reports are handed over).

5th August, 1916.

(Sgd). JAS.DAWSON, Lt.Colonel,
1/6th Bn. Gordon Highlanders.

At 3.P.M. to-day I inspected the extension of No.6. Sap and found that it had been extended until it reached the outskirts of the WOOD where it struck a trench which had been dug during our previous occupation of the WOOD. This trench extends along the egde of the WOOD till it reaches a point about 100 yards from the N.W. corner.

On the right front the enemy trench enters the WOOD and comes with a V shaped round the old Gun emplacements. A sap seems to to runs out from thisY and the patrol was fired on from here. Numerous dead bodies - British and German were to be seen here. Our men were walking about freely in the WOOD at S.4.c.2.6. without being fired on .

5/8/16.

(Sgd). JAS.DAWSON, Lt.Colonel,
Commanding 1/6th Bn. Gordon Highlanders.

Copy No...1...

Operation Orders No 52
by Lieut/Colonel J. Dawson, D.S.O.
Commanding 6th Gordon Highlanders.
Betaincourt, 10th August, 1916.

Map Reference 1/250.000 Europe Sheets 1 and 3

1. **OPERATION:-**
   The Battalion will move by rail to the 2nd Army area on the 12th instant.
   The Entraining station is LONGPRE, and the Detraining Station THIENNES.

2. **PARADE:-**
   The Battalion will parade at 3.41 a.m. in the main street facing North in the following order:-
   Headquarters, D. C. B. A.

3. **BILLETING:-**
   A Billeting party under Captain Cowie will proceed in advance to THIENNES by train leaving LONGPRE at 11.00 hours on the 11th instant.
   Captain Cowie will report to the Staff Captain at THIENNES Station on arrival.

4. **TRANSPORT:-**
   Transport will arrive at LONGPRE Station at 2.21 hours on 12th instant, and be loaded by a fatigue party from 8th Argyll & Sutherland Highlanders.

5. **LEWIS GUNNERS:-**
   Lewis Gunners will march with the Transport.

6. **BAGGAGE:-**
   All baggage will be taken to the Transport and loaded by 10 p.m. on the 11th instant.

7. **RATIONS:-**
   Rations for the 12th instant will be carried on the man. Rations for the 13th will be carried in the supply wagons on the train.

8. **BREAKFASTS:-**
   Breakfasts will be issued at the Entraining Station

9. **TRAIN:-**
   Train leaves the Entraining Station at 5.21 hours 12th instant.

   ...., Capt. & Adj.
   6th Gordon Highlanders.

Copy No. 1   Adjutant
       2 to 5 O's/C Companies.
           6 I.O.C. and Grenade Officer
           7 Transport Officer and Quartermaster
           8 Captain Cowie.

Copy No...... 1

Operation Orders No 53
by Lieut/Colonel J. Dawson, D.S.O.
Commanding 6th Gordon Highlanders.
BLARINGHEM, 17th August, 1916.

Map Reference   1/100,000 Hazebrouck 5A

1. **OPERATION:**
    The Battalion will move into Divisional Reserve in ARMENTIERES on the 18th instant. The Battalion less Transport will move by train from EBLINGHEM to STEENWERK.

2. **PARADE:**
    Battalion will parade at 8.40 a.m. ready to march off on the STEENBECQUE - LYNDE Road; head of column to be at Cross roads 400 yards North of U in LE CROQUET. Order of march:-
    Headquarters, "D", "B", "C", "A".

3. **TRAIN:**
    Train is due to leave EBLINGHEM at 10.40 hours, and arrive at STEENWERK at 11.36 hours.

4. **TRANSPORT:**
    Starting Point for Brigade Transport is junction of roads at LE CROQUET at 5.30 a.m. Transport, 6th Gordon Highlanders, will follow after the No 2 Section Divisional Signal Company.
    Route:- STEENBECQUE STATION - CROIX MARAISSE - MERVILLE - LA GORGUE, thence south of River LYS to ARMENTIERES.

    Column will halt when its head reaches west end of LA GORGUE, resuming its march at 2 p.m. A guide will meet the Battalion Transport at the railway crossing outside ARMENTIERES.

5. **LEWIS GUNS:**
    Lewis Gun handcarts will be taken in the train.

6. **BAGGAGE:**
    All baggage will be loaded by 9 p.m. to-night.

7. **BILLETS:**
    Billets are to be left scrupulously clean. The usual certificates as to their cleanliness will be required.

                                                    Capt. & Adj.
                                            6th Gordon Highlanders.

Copy No 1   Adjutant
       2 - 5 Os/C Companies.
       6   L.G.O.
       7   Grenade Officer
       8   Transport Officer and Quartermaster.

Operation Orders No 54 Copy No. 1
by Lieut/Colonel J. Dawson, D.S.O.
Commanding 6th Gordon Highlanders
In-the-Field, 25th August, 1916.

Map Reference 1/10,000 Trench Maps BOIS GRENIER and HOUPLINES.

1. The 6th Gordon Highlanders will relieve the 4th Seaforth Highlanders in the right sector of the Subsidiary Line on the 26th instant.

2. The relief will be carried out in accordance with the attached Table of Reliefs.

3. Duties will be taken over in accordance with the attached Table of Work Parties.

4. 170 rounds S.A.A., 1 day's rations, and a full waterbottle will be carried by all men.

5. 1 officer per Company will report to Headquarters, 4th Seaforth Highlanders, in Subsidiary Line near end of LUNATIC LANE (Route V) by 10 a.m. to-morrow, to reconnoitre his company front, and learn all particulars regarding food, water, etc., and to take over Trench Stores and ammunition.

6. The Quartermaster will arrange for 1 watercart, filled, to be sent up after dark.

7. (a) The Grenade Officer will detail 3 Company N.C.Os. to take over the 3 Brigade Bomb Stores in the Subsidiary Line. He will report with these to the Grenade Officer, 4th Seaforth Highlanders, at 10 a.m. and take over stores.

(b) The Light Section Officer will detail 1 N.C.O. and 2 men to take over Observation Post in SQUARE FARM at 6 a.m.

(c) The Lewis Gun Officer will report at Orderly Room at 9 a.m. when he will take over 2 guns and teams of 5th Seaforth Highlanders to relieve guns of 4th Seaforth Highlanders in PORT EGALE and BUTERNE FARM, strong points. He will inform L.G.O. of 4th Seaforth Highlanders that he may remove his other guns without relief

8. Headquarters Company and No 6 Platoon will remain in their present billets.

9. All parties moving to and from the trenches must do so as formed bodies. This applies to officers' servants as well as to others.

10. (a) 1 Captain and 4 subalterns per Company will betaken to the trenches.

(b) 4 N.C.Os. per Company will remain in ARMENTIERES. Further instructions regarding these will be issued later.

                                                Capt. & Adj.
                                            6th Gordon Highlanders.

Copy No 1.   Adjutant
    2 to 5   Os/C Companies.
       6   O/C Headquarters Coy.
       7   Quartermaster and L.G.O.
       8   Grenade Officer, and Light Section Officer
       9   Medical Officer.

SECRET
No. 134
152nd INF. BDE.

WAR DIARY
of
1/6th Battn. GORDON HIGHLANDERS.

From
1st September, 1916

To
30th September, 1916.

6th GORDON HIGHLANDERS.

WAR DIARY
—or—
INTELLIGENCE SUMMARY
(Erase heading not required.)

Army Form C. 2118

Place	Date	Hour	Summary of Events and Information	Remarks and references to Appendices
ARMENTIERES	1-5		Battalion held Subsidiary Line East of ARMENTIERES from C.28.c.7.2. to I.9.c.8.8. (France 36 N.W.)	
near BAILLEUL	6-19 20-30		Battalion held Front Line Trenches from I.5.c.2½.1½ to I.16.b.1.4. In Training Camp, South East of BAILLEUL (S.27.a.8.6; Trench Map 28 S.W.)	
near ARMENTIERES	15th		A raid, to be carried out on GERMAN MUSHROOM (ARMENTIERES, I.11.c.) by 4 officers and 43 other ranks, failed, owing to the wirecutting torpedoes not being strong enough to handle in the time allowed for getting them into position.	
"	22/23		Another attempt on GERMAN MUSHROOM partially successful, the German trench being entered in one place and bombed in other two.	
near BAILLEUL	25th		A Draft of 89 other ranks joined this Battalion from No 11 Entrenching Battalion	
"	26th		A Draft of 39 other ranks joined thisBattalion from No 3 Entrenching Battalion	
"	28th		Inspection of 152nd Brigade by IInd Army Commander - presentation of Military Medal Ribbons to two men of Battalion for conduct in raids.	
"	30th		Entrain for DOULLENS.	

Lieut/Colonel,
Commanding 6th Gordon Highlanders.

Confidential

MEMORANDUM.

30th Sept. 1916

From O.C. 6th Gordon Highrs.

To Head Qrs.
152nd Brigade.

Herewith War Diary for the month of September 1916 appertaining to this Battalion.

Jas Dawsen Lieut. Colonel.
Comdg 6th Gordon Highrs.

Copy No..1..

Operation Orders No 55
by Lieut/Colonel J. Dawson, D.S.O.
Commanding 6th Gordon Highlanders
In-the-Field, 4th Septr 1916.

1. OPERATION:-
   The 6th Battalion Gordon Highlanders will relieve the 6th Battalion Seaforth Highlanders in the trenches on the 5th inst.

2. RELIEFS:-
   A, B, C, and D Companies 6th Gordon Highlanders will relieve D, C, B, and A Companies 6th Seaforth Highlanders respectively.

3. TIMES OF STARTING:-
   Companies and sections will move off as follows:-

	Time	Route
Lewis Gunners	10 a.m.	LOTHIAN AVENUE and PORTE EGALE AVENUE
Light Section	9 a.m.	LOTHIAN AVENUE
"B" Company	2 p.m.	LOTHIAN AVENUE
"C" "	2 p.m.	PORTE EGALE AVENUE
"A" "	2.40 p.m.	LOTHIAN AVENUE
"D" "	2.40 p.m.	PORTE EGALE AVENUE
Headquarters Company	2.45 p.m.	SUBSIDIARY LINE

   Companies will move by platoons at 10 minutes intervals

4. GUIDES:-
   No guides will be provided for Companies or Light Section
   Guides for the 4 right Lewis Guns will be at the foot of LOTHIAN AVENUE at 10 a.m., and for the 4 left Lewis Guns at foot of PORTE EGALE AVENUE at 10 a.m.

5. CLEANLINESS OF LINES:-
   Os/C Companies will ensure that their lines and dug-outs are left scrupulously clean. A certificate as to their cleanliness will be rendered by Os/C Companies before moving off.

6. TRENCH STORES:-
   Os/C Companies will forward to Battalion Headquarters duplicate receipts of all Trench Stores taken or handed over.

7. SENTRY GROUPS:-
   Sentry Groups should be told off before Companies move.

8. COMPANY BOMBING SECTIONS:-
   Company Bombing Sections are not to be used on any work except with the permission of the Battalion Bombing Officer.
   They will be employed on the Rifle Grenade Batteries, and are not to be used at Bombing Posts.

9. BOMBS:-
   Battalion Bombing Officer will take over all Bomb Stores and Rifle Grenade Batteries to-morrow morning.

                                            Capt. & Adj.
                                            6th Gordon Highlanders.

Copy No 1   Adjutant
       2 - 5 Os/C Companies
         6   O/C 6th Seaforth Highlanders
         7   L.G.O. and Light Section Officer
         8   O/C Headquarters Company and Grenade Officer

Operation Order No. 56,
by Lieut. Colonel J. Dawson, D.S.O.
Commanding SNIPE,
In-the-Field, 14th. September, 1916.
-o-o-o-o-o-o-o-

1. **INTENTION.**
It is intended to carry out a raid on the enemy's trench from I.11.c.3½.2. to I.11.c.4.4. with the object of destroying or capturing the garrison and gaining information regarding garrison, trench equipment, etc..

2. **STRENGTH.**

		Officers	N.C.O's.	Men.
N.	Torpedo Party.	1	-	2
N.	Blocking Party	-	1	4
N.	Raiding Party	-	1	8
S.	Corresponding Party	1	2	14
	Centre Party	1	1	9
		3	5	37

3. There are three distinct parties:-
No. 1 or S. Party commanded by Lieut. Matheson.
No. 2 or Centre Party   "   "   "   Grant.
No. 3 or N. Party   "   "   "   McQueen.

Captain Clark will be in charge of whole operation, and will be stationed at East end of MUSHROOM Entrance Trench.

4. **EMERGENCY PARTY**
1 N.C.O. and 8 men will be in readiness in MUSHROOM TRENCH near O/C Raid, in case of emergency.

5. **PARADE.**
All officers and other ranks taking part will be at Battalion Headquarters by 5 p.m. on date fixed - parties at 10 minutes interval, in order 1, 2, 3, and Emergency party.

6. **DRESS, EQUIPMENT, etc.**
(a) No documents of any kind will be carried by officers or men.
(b) Gas Helmets in "Alert" Position.
(c) Faces and knees will be blackened.
(d) Kilt, without apron, will be worn, except by 3 T. men who wear trousers etc., and hedging gloves.
(e) Helmets and bayonets will be blackened.
(f) Helmet straps will be tight below chin.
(g) Bayonet men and carriers will wear equipment, and carry 50 rounds ammunition, plus 9 in magazine and 1 in breech.
(h) Throwers will carry revolvers only.
(i) Each Blocking party will carry 80 Mills and 4 N.D. bombs
(xxxxOfficersxwillxcarryxelectricxtorches.
Each Raiding party will carry 72 Mills and 4 N.D. bombs
Centre party will carry   100 Mills and 4 N.D. bombs
(j) Officers will carry electric torches.
(k) 6 bayonet men will carry electric torches fixed to /each rifle.
(l) One man of/Torpedo laying party will carry wire shears.

7. **TORPEDO.**
Wire to mark route will be laid, and torpedo placed in convenient position on night preceeding raid.

8. As soon as sufficiently dark on night of raid, the officer and 2 men from each party will proceed to place Torpedo in position, following the line of the wire already laid.

9. When this is accomplished the party will retire; the two men to the check on wire, and the officer to the O/C Raid, reporting Torpedo in position.

Page 2.

10. The two men will remain out as guards in each case.

11. 15 minutes from Zero the officer will conduct the Blocking and Raiding parties to their positions behind Torpedo, following its wires till check is reached.

12. At ZERO, the discharge of the Torpedoes will be the signal for (1) The parties to rush in at gaps made, and
(2) Mortars, etc., to commence firing.

13. The order within First and Third parties will be :-
   (a) Wire cutting man with shears,
   (b) Blocking party.
   (c) Officer and spare man.
   (d) Raiding party.

14. The Centre party has :-
   (a) Wireman.
   (b) Crater men.
   (c) Trench men.

   Wiremen enter gaps and cut any unbroken strands.

15. After this the two men who first came out with officer are at his disposal for trench investigation, removal of prisoners, wounded etc.

16. N. and S. Raiding parties work towards centre of salient at which the Centre party is stationed; Blocking parties keep entrance gap clear; Centre party bomb trench in front of them and more especially head of communication trench, two shovel men pushing in as much as possible of the enemy's parapet. No unnecessary bombing is to be indulged in by Raiding Parties.

17. Last man of each party will report "All Clear" to Officer in charge of Centre party, who will then blow whistle and light portfire.

18. O/C Raid will blow whistle and discharge 3 Gold and Silver Rain Rockets, on which all men will return to their own lines. *2 Red all Clear*

19. Each man will report to O/C Raid at East end of MUSHROOM Entry Trench; passing to Battalion Headquarters where Roll will be called.

20. Four Stretcher Bearers will be at East end of MUSHROOM Entry trench, and four at West end of same.

21. Watches will be checked at 7.30 p.m.

22. Password:- CRAIGELLACHIE.

(Signed) Jas. Dawson, Lieut. Colonel,
Commanding SNIPE.

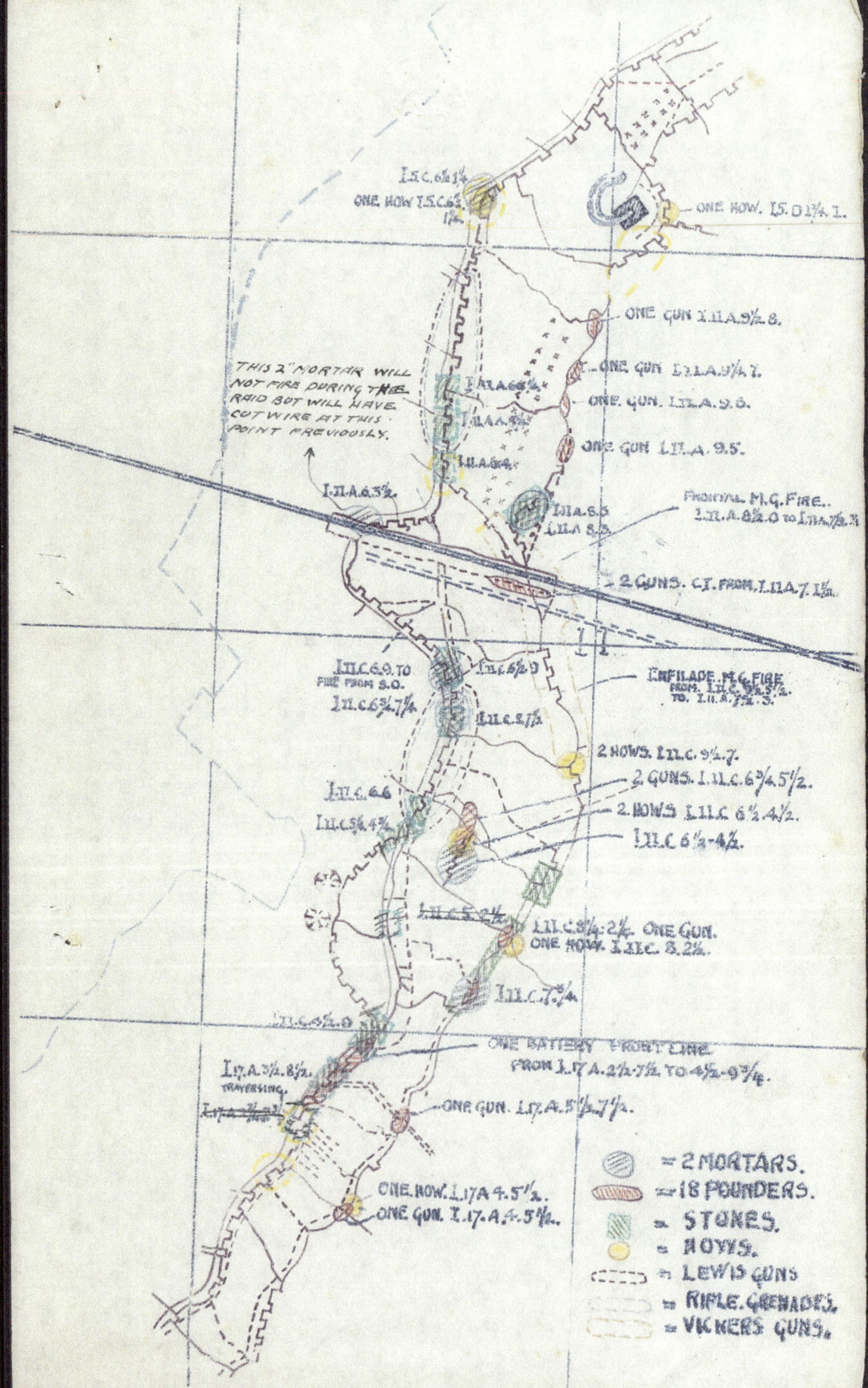

WAR DIARY

of

1/6th Battn., The GORDON HIGHLANDERS.

From

1st October, 1916

To

31st October, 1916.

Army Form C. 2118

WAR DIARY
or
INTELLIGENCE SUMMARY
(Erase heading not required.)

CONFIDENTIAL
No 2/(A)
HIGHLAND DIVISION

Instructions regarding War Diaries and Intelligence Summaries are contained in F. S. Regs., Part II. and the Staff Manual respectively. Title Pages will be prepared in manuscript.

Place	Date	Hour	Summary of Events and Information	Remarks and references to Appendices
Mitchell	1		Billetted at LONGUEVILETTE	
	2-3		In bivouac at BOIS DE WARNIMONT near AUTHIE	
	4-6		In trenches S.E. of HEBUTERNE from JOHN COPSE to CHASSEURS HEDGE [Map zone 57d, N.E. 3 + 4]	
	7		Bivouac at COLINCAMPS	
	8-11		Billets at LOUVAINCOURT } practising attack	
	12-16		Huts at BUS LES ARTOIS	
	17-20		Holding trenches near AUCHONVILLERS from LONG ACRE to BROADWAY (Map 57d S.E)	
	21		Huts at FORCEVILLE	
	22-24		Bivouac S.W. of MAILLY-MAILLET [Q.17 c & 5. Map 57d S.E.]	
	24-25		5th Battalion in AUCHONVILLERS } employed in trench fatigues at " at FORCEVILLE	
	26-30		Huts at FORCEVILLE	
	31		In trenches near AUCHONVILLERS opposite BEAUMONT HAMEL	

OPERATION ORDERS. NO. 60.
BY LIEUT/COLONEL J. DAWSON, D.S.O.
COMMDG. 6th GORDON HIGHLANDERS.
BAILLEUL, 29th SEPTR. 1916.

Copy No 1

Map Ref. 1/100000 HAZEBROUCK 5 a.
  and 1/100000 LENS - 11.

1. OPERATION.
   The Battalion will move on the 30th inst. by rail to LONGUEVILLETTE.

2. ENTRAINMENT AND DETRAINMENT.

   Entraining Station - BAILLEUL MAIN.
   Train leaves - 20.28 Hours - 30.9.16.

   Detraining Station - DOULLENS.
   Train arrives - 2.34 Hours. - 1.10.16.

   Transport Officer will arrange to be at the Entraining Station 3 hours before the departure of the train. Lewis Gunners will accompany the Transport.

3. PARADE.
   Battalion will parade in mass to South of the Lines ready to move off at 6.30 p.m.
   Steel helmets will be carried on the pack.

4. LOADING AND UNLOADING.
   All loading and unloading will be done by parties found by 8th Argyll & Sutherland Highlanders, and 5th Seaforth Highlanders, respectively.

5. CLEANLINESS OF LINES.
   Officers Commanding Companies are responsible that their lines and tents are left in a thoroughly clean state.
   The Orderly Officer will inspect the lines and tents after the Battalion is on parade, and report to Battalion Headquarters any Company whose tents or lines are not clean.

6. RATIONS.
   Rations for the 1st Octr., will be carried on the Supply Wagons and will be issued on arrival at LONGUEVILLETTE.

7. REFILLING POINT.
   Refilling Point on 1st October will be at the O in LONGUEVILLETTE.

8. BLANKETS.
   Blankets will be carried on the man to the Entraining Station. Transport will be provided for carriage of blankets from Detraining Station.
   All blankets are to be rolled up in the train before arrival at the Detraining Station.

9. GUARDS.
   Officers Commanding "H.Q". Coy. and "D" Coy. will each detail a guard of 1 N.C.O. and 4 men.
   2 men will be posted at each side of the train, and at either end immediately the train halts.
   They will prevent any men leaving the train without permission, and turn back all stragglers.

10. BAGGAGE.
    All baggage will be loaded by 4.30 p.m.

                                          Capt & Adjt.
                                          6th Gordon Highlanders.

Copy No 1 Adjutant.
"   " 2 OC "A"
"   " 3 " "B"
"   " 4 " "C"
"   " 5 " "D"
"   " 6 " "H.Q"
"   " 7 Transport Officer
Cop. no 8 Quartermaster
"   " 9 file

OPERATION ORDER NO. 61.
BY LIEUT/COLONEL J. DAWSON, D.S.O.
COMMANDING 6th GORDON HIGHLANDERS.
LONGUEVILLETTE, 1st. OCTOBER, 1916.

Copy No.

Map Ref. 57 D. 1/40,000
" LENS 11. 1/100,000.

1. OPERATION.

   The Battalion will move to AUTHIE tomorrow.

2. PARADE.

   The Battalion will parade in the main street, ready to move off at 8.15 a.m. Head of column to be at "D" Coys billets.
   Order of march - "H.Q.", "D", "C", "B", "A", Transport.

3. BAGGAGE and BLANKETS.

   All baggage will be ready for loading by 6.45 a.m.

   Blankets will be rolled as usual and ready for collection at same hour.

4. CLEANLINESS OF BILLETS.

   All billets will be thoroughly cleaned before the Battalion parades and a certificate as to their cleanliness handed in before the Battalion marches off.

5. BREAKFAST.

   Breakfast will be at 6.30 a.m.

                                            Capt. & Adj.,
                                       6th Gordon Highlanders.

Copy No. 1. Adjt.
  "   " 2. "A"
  "   " 3. "B"
  "   " 4. "C"
  "   " 5. "D"
  "   " 6. "H.Q."
  "   " 7. Transport Officer
  "   " 8. Quartermaster
  "   " 9. R.S.M.

Copy No. 1

Operation Orders No 62
by Lieut/Colonel J. Dawson, D.S.O.
Commanding 6th Gordon Highlanders
In-the-Field, 4th October 1916.

Map Reference FRANCE 57 D.

1. **RELIEF:**
    The Battalion will relieve the 13th Battalion Essex Regt. in the right sub-sector of trenches S.E. of HEBUTERNE to-day.

2. **PARADE**
    The Battalion will parade facing West on the road to the South of the camp, ready to move off at 11 a.m. Head of the column will be opposite German prisoners' enclosure.
    Order of march will be:- C. D. A. B. H.Q. Companies.

    Lewis Guns and teams will parade at 8 a.m.

    Transport and Q.M Stores will be taken over in BUS LES ARTOIS. 1 N.C.O. will report to the Town Major's Office there at 9 a.m., and will arrange with Transport Officer and Quartermaster for time of move.

3. **ROUTE:**
    Route of all units, except Transport, will be via ST LEGER LES AUTHIE, and SAILLY AU BOIS.

4. **GUIDES:**
    Guides from 13th Battalion Essex Regiment will meet Lewis Guns at Road Junction, SAILLY AU BOIS, (Map Reference J.18.b.2.3.) at 10.30. a.m., and the Battalion at the same place at 2 p.m.

5. **DINNERS:**
    Dinners will be served on arrival at SAILLY AU BOIS.

6. **DRESS:**
    Dress will be full marching order with packs. Kilt aprons and steel helmets will be worn.

7. **BLANKETS:**
    Officers' baggage and blankets will be sent to Transport by 10 a.m.

8. **CLEANING:**
    Huts and tents must be left scrupulously clean. The usual certificates will be rendered.

D Mackenzie   Lieut. & A/Adj.
6th Gordon Highlanders.

Copy No 1   Adjutant
      2   13th Battalion Essex Regiment
    3 - 7   Os/C Companies.
      8   Quartermaster and Transport Officer
      9   L.G.O.

Operation Orders No. 63.
by Lieut/Colonel J. Dawson, D.S.O.
Commanding 6th Gordon Highlanders,
Louvencourt, 11th October, 1916.

Copy No. 1.

Map Reference FRANCE Sheet 57d.

1. MOVE.
   The 6th Battalion Gordon Highlanders will move to BUS LES ARTOIS tomorrow 12th October, 1916.

2. PARADE.
   Order of the march will be :—   H.Q. Company.
                                          "A" Company.
                                          "B" Company.
                                          "C" Company.
                                          "D" Company.

   The head of the H.Q. Company will pass Cross Roads LOUVENCOURT at 3.30 p.m.
   Officers Commanding Companies will arrange their parades to follow in above order. No forming up or halting in Main Street will be possible owing to the congestion of Traffic.

3. TRANSPORT &C.
   The Transport and Quartermaster's Stores will remain in their present Quarters.

4. BLANKETS.
   Officers' baggage and blankets will be packed by 2.30 p.m.

5. CLEANING.
   Billets will be left scrupulously clean. The usual certificates will be rendered.

6. REPORTS.
   Companies will report their arrival in Billets, to Battalion Headquarters.

Copy No. 1 File
2 to 6. A.B.C.D. H.Q. Coys
7. Transport Offr
8. Quartermaster

MacKenzie Lieut and a/Adjutant.

Operation Order No. 64
by Lieut. Colonel J. Dawson, D.S.O.
Commanding 6th Gordon Highlanders,
BUS-LES-ARTOIS, 16th October, 1916.

Copy No. 1

Reference :- France 57d S.E.

1. **MOVE.**

    The 6th Battalion Gordon Highlanders will relieve the DRAKE BATTALION, 189th Brigade NAVAL DIVISION, tomorrow, 17th October in right sub-sector of BEAUMONT HAMEL SECTION.

2. **PARADES.**

    6 a.m.   Sick Parade.

    Breakfasts at 6.30 a.m.

    The Battalion will parade ready to march off at 8 a.m.

    Order of the march will be "HQ", "A", "B", "C", "D" Companies. After leaving MAILLY MAILLET, an interval of 5 minutes between platoons will be maintained.
    DRESS :- Full marching Order. Steel Helmets and kilt aprons will be worn.

3. **RELIEF.**

    Companies will relieve corresponding Companies of DRAKE Battalion.
    Platoon guides will meet the Battalion at AUCHONVILLERS STATION Q.8.d.5.9½, at 10 a.m.

4. **BAGGAGE.**

    Blankets and Officer's baggage will be collected at 7 a.m.

5. **AMMUNITION.**

    Companies will ensure that all men carry 170 rounds, S.A.A.

6. **CLEANING.**

    Huts and Tents will be left scrupulously clean. The usual certificates will be rendered.

7. **REPORTS.**

    Companies will report to Battalion Headquarters immediately the relief is completed. Batt'n H.Q. will be in HAYMARKET Q.10.c.1.1½

O. MacKenzie, Lieut & a/Adj,
6th Gordon Highlanders.

Copy No. 1   File.
     2 to 6   Companies.
        7.   Transport Officer.
        8.   Quartermaster.
        9.   R.S.M.

Copy No. 1

Operation Orders by Lieut. Colonel J. Dawson, D.S.O.,
Commanding 1/6th Gordon Highlanders,
Forceville, 21st October 1916.   O.O.45.

1. **MOVE.**

   The Battalion will leave its present billets today.
   The Battalion will parade at 1-30 p.m., in the Orchard West of the Camp.
   H.Q., A and B Coys and 1 Platoon of C Coy. will move to P.17.d.5.7.
   D Coy. and C Coy. less 1 Platoon will move to AUCHONVILLERS.
   This Detachment will be under Major J.W.Adams.
   Guides for this party will be at AUCHONVILLERS Station at 3.30 p.m.
   The order of the march will be – C, D, A, B, H.Q. Coys.

2. **BAGGAGE.**

   Baggage and Blankets will be ready for collection at 1 p.m.
   Camp Kettles for C and D Coys will be taken to AUCHONVILLERS by limber.

3. **LEWIS GUNS.**

   Lewis Guns of C and D Coys. will accompany these Coys.

4. **DINNERS.**

   Dinners will be at 12 noon.

5. **BILLETS.**

   Billets, Cookhouses and Latrines will be left scrupulously clean.
   The usual certificates will be rendered.

6. **GUIDES.**

   On arrival at new billets A Coy. will detail a guide to return to Divisional Grenade Dump at P.22.a.2.5 to guide the party of 3 Officers and 80 O.R. to new billet.

7. **Reports.**

   Coys will report to Battalion or Detachment Head Qrs. immediately relief is completed.

                                        O.MacKenzie Lieut. &
                                               A/Adjutant
                                        6th Gordon Highlanders.

Copy No. 1 File
 "   2-6   Coys.
 "   7   Transport Officer
           & Quartermaster.
 "   9   R.S.M.

Copy No. 1

Operation Orders No 66.
by Lieut.Colonel J. Dawson, D.S.O.
Commanding 6th Gordon Highlanders
FORCEVILLE, 29th Octr., 1916.

Map Reference:- FRANCE 57 D S.E.

1. **MOVE**:

    The 1/6th Battalion The Gordon Highlanders will relieve the 1/6th Battalion The Black Watch in bivouacs at P.17.c. central to-morrow.

2. **PARADE**:

    The Battalion will move off by Companies, H.Q. Company leaving at 10.40 a.m.
    Companies will move at 5 minutes' intervals.
    The order of march will be:- H.Q., "A", "B", "C", "D"

3. **ADVANCE PARTY**:

    One N.C.O. per Company will parade at Orderly Room at 9.30 a.m. under 2/Lieut Carnie, and proceed to P.17.c. as Advance Party to take over and allot billets. They will report at Headquarters, 1/6th Black Watch at 10 a.m.

4. **BAGGAGE**:

    Blankets and Officers' baggage will be ready for collection at 10 a.m.
    These must be clearly marked.

5. **STORES**:

    O/C H.Q. Company will detail Headquarters Bombers to remain in present billets as a guard over Bomb Stores.

6. **WORKING PARTIES**:

    Parties on fatigue at 1 a.m. and 7 a.m. will carry rifle and equipment, and will have all blankets collected and kits packed before going on fatigue. Packs will be taken to the new camp by Transport.
    These parties on returning from fatigue will report at P.17.c. central

7. **TRANSPORT**:

    Transport and Quartermaster's Stores will not move.

8. **BILLETS**:

    The Camp, including huts, tents, cookhouses, latrines, etc. will be left scrupulously clean.
    The usual certificates will be rendered.

9. **REPORTS**:

    Companies will report to Battalion Headquarters immediately relief is complete.

D. Mackenzie, Lieut & A/Adj.
6th Gordon Highlanders.

Copy No 1.   Adjutant
      2 - 6   Os/C Companies.
      7   2/Lieut Carnie
      8   Transport Officer
      9   Quartermaster.

No. 67

Operation Orders by Lieut. Colonel J. Dawson D.S.O.,
Commanding 1/6th. Bn. Gordon Highlanders,
Forceville, 30th Octr. 1916.

1. MOVE.

1/6th Bn. The Gordon Highlanders will move into Trenches in the Left Sub-sector of AUCHONVILLERS area today.

2. PARADE.

The Battalion will move off by platoons at 50 yards intervals. A Coy. leaving Camp at 11-30 a.m.
Order of march - A B C D H.Q.
Lewis Guns will leave at 10-30 a.m.

3. GUIDES.

Guides will meet the Battalion at the WINDMILL Q.1.d.8.a. at 1 p.m.

4. DRESS.

Full marching order with packs will be carried.

5. BAGGAGE.

Blankets and Officers Baggage will be collected at 11 a.m.
Cooks will accompany the Limber with camp kettles.

6. CLEANLINESS.

The Camp including Huts, Tents, Cook Houses, Latrines &c., will be left scrupulously clean. The usual certificates will be rendered.

7. REPORTS.

Companies will report to Battalion Head quarters immediately the relief is completed.

D. Mackenzie   Lieut. & A/Adj.
1/6th Bn. The Gordon Highlanders.

WAR DIARY

of

1/6th Battn. The GORDON HIGHLANDERS.

NOVEMBER. 1916.

Confidential.

6th Gordon Highlanders.

Army Form C. 2118.

WAR DIARY
or
INTELLIGENCE SUMMARY.
(Erase heading not required.)

Instructions regarding War Diaries and Intelligence Summaries are contained in F. S. Regs., Part II. and the Staff Manual respectively. Title pages will be prepared in manuscript.

Hour, Date, Place	Summary of Events and Information	Remarks and references to Appendices
In the Field Nov. 1-4	In Trenches near AUCHONVILLERS opposite BEAUMONT HAMEL.	
5-12	In Camp near FORCEVILLE.	
13-15	Attack and capture of BEAUMONT HAMEL. The 51st (Highland) Division captured BEAUMONT HAMEL. The 152nd and 153rd Infantry Brigades made the attack, the 154th Brigade being held in reserve. The 152nd Brigade attacked on a 2-Battalion front with one Battalion in support and one Battalion in reserve. The 6th Gordon Highlanders were the Battalion in reserve, and lost 3 officers killed and wounded (Captain A. GRANT, and 2/Lieut R.F. WILSON killed; 2/Lieut D.C. COOPER wounded) 115 O.R. killed and wounded.	
16-18	In Camp at MAILLY WOOD (EAST)	
19-24	Holding defences of BEAUMONT HAMEL. (10 O.R. killed, 30 O.R. wounded)	
24-29	In Billets at FORCEVILLE.	
29-30	In Billets at BOUZINCOURT.	

John W. Adam, Major,
Commanding 6th Gordon Highlanders.

30 NOV 1918

Copy No. 1

Operation Order No. 68.
by Lieut. Colonel J. Dawson, D.S.O.
Commanding 6th Gordon Highlanders
Forceville, 9th November, 1916.

1. **MOVE.**

    The 6th Battalion Gordon Highlanders will relieve the 4th Battalion Gordon Highlanders in HUTMENTS in MAILLY WOOD tomorrow.

2. **PARADE.**

    Lewis Gunners will move at 10.30 a.m.
    Companies will move independently by Platoons at two minutes' intervals, commencing at 10.45 a.m.
    Order of the march will be "A", "B", "C", "D" "HQ. Details".

3. **ROUTE.**

    Companies will move across fields.
    Point Guides will be posted at Road Junctions.
    Platoons will move in file.

4. **ADVANCE PARTY.**

    Captain Grey and 1 Officer from "A", "B", "D", and "HQ" Coys. as Advance Party will report to Camp Commandant MAILLY WOOD at 10 a.m.

5. **CAMP LINES.**

    All tents, cookhouses, latrines &c. must be left scrupulously clean. A Certificate to this effect is required from each Company.

6. **BAGGAGE.**

    Blankets and Officers' baggage will be ready for collection by 9 a.m.

7. **REPORTS.**

    Companies will report to Battalion Headquarters in MAILLY WOOD, immediately the relief is complete.

Cancelled

D MacKenzie Lieut. & a/Adj.,
6th Gordon Highlanders.

Copy No. 1 File.
" 2 - 6 Companies.
    7 Transport Officer.
    8 Quartermaster.
    9 R.S.M.

Copy No. 1

Operation Orders No 69
by Lieut.Colonel J. Dawson, D.S.O.
Commanding 6th Gordon Highlanders.
In-the-Field, 11th November 1916.

----------oOo----------

1. **MOVE:**

    The 6th Battalion Gordon Highlanders will move to the trenches to-morrow afternoon.

    Lewis Gun Teams selected by L.G.O. will parade ready to march off at 1 p.m. Remainder of the Battalion, except parties detailed below, will move off by Companies at 5 minutes intervals commencing at 4 p.m.

    Order of March:- "A", Right half of "B", left half of "B", "C", "D" Companies, and H.Q. Details.

2. **DUTIES:**

    Right half of "B" Company will take over posts from HUNTER TRENCH to BROADWAY.

    "D" Company will take over posts in HUNTER TRENCH.

    1 N.C.O. and 6 men will be detailed for each post, of which there are four in each Company front; men detailed for these posts will move off at 1 p.m. 1 Officer will be sent with each party. Gum boots for men in posts and Lewis Gunners will be drawn at MAILLY Boot Store.

    These Companies are also responsible that our own wire where necessary in front of both front and support lines is sufficiently cut to permit the passage of troops.

3. **WORK:**

    (a) 35 Trench Bridges will be carried up from AUCHONVILLERS DUMP by "A" Company and placed over MARLBOROUGH and SEAFORTH TRENCHES in positions which have previously been selected by an officer sent in advance.

    15 Trench Bridges will be taken from same dump by "C" Company and placed over HUNTER TRENCH.

    (b) "A" Company is responsible that SECOND AVENUE is kept open from 88th TRENCH to MARLBOROUGH.

    "C" Company is responsible that KING STREET, CLIVE TRENCH and MIDDLE STREET are kept open. These trench clearing parties will be withdrawn when other Battalions move up to positions of assembly.

    (c) "A" and "C" Companies will also arrange to take from AUCHONVILLERS DUMP 50 sticks each to ESSEX and WHITE CITY DUMPS respectively. Parties will be detailed by these Companies to wind half-coils of barbed wire on these from full coils on these dumps.

4. **DISCIPLINE:**

    The greatest effort must be made to prevent any of these operations being seen by the enemy. Absolute silence will be maintained during the progress of the work. No smoking in the trenches will be allowed, nor will torches be used in the forward area.

5. **GENERAL:**

    Normal trench activity will be maintained throughout the night so far as altered circumstances permit.

    Each man will have 5 rounds in the magazine before leaving camp. Bayonets will be fixed at 15 minutes before ZERO.

    Attention is again directed to the Information and Instructions already issued.

    Lieut. & A/Adjt.
    6th Gordon Highlanders.

Copy No 1 Adjutant   7 L.G.O.
     2 - 6 Companies   8 H.Q. Mess
                              9 File.

Operation Orders No. 70.   Copy No....1....
by Lieut. Colonel J. Dawson, D.S.O.
Commanding 6th Gordon Highlanders.
MAILLY WOOD, 18th November, 1916.

1. **MOVE.**

    The 6th Bn. The Gordon Highlanders will relieve the 4th Bn. Seaforth Highlanders in the trenches East of BEAUMONT HAMEL today.

2. **PARADE.**

    Battalion will leave its present billets at 11-45 a.m. Intervals of 50 yards will be maintained between platoons. Order of March will be :- B C D A Coys. Head Qrs. Details. Lewis Gun Teams will move along with coys.

3. **ROUTE.**

    Route will be STOCKTON DUMP where guides will be met. - Light Trench Railway near 2nd AVENUE.

4. **DISPOSITION.**

    The Battalion will be disposed - B and C Coys. in GREEN LINE, D and A Coys. and Battalion Head Quarters in BEAUMONT HAMEL.

5. **DRESS.**

    Overcoats will be worn. One Blanket will be carried in the pack. If weather remains wet, waterproof sheets will be worn.

6. **TRENCH EQUIPMENT.**

    Very pistols, Periscopes &c. will be drawn from Orderly Room at 9.30 a.m. Camp Kettles will be carried under Coy. arrangements, cooks joining their platoons.

7. **DINNER.**

    Dinners will be at 11 a.m.

8. **BILLETS.**

    Huts, Tents, Cookhouses and the Camp generally will be left scrupulously clean. Certificates to this effect will be rendered to Orderly Room.
    O.C. Details will render by 11 a.m. a list of Huts, Tents and Camp Equipment.

9. **BLANKETS &c.**

    The second blanket of the men will be collected in one of the Coy. Huts, and Officers' Baggage in one of the Officers' Huts by 11.15 a.m. under the supervision of the Quarter Master, who will have the Band at his disposal for guard and loading. The necessary arrangements for removal will be made by Transport Officer and Quarter Master.

10. **REPORTS.**

    Coys. will report to Bn. Head Qrs. immediately their relief in the trenches is complete.

D. MacKenzie Lieut. & A/Adjt.
6th Bn. Gordon Highlanders.

Copy No 1 File
2-6 Coys
7 H.Q. Mess
8 Q Master
9 Transport Officer.

Operation Orders No 171
by Lieut Colonel J. Dawson, DSO
Commanding PUFF
In - the - Field, 22nd Novr 1916

1. <u>Move</u>

The Battalion will be relieved by the 2nd Battalion Queens to morrow.

Arrangements for guides on attached sheet

2. <u>March</u>

On relief the Battalion will move independently by platoons in file to FORCEVILLE by NEW BEAUMONT ROAD — AUCHONVILLERS — MAILLY MAILLET.

Guides will meet platoons at point where MAILLY ROAD enters FORCEVILLE.

3. <u>Packs Blankets &c</u>

All overcoats will be in packs, blankets and waterproof sheets attached. Packs will be collected and loaded under the supervision of CSMs. at Company Dumps along BEAUMONT ROAD near Ration Dump (between old British and old German front lines). This must be completed by 9.30 AM, and as not more than 12 men can be employed by one company for this purpose at one time, collection should be begun early. Each man should be able to carry several packs. One GS wagon will be provided for the packs of each Company Men will retain nothing but fighting kit.

Page 2.

4. <u>Cooks etc</u>:

All cooking utensils and unconsumed portion of the days rations will be taken to each of above Company dumps by 9.30 AM. The cooks of each Company will act as loading party, and accompany wagons to FORCEVILLE.

On arrival they will at once prepare dinners for the men.

5. <u>Lewis Guns</u>

On relief each Lewis Gun team will move independently to AUCHONVILLERS STATION where they will await limbers.

Magazines will be taken out EMPTY.

6. <u>Stores</u>.

All bandoliers, bombs, and the usual Trench Stores will be handed over on relief & receipts obtained.

Battalion stores, e.g. Periscopes, Very Pistols, Wiring Gloves, Wiring Shears, will be taken out, handed in to Q.M. Stores, and a receipt obtained.

4 full petrol tins of water will be handed over by each Company on relief.

7. <u>DugOuts etc</u>

All Dugouts, Cookhouses, & Latrines will be left scrupulously clean. O/C Companies will inspect these personally.

8.

8. **Relief**

Immediately relief is complete Companies will report to Battalion Headquarters by wire where possible, using surname of O/C Company as Codeword.

9. **Garrison**

The Garrison of Post in BEAUMONT ALLEY will be relieved as early as possible after dark. A guide will be left by A Company to guide relief. On relief the garrison will march to AUCHONVILLERS STATION where a G.S. wagon will meet them.

O MacKenzie
Lieut & A/Adj.
PUFF

Operation Orders No. 72,
by Lieut. Colonel J. Dawson, D.S.O.
Commanding 6th Gordon Highlanders.
Forceville, 26th Novr, 1916.

Copy No. 1

Reference Maps:-
FRANCE 57c S.W. 1/20,000.
" 57d S.E. 1/20,000.
Trench Map. LE SARS 1/10,000.

1. **MOVE.**

   The 6th Battalion Gordon Highlanders will move to BOUZINCOURT tomorrow 27th Novr.

2. **PARADE.**

   Companies will parade independently and will not form up on the street.
   The order of the march will be "A"; "C"; "B"; "D" & "HQ" Coys. Lewis Guns will accompany "HQ" Coy.
   Transport will march 200 yards in rear of Battalion, the head of the Transport column will be at road junction at P.21.d.3.6. at 2.40 p.m.

3. **MARCH.**

   The Battalion will march in file, 20 paces distance between platoons and 100 paces between Companies. The head of the Battalion will pass the junction of the road and track at P.27.b.5.7. at 2.30 p.m.

4. **DRESS.**

   Dress will be full marching order. Leather jerkins and steel helmets will be strapped to packs.

5. **BILLETING PARTY.**

   A party of Sgt. Dalgarno and 1 N.C.O. from each Company (including "HQ") will parade at the Orderly Room at 8.30 a.m. under 2/Lieut. D. MacDuff, and will proceed to BOUZINCOURT to report to the Town Major at 10 a.m.
   This party will meet the Battalion and guide Companies to billets.

6. **BAGGAGE.**

   All blankets will be tightly rolled up and collected in one billet per company by 10.30 a.m.
   Cooking utensils and Officers' baggage will be ready for collection at 1 p.m.

7. **BILLETS.**

   All billets, cookhouses, latrines and the vicinity of these will be left scrupulously clean. O/C Companies will render certificate to this effect on the pro forma issued.

8. **REPORTS.**

   Os/C Companies will report to Battalion Headquarters immediately new billets are taken over.

D. MacKenzie.
Lieut. & a Adj,
6th Gordon Highlanders.

Copy No. 1   File.
     2 - 6   Coys.
        7.   Transport Officer.
        8.   "HQ" Mess.
        9.   Quartermaster.

WAR DIARY

of

1/6th Battn. The GORDON HIGHLANDERS.

From

1st December, 1916.

To

31st December, 1916.

WAR DIARY

Army Form C. 2118.

WAR DIARY
or
INTELLIGENCE SUMMARY.
(Erase heading not required.)

Instructions regarding War Diaries and Intelligence Summaries are contained in F.S. Regs., Part II. and the Staff Manual respectively. Title pages will be prepared in manuscript.

Hour, Date, Place	Summary of Events and Information	Remarks and references to Appendices
	Map Reference FRANCE 1/2,400 57 D.S.E. and 57 C S.W.	
December, 1916		
1 – 3 FAUZINCOURT	Battalion in billets.	
3 – 9 near AVELUY	In BRUCE HUTS (W.16.a.)	
9 – 12 COURCELETTE	In support near Courcelette (CHALK MOUND, R.29.a. and surroundings) Lewis gunsteams took over Posts in front line on night of 11/12th, being relieved on night of 14/15th.	
12 – 15/16th	In front line from M.13.b.2.3. to M.14.b.6.3. Unit on left SEAFORTH HIGHLANDERS; Division on right.	
16th near VILLERS	In VILLERS HUTS. (X.7.d.)	
16 – 21 FAUZINCOURT	In billets	
21 – 27 near AVELUY	In BRUCE HUTS.	
27 – 31	"A" Company in dugout in COURCELETTE "B" Company in FRASER'S POST (near COURCELETTE) R.29.d. "C" and "D" Companies in VILLERS HUTS (X.7.d.)	
31	Ten Lewis Rifle teams occupied posts in front line for 48 hours.	

John W. Adams, Major,
Commanding 6th Gordon Highlanders.

Operation Orders No. 73. Copy No........
By Major J. W. Adams,
Commanding 6th Gordon Highlanders,
Bouzincourt, 2nd December, 1916.

Reference Trench Map.
Sheet 57d S.E. 1/20,000.

1. **MOVE.**

    The 6th Bn. Gordon Highlanders will relieve the 4th Bn. Seaforth Highlanders in BRUCE HUTS at W.16.a. tomorrow, 3rd December, 1916.

2. **PARADE.**

    Battalion will be clear of BOUZINCOURT by 10 a.m.
    Battalion will move by platoons in file; at 20 paces distance between platoons and 100 paces distance between Companies.
    The order of the march will be "B"; "D"; "C"; "A" and "HQ" Companies.
    The leading platoon of "B" Company will pass the Church at 9.30 a.m.

3. **DRESS.**

    Full marching order will be worn. Leather jerkins and steel helmets will be strapped to the packs. Kilt aprons will not be worn.

4. **BAGGAGE.**

    Cooks' utensils, blankets and Officers' baggage will be ready for collection by 8.45 a.m.

5. **BILLETS.**

    All billets will be left scrupulously clean.
    Certificates that billets have been personally inspected by Officers Commanding Companies, will be rendered to the Orderly Room.

6. **BILLETS.**

    Officers Commanding Companies will report to Orderly Room immediately they have taken over new billets.

                                    D. Mackay, Lieut. & a/Adjt,
                                    6th Gordon Highlanders.

Copy No. 1   File.
        2 - 6 Companies.
        7   H.Q. Mess.
        8   Transport.
        9   Quartermaster.

No. 74

Operation Orders by Major J. W. Adams,
Commanding 6th Gordon Highlanders,
near AVELUY, 8th Decr. 1916.

---

1. **RELIEF.**

   The 6th Gordon Highlanders will relieve the 4th Gordon Highrs. in the support position near COURCELETTE tomorrow. Companies will relieve corresponding companies of the 4th Gordon Highrs.

2. **MOVE.**

   The Battalion will move in platoons in file at 5 minutes intervals. Order of the march will be :— A. B. C. D. H.Q. Coys., S.B'S. and Signallers marching with the companies to which they are attached.   Route — AVELUY — CROMWELL HUTS — OVILLERS.
   The leading platoon of A Company will leave at 5.20 p.m., and will, at 7.10 p.m., reach the GUM BOOT STORE at POZIERES x.4.c.5.3., where Platoon Guides will meet the Battalion.

3. **DRESS.**

   Fighting Order with Great Coats and Jerkins will be worn. Two days' rations, full Water Bottles, two dry pairs of socks and two Sandbags will be carried on the man.
   All Blankets, Kilts, Packs and Baggage will be clearly marked and ready for collection by 2 p.m.
   One pair of Gum Boots will be carried — not worn — by each man.

4. **TRENCH STORES.**

   Sandbags, Periscopes, Very Pistols and Ammunition will be drawn by companies and Lewis Gunners during the forenoon.

5. **BILLETS.**

   The Camp and its surroundings will be left scrupulously clean. The usual Certificates will be rendered before the companies move off.

6. **GENERAL.**

   O. C. Companies will ensure that, before moving off, each man has his feet and legs rubbed well with Whale Oil.
   No lights may be shown, and no smoke visible, in the new area. This must be made known to all ranks.

7. **RELIEF.**

   Immediately the relief is completed, Companies will report to Battalion Head Quarters, using the name of the O. C. Company as a Code Name.

D. MacKenzie. Lieut. & A/Adjt.
6th Gordon Highlanders. (T. F.)

TABLE of RELIEFS issued with OPERATION ORDERS No 76.

Company	To	Unit Relieved	Time first platoon leaves.
"H.Q"	OVILLERS HUTS	7th A. & S. Hrs.	1.35 p.m.
"C"	do.	do.	1.39 p.m.
"D"	do.	do.	1.47 p.m.
"A"	COURCELETTE	4th Seaforth Hrs.	4.20 p.m.
"B"	FRASER POST	4th Gordon Hrs.	4.28 p.m.

Warning Order by Major J. W. Adams,
Comdg. 6th Gordon Highlanders,
near AVELUY, 7th Decr. 1916.

1. MOVE.

The Battalion will move to a position in support on the night 9/10th December 1916.

2. PARADES.

All parades for the 8th December are cancelled. All Night Fatigue parties will be waked by 11 a.m.

3. DRESS.

Trousers, Puttees and Body Belts will be issued at 11 a.m. on the 8th to all ranks proceeding to the Line. Fighting Order will be worn in the Line. All Kilts will be collected in bundles of 10 and clearly marked under Company arrangements. Kilts and packs will be removed to Q.M. Stores by 2 R.S. Wagons at 2 p.m. on the 8th.
Balmorals will be placed in packs. Spare Socks will be retained, and not left in Packs. Men going on leave on 8th and 9th December will retain their ~~kits~~ Kilts and packs.

4. EQUIPMENT.

All Officers will ensure that their commands are fully equipped, and that any deficiencies are made up.

5. ADVANCE PARTY.

An Advance Party consisting of 2nd Lieuts. 19 THOMSON, BRUCE, DUNCAN and WOOD, 1 N.C.O. per platoon and Corporal DON will parade in Camp at 1.30 a.m. on the morning of 9th December, and proceed to report at Head Quarters, 154th Infantry Brigade at R.29. Central by 4 a.m.
The Servants of above mentioned Officers will accompany this party.
3 days' Rations and full Water Bottles will be carried.
This party will obtain full information regarding the positions of all DUMPS, and all arrangements about Rations, Water Supply, and Quarters.

6. GENERAL.

Blankets and Officers' Baggage will be collected on 9th.
Clean Socks will be issued and dirty Socks withdrawn on 9th.

Detailed Operation Orders will be published later.

D. MacKenzie. Lt. & Adjt.
6th Gordon Highlanders.

Copy No. 1

Operation Orders No 75.
by Major J.W. Adams.
Commanding 6th Gordon Highlanders
BOUZINCOURT, 20th December, 1916.

Map Reference:- FRANCE 57 D.S.E. 1/20,000.

(1) MOVE:

The 6th Battalion Gordon Highlanders will relieve the 9th Battalion Royal Scots in Bruce Huts at W.16.a. to-morrow 21st December.

(2) PARADE.

The Battalion will be clear of BOUZINCOURT by 10a.m.
Battalion will move in file at 20 paces distance between platoons and 100 paces distance between Companies.
Order of march will be A. B. C. D. and H.Q. Coys.
The leading platoon of B Company will pass the road junction 100 yards N.E. of BOUZINCOURT Church at 9.30a.m.

(3) DRESS.

Full marching order. Steel Helmets will be carried strapped to the pack. Kilt aprons will not be worn.

(4) BAGGAGE:

Cooks' utensils, blankets, and officers' baggage will be ready for collection by 8.45 a.m.
Three G.S. wagons will report at Headquarters at 9 a.m. to-morrow for blankets.

(5) BILLETS:

All billets will be left scrupulously clean, and the usual certificates of cleanliness or otherwise rendered by Os/C Companies.

(6) BILLETING PARTIES:

A Billeting Party of 1 officer and 4 men per Company will report to Lieutenant Minty at Headquarters at 8.30 a.m. to proceed in advance and take over the huts.

McPherson Capt. & Adj.
6th Gordon Highlanders.

Copy No 1. Adjutant
2 - 6 Companies.
7 Quartermaster and a/Transport Officer.
8 & 9 Spare.

Copy No. 1

Operation Orders No 76
by Major J. W. Adams,
Commanding 6th Gordon Highlanders
In-the-Field, 26th December, 1916.

Map References 57 C. S.W. 1/20.000
57 D. S.W. 1/20.000

1. **OPERATION:**

   The 6th Battalion Gordon Highlanders will relieve Companies of the 154th Infantry Brigade during the night 27/28th December 1916, in accordance with the attached table.
   Platoons will move at 200 yards distance.

2. **GUIDES:**

   Platoon Guides from 4th Seaforth Highlanders for "A" and "B" Companies will be at the Red Cross Flag, POZIERES, at 6 p.m.

3. **GUM BOOTS:**

   Gum Boots will not be worn on the march.

4. **BLANKETS:**

   All blankets will be rolled in bundles by 10 a.m.
   Those of "A" and "B" Companies will be taken to the Quartermaster's Store.
   Those of the remainder of the Battalion will be taken to OVILLERS HUTS.
   2 G.S. wagons will be at BRUCE HUTS at 9 a.m.

5. **KILTS:**

   Kilts of "A" and "B" Companies will be stored in the Quartermaster's store along with their blankets.

6. **KITS:**

   Officers' baggage and Mess kit will be packed and ready for loading by 1.15 p.m.

7. **TRANSPORT:**

   Horses for Lewis Gun Limbers will be at BRUCE HUTS at 1.15 p.m.

8. **RATIONS:**

   "A" and "B" Companies will carry the following day's rations on the man with the exception of fuel.

9. **HANDING OVER BILLETS:**

   Companies will leave a party of 1 officer and 4 men to hand over their billets and obtain receipts for all stores.
   1 officer from "C" and "D" Companies and 4 men per platoon, and 1 N.C.O. from Headquarters Company will proceed two hours in advance of the Battalion to take over huts at OVILLERS.

10. **CLEANLINESS OF HUTS:**

    The usual certificates as to the cleanliness of huts will be required.

11. **REPORTS:**

    Completion of all moves will be reported to Battalion Headquarters.

                                        Capt & Adj.
                                        6th Gordon Highlanders.

Copy No. 1   Adjutant
       2 - 6   Companies
          7   Quartermaster
          8   Transport Sergeant
          9   Spare.

Copy No. 1

Operation Orders No 77
by Major J. W. Adams,
Commanding 6th Gordon Highlanders,
In-the-Field, 31st December 1916.

Map References FRANCE 1/20,000
57 D. S.E. and 57 C S.W.

1. **OPERATION:**
   The 6th Battalion Gordon Highlanders will relieve the 6th Battalion Seaforth Highlanders in the right subsector of the line on the night of 31st Decr/1st January.

2. **RELIEF:**
   "C" Company will relieve the right Company of 6th Seaforth Highlanders; "D" Company the left Company.

3. **MARCH:**
   The order of the march will be:-
   "C", "D", and "H.Q".
   Companies will move by platoons at 5 minutes' interval.
   First platoon of "C" Company to move off at 2.40 p.m.

4. **GUM BOOTS:**
   Gum Boots will be carried to the junction of the WATTLE TRACK and the ALBERT – BAPAUME Road when they will be put on. Platoons will be allowed 2 minutes for changing boots. This time must be strictly adhered to.
   Platoon Commanders are responsible that an interval of 150 yards is maintained while they are halted to change boots.

5. **GUIDES:**
   Platoon Guides will be at the SOUP KITCHEN near Brigade Headquarters at 4.30 p.m.

6. **LIGHT SECTION:**
   Half the Light Section will be attached to each of "C" and "D" Companies. Cpl Don will report to Lieut Duncan at Battalion Headquarters in the line.

7. **BAGGAGE:**
   All baggage and officers' kits will be packed and ready for loading by 2 p.m.

8. **TRANSPORT:**
   Cookers and Watercarts with the Cooks of "C" and "D" Companies will return to the Transport lines.

9. **RATIONS and WATER:**
   Two days' rations will be carried on the man.
   All waterbottles will be filled, and Companies will, in addition, carry up the following day's supply.
   The Quartermaster will arrange for the transport of the necessary water.

10. **HANDING OVER:**
    The usual Handing Over Certificates and certificates as to cleanliness of billets will be rendered.
    Lieutenants Grey and Minty will remain behind to hand over the huts to 8th Argyll & Sutherland Highlanders.

11. **FEET:**
    The feet of all officers and men are to be well rubbed with whale oil during the forenoon.

12. **REPORTS:**
    OS/C "C" and "D" Companies will report the completion of the relief to Battalion Headquarters in code.

    Capt. & Adjt.
    6th Gordon Highlanders.

152nd Inf. Bde. SECRET No. 134.

WAR DIARY
of
1/6th Bn. The GORDON HIGHLANDERS.

CONFIDENTIAL.
No 21(A)
HIGHLAND DIVISION.

FROM
1st JANUARY, 1917.

TO
31st JANUARY, 1917.

Army Form C. 2118.

CONFIDENTIAL.

No 21(?)

WAR DIARY
or
INTELLIGENCE SUMMARY.

HIGHLAND DIVISION.

(Erase heading not required.)

Instructions regarding War Diaries and Intelligence Summaries are contained in F. S. Regs., Part II. and the Staff Manual respectively. Title pages will be prepared in manuscript.

Place	Date	Hour	Summary of Events and Information	Remarks and references to Appendices
Front line	1-2		In Front line, North of COURCELETTE, M.13.b.2.3. — M.14.b.6.3. (FRANCE 57 D. S.E.) 8th F.O.S.H., 15th Division on right, 5th Seaforth Highlanders, 51st Division, on our left.	
OVILLERS HUTS	2-3		Rested night at OVILLERS HUTS	
BOUZINCOURT	3-7		At rest in BOUZINCOURT	
BRUCE HUTS	8-12		In BRUCE HUTS, AVELUY, General Fatigue.	
BOUZINCOURT	12-13		Night at BOUZINCOURT, Preparatory to march to Training Area at HAUTVILLERS.	
RAINCHEVAL	13-14		At RAINCHEVAL	
BOIS BERGUES	14-15		At BOIS BERGUES	
YVRENCH	15-16		At YVRENCH	
HAUTVILLERS	16-31		Refitting and Training at HAUTVILLERS	

J. Dawson Lieut Colonel
Commanding 6th Gordon Highlanders.

"A" Form.   Army Form C. 2121.

MESSAGES AND SIGNALS.

Confidential

TO **Headquarters 152nd Brigade**

Sender's Number: GR.7. 76.
Day of Month: 1st
AAA

Herewith War Diary for January.

From **Commanding 6th Gordon Highlanders**
Time 9 AM

Lt Colonel

SECRET
No. 134
152nd INF. BDE.

WAR   DIARY

of

1/6th Bn.   GORDON   HIGHLANDERS.

from

1st FEBRUARY 1917.

to

28th FEBRUARY 1917.

———————————

Army Form C. 2118.

WAR DIARY
or
INTELLIGENCE SUMMARY.
(Erase heading not required.)

Instructions regarding War Diaries and Intelligence
Summaries are contained in F. S. Regs., Part II.
and the Staff Manual respectively. Title pages
will be prepared in manuscript.

Place	Date February 1917	Hour	Summary of Events and Information	Remarks and references to Appendices
HAUTVILLERS	1-5		In Billets. Training.	
GAPENNES	5/6		March to New Area	
	6/7		Billets.	
BOIRE AU BOIS	7/8		Do.	
FRAMECOURT	8/9		Do.	
GRENCOURT	9/10		Do.	
HERMIN	10/11		In Huts S.W. of Village.	
ECOIVRES	11-16		" Billets.	
MAROEUIL	17-23		" Trenches N.E. of ROCLINCOURT. A very quiet part of the line.	
MAROEUIL	24-27		" Billets.	
ACQ	27-28		" Do.	Battn. billeted at MAROEUIL and ACQ.

A5834 Wt.W4973/M687 750,000 8/16 D.D.& L. Ltd. Forms/C.2118/13

Operation Orders and Instructions for carrying out a Brigade Attack
Practice February 3rd, 1917.

Hautvillers 2nd. February 1917.

1. The Battalion will take part in a Brigade practice attack to-morrow 3rd. inst.

2. The Battalion will parade on main road opposite Q.M. stores at 8-15 a.m. The order of march will be A.C.B.D. Companies.

3. Assembly positions have been pointed out; these will be occupied and troops ready to advance by 9 a.m.

4. Frontages and objectives as arranged.

5. Dress. Fighting Order with Steel Helmets.
Jerkins will be worn.
Kilt Aprons will not be worn.

6. Ammunition etc. All S.A.A. will be withdrawn and rifles and pouches inspected by an officer before marching off.
Bomb buckets but no bombs will be carried: Battalion Bombing Officer to arrange for distribution.
Lewis Gun drums will be carried but will be empty. Battalion L.G.O. to issue definite orders regarding carrying of these, but Company Officers are responsible that they are empty.

7. Each attack will be started by the "Advance" sounding, and at the end of each attack, on the "No Parade" being sounded, units will return to their position in the assembly trenches.

8. Boundary lines between stubble and plough will be held to represent Communication trenches.
Dug-outs will be marked by notice boards and the Barrage by flagmen.
Drums will be used to represent a Vickers Gun in action.

9. The fullest use will be made of Scouts & Runners by all Commanders.

10. It must be impressed upon every man that the leading line must be not more than 50 yards from the Barrage, the line conforming to the line of the Barrage and not taking its dressing from the right or left.

11. All officers will have a few message forms ready addres--sed and signed.

12. Flares will be issued to C and D companies, and will be used when the objective is reached and then only before the Argyll's pass through them; that is, when the Gordons are the leading line. Half will be used in each attack.

13. Stretcher-bearers carrying stretchers, will accompany the advance. Casualty tickets will be issued. The Aid Post will be near Battalion H.Q.

14. Battalion Headquarters will be in Second Assembly Trench, near Bushes pointed out to-day.

15. All Pipers and Big Drummer will report to Staff Captain at Assembly Trenches at 9 a.m. Pipes will be taken.
Two side drummers, with drums, will report to O/C 2nd M.G. Company at Assault Trenches at 9 a.m.
Remaining side drummer, with drum, will parade with a "D" Company Lewis Gun Team.
Bugler will report to Brigade Major at Assembly Trenches at 9 a.m.

Page 2.

16. A second attack will be made at 11.30 a.m. The enemy will be represented by the 6th Seaforth Highlanders. Every precaution must be taken against counter-attacks, especially from a flank. Any such must be resolutely dealt with.

17. Dinners will be at 2 p.m.

D MacKenzie Lieut & A/Adj.
6th Gordon Highlanders

Copy No. 1

Operation Orders No 86
by Lieut Colonel J. Dawson, D.S.O.
Commanding 6th Gordon Highlanders
HAUTVILLERS, 4th February, 1917.
———oOo———

1. **MOVE**

    The Battalion will move from present billets to CAPENNES to-morrow 5th instant.

2. **STARTING POINT and TIME**

    The Battalion will be formed up on road through village, ready to move off at 10 a.m.; the head of the column at Church. Order:- H.Q., "A", "B", "C", and "D" Companies.

3. **ORDER OF MARCH**

    The Battalion will move closed — 10 paces between Companies: Lewis Gun carts behind Companies and before Transport.

4. **BAGGAGE**

    Company blankets will be collected in one of the billets, and 2 men (not likely to stand the march) detailed to take charge. H.Q. Details' and Band's blankets to be collected at Q.M. Stores, and 1 man left in charge.

    Pipe Major Howarth will be responsible for collection and delivery of blankets.

    Officers' valises, Company blankets etc., will be ready for collection by 8.30 a.m.

5. **ADVANCE PARTY:**

    2/Lieut Archibald, Sergt Dalgarno, and 4 orderlies will leave at 9 a.m.

6. **CERTIFICATES**

    The usual certificates regarding cleanliness of billets will be rendered before marching off.

7. **RETURN**

    On completion of march OS/C Companies will send to Orderly Room a return showing number of men who have fallen out on the march.

    The Battalion established a record on its march down country in not losing a man en route. It is hoped that an endeavour will be made to finish the up journey also with Nil returns.

8. **PARADES:**

    Sick Parade   8.15 a.m.

    Orderly Room   9 a.m.

9. DRESS Full marching order: Balmorals and leather jerkins will be worn. Kilt aprons will not be worn.

    [signature] Lieut & A Adj.
    6th Gordon Highlanders.

Copy No 1   File
        2-5 Companies
        6   Transport Officer
        7   Quartermaster
        8   L.G.O.

Copy No. 1

Operation Orders No. 87
by Lieut. Col. J. Dawson, D.S.O.,
Commanding 6th. Gordon Highlanders.
GAPENNES, 5th. February 1917.

Reference Maps FRANCE,
ABBEVILLE 14, LENS 11.

1. MOVE.

    The 6th. Battalion Gordon Highlanders will move on the 6th. February to BUIRENAU-BOIS.

2. PARADE.

    The Battalion will be formed up on the road through the village ready to move off at 8a.m. The head of the column will be at the Church. The order of march will be Headquarters, B, C, D, & A Companies.

3. BAGGAGE.

    All baggage and blankets will be ready for collection by 7 a.m.

4. ADVANCE PARTY.

    The usual billeting party will leave at 8 a.m.

5. GENERAL.

    The instructions issued in Operation Order No 86 — issued yesterday — regarding Dress, Certificates, Returns, and collection of blankets will hold good during the remainder of the march, unless otherwise ordered.

    Pipe Major Howarth will meet the motor lorries at the Church at 7 a.m.

                                            D Mackenzie Lieut & A/Adj.
                                                         6th Gordon Highlanders.

    Copy No 1   File
           2 - 5 Companies
             6   Transport Officer
             7   Quartermaster
             8   L.G.O.

Copy No 1...

Operation Orders No. 88
by Lieut. Colonel J.Dawson, D.S.O.,
Commanding 6th. Gordon Highlanders.
BUIRE-AU-BOIS 6th. February, 1917.

---

1. **MOVE.**

    The 6th. Battalion Gordon Highlanders will move from its present billets to-morrow, 7th. February. Battalion less "D" Company, will move to FRAMECOURT and PETIT-HOUVIN; "D" Company to SERICOURT.

2. **PARADE.**

    The Battalion will be formed up on the road through the village ready to march off at 9.15 a.m. The head of the column will be at the church. The order of march, from the North, will be H.Q., "D", "C", "A" and "B" Companies.

3. **BAGGAGE**

    All blankets and baggage will be ready for collection by 8 a.m. One motor lorry will be detailed to take all "D" Company's blankets, baggage, officers' kits, camp kettles, rations, etc.
    Pipe Major Howarth will supervise the collection and delivery of all blankets, except "D" Company's. O/C "D" Company will detail a N.C.O. for this purpose.

4. **ADVANCE PARTY**

    An Advance Party of 2/Lieut J. Archibald, Sergt Dalgarno, and 3 orderlies will leave at 8.30 a.m. O/C "D" Company will detail an Officer to go in advance with this party to arrange for billets in SERICOURT.

5. **LEAVE PARTY**

    The party going on leave will join "D" Company. 2/Lieut K. MacKay will take charge of this party, and will march them from SERICOURT to FREVENT during the afternoon.

6. **GENERAL**

    The instructions already issued regarding dress, march discipline, returns and certificates, will be observed.

    D. Mackenzie   Lieut & A/Adj.
    6th Gordon Highlanders

Copy No 1   File
       2   H.Q. 152nd Inf. Brigade.
     3 - 6 Companies
       7   Transport Officer
       8   Quartermaster
       9   L.G.O.
      10   Pipe Major Howarth

Copy No. 1.

Operation Orders No. 89,
by Lieut. Colonel J. Dawson, D.S.O.,
commanding 6th. Gordon Highlanders.

Map Reference, FRANCE,
1:100,000.   LENS 11.

1. MOVE.

The 6th. Battalion Gordon Highlanders will move from its present billets to-morrow 8th. February to ORLENCOURT.

2. PARADE.

The Battalion will be formed up ready to move off at 9a.m., on the road running S.E. through the village. The head of the column will be at the cross-roads due west of the P. in Pt. HOUVIN. C. and D Companies will arrange to rendezvous at the cross-roads ~~by the order of~~ by 9a.m.
The order of march will be H.Q., C.D.A.B companies.

3. BAGGAGE.

All Blankets and Baggage will be packed ready for collection by 8 a.m. The Transport Officer and Quarter Master will arrange for the collection, conveyance and delivery of blankets.

4. ADVANCE PARTY.

2/Lieut. J. Archibald and the usual billeting party will proceed to ORLENCOURT on the afternoon of the 7th February.

5. BILLETS.

Officers commanding companies are reminded that it is their duty personally to inspect all billets occupied by men under their command before moving off. This inspection should be independent of the inspection of billets by Platoon Commanders, and will be made in sufficient time to allow any instructions they may issue to be carried out.

6. GENERAL.

The instructions already issued regarding Dress, March Discipline, Returns and Certificates will be observed.

Lieut. & A/Adj.
6th Gordon Highlanders.

Copy No. 1 - File.
2 - Head Qrs. 152nd Brigade.
3- 6 - Companies.
7. Transport Officer.
8. Quarter Master.
9. Lewis Gun Officer.

AMENDMENTS to O.O. No 89

The following alterations are made in the times stated in O.O. No 89

1. All blankets and baggage will be ready for collection by 9.30 a.m.
2. The Battalion will be ready to move off in the order already given from the appointed rendezvous at 11.15 a.m.

Mackenzie Lieut & A/Adj.
6th Gordon Highlanders

SECRET.

6th GORDON HIGHRS.

On February 8th the 152nd Inf. Brigade Group marches through ST. POL where the Third Army Headquarters are situated.

The Brigadier General Comdg. wishes Commanders to ensure that proper march discipline is observed and that units march well closed up.

If the column is checked in the town itself care must be taken that the side streets leading into the route are not blocked by the halted troops or vehicles.

[signature]

Captain,
Brigade Major,
152nd Infantry Brigade.

6th February, 1917.

Copy No. 1

Operation Orders No. 90,
by Lieut. Colonel J. Dawson D.S.O.
commanding 6th. Gordon Highlanders
ORLENCOURT 8th February 1917.

1. MOVE

    The 6th. Battalion Gordon Highlanders will move from present billets to HERMIN on Friday 9th. February.

2. PARADE.

    The Battalion will parade on the street through the village, ready to march off at 10ᵃ a.m.   The head of the column will be at the most easterly billet of "C" Company.   The order of march will be H.Q., A, B, C, D Companies.

3. BAGGAGE.

    All Baggage and Blankets will be ready for collection by 9a.m.   The Transport Officer and Quartermaster will arrange for the conveyance of blankets.   The loading and delivery of blankets will be supervised by Pipe Major Howarth.

4. ADVANCE PARTY.

    2/Lieut. Archibald and the usual billeting party will move in accordance with instructions already issued.

5. GENERAL.

    The usual instructions regarding DRESS, March Discipl-ine, Certificates and Returns will be observed.

                                        _____, Lieut. & A/Adjt.
                                                6th. Gordon Highlanders.

Copy No. 1.   File.
          2.   H.Q. 152nd. Inf. Bde.
          3-6 Companies.
          7.   Quarter Master.
          8.   Transport Officer.
          9.   L.G.O.

Operation Orders No. 91,
by Lieut. Colonel J. Dawson D.S.O.
Commanding 6th. Gordon Highlanders.
HERMIN 9th. February 1917.

Copy No. 1.

1. MOVE.

The 6th. Battalion Gordon Highlanders will move from its present billets to ACQ to-morrow February 10th.

2. PARADE.

The Battalion will parade ready to march off at ~~10am~~ 9.30am in the street through the village. the head of the column will be at the bridge on the CAUCOURT road, North East of the village. The order of march will be H.Q., B, C, D and A Coys.

3. BAGGAGE.

All baggage and blankets will be ready for collection by 8.15a.m. The Quartermaster and Transport Officer will arrange for the conveyance and delivery of blankets. All transport will be at the top of the hill immediately East of the village by ~~10a.m.~~ 9.30am.

4. ADVANCE PARTY.

2/Lieut. Archibald and the usual billeting party will move in accordance with instructions already issued.

5. GENERAL.

The instructions already issued regarding Dress, March Discipline, Certificates and Returns will be observed.

D. MacKenzie .... Lieut. & A/Adjt.
6th. Gordon Highlanders.

Copy No.   1. File.
2. H.Q. 152nd. Inf. Bde.
3. -6 Companies.
7. Transport Officer.
8. Quartermaster.
9. L.G.O.
10. H.Q. Mess.
11. Pipe Major.

Operation Orders No. 92   Copy No. 1
by Lieut. Colonel J. Dawson, D.S.O.
Commanding 6th. Gordon Highlanders.
ECOIVRES 10th. February 1917.

1. **MOVE.**

    The 6th. Battalion Gordon Highlanders will move from its present quarters to MAROEUIL to-morrow, February 11th. 1917.

2. **PARADE.**

    Companies will parade on the road near the camp at the under mentioned hours, and will move by platoons at 100 paces interval. H.Q. Details will move in the rear of A Company.

    A.Coy.   1.45 p.m.
    B.Coy.   1.50 p.m.
    C.Coy.   1.55 p.m.
    D.Coy.   2.   p.m.

    Each Company will send one officer to reconnoitre the route during the forenoon.

3. **BAGGAGE.**

    All Baggage and blankets will be ready for collection by 10 a.m.. The Transport Officer will arrange for the conveyance and delivery of these. This will be complete by 4 p.m.

    Each Company will detail one N.C.O. and 2 men to move with the waggons and to act as guard over the company blankets.

    Cookers and Mess Cart will move in the rear of the Battalion.

4. **ADVANCE PARTY.**

    W/Lieut. Archibald, Sgt. Dalgarno and one N.C.O. per Company will report to the Town Major, MAROEUIL at QP 10.30 a.m. N.C.O's will parade at the Orderly Room at 9.40 a.m.

5. **GENERAL.**

    The instructions regarding Dress, March Discipline, Returns and Certificates will be observed.

                     D. MacKenzie   Lieut. & A/Adjt.
                                6th. Gordon Highlanders.

Copy No.   1.   File.
            2.   H.Q. 152nd. Inf. Bde.
            3.-6   Companies.
            7.   Transport Officer.
            8.   Quartermaster.
            9.   L.G.O.
           10.   Spare.

Copy No. 1

Operation Orders No 93
by Lieut Colonel J. Dawson, D.S.O.
Commanding 6th Gordon Highlanders
MAROEUIL, 14th February, 1917.

Cancelled by No 94

1. **OPERATION:**
   The 6th Battalion Gordon Highlanders will relieve the 6th Battalion Seaforth Highlanders in the forward area to-morrow 15th February.

2. **RELIEF:**
   Companies and Platoons of this Battalion will relieve corresponding platoons and companies of the 6th Seaforth Highlanders. "B", and "D" Companies will take over the front line trenches. "D" Company on the right, "B" Company on the left. "A" Company and Battalion Headquarters will be in ROCLINCOURT, "C" Company in ANZIN.

3. **PARADE:**
   The Battalion will move by platoons at 100 paces interval. The order of march will be:- H.Q. Details, "D" "B", "A", and "C" Companies. The leading platoon of "D" Company will leave at 1.45 p.m.

4. **GUIDES**
   Guides at the rate of 1 per platoon will meet the Battalion at ANZIN CHURCH at 2.30 p.m.

5. **LEWIS GUNS:**
   4 Lewis Guns will move with "B" Company, 4 with "A" Company, 3 with "D" Company, and 1 with "C" Company, the L.G.O. to make the necessary arrangements: Gun teams will move along with platoons in whose area their positions are. Lewis Gun magazines will not be carried.

6. **DRESS:**
   Full marching order. Leather Jerkins and kilt aprons will be worn. Full water bottles will be carried.

7. **TRENCH EQUIPMENT:**
   "A", "B", and "D" Companies will each draw from the Q.M. Stores in the forenoon 2 1" Very Pistols, 1 1½" Very Pistols, 4 Box, 12 Vigilant and 1 Life Guard periscopes. (The last for the use of Officers)

8. **TRANSPORT:**
   1 Travelling Kitchen will accompany "C" Company. Camp kettles for the remaining Companies will be taken up with the rations. The cooks of "A", "B", and "D" Companies will accompany the ration limbers with the exception of the Sergeant Cook, and 1 per Company who will move with Headquarters Details to find the exact location of cookhouses.
   The tool wagon, with picks and shovels, will be sent up with ration limbers. "C" Company's blankets will accompany that Company to ANZIN.

9. **BAGGAGE:**
   Officers' baggage and blankets will be ready for collection by 11 a.m. Each Company will detail a loading party. The Quartermaster and the Transport Officer will arrange for their collection and removal to the Q.M. Stores.

10. BILLETS/

Page 2.

10. BILLETS
All billets, cookhouses, and latrines will be left scrupulously clean. Companies will render certificates to this effect to the Orderly Room before moving off.

11. REPORTS:
Companies will report to Orderly Room by Runner immediately relief is complete. Two Runners per Company should be sent in order to reconnoitre the route to Battalion Headquarters.

D. Mackenzie
Lieut & A/Adj.
6th Gordon Highlanders

Copy No 1   File
       2   H.Q. 152nd Inf. Bde.
  3 - 6   Companies
       7   Transport Officer
       8   Quartermaster
       9   L.G.O.
     10   H.Q. Details.
     11   H.Q. Mess

COPY NO. 1

Operation Orders No. 94
by Lieut. Colonel J. Dawson D.S.O.
Commanding 6th Gordon Highlanders.
MAROEUIL 16th. February 1917.

1. **OPERATION.**
   The 6th. Battalion Gordon Highlanders will relieve the 6th. Battalion Seaforth Highlanders in the forward area to-morrow 17th. February.

2. **DISPOSITION.**
   "B" and "D" Companies will take over the front line trenches - "D" Company on the right, "B" Company on the left. "A" Company and Battalion Headquarters will be in ROCLINCOURT, "C" Company in ANZIN.

3. **PARADE.**
   The Battalion will move by platoons at a hundred paces interval. The order of march will be:- H.Q. Details, "D", "B", "A" and "C" Companies. The leading platoon of "D" Company will leave at 1.45p.m.

4. **GUIDES.**
   Guides at the rate of 1 per platoon, and 1 per Company Headquarters will meet the Battalion at ANZIN CHURCH at 2.30p.m.

5. **LEWIS GUNS.**
   4 Lewis Guns will move with "B" Company, 4 with "D" Company, 3 with "A" Company and 1 with "C" Company, the L.G.O. to make the necessary arrangements. Gun teams will move along with platoons in whose area their positions are. Lewis Gun Magazines will not be carried.

6. **DRESS.**
   Full marching order. Leather Jerkins and Kilt Aprons will be worn. Full water bottles will be carried.

7. **TRENCH EQUIPMENT.**
   "A", "B" and "D" Companies will each draw from the Q.M. Stores in the forenoon two 1" very pistols, one 1½" very pistol, 4 Box, 12 Vigilant, and 1 Lifeguard, periscopes. (The last for the use of officers).

8. **TRANSPORT.**
   1 Travelling Kitchen will accompany "C" Company. Camp Kettles for the remaining Companies will be taken up with the rations. The cooks of "A", "B" and "D" Companies will accompany the ration limbers, with the exception of the Sergt. Cook and 1 per Company who will move with H.Q. Details to find the exact location of Cook-houses.
   "C" Company's blankets will accompany that Company to ANZIN.

9. **BAGGAGE.**
   All blankets and officers' baggage will be removed to the Q.M. Stores under Company arrangements, by 12 noon.

10. **BILLETS.** All Billets, Cook-houses and latrines will be left scrupulously clean. Companies will render certificates to this effect to the Orderly Room before moving off.

11. **REPORTS.**
    Companies will report to Orderly Room by Runner immediately relief is complete. Two Runners per Company should be sent in order to reconnoitre the route to Battalion Headquarters.

D. Mackenzie
Lieut. & A/Adjt.
6th. Gordon Highlanders.

Copy No. 1

Operation Orders No. 95,
by Lieut. Colonel J. Dawson, D.S.O.
Commanding 6th. Gordon Highlanders.
ROCLINCOURT trenches, 19th. Feb. 1917.

---

1. RELIEF.

    An inter-company relief will be carried out to-morrow 20th. February. "A" Company will relieve "B" Company, and "C" Company will relieve "D" Company.

2. GUIDES.

    Guides at the rate of 1 per platoon and 1 per Company Headquarters will rendezvous at the Ration Dump to meet "A" Company at 2.30 p.m. and to meet "C" Company at 2.45 p.m.
    "B" and "D" Companies will one junior N.C.O. per platoon during the forenoon to take over new areas and to guide guide their Companies in, on relief. "B" Company will send an officer during the forenoon to take over the defences of ROCLINCOURT.

3. MARCH.

    Platoons will move at an interval of at least a hundred yards along trenches.

4. LEWIS GUNS.

    The Lewis Gun Officer will make the necessary arrangements for the disposition of Lewis Guns.

5. COOKING.

    "C" Company will take over "D" Company's cook-house, camp-kettles and vice-versa.

6. BAGGAGE.

    "C" Company's blankets and officers' baggage will be ready for collection by 11 a.m. The Transport Officer will send up "D" Company's blankets and officers' kits. Echelon B will remain at ANZIN.

7. WORK.

    All working parties will cease work at 12 noon. "A" and "C" Companies will arrange to carry on the usual work of patrol, wire-cutting and improvement of trenches. "B" and "D" Companies will take over the working parties of "A" and "C" Companies. These will not be required on the night of 20th.-21st., with the exception of the food and ration parties which will be supplied by "B" Company.

8. SCHEMES.

    Each relieving Company will get from the Company relieved a full scheme of the work in hand, and a list of stores.

9. BILLETS.

    Billets, dug-outs, cook-houses, latrines and the trenches generally will be left scrupulously clean.

10. REPORTS.

    The completion of relief will be at once wired to Battalion Headquarters, the code word "SAP" being used.

                                    D. MacKenzie Lieut. & A/Adjt.
                                         6th. Gordon Highlanders.

Copy No. 1.   File.
  "   2.   H.Q. 152nd. Bde.
  "   3-6.   Coys.
  "   7.   Transport Officer.
  "   8.   Quartermaster.
  "   9.   L.G.O.
  "   10.   H.Q. Mess.

Copy No. 1

Operation Orders No. 26
by Lieut. Colonel J. Dawson D.S.O.
Commanding 6th. Gordon Highlanders.
Roclincourt trenches 22nd Feb. 1917.

1. RELIEF.

    The 6th. Battalion Seaforth Highlanders will relieve the 6th. Battalion Gordon Highlanders in the forward area to-morrow 23rd. February.

2. MOVE.

    Immediately relief is complete Companies will move by platoons to MAROEUIL and occupy the same billets as when last there. "D" Coy. will leave ANZIN by 11a.m. 1 N.C.O. per platoon and 1 officer will be left by "D" Company to hand over.

3. GUIDES.

    Guides at the rate of one per platoon and one per Coy. Hd. Qrs. will rendezvous at the baths ROCLINCOURT at 2.30p.m. 2/Lieut. Duncan will marshal the guides.

4. LEWIS GUNS.

    All Lewis Gun Magazines taken over from the 6th. Seaforths will be handed back to them on relief. Each Company will obtain a receipt for all magazines and buckets handed over by teams in its lines.

5. TOOLS ETC.

    Work will cease at 11.30 a.m. All tools will be handed over to the R.S.M. at the Tool Dump by 12 noon.

6. STORES.

    A duplicate list of stores will be prepared by each Company. Receipts will be sent to the Orderly Room immediately on arrival at MAROEUIL. Company commanders will also hand over to incoming Companies, schemes of dispositions, gaps in enemy's wire, work in hand and work contemplated.

7. WIRE CUTTERS ETC.

    All Very pistols and periscopes will be taken out. Wire Cutters and Hedging Gloves will be handed over, not as trench stores, but as a separate item and receipts obtained.

8. ADVANCE PARTY.

    2/Lieut. Archibald and 1 N.C.O. from "A", "B" and "C" Companies will leave Battalion Headquarters at 9.30a.m. and proceed to MAROEUIL to take over from the 6th. Seaforths.- O.C. "D" Coy. will send an officer in advance to make arrangements for his Company.

9. TRANSPORT.

    The Transport Officer will arrange for the conveyance of "D" Company's baggage from ANZIN to MAROEUIL, and for the conveyance of tools and camp-kettles from ROCLINCOURT.

10. BAGGAGE.

    O.C. "D" Company will arrange to have the blankets and officers' kits of the various Companies conveyed to the Coy. billets.

11. COOKS ETC.

    Immediately after dinners, all cooks except one per Company will move to MAROEUIL as a formed body under the Sgt. cook and prepare teas. The remaining cooks will assist in loading camp-kettles. O.C. "B" Coy. will detail 4 men to remain to load the tool wagons.

12. CLEANLINESS.

    Trenches, dug-outs, latrines etc. will be left scrupulously clean.

13. REPORTS.

    Immediately relief is complete Companies will wire Battalion Headquarters, the code word being MAC. Companies will also advise Battalion Headquarters as soon as they reach new billets.

    O. MacKenzie Lieut. & A/Adjt.
    6th. Gordon Highlanders.

Copy No. 1 File.
" 2 Hd. Qrs. 152nd. Bde.
" 3-6 Companies.
" 7 Transport Officer.
" 8 L.G.O.
" 9 Quartermaster.
" 10 H.Q. Mess.

Copy No. 1

Special Operation Orders
by Lieut Colonel J. Dawson, D.S.O.
Commanding 6th Gordon Highlanders,
ACQ, 27th February, 1917.
------oOo------

1. OBJECT:

    To gain information regarding the enemy and his trenches; to obtain prisoners, and to damage trenches and dugouts.

2. OBJECTIVE

    The German front line from A.23.d.80.10. to A.30.a.25.33., and the second line from A.23.d.90.20. to A.30.a.33.40.

3. ZERO HOUR and DATE:

    The raid will take place on 3RD March; Zero hour will be intimated later.

4. TIME TABLE:

    Zero minus 1 — Artillery barrage on German front line.
    Zero — Barrage lifts to German second line. Troops move from old French Trench.
    Zero plus 3 — Barrage lifts to German third line. Troops for second German line move from first German line.
    Zero plus 15 — Troops from second German line commence to move back to own lines.
    Zero plus 25 — Troops from first German line commence to move back to own lines.

5. STRENGTH:

    12 officers and 300 men.

6. O/C RAID:

    Captain I. G. Fleming, MC, will command the Raiding Party from Old French Trench at head of No 5 sap.

7. FORMING UP:

    All troops taking part will be housed for the night in FISH TUNNEL, and will commence to move at 1 hour 15 minutes before Zero to assembly positions in Saps and Old French Trench, as shown in Appendix A. Absolute silence will be observed during the movement to positions of assembly. Smoking is forbidden.

8. ACTION:

    All men engaged are arranged in groups (1 N.C.O. and 8 men) with definite objectives — each area being an officer's command as shown in Appendix B. all

    First line groups and Communication Trench Groups move first, followed by those who are to occupy German Second line. The second line groups re-organise in German first line; those between ALLGAUER TRENCH (inclusive) and KOMMANDUER TRENCH (inclusive) moving forward by means of Communication Trenches; those North of ALLGAUER TRENCH over the open.

9. MOPPING UP:

    When parties reach their objectives they rush along trench and secure entrances to dugouts, 2 sentries being left at each. Occupants are invited to come out; if they hesitate, a Mills bomb is thrown down the entrance and a further opportunity of coming up given. If no response, the entrances are guarded, and just before time of withdrawal petrol and "P" Bombs are used at one entrance, the other being left open for occupants being driven up. "W.S" Bombs will be thrown in just before leaving.

    Mobile charges will be used for tunnels and front line dugouts. If occupants come up readily, the dugouts will be searched for identifications and documents, before being destroyed.

10. EQUIPMENT/

10. EQUIPMENT

Men will not wear any equipment. Rifle with bayonet fixed will have 9 rounds in magazine and 1 in breech — safety catches down. 10 rounds will be carried in left tunic pocket.

2 Mills Bombs will be carried by each man in the right tunic pocket.

P.H. helmets will be worn in "Gas Alert" position

Blocking Groups I.A., IV.A., V.A., IX.D., X.A., and XI.C. will carry 42 Mills, 12 Rifle Grenades, 1 pick, 1 shovel. Each other group will carry 42 Mills Bombs in 2 Bucket Carriers.

Throwers will wear waistbelt and side arms. Of the other groups 2 men carry petrol; 3 men 2 "P" Bombs and 1 "W.S" Bomb each; 2 Mobile Charges.

Parties IV, V, and VI, carry 2 ladders each for use in scaling the parados of front line German trench.

Each second line man will have the number of his group on cardboard disc sewn on back of tunic.

11. DOCUMENTS, PRISONERS, etc.

All available documents, maps etc., are to be brought back; prisoners are to be searched and all weapons and papers removed; prisoners will be headed towards FISH TUNNEL — escort 1 per 20; where a party will be detailed to receive them. Every endeavour must be made to get as many prisoners as possible. Machine Guns and Trench Mortars must be carried back to the British lines immediately on capture.

12. MEDICAL ARRANGEMENTS:

Every effort will be made to bring back casualties. Two stretchers will accompany last wave to first German line near ALLGAUER TRENCH. First Aid Post will be established in FISH TUNNEL.

13. IDENTIFICATION:

All papers, letters, identity discs and shoulder titles will be left behind. Each man will carry in his pocket a paper stating his number, rank, name, and GORDON HIGHLANDERS only — no reference to Battalion. If a man is captured, the statement on his paper is the only information he is obliged to give. Nothing whatsoever about trenches, disposition, or any other information must be disclosed.

14. SYNCHRONISATION OF WATCHES:

All watches will be synchronised before leaving FISH TUNNEL.

Zero minus 1 will be taken from first salvo of artillery.

Copy No 1   File
2   H.Q. 152nd Inf. Brigade.
3   B Company
4   D "
5   6th Seaforth Highlanders
6   spare.

SECRET
No. 134
152nd INF. BDE.

152/51

Vol 29

WAR DIARY.

of

1/6th Bn. GORDON HIGHLANDERS.

From

1st MARCH, 1917.

to

31st MARCH, 1917.

****

Army Form C. 2118.

WAR DIARY

INTELLIGENCE SUMMARY.

(Erase heading not required.)

Instructions regarding War Diaries and Intelligence Summaries are contained in F. S. Regs., Part II. and the Staff Manual respectively. Title pages will be prepared in manuscript.

Place	Date	Hour	Summary of Events and Information	Remarks and references to Appendices
A.C.Q	1.3.17		In Billets. Preparations in progress for raid on German Trenches. Scheme of trenches laid out on fields at MARŒUIL where men practice attack	
do	4.3.17		The men who were to take part in raid marched to the trenches at BtCLIN) -COURT. They were arranged in FISH TUNNEL for the night and equipped with explosives, etc. 300 men and 13 officers took part.	
			For days before wire cutting had been proceeding. Artillery and trench mortars were used but wire in front of the British line (old French trench) had to be cut by hand. This work was under the supervision of Captain D.G.Clark and was carried out by a special squad of men. The Saps from B.NNAL Trench to the old French Trench, and this latter trench itself, had been cleared for the assembly of the raiders and they took up position without a hitch in the dark. An artillery Barrage had been arranged. Heavies, 18 pounders, Stokes and 60 pound Trench Mortars, and machine guns were all as used (see appendix II) Zero hour was 6.10 a.m. At Zero - 1 the artillery opened and punctually at the hour the first wave of raiders rushed over No-man's Land and for the most part got into the German trench before the defenders could get out of their dug-outs. The second wave followed about 50 yards behind the first. The raiding force was divided into XI groups, each group being under the command of a subaltern officer. These groups were again sub-divided into squads each under a N.C.O., and every squad had a definite objective given it. (See Appendix I) Captain I.G.Fleming, M.C. was in command of the force and he took up his position at the head of Sap 5 in old French trench. Considerable fighting took place in the German trenches, but the objects set before the raiders were gained. Sixty six German dead were counted and 21 prisoners captured including 1 officer. One German machine gun was brought back; one was smashed by a shell and 1 anti-aircraft gun was destroyed by bombs. (Appendix V) A considerable amount of damage was done to trenches and dug-outs. Twenty pound charges of Ammonal, Mills and "P" bombs and Stokes shells were used for this destruction. It was expected that the 104th. Regiment of Saxons would be in occupation of the trenches raided, but the occupants proved to be the 2nd. Bavarian Regiment. From prisoners it was learned that this regiment had relieved the other the previous evening, this relief being completed at 12 midnight. They had been warned to expect a raid but had not thought it would come so soon.	

Army Form C. 2118.

WAR DIARY
or
INTELLIGENCE SUMMARY.
(Erase heading not required.)

Instructions regarding War Diaries and Intelligence Summaries are contained in F. S. Regs., Part II. and the Staff Manual respectively. Title pages will be prepared in manuscript.

Place	Date	Hour	Summary of Events and Information	Remarks and references to Appendices
	4.3.17		The success of the raid was due to the completeness of the arrangements and the speed and smoothness with which they were carried out. Our loss was entirely due to the fighting qualities of the German Regiment found in the trenches. Our Casualties were :-	
			Officers. Other Ranks. Killed 10 Missing 1 6 Wounded 5 32 TOTAL 6 48 = 54	
			The following awards were made for gallantry displayed during the raid :-	

			Military Cross - 2
			     Distinguished Conduct Medal - 1
			     Bar to Military Medal - 1
			     Military Medal - 6	

			On the afternoon Field Marshall Sir Douglas Haig, G.C.B., G.C.V.O., K.C.I.E., Commander-in-Chief, British Armies in France, inspected the raiders at HAUTE-AVESNES and congratulated them heartily on the successful nature of the operation. The Divisional General, Major General G.M. Harper, C.B., D.S.O., and Brigadier General Pelham Burn, D.S.O., Commanding 152nd. Infantry Brigade, also conveyed their congratulations.	
AcQ	6-11.3.17		In Billets. Training and working parties.	
	11.3.17		Presentation by the Corps Commander, Lieut. General Sir Charles Fergusson, Bt., K.C.B. M.V.O., D.S.O., of awards to men of the 152nd. Infantry Brigade. The following were presented to this Battalion :-	

			Military Cross - 2.
			     Distinguished Conduct Medal - 1.
			     Military Medal - 5.	

Army Form C. 2118.

WAR DIARY
or
INTELLIGENCE SUMMARY.
(Erase heading not required.)

Instructions regarding War Diaries and Intelligence Summaries are contained in F.S. Regs., Part II. and the Staff Manual respectively. Title pages will be prepared in manuscript.

Place	Date	Hour	Summary of Events and Information	Remarks and references to Appendices
ACQ	12-14.3.17.		In Billets. Training and working parties.	
ROCLINCOURT	14-17.3.17.		In trenches N.E. of ROCLINCOURT. On the night of 16/17 the 8th. Argyle and Sutherland Highlanders raided the same German trenches as the 6th. Gordon Highlanders raided on the 5th. March. The raiding party numbered 12 officers and about 400 men. Ten prisoners were captured and much damage done to trenches and enemy's personnel.	
BOIS DE MAROEUIL	17/18.3.17		In Camp for the night on relief from trenches.	
AGNIERES & CAUCOURT.			Battalion in Billets. Headquarters and "A" and "B" Companies in AGNIERES and "C" and "D" Companies in CAUCOURT. Training for a contemplated attack on German trenches east of ROCLINCOURT was engaged in.	
ECOIVRES.	22.31.3.17		In Huts. Training for attack.	

J. Dawson Lieut. Colonel
Comdg. 6th Gordon Highlanders.

Bde file

152nd Infantry Brigade - Special Order.

The Brigadier General Commanding wishes to express to all ranks of 1/6th Bn. GORDON HIGHLANDERS his great appreciation of the very gallant and thorough manner in which the skilful and comprehensive arrangements of the Officer Commanding that Battalion were put into practice by his raiding party in the face of a most stubborn resistance by the enemy.

It should be a matter of great satisfaction to the Commanding Officer that the action, following so closely as it did the times he had laid down for it, was so complete a success.

The Brigadier General Commanding also much appreciates the excellent work of the units auxiliary to the raiding party by which success was made possible. All who took part in the raid are unanimous that the destruction of the wire, the moving barrage and the protective barrage were beyond criticism, and the greatest confidence in the skill of the artillery and Trench Mortar units concerned has been engendered in the infantry, which will be invaluable in future operations.

The support given by the 152nd and 154th Trench Mortar Batteries and the 152nd Machine Gun Company was considerable. The former fired 2,049 rounds in 34 minutes, almost certainly a record performance, and the latter 24,000 rounds. Further the Brigadier General Commanding considers that the assistance given by the 8th Bn. Seaforth Highlanders in the preparation of our own trench system for the raid was invaluable. He is especially pleased with the work done by Lieut. Wellwood in clearing the old French Trench of obstacles and with the valuable reports rendered by Lieut. Grant.

G. W. Bracken
Captain.
Brigade Major,
152nd Infantry Brigade.

8th March, 1917.

Battalion Orders by Lieut. Colonel J. Dawson, D.S.O.
Commanding 6th. Gordon Highlanders.
ACQ, 1st. March 1917.

1. Orderly Officer for to-morrow — 2/Lieut. W.M. Bruce.
   Next for duty   — 2/Lieut. M.A. Matheson.

2. PARADES.

   8.15 a.m. — Sick Parade.
   9 a.m.   — Orderly Room.

   Other parades and working parties will be detailed later.

3. SALUTING (C.R.O. 76.)

   "Officers Commanding will impress on all troops under their "Command that Cars flying flags should be saluted at sight, without "waiting to ascertain who is occupying the car."

   Sentries to be warned to present arms invariably when such "cars pass their posts."

   Facilities will always be given for the passage of motor cars "carrying the Union Jack or other distinguishing flag."

4. STRENGTH.

   The u/m N.C.O. having proceeded to D.G.T., BOULOGNE, is struck off, 1.3.17.
   10719 L/C Sandison W.R. (D)

   The u/m officers on transfer to U.K. are struck off.
   2/Lieut. A.M. Morrice 15.2.17.
   "   J.G. Thomson   "

   Capt. & Rev. R. Coulter taken on strength and posted to "A" Company 18.2.17.

   Capt. & Rev. Ferrigan having left Battalion is struck off 16.2.17.

   The u/M men having been transferred to U.K. are struck off.

1379	Pte.	Cumming	J.	(B)	Sick.	15.2.17.
12799	"	Grimshaw	A.	(C)	"	16.2.17.
13509	"	Begg	E.	(A)	"	7.2.17.
13519	"	Gaull	J.	(A)	"	15.2.17.
14100	"	Aitken	A.	(D)	"	15.2.17.

5. MOVEMENTS.

   13603 Pte. Law J. employed with A.P.M., having been admitted to hospital on 25.2.17, the u/m man has been sent as a substitute.
   977 Pte. Duncan A. (D) 1.3.17.

   The following are permanently detached for duty with Divl. Graves Record Officer.

1579	L/C	Edmond	J.	(D)	1.3.17.
11122	Pte.	Benzie	J.	(B)	"
235018	"	Doran	W.B.	(A)	"
235082	"	Duncan	G.	(A)	"
14012	"	Fletcher	W.	(A)	"
10794	"	Flett	W.J.	(B)	"
11095	"	Law	W.	(D)	"
L2177	"	Moir	J.	(B)	"
11018	"	Reid	D.	(D)	"
14079	"	Robertson	D.E.	(A)	"
10793	"	Smith	A.	(B)	"

   The following proceeded to Divisional School for General Training:-

235025	Pte.	Barclay	A.	(A)
285017	"	Birmingham	L.	(C)
13692	"	Campbell	R.	(A)
235035	"	Donald	W.	(A)
13639	"	Fraser	J.	(C)
235027	"	Geddes	J.	(A)
285041	"	Gorrie	C.	(C)
13300	"	Gowan	J.	(A)
13522	"	Hay	R.	(A)
13528	"	Lumsden	R.	(C)
235011	"	Martin	L.A.	(A)
285013	"	McCulloch	J.	(C)

2.

5. MOVEMENTS (contd.)

    285014 Pte - McEachern C. (C)
    235007 " - McKay   F. (C)
    285028 " - McMengle   R. (A)
    285031 "   Richmond   M. (A)   3.3.17
    285032 " - Scott   J. (C)   B.122 sent
    14087   " - Simpson   H. (A)
    285035 " - Speirs   A. (A)
    13633   " - Staines   W. (C)
    285036 " - Taylor   A. (A)
    235017 " - Taylor   W. (A)
    11552   " - Thow   W. (C)
    285006 " - Walker   J. (C)
    12798   " - Williamson T. (C)

    The following Officers and O.R. proceeded to Courses of Instruction as under:-

    2/Lieut. T.Anderson   Lewis Gun Course.
    2/Lieut. J.S.B.Ward   T.M.Course.
    13501 L/C Baird   W. (A)   "
    11435 Pte. Fraser   H. (A)   "
    13616 " Kelly   P. (B)   "
    13601 " McMillan J. (B)   "
    12836 " Leason J. (D)   "
    14055 " Davidson A. (D)   "

6. ADMISSIONS TO HOSPITAL

    The u/m men attached 152 T.M.Battery were admitted to hospital 28.2.17.

    12799 Pte. Griffiths J.H. (B)
    12114 " Wilson   A.   (C)

7. EVACUATIONS

    12355 Pte. Mair G.T. to XI11 Corps Rest Station.

D.MacKenzie
Lieut. & A/Adjt.
6th. Gordon Highlanders.

Battalion Orders by Lieut. Colonel J. Dawson, D.S.O.
Commanding 6th. Gordon Highlanders.
ACQ 2nd. March 1917.

Orderly Officer for to-morrow   2/Lieut. M.A.Matheson.
Next for duty   "   W.K.Leggat

1. PARADES.

       8.15a.m.   Sick Parade
       9 a.m.   Orderly Room.
       10 a.m. - 12 noon   The Party under special training will have Physical Training, Bayonet Fighting and Wire Cutting Practice. Wire Cutting will be practised at the Snipers' Panopticum on the ACQ) HAUTES: :AVESNES ROAD, S.W. of ACQ. 40 Pairs of Wire Breakers will be drawn from Orderly Room. Capt. I. G. Fleming will arrange details.

2. STRENGTH.

     The u/m man having been taken on the strength of Brigade Head Quarters is struck off the strength of the Battalion :-
     10725 - Pte Pirie:A. (D)

3. DISCIPLINE.

     Men off duty will, at all times, move smartly in the neighbourhood of Billets, and not lounge about street corners. P. H. Helmets will always be worn. The strictest attention will be paid to saluting.

4. CONDUCT SHEETS.

     O. C. Coys. will send to Orderly Room tomorrow the Conduct Sheets of all N.C.Os. and Men struck off the strength in their possession.

                                                Lieut. & A/Adjutant.
                                        6th Gordon Highlanders.

Battalion Orders by Lieut. Colonel J.Dawson, D.S.O.
Commanding 6th. Gordon Highlanders.
ACQ, 3rd. March 1917.

Orderly Officer for to-morrow — 2/Lieut. W.K.Leggat
Next for duty — 2/Lieut. T.Mack.

1. PARADES.
   10a.m. — Service for all C.of E. men at Empire Hall. Parties will be marched to the Hall under Company arrangements.

   11a.m. — Service for men of Attack Practice only, at the Empire Hall. Parties will be marched to the Hall under Company arrangements.

2. STRENGTH.
   The u/m man being posted to 8/10th. Gordon Highlanders, is struck off the strength 30.7.16.
   14021 Pte. Earsman J. (B)

3. CORRECTIONS.
   Reference Battalion Orders of 21.1.17. para. 2:—

   for 13608 Cpl. Blyth   D.   (B)
   read 13608 Pte. Blyth   D.   (B)

   for 13619 L/C Shields   R.   (B)
   read 13619 Pte. Shields R.   (B)

   for 13629 L/C Cormack   G.   (C)
   read 13629 Pte. Cormack G.   (C)

   Reference Battalion Orders of 19.1.17. para 5.

   for 11051 Cpl. Robb   J.   (A)
   read 11051 L/C (unpaid) Robb J.   (A)
   Date of reversion 17.1.17.

4. REVERSIONS
   The following N.C.O's revert to permanent grade of private from the dates stated to the right of their names.

   13502 L/C Cooper J.   (A)   2.10.16.
   13545 "   Irvine W.S. (B)   3.12.16.

5. REGIMENTAL NUMBERS.
   The correct Regimental Number of the u/m man is as stated and not 285003 which belongs to Pte. Robertson A. (C)

   285045 Pte. Stewart C. (B).

                                    Lieut. &A/Adjt.
                              6th Gordon Highlanders.

Battalion Orders by Lieut. Colonel J. Dawson, D.S.O.
Commanding 6th. Gordon Highlanders.
ACQ, 4th. March 1917.

    Orderly Officer for to-morrow   —   2/Lieut. T. Mack.
    Next for duty   —   2/Lieut. J.G. Gordon.

1. PARADES.

    Parades and Working Parties will be notified later.

2. STEEL HELMETS. (D.R.O. 719.)

"The chain visors of Steel Helmets are not to be worn at the "back of the head. They are to be worn properly looped up "at the front of the helmet when not required for the protection "of the eyes."

3. STRENGTH.

    The u/m man having been transferred to the U.K. is struck off.
    10748 Pte. McIntosh A. (C) 14.2.17 Sick.

4. PROFICIENCY PAY.

    The u/m men are granted proficiency pay Class 2 from dates stated.
    14096 Pte. Forbes A. (A) 14.12.16.
    14098 " Thomson W.J. (A) 7.12.16.

5. PUNISHMENTS

    13628 Pte Ferns J. (B) Awarded 4 day's F.P. No. 2 for:—
When on Active Service being absent off parade at 9.40 a.m. 4.3.17.

    235015 Pte. Will F. (B)   Deprived of 3 day's pay for:—
    235028 " Kynoch A. (B)   When on Active Service being
    13546 " Simpson G. (B)   deficient of Grocery Ration.
    13628 " Ferns J. (B)

6. ADMISSIONS TO HOSPITAL

    235025 Pte. Barclay A. (A) Admitted to Hospital 2.3.17.
from 51st. (H) Divisional Depot Battalion.

    285031 Pte. Richmond M. (A) Admitted to Hospital from
51st. (H) Divisional Depot Battalion 3.3.17.

7. MOVEMENTS.

    The u/m man is detached for duty at the Divisional Gas School as Orderly.
    12111. Pte. Robertson W. (C)

Lieut. & A/Adjt.
6th. Gordon Highlanders.

Notes.

Overcoats will be worn, and Mess Tins carried on the march up to the Trenches. Neither Leather Jerkins nor Kilt Aprons will be worn. P.H. Helmets will be worn in the ALERT position. Safety Pins can be ~~carried~~ drawn from the Orderly Room at 1 p.m. Box Respirators will be carried on the march. Equipment will not be worn except by Throwers, Blocking Bombing Sections, who will wear Waistbelt and Bayonet.

Bayonets will be fixed before moving off. Scabbards will be worn.

The number of the Battalion will be stamped out of the Identity Discs of all ranks. If this is done, Identity Discs will be worn. Each Officer will inspect his command before ~~leaving~~ moving off to see that no identity could be established.

Rifles will have 10 rounds in the Magazine before leaving Billets. Each man will carry 10 rounds in his left pocket.

Groups will be arranged in the Tunnel, as already ~~arranged~~, detailed, leaving ACQ in that order at 3.30 p.m., each Sap Group moving as a separate unit at 100 yards intervals. A halt of 10 minutes will be made from 4.20 p.m. to 4.30 p.m.

Teas will be taken before moving off. Route from ANZIN CHURCH will be by the Track on the right side of ANZIN AVENUE - ROCLINCOURT - FISH AVENUE. Touch will be maintained between Groups. Men will be roused at 4 a.m. on Z Day. Tea will be provided. Equipment of Groups and of individuals will be proceeded with.

4 men per squad will carry one half candle each.

Officers will wear mens' S.D. Jackets.

Officers will carry either Rifles or Revolvers.

All Ammonal and P Bombs will be used for destruction of dug-outs, M.G. Emplacements, Ammunition and Bomb Stores &c. All Bombers Buckets, Wire Cutters and unexpended MILLS Bombs must be brought back.

4.3.17.

APPENDIX A.

Sap:	First two waves	Second two waves
I	XI^C, IX^D	IX^C, XI^B
II	IX^A, IX^B	XI^A, VIII^D
III	VIII^A, VIII^B	VIII^C, VIIIE
IV	VII^A, VII^B	VII^C
V	III^B, X^A	X^B, X^C
VI	III^A, VI^A	VI^B, VI^C
VII	II^A, II^B	II^C, II^D, V^C
VIII	I^B, V^A, V^B	IV^B, IV^C
IX	IV^A, I^A	

(2) Order in Fish Tunnel from BONNAL END.

1. Sap I Party
2. " IX "
3. " II "
4. " VIII "
5. " III "
6. " VII "
7. " IV "
8. " VI "
9. " V "

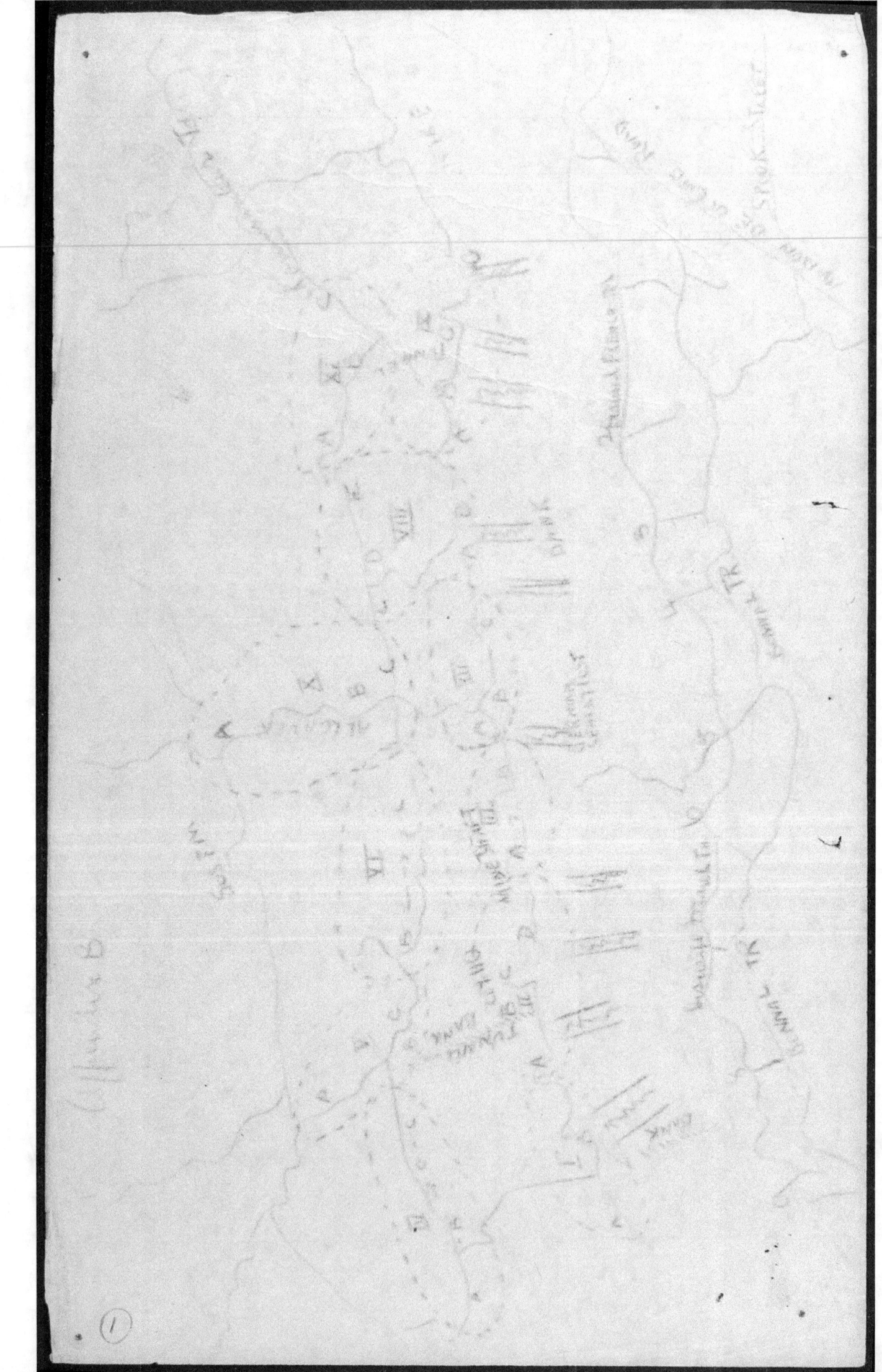

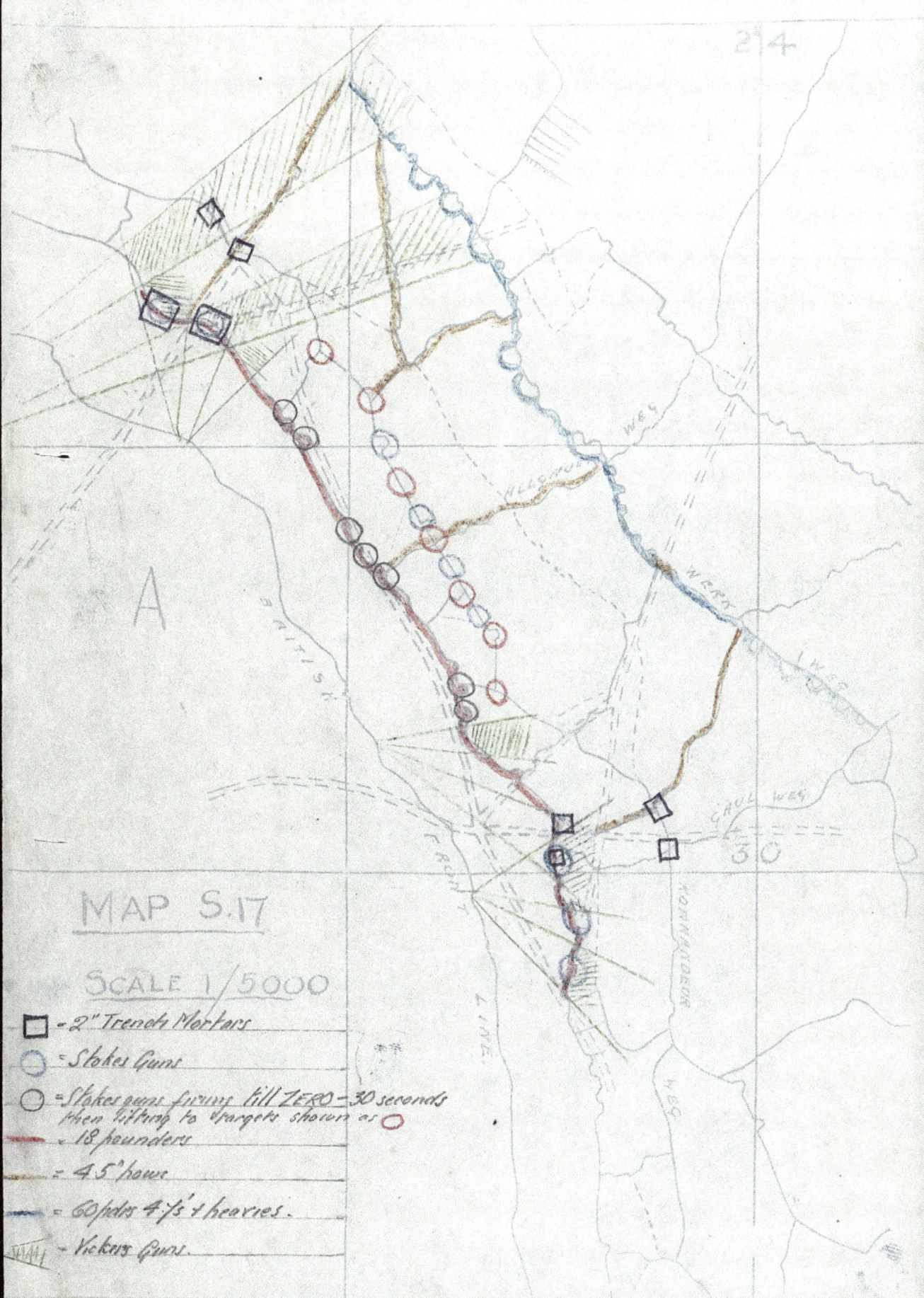

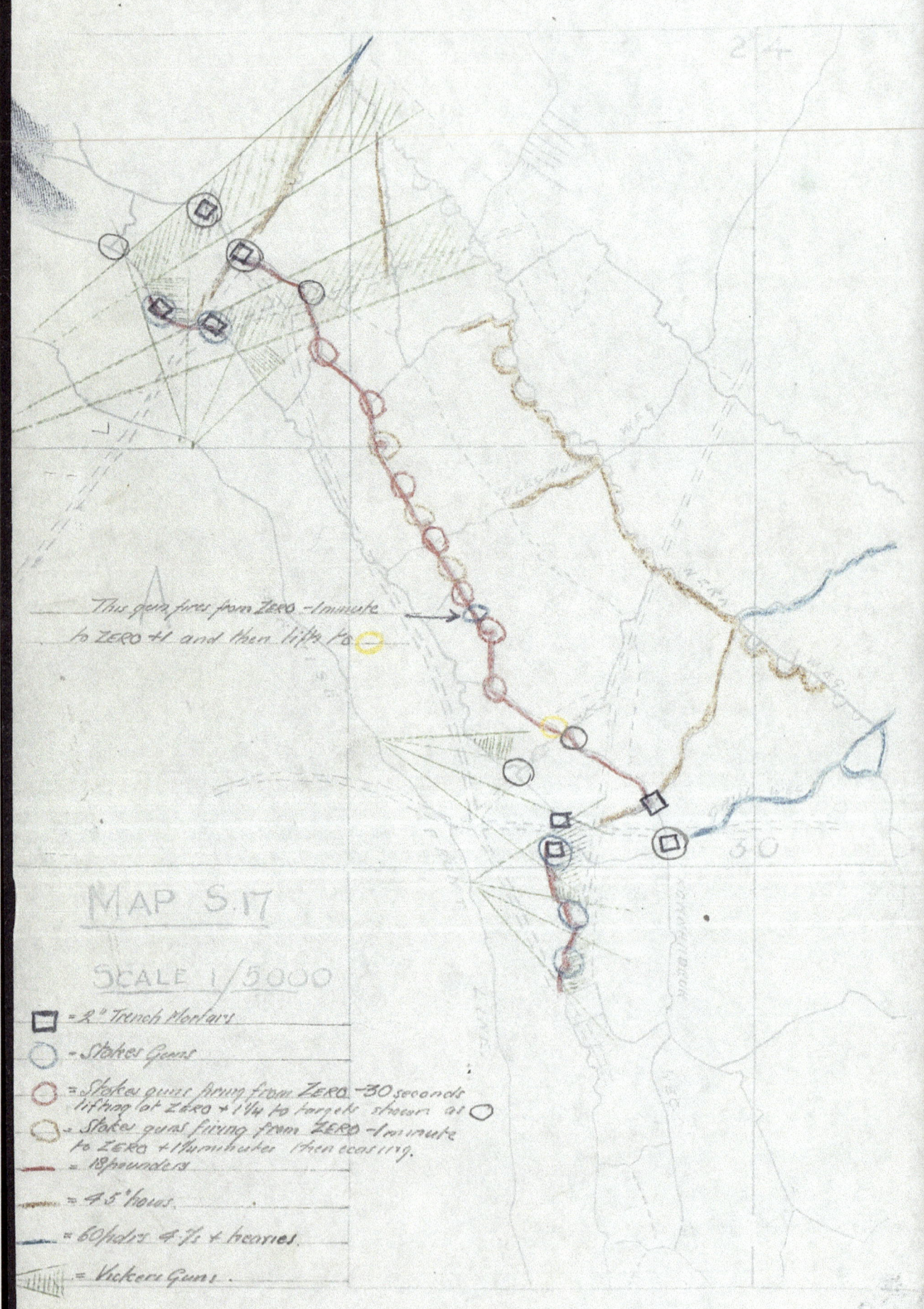

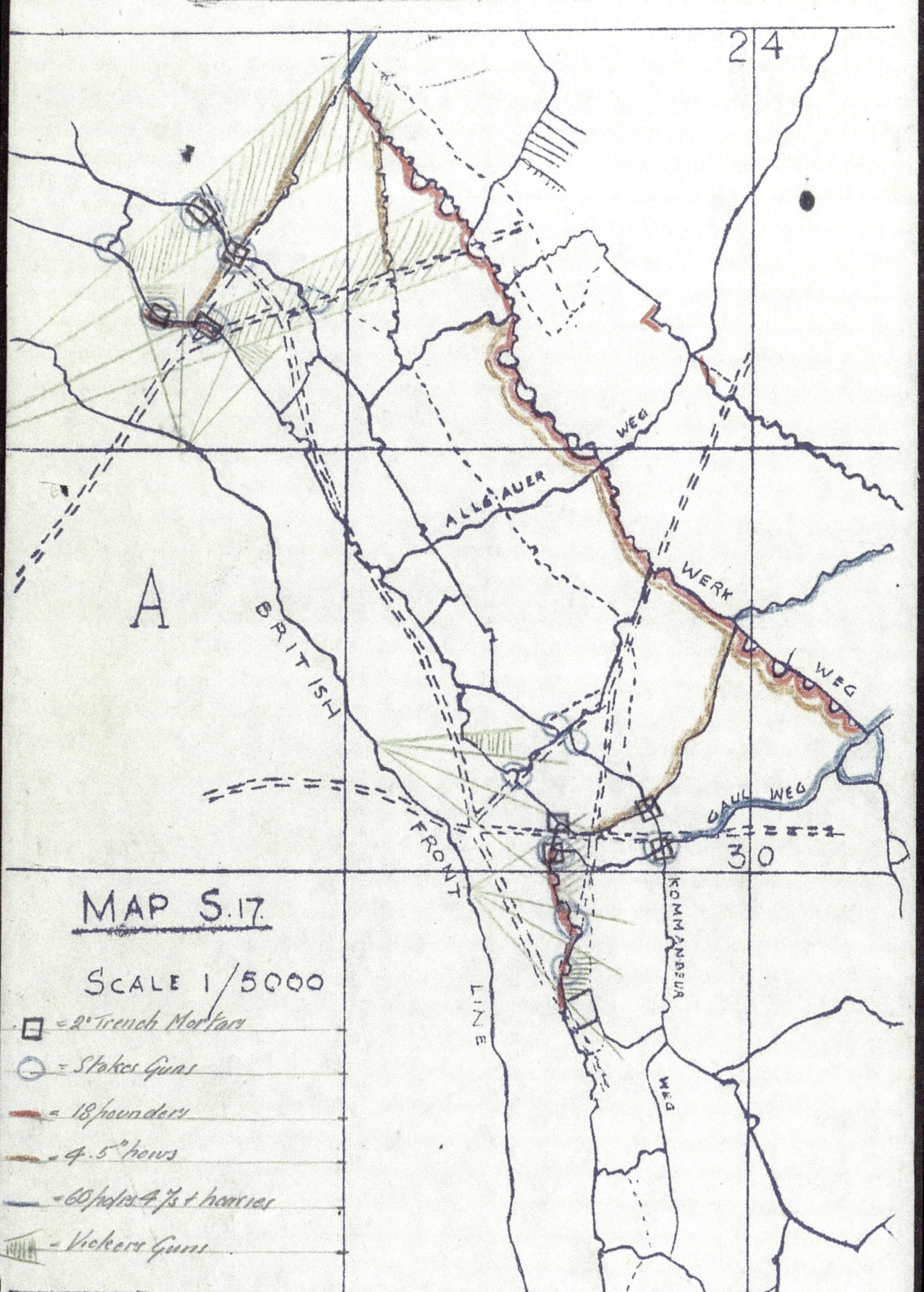

Refce: ROCLINCOURT
51B N.W.I

Annotated Map of Raided Area.

"X" indicates Trench fire stepped.

GROUP EQUIPMENT. IV

Group	No. 5	No. 23.	Amm.	P. & Petrol	Picks & Shovels.	Ladders.
I A	42	12	–	4 & 1	1 of each	–
I B	34	–	1	4 & 1	–	–

Group	No 5	No. 23	Amm.	P. & Petrol	Picks & Shovels.	Ladders.
II A	34	–	2	4 & 1	–	–
II B	42	–	2	4 & 2	–	–
II C	34	–	2	4 & 1	–	–
II D	34	–	1	4 & 1	–	–

Group	No.5	No. 23	Amm.	P. & Petrol	Picks & Shovels.	Ladders.
III A	34	–	1	4 & 2	–	–
III B	34	–	1	4 & 1	–	–

IV A

Group	No. 5	No. 23	Amm.	P. & Petrol	Picks & Shovels.	Ladders
IV A	42	12	–	4 & 1	2 of each.	–
IV B	34	–	–	6 & 2	–	1
IV C	34	–	1	6 & 2	–	1

Group	No. ~~XXX~~ 5	No.23	Amm.	P & Petrol	Picks & Shovels	Ladders.
V A	42	12	–	4 & 1	1 of each.	1
V B	34	–	2	4 & 2	–	1
V C	34	–	–	6 & 2	–	1

Group	No. 5	No. 23.	Amm.	P & Petrol.	Picks & Shovels.	Ladders
VI A	34	–	–	6 & 2	–	1
VI B	34	–	1	6 & 2	–	–
VI C	34	–	–	6 & 2	–	1

Group	No. 5	No. 23.	Amm.	P & Petrol	Picks & Shovels.	Ladders.
VII A	34	–	2	4 & 1	–	–
VII B	34	–	1	4 & 2	–	–
VII C	34	–	1	4 & 1	–	–

Group	No 5	No. 23	Amm.	P. & Petrol	Picks & Shovels.	Ladders.
VIII A	34	–	2	4 & 2	–	–
VIII B	34	–	2	4 & 1	–	–
VIII C	34	–	–	6 & 2	–	–
VIII D	34	–	1	6 & 2	–	–
VIII E	42	–	–	6 & 2	–	–

Group	No 5	No. 23	Amm.	P. & Petrol.	Picks & Shovels.	Ladders.
IX A	34	–	2	4 & 1	–	–
IX B	34	–	2	4 & 2	–	–
IX C	34	–	2	4 & 2	–	–
IX D	42	12	1	4 & 1	1 of each.	–

3.

Group	No. 5	No. 23.	Amm.	P. & Petrol.	Picks & Shovels.	Ladders.
X A	42	-	3	4 & 1	-	-
X B	34	12	-	6 & 2	1 of each.	-
X C	34	-	1	6 & 2	-	-

Group	No. 5	No. 23.	Amm.	P. & Petrol.	Picks & Shovels.	Ladders.
XI A	34	-	1	6 & 2	-	-
XI B	34	-	2	4 & 2	-	-
XI C	42	12	-	4 & 1	1 of each.	-

COPY NO. 1.

Operation Orders No. 98
by Lieut. Colonel J. Dawson, D.S.O.,
Commanding 6th. Gordon Highlanders.
ACQ, 14th. March 1917.

1. OPERATION.

The 6th. Battalion Gordon Highlanders will relieve the 5th. Battalion Seaforth Highlanders in the trenches East of ROCLINCOURT tomorrow 15th March 1917.

2. DISPOSITION.

A and C Coys. will take over the front line, C Coy on the right, A Coy on the left. B Coy and Battalion Head Quarters will be in ROCLINCOURT, D Coy in ANZIN.

3. PARADE.

The Battalion will move by Platoons at 100 yards interval. The order of march will be H.Q. Details, C, A and B Coys. The leading platoon of C Coy. will leave ACQ at 2 a.m. D Coy will leave at 9 a.m.

4. ROUTE.

Route will be — MAROEUIL — ANZIN — XXXXXXXX — TRACK on right of ANZIN AVENUE — FILATIER — ROCLINCOURT.

5. DRESS.

Full marching order with leather jerkins will be worn, Great Coats in Packs.

6. EQUIPMENT.

Very Pistols and Periscopes as issued will be taken up by A, B and C Coys.

7. LEWIS GUNS.

O.C. D Coy. will detail one trained Lewis Gun/Team with Gun to go with A Coy. This Team will report to O.C. A Coy. by 1.30 a.m. 2 Limbers with Lewis Guns of A, B and C Coys. will accompany H.Q. Details to ANZIN, from which Lewis Guns will be carried forward by Teams. Teams will move with companies to which they belong, or are attached. A, B and C Coys. will take over Lewis Gun Magazines and the Carriers from the 5th Seaforth Highlanders on relief, giving a receipt. A duplicate of the receipt will be sent to Orderly Room immediately relief is complete. The 3 remaining Lewis Guns of D Coy. will accompany that Company to ANZIN.

8. BAGGAGE.

All Blankets will be collected in one Billet per Coy. before marching off. Two of the Band will report to A, B and C Coys. and to Bn. Head Qrs at 6 p.m. tonight for instructions regarding these.
Officers Valises will be collected along with Blankets.
The Band will act as Guard and Loading Party for Blankets. The Transport Officer will make the necessary arrangements for transport of Baggage, Blankets, and Orderly Room. D Coy's Blankets will be conveyed to ANZIN.

9. TRANSPORT.

The Sergeant Cook and all Cooks of A, B and C Coys. less one per Coy. will be prepared to move at 5 p.m. today with the necessary Camp Kettles and Rations.
Officer's Mess Cart will leave at midnight accompanied by 2 Officers' Servants from each of A, B and C Coys. D Coy. will make its own arrangements.

10. CLEANLINESS.

Platoon and Coy. Officers will personally inspect all Billets, Cookhouses, &c., and render the usual certificate to Orderly Room before moving off.

11. REPORTS.

Coys. will report to Battalion Head Quarters immediately relief is complete, B.A.B. Code being used.

Lieut. & A/Adjutant
6th Gordon Highlanders.

Operation Orders No. 08
by Lieut. Colonel J. Dawson, D.S.O.,
Commanding 6th. Gordon Highlanders.
AOM, 14th. March 1917.

Copy No......

Copy No. 1 - File.
        2 - Head Quarters.
        3 - 6 - Companies.
        7 - Quarter Master.
        8 - Transport Officer.
        9 - RCM

1. OPERATION.

The 6th. Battalion Gordon Highlanders will relieve the 5th. Battalion Seaforth Highlanders in the trenches East of ROCLINCOURT tomorrow 15th March 1917.

2. DISPOSITION.

A and C Coys. will take over the front line, C Coy on the right, A Coy on the left. B Coy and Battalion Head Quarters will be in ROCLINCOURT, D Coy in ANZIN.

3. PARADE.

The Battalion will move by Plato ns at 100 yards intervals. The order of march will be H.Q. Details, C, A and B Coys. The leading plato n of C Coy. will leave ICQ at 8 a.m. D Coy will leave at 9 a.m.

4. ROUTE.

Route will be - MAROEUIL - ANZIN - XXXXXXXX - TRACK on right of ANZIN AVENUE - FILGIEL - ROCLINCOURT.

5. DRESS.

Full marching order with leather jerkins will be worn. Great Coats in Packs.

6. EQUIPMENT.

Very Pistols and Periscopes as issued will be taken up by A, B and C Coys.

7. LEWIS GUNS.

O.C. D Coy. will detail one trained Lewis/Team with Gun /Gun to go with A Coy. This Team will report to O.C. A Coy. by 1.30 a.m. 2 Limbers with Lewis Guns of A, B and C Coys. will accompany H.Q. Details to ANZIN, from which Lewis Guns will be carried forward by Teams. Teams will move with companies to which they belong, or are attached. A, B and C Coys. will take over Lewis Gun Magazines and the Carriers from the 5th Seaforth Highlanders on relief, giving a receipt. A duplicate of the receipt will be sent to Orderly Room immediately relief is complete. The 3 remaining Lewis Guns of D Coy. will accompany that Company to ANZIN.

8. BAGGAGE.

All Blankets will be collected in one Billet per Coy. before marching off. Two if the Band will report to A, B and C Coys. and to Bn. Head Qrs at 6 p.m. tonight for instructions regarding these. Officers Valises will be collected along with Blankets. The Band will act as Guard and Loading Party for Blankets. The Transport Officer will make the necessary arrangements for transport of Baggage, Blankets, and Orderly Room. D Coy's Blankets will be conveyed to ANZIN.

9. TRANSPORT.

The Sergeant Cook and all Cooks of A, B and C Coys. less one per Coy. will be prepared to move at 5 p.m. today with the necessary Camp Kettles and Rations.
Officer's Mess Cart will leave at midnight accompanied by 2 Officers' Servants from each of A, B and C Coys. D Coy. will make its own arrangements.

10. CLEANLINESS.

Platoon and Coy. Officers will personally inspect all Billets, Cookhouses, &c., and run or the usual certificate to orderly Room before moving off.

11. REPORTS.

Coys. will report to Battalion Head Quarters immediately relief is complete, R.L.B. Code being used.

Lieut. & Adjutant
6th Gordon Highlanders.

Operation Orders No. 98. Copy No 1
(Should be 99)
by Lieut. Colonel J. Dawson, D.S.O.,
ROCLINCOURT 16th March 1917.

1. RELIEF

The 5th Battalion Gordon Highlanders will relieve the 6th Battalion Gordon Highlanders in the trenches to-morrow, 17th March 1917. On relief, the 6th Battalion Gordon Highlanders will proceed to Camp in BOIS DE MAROEUIL.

2. ROUTE

Route will be ROCLINCOURT – FILATIERS – GENIE AVENUE – ANZIN. Men will not be allowed to move along the open unless the day is misty or unless it is dusk before the relief is complete.

3. GUIDES

One Guide from each platoon of A, B & C Coys. under Lt. Duncan will rendezvous at junction of GENIE and FILATIERS AVENUE at 2.30 p.m. leaving Battalion H.Q. at 1.45 p.m.

Guides from D Company will rendezvous at ANZIN CHURCH at 1.30 p.m.

4. LEWIS GUNS

All magazines, buckets and carriers will be taken out. These, along with Guns will be collected in ROCLINCOURT and one man per team left as guard and loading party. Transport Officer will arrange to collect after dark.

5. CAMP KETTLES, ETC.

All Camp kettles and Cooks' material will be collected by Transport from ROCLINCOURT. 2 Cooks per Company will be left as guard and loading party.

6. **TRENCH EQUIPMENT**

Companies will take out all periscopes, Very Pistols and Wire Cutters issued, and hand them in to Q.M. Stores on arrival in billets.

Bombers' Buckets and Cups will be handed over to Sgt. GOLDIE in ROCLINCOURT by 2 p.m. The Transport Officer will arrange for their removal.

7. **ADVANCE PARTY ETC.**

The Quartermaster & Coy. Q.M. Sergeants will report at BOIS DE MAROEUIL at 10 a.m. to take over the camp. O.C. "D" Coy will detail guides for other Companies from the main road to the Camp.

8. **HANDING OVER.**

Companies will hand over all work in hand, defence schemes, dispositions and posts to relieving Companies.

Duplicates of Stores handed over will be sent to Battn H.Q.

9. **DUG-OUTS**

Dug-outs and trenches will be left scrupulously clean.

10. **ASSEMBLY**

Companies will **not** assemble at ANZIN. Leading platoons will not halt till at least 800 yards beyond Church, other platoons closing up to 100 yards distance. When all are assembled, march will be continued with platoons at intervals mentioned.

11. **REPORTS**

Companies in line will report by B.A.B. code when relief is complete. All Companies will report immediately on arrival in Camp.

Copy No. 1. FILE
" " 2. H.Q. 152nd Bde.
" " 3-6 Companies
" " 7 Quartermaster
" " 8 Transport Officer

(Signed) D. MacKenzie Lt.
6th Gordon Highlanders a/Adjt.

Copy No 1 .....

Operation Orders No 99 (should be No 100)
by Lieut Colonel J. Dawson, D.S.O.
Commanding 6th Gordon Highlanders
BOIS DE MAROEUIL, 17th March 1917

Reference FRANCE 1/100.000, LENS 11

1. **MOVE**

    The 6th Battalion Gordon Highlanders will move from its present billets to-morrow 18th February.
    Battalion Headquarters, A. and B. Companies will proceed to AGNIERES; C. and D. Companies, Transport and Q.M. Stores to CAUCOURT.
    The detachment at CAUCOURT will be under Major J. W. Adams. The Signalling Class will be attached to A Company.

2. **PARADE**

    The Battalion will move at 9 a.m. The order of march will be:- H.Q., A, B, D, and C Companies.

3. **MARCH**

    An interval of 100 paces will be maintained between platoons, and 200 paces between Companies. All platoons will march in file.
    Route will be:- BRAY, ECOIVRES, ACQ, AGNIERES. The CAUCOURT detachment will continue its march by road through Y of AUBIGNY, L of MIGNOVAL, second E of VILLERS CHATEL.

4. **DRESS**

    Full marching order. Greatcoats will be carried in packs. Leather Jerkins will be worn. Kilt aprons will not be worn.

5. **ADVANCE PARTY**

    Lieut Archibald and 1 cycle orderly will report to Town Major, AGNIERES, at 9 a.m. Sgt Dalgarno, 1 cycle orderly, and 1 representative of Transport will report to Town Major, CAUCOURT at 10.30 a.m.

6. **TRANSPORT**

    Blankets, Officers' baggage, and cooks' utensils will be ready for collection by 8 a.m. Officers Commanding Companies will see that no greatcoats or other kit are packed with blankets. The Transport Officer will arrange for the conveyance of all baggage, and Q.M. Stores.

7. **MEDICAL INSPECTION**

    Sick Parade will be at 7.30 a.m. - in full marching order.

8. **CLEANLINESS**

    All tents, latrines, and the camp generally will be left scrupulously clean. The usual certificates will be rendered.

9. **REPORTS**

    Companies will report immediately on arrival in new billets to Battalion or Detachment Headquarters.

                                D. MacKenzie, Lieut & A/Adj.
                                6th Gordon Highlanders

Copy No 1   File
        2   Headquarters, 152nd Brigade
      3 - 6 Companies
        7   Transport Officer
        8   Quartermaster
        9
       10

Copy No. 1

Operation Orders No 100
by Lieut Colonel J. Dawson, D.S.O"
Commanding 6th Gordon Highlanders
AGNIERES, 21st March, 1917.

Reference FRANCE 1/100,000 LENS 11.

1. **MOVE.**
   The 6th Battalion Gordon Highlanders will move from its present billets to ECOIVRES huts to-morrow 22nd March.

2. **PARADE.**
   The Battalion will parade at the Attack Theatre at 10 a.m. in full marching order.

3. **MARCH.**
   After Attack practice Battalion will march to ECOIVRES by AGNIERES and ACQ. An interval of 100 paces will be maintained between platoons, and 200 paces between Companies. Platoons will march in file.

4. **DRESS**
   Full Marching Order. Greatcoats will be carried in packs. Leather Jerkins will be worn. Kilt aprons will not be worn.

5. **ADVANCE PARTY**
   Sergeant DALGARNO and 1 Cycle Orderly will report at ECOIVRES Huts at 10 a.m.

6. **TRANSPORT**
   Blankets and Officers' baggage will be ready for collection by 9 a.m. Two men per Company will be left as loading party for blankets. Lewis Gun and Bomb limbers will be loaded by 9 a.m. One man will be left with each limber. The Transport Officer will arrange for the conveyance of all baggage and Q.M. Stores.

7. **COOKS**
   Cooks, travelling kitchens, and cooks' utensils will move immediately after breakfast. Dinner will be ready for the Battalion in ECOIVRES Huts by 1.30 p.m.

8. **CLEANLINESS**
   All tents, latrines, and billets will be left scrupulously clean. The usual certificates will be rendered.

9. **REPORTS.**
   Companies will report immediately on arrival in new billets.

D. Mackenzie
Lieut & A/Adj.
6th Gordon Highlanders

Copy No	
1	File
2	Headquarters, 152 Infantry Brigade.
3	Major J. W. Adams
4 - 7	Companies
8	Transport Officer
9	Quartermaster
10	R.S.M.
11	Town Major, AGNIERES
12	Town Major, CAUCOURT

Copy No. 1

Instructions for Attack Practice

1. **ASSEMBLY.**
   The Battalion will be in position in the assembly trenches ready to attack at 11 a.m.

2. **DRESS**
   Rifles, bayonets, waistbelts, steel helmets, and leather jerkins, P.H. helmets, and ground sheets.

3. **PARADE**
   Only men to take part in attack will parade. Those left out will perform camp duties.

4. **BARRAGE**
   2/Lieut G. DUNCAN, R.S.M. H. DAVISON, and the usual barrage, with flags, and drums, will report to the Brigade Major at 10.15 a.m. This party will leave at 8 a.m.

5. **STORES**
   Bombing Squads will carry buckets but no bombs. Lewis Gunners will carry Lewis Guns but no magazines. Each platoon of C Company and the third platoon of A Company will each carry two ground flares. These will be issued by the Signalling Officer and will be lit only in the third German line.

6. **LEWIS GUN TEAMS**
   Only the team leader and four Lewis Gunners per team will be taken to the attack theatre, but two riflemen will be attached to each Lewis Gun team from the rifle sections of the platoon.

7. **MESSAGES, RUNNERS, etc.**
   All Company runners must know the position of Battalion Headquarters before practice begins. Frequent use will be made of messages and of runners. Four Headquarters runners will accompany Battalion Headquarters.

8. **LIAISON.**
   A contact aeroplane will be present. Headquarters Signallers will take signalling apparatus.

9. **DINNERS.**
   Dinners will be taken on the field. Cookers of A Companies with cooked dinners will be at practice ground at 12 noon. Other Companies will carry mid-day rations. Men of Companies for whom cooked dinners are provided will take messtins.

Lieut & A/Adj.
6th Gordon Highlanders

Copy No 1   File
        2   Major Adams
   3 - 6   Companies
        7   B.B.O.
        8   S.O.
        9   R.S.M.

WAR DIARY

of

1/6th Bn. GORDON HIGHLANDERS

for

APRIL, 1917.

****

Army Form C. 2118.

WAR DIARY
or
INTELLIGENCE SUMMARY.
(Erase heading not required)

Instructions regarding War Diaries and Intelligence Summaries are contained in F. S. Regs., Part II. and the Staff Manual respectively. Title pages will be prepared in manuscript.

April, 1917

Place	Date	Hour	Summary of Events and Information	Remarks and references to Appendices
ECOIVRES	1		In "X" Hutments.	Reference Map ROCLINCOURT 51B N.W.1. Scale 1/10000
Bois de MAROEUIL	2-7		In tents. Training and Range Practice, Wire Cutting, Bomb Throwing, Lectures on the "Attack".	
ROCLINCOURT	8-11		Took over the trenches on the night of the 7th/8th. The Battalion was 670 strong, and was accommodated in FISH TUNNEL and ROCLINCOURT. One Company remained in huts at BOIS de MAROEUIL.	Appendices I. II. III. IV.
			On the 9th the BATTLE of ARRAS opened. The objective given the Battalion was the front line system of trenches, viz:- Firing Line, Support Line, and Reserve Line, known as the "Black" line. The Battalion assembled for the attack in three double waves, each wave consisting of five Platoons, while 4 remaining platoon organised as three Bombing Squads and one Lewis Gun Squad was kept in FISH TUNNEL as a reserve. "D" Company and two platoons of "A" formed the right of the attack. "B" Company the left. These Companies formed the first two double waves. "C" Coy with one platoon of "A" Company formed the third double wave. The remaining platoon of "A" Company was the reserve in the hands of the Battalion Commander. At ZERO the advance was promptly begun, and, immediately the barrage lifted, the objectives were assaulted and cleared up effectively. A good deal of hard fighting took place, but the men had been so thoroughly trained that they were prepared for all eventualities, and speedily got the better of all opposition, though not without heavy loss. One disconcerting incident happened— a minnenwerfer ammunition dump was exploded, and formed a crater about 30 feet deep. Probably 20 casualties were caused by this explosion. About 100 prisoners were captured, as well as three machine guns and a number of trench mortars of varying sizes.	

Officers killed	3	
do. Died of Wounds	2	
do. Wounded	3	
do. Remaining at duty	8	
	16	

Killed
2Lieut J S Grant
" J Mack
" G Reid

Died of Wounds
2Lieut D McKillop
" R Henderson

Wounded
2Lieut D Anderson
" K MacKay
" H Milne

Army Form C. 2118.

WAR DIARY
or
INTELLIGENCE SUMMARY.
(Erase heading not required.)

Page 2

April, 1917.

Instructions regarding War Diaries and Intelligence Summaries are contained in F. S. Regs., Part II. and the Staff Manual respectively. Title pages will be prepared in manuscript.

Place	Date	Hour	Summary of Events and Information	Remarks and references to Appendices
ROCLINCOURT	8-11		Other Ranks casualties were:- Killed 53, Died of Wounds 22, Wounded 175, do. Remaining at duty 4, Missing 6. Total 260	yes
ECOIVRES	12.		Withdrawn from the line to huts.	Opd.
PENIN	13-15		In billets.	Opd.
ARRAS	16-18		In billets.	yes
Trenches	17-18		Took over first line trench system in Squares H.22.a. and b. (Reference 1/10,000 ARRAS and FAMPOUX) from the 7th Black Watch.	Opd. Reference Map.
ARRAS	19-22		In billets.	Opd. ARRAS and FAMPOUX
In the Field	22-24		The Battalion, which had been attached to the 153rd Infantry Brigade, marched to Assembly Trenches — PUDDING and PORT (H.16.b.) on the 23rd began the Battle East of FAMPOUX. The work assigned to the 6th Gordon Highlanders was the capture of the German trench running from I.20.b.7.5. to L.15.d.5.8. (known as the RED line), the capture of HAUSA and DELBAR WOODS and establishing posts on outer flank, and the digging of a support line 200 yards on the British side of the German trench. The order of advance of the 153rd Infantry Brigade was:- 7th Black Watch on the right, and 7th Gordon Highlanders on the left of the Brigade front. These were to take the BLACK, BLUE, and BROWN lines. The 6th Black Watch on the left were to pass over the 7th Gordon Highlanders and dig a trench in front of PLOUVAIN, while the 6th Gordon Highlanders were to pass over the 7th Black Watch and assault the objectives already named. The 154th Infantry Brigade advanced on the right of the/	Scale 1/10.000 Appendices I II III IV V VI VII

Army Form C. 2118.

WAR DIARY
or
INTELLIGENCE SUMMARY.
(Erase heading not required.)

April, 1917
Page 3.

Place	Date	Hour	Summary of Events and Information	Remarks and references to Appendices
In the Field	22-24			Reference Maps. ARRAS and FAMPOUX Scale 1/10,000 Appendices I, II, III, IV, V, VI, VII.

the 153rd Infantry Brigade, and the 37th Division were on the left. A heavy artillery barrage was prepared.

At ZERO plus 1 hour (5.45 a.m.) the 6th Gordon Highlanders left the assembly trenches in artillery formation in four lines of half platoons in file. Lieut Colonel J. Dawson, D.S.O. led the first two lines, which consisted of "A" (on right), and "B" (on left) Companies. "C" and "D" Companies formed the second two lines. The enemy's artillery barrage was heavy, but the Battalion did not suffer greatly, except in one case where a platoon of "B" Company was almost wiped out. It had been expected that extension would not be needed till the Battalion had passed the CHEMICAL WORKS, but long ere this position was reached, heavy machine gun fire rendered extension necessary, and the Companies were extended about H.18.a. and c. The Companies had to advance after this mainly by communication trenches. About 6 a.m. Lieut Colonel J. Dawson was severely wounded (about H.18.b.3.2.), and the command devolved on Captain J. Hutcheson. Under his command the advance continued for some distance, but this was only possible with the assistance of a Tank, which came in response to a signal and went forward and cleared the first German trench (BLACK LINE). Captain J. Hutcheson got as far as the CHEMICAL WORKS, and established his Headquarters at I.13.o.9.9., and posts were thrown out round the CHEMICAL WORKS. This was done about 9.30 a.m. Urgent messages were despatched for reinforcements, but none were forthcoming, and, as it was considered that the numbers in and around the CHEMICAL WORKS were too few to hold back a counter attack which was imminent, Captain J. Hutcheson decided to withdraw to the old British lines. This was done about 12 noon, but a strong post was left at Quarry (H.13.a.2.3.). Laterin the evening (8.30 p.m.) when another British advance took place, this post, which had held its ground all the time, took part in the advance. About 11.45 p.m. the Battalion was withdrawn to the British front line, and remained there during the night. At 12 noon next day the Battalion was relieved by the 25th Northumberland Fusiliers (103rd Brigade), and, after resting for some time in the support trenches; was withdrawn to bivouac in ST NICHOLAS.

From the foregoing it will be seen that the objectives were not gained. This failure was due to the fact that the BLACK and BLUE lines were not taken, but had to be fought for, and the time taken to do this lost to the attack the protection)

Army Form C. 2118.

WAR DIARY
or
INTELLIGENCE SUMMARY.

(Erase heading not required.)

April, 1917. Page 4.

Place	Date	Hour	Summary of Events and Information	Remarks and references to Appendices

In the field	22-24		protection of our own artillery barrage. The enemy machine gun fire was of an extremely galling nature. The Battalion went into battle 630 strong. The following officers were killed or wounded:-
			 Killed 2/Lieutenant A. H. Collyer
			 Wounded Lieut Colonel J. Dawson, D.S.O.
			 do. a/Captain J. H. Matheson
			 do. Lieutenant J. R. W. Gillan
			 do. " D. MacKenzie
			 do. 2/Lieutenant S. E. Hart
			 do. " M. A. Matheson
			 do. " T. Wylie
			 do. " J. Wood
			 do. " W. H. Hume
			 do. " T. J. Purdie
			 do. " J. McMurtrie (Remaining at duty)
			
			 The following are the figures of Other Rank Casualties:-
			 Killed 21
			 Died of Wounds 5
			 Wounded 184
			 do. Remaining at duty 3
			 Unaccounted for 28
			                       ___
			                       241	

ST. NICHOLAS	24-26		In bivouac. Lieutenant Colonel J. Dawson, D.S.O. having been severely wounded, Major J. W. Adams took over command.	
CAPELLE FERMONT	26-28		In billets.	
GOUY EN TERNOIS	28-30		In billets. Lieut Colonel Hon W. Fraser M.C. took over the command vice Major J. W. Adams.	

WAR DIARY
or
INTELLIGENCE SUMMARY.

(Erase heading not required.)

Army Form C. 2118.

April, 1917.   Page 5.

Place	Date	Hour	Summary of Events and Information	Remarks and references to Appendices
			Officers Other Ranks	
			Strength at beginning of month 41 970	
			Battle Casualties 19 494	
			Sick - evacuated - 16	
			19 510	
			22 460	
			Reinforcements 7 227	
			Strength at end of month 29 687	
			Lieut Colonel,	
			Commanding 6th Gordon Highlanders.	

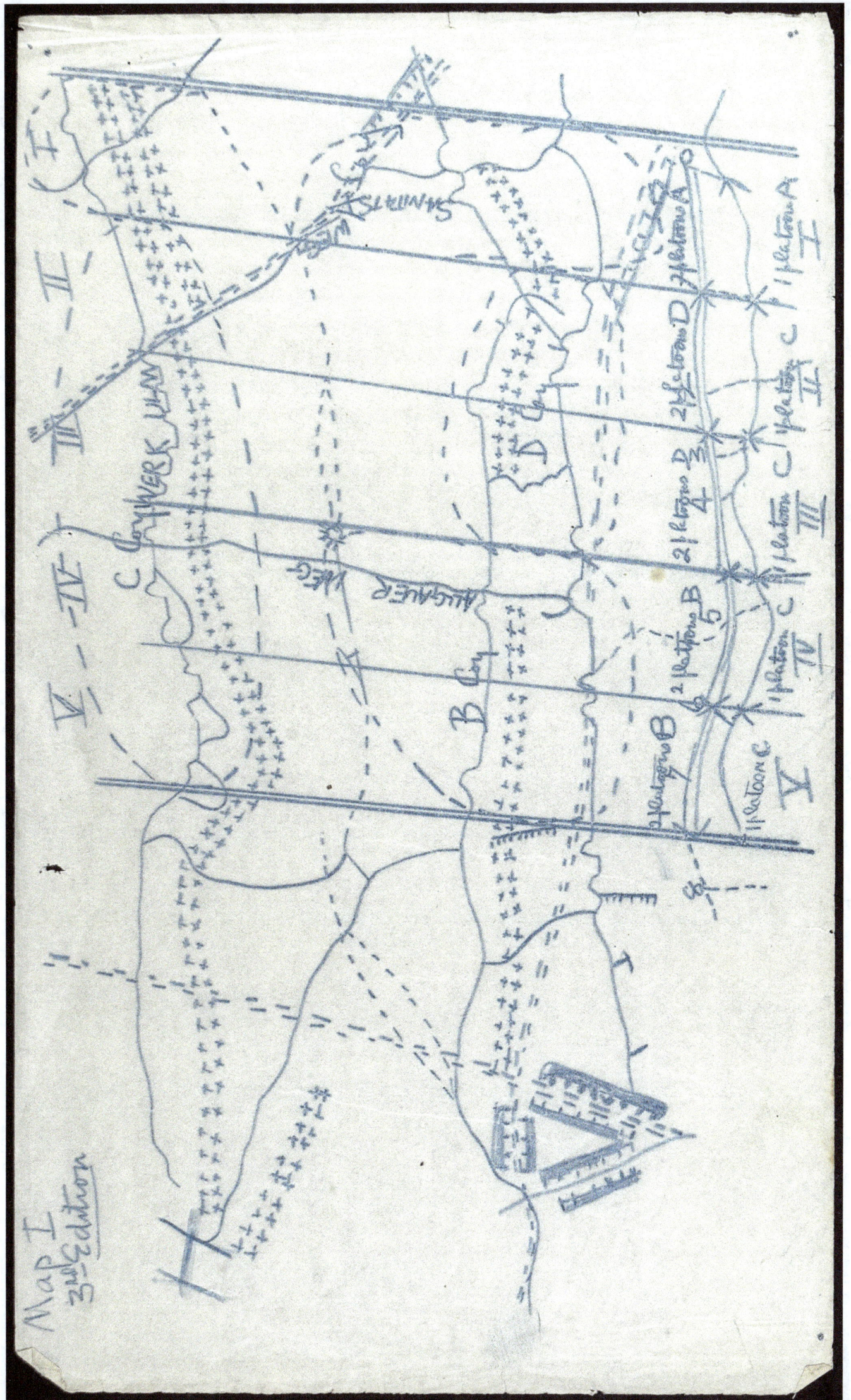

Copy No. 1

Operation Order No. 101,
by Lieut. Colonel J. Dawson, D.S.O.
Commanding 6th. Gordon Highlanders,
ECOIVRES, April 1st., 1917.

1. **MOVE.**
   The 6th. Battalion Gordon Highlanders will move from ECOIVRES HUTS to tents in MAROEUIL WOOD to-morrow 2nd. April, 1917.

2. **PARADE.**
   Companies will move by Platoons in the order B, C, A and D Companies, the leading platoon of B Company leaving at 3 p.m.

3. **DRESS.**
   Full marching order. Leather Jerkins will be worn. Blankets will be carried on the man.

4. **ADVANCE PARTY.**
   Captain FLEMING, 1 N.C.O. per Company and L/C LEITCH will report at camp in MAROEUIL WOOD at 10 a.m. to take over.

5. **TRANSPORT.**
   Officers' baggage will be ready for collection by 2.30 p.m. B.B.O. and L.G.O. will arrange for the move of Grenade and L.G. Limbers.

6. **Q.M. STORES.**
   Q.M. Stores will move to 12 Bridge St., MAROEUIL. The Quartermaster will arrange direct with Transport Officer.

7. **COOKS.**
   Cooks, Travelling Kitchens and cooks' utensils will move immediately after dinners.

8. **CLEANLINESS.**
   All huts, latrines, cookhouses and the camp generally will be left scrupulously clean. Companies will render the usual certificates. The Orderly Officer will inspect the camp after Battalion leaves, and report.

9. **REPORTS.**
   Companies will report immediately on arrival in new billets.

D. Mackenzie
Lieut. & A/Adjutant,
6th. Gordon Highlanders.

Copy No. 1   File.
"   " 2   H.Q. 152nd. Infantry Brigade.
"   " 3-6 Companies.
"   " 7.   Quartermaster.
"   " 8.   Transport Officer.
"   " 9.   Camp Commandant.

Copy No. 1

OPERATION ORDER No. 102a,
by Lieut. Colonel J. Dawson, D.S.O.,
Commanding 6th. Gordon Highlanders.
BOIS-DE-MAROEUIL, 6th. April, 1917.

---

1. MOVE.

"D" Company will leave its billets at 100 yards platoon intervals so as to be clear of MAROEUIL by 7.15 p.m. on 8/9th. April.

2. DESTINATION.

The Company will move to FISH TUNNEL where it will remain till hour of Assembly.

3. DRESS & EQUIPMENT.

Overcoats will be worn.
Fighting Kit as already detailed.
Periscopes, wire-cutters, Very Pistols as issued.
Arrangements for collection of Packs, Leather Jerkins and blankets will be issued separately.

4. ROUTE.

Route B, as per Maps already issued will be followed.

D. MacKay. Lieut. & A/Adjutant.
6th. Gordon Highlanders.

Copy No. 1 File.
"   " 2 D Company.
"   " 3 Major Adams.
"   " 4 Adjutant.

Copy No ......

OPERATION ORDERS, No. 102,
By Lieut. Colonel J. Dawson, D.S.O.,
Commanding 6th. Gordon Highlanders.
BOIS-DE-MAROEUIL, 6th. April, 1917.
-o-o-o-o-o-o-o-o-o-o-o-o-o-

1. RELIEF.
   The Battalion less "D" Company will proceed to trenches to take over battle area on night 7/8th. April.

2. ORDER AND TIME OF MARCH.
   Companies will move by platoons at 100 yards interval; order of march - Headquarters, "A", "B", "C". Headquarters will move off from camp at 7.30 p.m.

3. COMPOSITION.
   Only men going into action will proceed to trenches. Company Sergeant Majors will join their Companies but will return to Echelon B when equipping of Companies is completed on morning of Z Day.

4. DRESS AND EQUIPMENT.
   Overcoats will be worn.
   Fighting Kit as already detailed.
   Periscopes, wire-cutters, Very pistols as issued.
   Arrangements for collection of Packs, Leather Jerkins and blankets will be issued separately.

5. ROUTE.
   Route B as per Maps already issued, will be followed.

6. DISPOSITION.
                                                                    of "A" Coy.
   2 platoons of "A" Company, and 1 extra Lewis Gun Team from platoon in FISH TUNNEL, will hold the battle front.
   1 platoon of "A" Company will be in dugouts in FISH AVENUE.
   1 platoon of "A" Company will be in I Work (FISH TUNNEL)
   2 platoons of "B" Company will be in East end of TUNNEL.
   1 platoon of "B" Company will be in dugout on S. side of TUNNEL.
   1 platoon of "B" Company will be in West end of TUNNEL.
   "C" Company will occupy billets in ROCLINCOURT.

7. TAKING OVER.
   One Officer and 1 N.C.O. selected from those not going into action, per Company, will reconnoitre Company area by daylight and will return to ANZIN CHURCH to meet Companies there.

                                            D. MacIntyre
                                                      Lieut. & A/Adjutant,
                                            6th. Gordon Highlanders.

Copy No. 1 File.
  "   " 2 H.Q. 152nd. Inf. Bde.
  "   " 3-6 Companies.
  "   " 7 Transport Officer.
  "   " 8 Quartermaster.
  "   " 9 H.Q. Mess.

ASSEMBLY ORDERS

1. As ZERO hour has not yet been announced, the time for moving to Assembly positions cannot be given, but all will be in position 1 hour 30 minutes before ZERO hour.

2. 10 Rounds S.A.A. will be placed in Magazine before troops move from their Y Day Billets, and 1 Round will be placed in Breech when Bayonets are fixed, immediately before ZERO.

3. The utmost care must be exercised to minimise noise in moving to Assembly Trenches. Bayonets will not be fixed till immediately before ZERO. Silence must be observed, and full advantage of cover taken, to prevent warning being given to enemy. No smoking allowed

4. Rum will be issued immediately before leaving the tunnel.

5. Overcoats will be worn and at 30 minutes before ZERO these will be collected in bundles of half a dozen, tied in one of them, and left for future collection. Troops in BONNAL will collect those in that line and place them in shelters in the trench.

6. One N.C.O. and 2 privates per Platoon detailed for German front line will act as covering patrols, and first relief will be in position 15 minutes before troops move in.

7. Should hostile aeroplanes come over lines at dawn, men must not look up towards them but keep heads down.

8. All polished helmets are to be covered with mud.

Lieut Colonel,
Commanding 6th Gordon Highlanders

7.4.1917.

Operation Orders No. 103
by Lieut Colonel J. Dawson, D.S.O.
Commanding 6th Gordon Highlanders
ECOIVRES, 13th April, 1917.

Copy No. 1

Map Reference - LENS 11 1/100,000

1. **MOVE**

   The Battalion will move to billets in PENIN to-day.

2. **PARADE**

   Parade:- 11.45 a.m. on the road leaving S.W. Route
   ARRAS - ST POL Road - SAVY - PENIN.
   Order of March:- Headquarters, A, B, C, D Companies.
   An interval of 200 yards between Companies will be maintained.

3. **BAGGAGE**

   Blankets and Officers' baggage to be ready for collection by 11 a.m.

4. **SPARE PACKS.**

   All spare packs will be collected in "A" Company's Q.M. Sergeant's hut.

5. **CERTIFICATES**

   The usual certificates regarding cleanliness of billets will be handed in before moving off.

6. **DRESS**

   Steel Helmets will be worn.

   Capt. & Adj.
   6th Gordon Highlanders

Copy No 1 File
       2 H.Q. 152nd Inf Brigade.
   3 - 6 Companies
       7 Transport Officer
       8 Quartermaster
       9 Spare.

TRENCH ROUTINE.

The following points will be observed during this tour of Trenches:-

1. Normal procedure will be observed as far as possible.

2. Commanders of Platoons holding the line will allocate Gaps in German Wire to each of the 3 Lewis Guns and these must be kept under fire during hours of darkness. Only two drums will be used for this purpose and these will be kept filled from boxes of S.A.A. placed at Gun Positions.

3. On X/Y night from 8 - 10 p.m. and from 1 - 3 a.m., and on Y/Z night from 10 p.m. - Midnight, artillery, M.G's, and Trench Mortars will cease fire to enable patrols to be sent out. These patrols will report on nature of German wire and will endeavour to ascertain whether First line trench is held by enemy.

 A special patrol will be arranged for investigating Sunken Road on our Right Front, and cutting wire there if necessary.

4. Procedure during Assembly on Z Day will be issued separately.

Lieut. Colonel,
Commanding 6th Gordon Highlanders.

TRENCH EQUIPMENT.

PERISCOPES.- 2 Box, 16 Vigilant and 4 Lifeguard per Company.

1" Very Pistols -1 per Lewis Gun Team (already issued)
5 per Company, except "A" - 4.
One dozen rounds per pistol.

CANDLES. - 12 half candles per platoon - to be used only for searching enemy dug-outs.

WIRING GLOVES.- 1 pair for each man with wire-cutting shears.

SOLIDIFIED ALCOHOL.-20 tins per platoon for 4 platoons of "C" and third line platoon of "A" Company. This means one tin for two men, and are to be used only in enemy lines.

BREAKFAST RATIONS. - For "A", "B" & "C" Companies. Sausages and chocolate.

FLARES. - 12 for each 3rd. line platoon as above.

WATER BOTTLES.- To be filled during forenoon.
6 "P" Bombers and 2 additional rifle- grenadiers per platoon to have sandbag carriers.

LIST OF BATTLE CASUALTIES.

Killed in Action

X	2/Lieut	J. B. Grant		"B"	9.4.17	(3)
R	"	T. Mack		"A"	"	
R	"	G. Reid		"C"	"	

B₁₇₇ anginted	290464	Pte-Ferries	W.	"C"	7.4.17	
B₁₂₂ X	265515	" -Fulton	G.	"A"	9.4.17	
B₁₂₂ X	266202	" -Lumsden	J.	"A"	"	
B₁₂₂ X	40943	" -Forsyth	L.	"A"	"	
X	266242	" -Stewart	A.	"A"	"	
B₁₂₂ X	266650	" -Smith	A.O.H.	"A"	"	
B₁₂₂	241077	" -Lawrence	J.	"A"	"	
B₁₂₂ +	266147	Sgt Watt	P.G.	"B" ✓	"	
B₁₂₂ +	265065	Pte-Garrow	A.	"B"	"	
X	266608	" -Jones	A.E.	"B"	"	
B₁₂₂ R	265804	" -Pozzi	I.	"B"	"	
B₁₂₂ R	266829	" -Bruce	W.	"B"	"	
B₁₂₂ +	266117	" -Gordon	F.	"B"	"	
B₁₂₂ R	241605	" -McCann	W.	"B"	"	
B₁₂₂ X	265981	" -Ainslie	J.M.	"B"	"	
B₁₂₂ X	266620	" -Boyd	R.	"B"	"	
B₁₂₂ X	266950	" -Graham	A.	"B"	"	
B₁₂₂ +	265458	Cpl Harper	J.	"C" ✓	"	
B₁₂₂ +	265512	" Sutherland	W.	"C" ✓	"	
B₁₂₂ X	266847	" Mann	G.	"C" ✓	"	
B₁₂₂ +	265102	" Don	G.	"C" ✓	"	
B₁₂₂	266308	Pte-Anderson	J.	"C"	"	
B₁₂₂	265404	" -Bain	J.	"C"	"	
	266908	" -Blair	A.	"C"	"	
B₁₂₂ +	265643	" -Calder	A.B.	"C"	"	
B₁₂₂ +	265088	" -Cruickshank	G.	"C"	"	
B₁₂₂ X	285012	" -Campbell	F.	"C"	"	
B₁₂₂ X	265227	" -Cameron	G.	"C"	"	
B₁₂₂ X	266804	" -Pirie	R.	"C"	"	
B₁₂₂ X	266824	" -Howie	C.	"C"	"	
B₁₂₂ X	266671	" -Hoyle	T.A.	"C"	"	
B₁₂₂ R	265705	" -Inglis	A.	"C"	"	
B₁₂₂ X	285006	" -Miller	J.	"C"	"	
B₁₂₂ +	266834	" -Middleton	W.	"C"	"	
B₁₂₂ X	266107	" -Moretrie	J.D.	"C"	"	
B₁₂₂ R	266902	" -Riddell	J.	"C"	"	
B₁₂₂ X	265258	" -Smith	A.	"C"	"	
B₁₂₂	265104	" -Still	C.	"C"	"	
B₁₂₂	285032	" -Scott	J.	"C"	"	
X	266178	" -Skinner	A.	"C"	"	
B₁₂₂ X	266896	" -Screen	F.	"C"	"	
B₁₂₂ X	266912	" -Smith	R.	"C"	"	
B₁₂₂ X	266703	" -Stringfellow	H.V.	"C"	"	
B₁₂₂ +	285006	" -Walker	J.	"C"	"	
B₁₂₂ X	40904	P/c-Neyland	J.L.	"D"	"	
B₁₂₂ X	266255	L/C-Duncan	J.	"D" ✓	"	
B₁₂₂ X	265628	Pte-Shand	W.	"D"	"	
B₁₂₂ X	241841	" -Nicol	R.	"D"	"	
B₁₂₂ X	266278	" -Inglis	F.	"D"	"	
B₁₂₂ X	265196	" -Meldrum	J.	"D"	"	
B₁₂₂ X	40918	" -Crawford	R.	"D"	"	

Marginal notes: add to le / x marker / Watt = S⁴ / at A.23.D.9.0 contains 49 bodies marked X of which 3 are unknown (1 of whom is a raider) and 2 are Sgt Smith & Irish K in A on 5.3.17 also A/c Smith L.

Died of Wounds.

B₁₂₂ R	265264	L/C-Row	A.G.	"A" ✓	9.4.17	
X B₁₂₂	266266	Pte-Banks	J.	"D"	"	
B₁₂₂ Hdk known	266858	" -Ellis	F.	"A"	"	
last Notes B₁₂₂	266904	" -Staines	W.	"C"	"	
B₁₂₂ R	266077	" -Middleton	J.	"C"	10.4.17	(12)
B₁₂₂ R	266045	" -Thom	W.	"D" ✓	"	
B₁₂₂ R	265601	Sgt Riddell	J.	"C"	"	
B₁₂₂ A	285013	Pte-McCulloch	J.	"	"	
B₁₂₂	266010	" -Fraser	J.	"A"	"	
B₁₂₂ A	266319	" -Simpson	A.	"C"	"	
B₁₂₂ A	40000	" -McLelland	A.	"C"	"	
do Noth B₁₂₂	265242	" -Jamieson	J.	"C"	"	

Page 2.

CASUALTY LIST. Continued.

Wounded

	2/Lieut	T. Anderson	"D"	9.4.17	
	"	K. MacKay	"D"	"	
	"	R. J. Milne	"B"	"	
	"	L. B. Kilborn	"B"	"	
	"	R. Henderson	"C"	"	
	"	A. E. Paterson	"C"	"	Remaining at duty
	"	J. S. B. Ward	"A"	"	do.
	"	W. F. Leggat	"C"	"	do.
	"	W. H. Hume	"D"	"	do.
	"	M. A. Matheson	"B"	"	do.
				(enemy barbed wire)	
	"	J. Collins	"D"	9.4.17	Remaining at duty
	"	R. W. McWatters	"A"	"	do.

40012	Pte-Leighton	G.T.	"C"	7.4.17
267006	" -Simpson	H.	"C"	"
266604	" -Bancroft	H.	"A"	9.4.17
266010	" -Bremner	J.	"A"	"
266505	" -Grant	A.	"A"	"
265095	" -Milton	G.	"A"	"
40937	" -Stewart	A.	"A"	"
290351	" -Davidson	A.	"A"	"
40921	" -Fitton	R.	"A"	"
266857	" -Watson	A.	"A"	"
265156	" -Gavin	J.	"A"	"
40939	" -Shaw	J.J.	"A"	"
266868	" -Harkin	H.	"A"	"
265588	Sgt-Sim	C.	"A"	"
265025	Pte-Lauderdale	D.	"A"	"
290374	" -Sharp	G.	"A"	"
266812	" -Corbett	T.	"A"	"
266783	L/C-Baird	W.	"A"	"
266651	Pte-Cavanagh	J.	"A"	"
266104	" -Rattray	C.	"A"	"
265342	L/C-Mearns	F.	"A"	"
267009	Pte-Dalgleish	R.	"A"	"
266345	" -McGregor	G.	"A"	"
265007	" -Smith	F.	"A"	"
265641	L/C-Flett	F.B.	"A"	"
265505	Sgt-Wallace	J.	"A"	"
265513	Pte-Soutar	C.	"A"	"
265789	" -Barclay	G.	"A"	"
265841	" -Bell	J.	"B"	"
265703	" -Callum	J.N.	"B"	"
266317	" -Collie	R.	"B"	"
40915	" -Court	J.S.	"B"	"
265271	" -Gifford	G.	"B"	"
266280	" -McRae	E.	"B"	"
266065	" -Stronach	G.	"B"	"
266710	" -Shires	H.	"B"	"
266084	" -Annand	J.	"B"	"
265651	" -Bremner	R.	"B"	"
266040	" -McDonald	R.	"B"	"
265913	Sgt-Shand	J.	"B"	"
265980	L/S-Lemon	R.	"B"	"
266126	Pte-Barron	G.	"B"	"
266642	" -Crisp	J.H.	"B"	"
266977	" -Cooper	D.	"B"	"
266884	" -Forbes	J.	"B"	"
265850	" -Shearer	W.	"B"	"
266872	" -McMillan	J.	"B"	"
265452	" -Finnie	A.	"B"	"
266143	Sgt-Gordonan	D.I.	"B"	"
265397	Cpl-Meldrum	G.	"B"	"
266617	L/C-Bilton	A.	"B"	"
265054	Pte-Gann	W.	"B"	"
265661	" -Gregg	C.A.	"B"	"
265790	" -Gray	J.	"B"	"
266638	" -Cooper	J.	"B"	"

Page 3.

CASUALTY LIST. Continued

Wounded.

266876	Pte.-Hunter	W.	"B"	9.4.17
266817	" -Irvine	W.	"B"	"
266085	" -Kaye	A. F.	"B"	"
265563	" -Milne	J.	"B"	"
266006	" -McDonald	J.	"B"	"
265746	" -Stronach	J.	"B"	"
266168	" -Stewart	E. G.	"B"	"
266709	" -Shaw	H.	"B"	"
266155	" -Watt	J.	"B"	"
266001	Sgt.-Brebner	L.	"C"	"
265052	" -Watt	J. M.	"C"	"
265594	" -Gilbert	J.	"C"	"
266504	Cpl.-Stott	G.	"C"	"
265861	" -Benzie	R. J.	"C"	"
265914	" -Lemon	J.	"C"	"
40905	Pte.-Smith	L. F.	"C"	"
265062	L/C-Davidson	W.	"C"	"
266102	" -Johnstone	W.	"C"	"
40932	Pte.-Baillie	D. C.	"C"	"
285001	" -Bowman	J.	"C"	"
285010	" -Birmingham	L.	"C"	"
266031	" -Bruce	A.	"C"	"
265327	L/C-Catto	J. M.	"C"	"
265034	Pte.-Cryle	J.	"C"	"
285010	" -Darrach	J.	"C"	"
266644	" -Dawson	H.	"C"	"
265837	" -Duncan	A.	"C"	"
40010	" -Fraser	J.	"C"	"
285041	" -Gorrie	C.	"C"	"
266413	" -Gordon	J.	"C"	"
265595	" -Gray	W. G.	"C"	"
265044	" -Grant	J.	"C"	"
266828	" -Irvine	A.	"C"	"
266809	" -Kelly	F.	"C"	"
267008	" -Ledingham	A.	"C"	"
265968	" -Littlejohn	W.	"C"	"
265677	" -Murison	W.	"C"	"
265921	" -Massie	W. L.	"C"	"
265180	" -McDonald	D.	"C"	"
266370	" -McKay	H.	"C"	"
266245	" -Moiretrie	J.	"C"	"
266550	" -Nicol	W.	"C"	"
265896	" -Petrie	J.	"C"	"
267005	" -Rae	T.	"C"	"
266932	" -Sandison	J.	"C"	"
265400	" -Ross	W. G.	"C"	"
241090	" -Peterson	A.	"C"	"
285028	" -McMonigle	R.	"C"	"
266568	" -Clark	J.	"C"	"
266000	" -Thomson	A.	"C"	"
266006	" -Torrie	J.	"C"	"
265020	Sgt.-George	A.	"D"	"
265015	Cpl.-Howitt	J.	"D"	"
265161	" -Spence	W.	"D"	"
265117	" -Milne	W.	"D"	"
266046	L/C-Lumsden	J.	"D"	"
265116	" -Aitken	J.	"D"	"
266327	" -Tough	W.	"D"	"
266067	" -Ironside	W.	"D"	"
266923	" -Austin	J.	"D"	"
266914	Pte.-Copland	A.	"D"	"
40930	" -Linn	A.	"D"	"
40929	" -Logan	F.	"D"	"
266064	" -Runcie	G.	"D"	"
266911	" -Grundy	A.	"D"	"
265730	L/C-Peterkin	G.	"D"	"
266712	Pte.-Sherlock	J.	"D"	"
240661	" -Thoirs	G.	"D"	"

Page 4.

CASUALTY LIST. Continued

Wounded

265785	Pte-Barron	W.	"D"	9.4.17
266604	" -Leighton	J.B.	"D"	"
266350	L/C.McDonald	W.	"D"	"
265919	Pte-McLeod	C.	"D"	"
266240	" -Cormack	R.	"D"	"
266690	" -Small	J.	"D"	"
266668	" -Halliday	F.	"D"	"
266111	" -Cammack	G.	"D"	"
266052	" -Ellis	I.	"D"	"
265343	" -Leggie	J.	"D"	"
266844	" -McRitchie	J.	"D"	"
266093	" -Godsman	W.	"D"	"
265666	" -Rodger	G.	"D"	"
266916	" -Livingstone	G.	"D"	"
292563	" -Hutcheson	F.	"D"	"
S/15616	" -Meggie	J.	"D"	"
40013	" -Fraser	E.R.	"B"	"
266357	" -Valentine	H.	TMB	"
265401	" -Tobin	T.	"D"	"
265300	" -Findlay	A.	"A"	8.4.17
40914	" -Dencon	D.	"C"	9.4.17 Adm. 12.4.17
265756	" -Cowie	F.	"C"	" Remaining at duty
266015	" -Higson	R.	"C"	"
265570	L/C-McLean	N.	"A"	"
266176	Pte-Blaikie	F.	"A"	"
266293	" -Gill	R.	"A"	"
12146	" -Grant	J.	"A"	"
285030	" -Budie	J.	"A"	"
266789	" -Cameron	A.	"A"	"
265892	" -Fraser	H.	"A"	"
266832	" -Ross	M.	"A"	"
241589	" -Marr	N.C.	"B"	"
266048	" -Wishart	J.	"B"	"
267010	" -Aird	N.	"B"	"
266044	" -Copperwhite	R.	"B"	"
266261	" -Gray	G.	"B"	"
265151	" -McMann	F.	"B"	"
40911	" -Miller	D.J.	"B"	"
266842	" -Luthwood	G.	"C"	"
265653	" -Geddes	G.	"C"	"
266667	" -McDougall	J.	"C"	"
266891	" -McKay	T.	"C"	"
266426	" -Murdoch	A.	"C"	"
201276	" -Taylor	W.	"C"	"
285039	" -Young	T.	"C"	"
266448	" -Balfour	F.	"D"	"
S/15984	" -McFarlane	G.	"D"	"
266924	" -Carr	A.	"D"	"
266928	" -Harkness	F.	"D"	"
266925	" -Little	J.	"D"	"
266490	" -Proctor	J.	"D"	"
40941	" -Henderson	J.	"D"	"
40942	" -Caldwell	W.	"D"	"
S/10081	" -Barnett	J.	"B"	"
266407	" -Mair	G.T.	"B"	
290981	" -Wilson	H.	"B"	

OPERATION ORDERS No. 105,
by Lieut. Colonel J. Dawson, D.S.O.
Commanding 6th. Gordon Highlanders.
ARRAS, 18th. April, 1917.

Copy No. 1

Reference 1/10,000 ARRAS & FAMPOUX.

1. MOVE.
   The 6th. Battalion Gordon Highlanders will relieve the 7th. Black Watch in the front trench system in Squares XXXXXXXX H. 22. a and b to-night, 18th. April, 1917. Companies will relieve corresponding Companies.

2. PARADES.
   The Battalion will parade at Barracks at 6 p.m., and will move by platoons in file to H.Q. 153 Infantry Brigade at ATHIES where guides will meet the Battalion. Order of march will be, Headquarters, D, A, C, and B Companies.

3. DRESS.
   Fighting kit, great coats and kilt aprons will be worn. Great coats will be hooked back. If weather is wet, ground sheets will be worn.

4. EQUIPMENT ETC.
   Each Company will carry 50 shovels and 25 picks. Lewis Gun and Bomb Limbers will proceed to ATHIES during the afternoon. Company Lewis Gun and Bombing Instructors will proceed with the limbers, and will have all Lewis Guns, L.G. Magazines and Bombing Buckets ready for distribution near 153 Brigade H.Q.
   Rations for the 19th. and filled water bottles will be carried.

5. BAGGAGE.
   Packs and blankets will be removed to the Q.M. Stores - RUE DES AGACHES - by 4.30 p.m. under Company arrangements. Officers' kits will be ready for collection by 5.30 p.m.

6. TRANSPORT.
   Transport will not move.

7. BILLETS.
   Billets and their neighbourhood will be left scrupulously clean. The usual certificates will be rendered.

8. REPORTS.
   Companies will report immediately relief is complete.

R. Mackenzie, Lieut., & A/Adjt.
6th. Gordon Highlanders.

Copy No. 1 File
        2 H.Q. 152 Brigade.
      3-6 Companies.
        7 Transport Officer.
        8 Quartermaster.
        9 H.Q. Mess.
       10. R.S.M.

Copy No. 1.

6th GORDON HIGHLANDERS.

OPERATION ORDERS No. 106.

1. MOVE.

    The 6th. Battalion, Gordon Highlanders will move to Assembly Trenches in H. 16 b. to-night, 22nd. April, 1917.

2. PARADE.

    Companies will parade ready to move off at 7.15 p.m. Order of the march will be Headquarters, B, A, D and C Companies. Battalion will move by platoons at 100 paces interval, care being taken to maintain touch.

3. ROUTE ETC.

    Route will be Railway Bridge over SCARPE at G. 22. a. 5.0. 6.5. (Starting point) - Tow Path along North Bank of SCARPE to path at H. 13. d. 4. 5. - HERVIN FARM. Head of the column will pass starting point at 7.30 p.m. Tea will be issued at HERVIN FARM. Battalion will leave HERVIN FARM in the same order at 10.30 p.m. and will proceed to Assembly Positions via RAILWAY BRIDGE at H. 14. a. 4.0. 2.5., and overland track commencing H. 14. a. 1. 5.

4. TRANSPORT ETC.

    Cookers with 2 cooks per Company and Lewis Gun Limbers will leave ARRAS at 2 p.m. and await Battalion at HERVIN FARM. Company Lewis Gun Instructors will accompany Limbers and distribute Lewis Gun Magazines at HERVIN FARM.

5. BAGGAGE.

    Packs, blankets and Officers' kits will be sent to Q.M. Stores by 6 p.m.

6. DISCIPLINE.

    No singing, noise or smoking will be allowed on the march. One Latrine per platoon will be dug immediately Assembly Positions are reached.

7. REPORTS.

    Companies will report their arrival in Assembly Positions to Battalion Headquarters, H. 16. b. 7. 9.

                                    D. MacKenzie
                                          Lieut. & A/Adjutant,
                                          6th. Gordon Highlanders.

Copy No. 1   File
           2   H.Q. 153 Infantry Brigade.
   3 - 6   Companies.
           7   Transport Officer.
           8   Quartermaster.
           9   H.Q. Mess.
         10   Spare.

LIST OF BATTLE CASUALTIES.

Killed in Action

	S/16407	Sgt. Thorne	E.W.	"C"	23.4.17
	265614	L/C McGlashan	A.	"C"	"
	285069	Pte. Anderson	G.	"C"	"
	266632	" Cooper	R.	"C"	"
	266339	" Donald	A.	"C"	"
	265970	" Ellis	G.B.	"C"	"
	266815	" Scott	G.	"C"	"
	265602	L/C Mackie	A.	"B"	"
	265763	Pte. Allan	J.	"B"	"
	292186	" McGee	J.	"B"	"
	266030	" Philip	A.N.	"B"	"
	265562	" Watt	R.	"B"	"
	265890	" Hendry	R.	"A"	"
	265060	" Hepburn	A.	"A"	"
	265270	" McKay	S.	"A"	"
	266576	" Smith	W.	"A"	"
	265975	a/Sgt. Duguid	W.	"D"	"
	290259	Pte Watson	J.	"D"	"
	266852	" McDonald	T.	"D"	"
	265898	" Robertson	J.	"D"	"

Died of Wounds

		2/Lieut A. H. Collyer		"C"	23.4.17
	17033	Pte Milne	J.	"B"	"

Wounded

		Lieut Colonel J. Dawson, D.S.O.			23.4.17
		a/Captain J. H. Matheson			"
		Lieutenant J. R. W. Gillan			"
		" D. MacKenzie			"
		2/Lieut S. E. Hart			"
		" M. A. Matheson			"
		" T. Wylie			"
		" J. Wood			"
		" W. H. Hume			"
		" T. J. Purdie			"
	S/5628	L/S Pearson	T.W.	"C"	23.4.17
	265416	L/C Smith	W.	"C"	"
	265164	" Fordyce	W.	"C"	"
	285046	Pte. Brodie	J.M.	"C"	"
	285078	" Ferguson	S.	"C"	"
	285070	" Gray	D.	"C"	"
	S/15862	" McGuire	A.	"C"	"
	285136	" McKechnie	G.	"C"	"
	266286	" Smith	R.	"C"	"
	265529	" Thomson	J.	"C"	"
	266602	" Austin	J.	"C"	"
	266555	" Gilbert	C.	"C"	"
	265309	" Jaffray	A.	"C"	"
	17053	" Moir	J.	"C"	"
	285054	" McKenzie	J.C.	"C"	"
	285131	" McLean	J.	"C"	"
	285052	" McDonald	W.	"C"	"
	285064	" Slattery	M.	"C"	"
	291176	" Brookes	F.	"C"	"
	201721	" Gavin	W.	"C"	"
	285111	" Hamil	C.J.	"C"	"
	266837	" Irvinge	W.	"C"	"
	266898	" Moore	W.	"C"	"
	285066	" Rose	H.	"C"	"
	265756	" Cowie	P.	"C"	"
	40914	" Denoon	D.	"C"	"

Page 2

BATTLE CASUALTIES (continued)

WOUNDED

S/15360	Pte.	-Imray	J.	"C"	23.4.17.
285115	"	-Wright	W.	"C"	"
266090	"	-Graham	J.	"C"	"
265932	Cpl.	-Will	G.	"B"	"
266122	L/C	-Bennett	G.	"B"	"
265199	Sgt.	-Runcie	A.	"B"	"
14808	Pte.	-Wilkinson	W.	"B"	"
265188	L/C	-Webster	F.	"B"	"
266406	"	-Scott	A.T.	"B"	"
17027	Pte.	-Fairbairn	W.	"B"	"
266899	L/C	-Ferns	J.	"B"	"
266356	Pte.	-Brown	R.	"B"	"
290837	"	-Brown	J.	"B"	"
10417	"	-Burns	J.	"B"	"
11211	"	-Calder	G.	"B"	"
266095	"	-Clark	C.	"B"	"
285043	"	-Barnett	D.	"B"	"
266481	"	-Duncan	W.C.	"B"	"
266451	"	-Farquhar	J.	"B"	"
266218	"	-Gordon	J.	"B"	"
S/40924	"	-Gilmour	E.S.	"B"	"
266060	"	-Henderson	G.	"B"	"
40922	"	-Harris	J.K.	"B"	"
200209	"	-Kynoch	A.	"B"	"
292445	"	-Kirby	G.	"B"	"
266160	"	-Keggans	P.	"B"	"
265567	"	-Low	W.	"B"	"
266882	"	-Mullan	R.	"B"	"
292465	"	-Moseley	C.	"B"	"
17048	"	-Murphy	F.	"B"	"
266883	"	-Peel	R.	"B"	"
266086	"	-Smith	J.	"B"	"
265646	"	-Sutherland	J.	"B"	"
265832	"	-Smith	C.	"B"	"
15613	"	-Shepherd	J.	"B"	"
9558	"	-McNally	J.	"B"	"
265032	"	-McLaren	J.	"B"	"
265778	"	-McAllister	P.	"B"	"
265945	"	-McKenzie	A.	"B"	"
266554	"	-Taylor	P.	"B"	"
265997	"	-Teunion	D.	"B"	"
266041	"	-Walton	G.	"B"	"
265656	"	-Wilson	E.	"B"	"
265767	L/C	-Paterson	P.	"B"	"
266870	Pte.	-Allan	R.	"A"	"
265325	Sgt.	-Burnett	A.G.	"A"	"
266623	Pte.	-Briggs	H.	"A"	"
266173	"	-Barron	W.	"A"	"
266853	"	-Campbell	J.	"A"	"
7212	"	-Craig	R.	"A"	"
265955	L/C	-Charlesworth	T.	"A"	"
266291	Pte.	-Clark	J.	"A"	"
15294	"	-Dunnet	B.	"A"	"
241206	"	-Ewen	G.	"A"	"
265946	"	-Emslie	D.	"A"	"
266861	"	-Gavin	C.	"A"	"
266216	"	-Gray	C.	"A"	"
266951	L/C	-Grierson	A.	"A"	"
266903	Pte.	-Gibson	J.	"A"	"
266676	"	-Hinchcliffe	C.	"A"	"
285023	"	-Hudson	A.	"A"	"
952	"	-King	G.	"A"	"
285027	"	-Knox	J.	"A"	"
266294	Cpl.	-Johnstone	H.	"A"	"
265147	L/C	-Walker	W.	"A"	"
266183	Pte.	-Kennedy	A.	"A"	"
40938	"	-Lindsay	A.	"A"	"
265226	"	-Lawson	W.	"A"	"
266558	"	-Jamieson	W.	"A"	"
266860	"	-McMillan	A.	"A"	"

Page 3.

BATTLE CASUALTIES (continued)

WOUNDED

5325	Pte.	-McGuire	J.	"A"	23.4.17.
15140	"	-Ness	F.	"A"	"
265276	"	-Porter	A.	"A"	"
266862	"	-Richardson	F.	"A"	"
265719	"	-Stronach	W.	"A"	"
266441	"	-Stewart	D.	"A"	"
266231	"	-Stewart	J.	"A"	"
266121	"	-Shearer	W.	"A"	"
285036	"	-Taylor	H.	"A"	"
266402	"	-Urquhart	H.	"A"	"
265762	"	-Wood	A.	"A"	"
266865	"	-Wallace	A.	"A"	"
266527	"	-Jones	J.	"A"	"
266866	"	-Campbell	T.	"C"	"
285055	"	-Steel	A.	"C"	"
266174	"	-Grant	L.	"D"	"
266918	"	-Bergen	P.	"D"	"
285101	"	-Bland	A.J.	"D"	"
265051	"	-Blackhall	G.	"D"	"
266164	"	-Beaton	F.	"D"	"
265514	L/C	-Bell	D.	"D"	"
265474	Sgt.	-Clark	R.	"D"	"
285104	Pte.	-Currie	A.	"D"	"
266321	"	-Donald	J.	"D"	"
285117	"	-Donley	T.	"D"	"
266930	L/C	-Fraser	C.	"D"	"
266061	Pte.	-Henderson	J.	"D"	"
265843	Cpl.	-Innes	T.M.	"D"	"
266264	Pte.	-Innes	A.	"D"	"
285105	"	-McKeand	T.	"D"	"
285133	"	-McLay	A.	"D"	"
285109	"	-Manson	J.	"D"	"
285098	"	-Paterson	A.	"D"	"
266401	"	-Peddie	A.	"D"	"
266846	"	-Philip	A.	"D"	"
S/15021	"	-Paterson	W.H.	"D"	"
40935	"	-Rose	F.	"D"	"
266716	L/C	-Thompson	F.	"D"	"
266838	"	-Thomson	A.	"D"	"
266313	Pte.	-Thomson	J.	"D"	"
266409	"	-Masson	J.L.	"D"	"
285084	"	-McDowell	F.	"D"	"
265710	Sgt.	-Whyte	J.	"D"	"
S/15208	Pte.	-Wrafter	P.	"D"	"
17042	"	-Walls	H.	"D"	"
266154	"	-Stewart	W.	"D"	"
265345	"	-Watt	A.R.	"D"	"
17022	"	-Yeats	H.	"D"	"
15981	"	-Lynen	F.	"D"	"
266826	"	-Sherriffs	G.	"D"	"
265359	"	-Tytler	R.	"D"	"

WOUNDED - REMAINING AT DUTY

265395	Sgt Ross	J.	"C"	23.4.17	G.S.W.	Back
285094	Pte McKay	A.	"D"	"	do.	Knee

over.

Page 4.

BATTLE CASUALTIES, Continued.

UNACCOUNTED FOR

285061	Pte	Dudmon	W.H.	"C"	23.4.17
285138	"	Watt	W.	"C"	"
266875	"	Brown	D.	"C"	"
201492	"	Donald	W.	"C"	"
285079	"	Irving	J.	"C"	"
15996	"	Jamieson	W.	"C"	"
285014	"	McEachern	G.	"C"	"
285067	"	McDowell	S.	"C"	"
S/12825	"	McKenzie	T.	"C"	"
17043	"	Smith	A.	"C"	"
265779	"	Bruce	J.	"C"	"
266658	"	Gaunt	L.W.	"C"	"
17069	"	Hay	W.	"C"	"
266495	"	Milne	G.	"C"	"
8317	"	McLaughlin	T.	"C"	"
285057	"	Towner	J.H.	"C"	"
S/14210	"	Fletcher	A.	"C"	"
285035	"	Spiers	A.	"C"	"
S/7612	L/C	Bisby	S.	"B"	"
6709	Pte	Gray	J.	"B"	"
13175	"	Hilton	J.	"B"	"
8904	"	Oliphant	W.	"B"	"
11332	"	Pilkington	J.	"B"	"
240474	"	Will	F.	"B"	"
9636	"	Sibbald	D.	"B"	"
290398	"	Cargill	C.	"A"	"
15796	"	Calder	A.	"A"	"
15636	"	Duguid	W.	"A"	"
266130	"	Davidson	J.	"A"	"
266988	"	Fordoun	A.	"A"	"
15115	"	Hook	G.	"A"	"
5709	"	Lister	T.	"A"	"
13223	"	Lind	A.	"A"	"
266063	"	Mitchell	J.	"A"	"
265447	"	McKenzie	R.	"A"	"
285029	"	McRae	J.	"A"	"
265768	"	McWilliam	J.	"A"	"
266999	"	McQueen	J.	"A"	"
265435	"	McKenzie	P.	"A"	"
266104	"	Sutherland	A.	"A"	"
290582	"	Selby	W.	"A"	"
285034	"	Stewart	A.	"A"	"
266172	"	Thomson	J.	"A"	"
290994	"	Watt	L.	"A"	"
267014	"	Whitelaw	R.	"A"	"
265177	Cpl	Watt	W.	"A"	"
285038	Pte	Wilson	A.	"A"	"
265908	"	Watt	G.	"A"	"
13625	"	Wells	C.	"A"	"
266312	"	Priest	A.	"A"	"
285047	"	Allan	J.	"D"	"
285093	"	Cawley	A.G.	"D"	"
S/14531	"	Cormack	W.	"D"	"
285092	"	Graham	W.A.	"D"	"
266493	"	Innes	G.	"D"	"
285099	"	Howie	L.	"D"	"
266203	"	Fraser	G.	"D"	"
265399	Cpl	Milne	W.	"D"	"
291536	Pte	McKay	D.	"D"	"
266927	"	Petrie	J.	"D"	"
14851	"	Kerr	J.	"D"	"
285080	"	O'Rourke	J.	"D"	"
266380	L/C	McConnachie	J.	"D"	"
240234	Pte	Reid	W.	"D"	"
265508	"	McKenzie	J.	"D"	"
40925	"	Robeson	G.H.	"D"	"
285108	"	Stewart	J.	"D"	"
285095	"	Low	J.	"D"	"

Copy No. 1

6th. GORDON HIGHLANDERS.

OPERATION ORDERS NO. 107

28th. April, 1917.

Map Reference - 1/100,000 LENS.

1. MOVE.

    The Battalion will move to GOUY-EN-TERNOIS today.

2. STARTING POINT.

    CAPELLE FERMONT - AGNIERES Road; just clear of the former village.

    Time   10.30 a.m.

    Order of March   D, B, C, A Companies.
    An interval of 200 yards will be maintained between Companies.

    Route   AGNIERES - SAVY - BERLES - PENIN.

3. TRANSPORT

    Transport will march 200 yards in rear of the rear Company.

4. BAGGAGE

    Officers' kits, baggage, and blankets will be ready for loading at 9.30 a.m.

5. Q.M. STORES

    A lorry will report at Brigade Headquarters in FREVIN CAPELLE at 3 p.m. to move Q.M. Stores.
    Quartermaster will detail a guide to meet this 'bus and take it to his store.

6. BILLETS

    Usual certificates re billets are required.

                                                    Capt. & Adj.
                                            6th Gordon Highlanders.

```
Copy No  1    File
         2    H.Q. 152nd Inf. Brigade
       3 - 6  Companies
         7    Transport Officer
         8    Quartermaster
         9    H.Q. Mess
         10   spare.
```

Copy No...... 6.

Instructions for Offensive Operations.

Reference. Map RACLINCOURT 51 B. N.W. 1.
Scale 1/10,000.

II

1. **OBJECTIVE.** The objective of the 6th. Gordon Highlanders is the MEASY LINE, which includes the German Front Line System of trenches, viz:- Firing line, Support line and Reserve line. (See Map.)

2. **ASSEMBLY.** The Battalion will assemble for the attack in three double waves, each wave consisting of 5 platoons (See Map 1.) The 4th. platoon of A Company, organised as three Bombing Squads and one Lewis Gun Squad will assemble in "I" Work (FISH TUPPEN), where they will be at the disposal of the Battalion Commander to be used for reinforcing, carrying etc.
   Platoons in Sector I will use Map 0
   No. II   do. 1
   No. III   do. 2
   No. IV   do. 3
   No. V   do. 4
   and forming up will be arranged accordingly.

3. **COMMAND.** The two platoons of "A" Company detailed for 1st and 2nd lines will come under command of O/C "D" Company, on reaching assembly positions.
   The one platoon of "A" Company detailed for the 3rd line will be under the command of O/C "C" Company on reaching assembly positions.

4. **METHOD OF ATTACK**
   (a) The method adopted for the attack will be the "Leap Frog" system. The first double wave will capture the German 1st line.
   The 2nd double wave will pass over the 1st wave and capture the German 2nd line.
   The 3rd double wave, which will move from BUNYAN in to the OLD FRENCH TRENCH immediately it is vacated by 2nd wave, will pass over the 1st and 2nd waves and will capture the German 3rd line - MEASY LINE.
   (b) In the advance the distance between double waves will at all times be a minimum of 50 yards to ensure that one double wave does not become implicated in any fighting in which the double wave in front of it may be engaged.

5. **TIME TABLE FOR THE ATTACK.**
   Opening of Barrage on German front line   -   ZERO

   Barrage lifts off first line }   Z plus 4
   Assault of first line

   Barrage lifts off second line }   Z plus 7
   Assault of second line

   Creeping Barrage lifts off intermediate
       position   Z plus 10

   Barrage lifts off third line }   Z plus 34
   Assault of third line

6. **ACTION TO BE TAKEN ON CAPTURE OF OBJECTIVES**
   (a) Each double wave will be responsible for the clearance of the line allotted to it.

   (b) When the first two lines are cleared, care being taken that every dugout is empty, the sections will be re-organised and got ready for carrying, reinforcing, or for any other purpose.

   (3)/

6. ACTION TO BE TAKEN, continued
    (c) When the third wave has captured and cleared its trench, the work of consolidation must begin at once, attention being first paid to the construction of firesteps sufficient for every man to use his rifle effectively.

7. CO-OPERATION WITH AIRCRAFT
    The contact aeroplanes working with the Division are marked with 1 BLACK Band under the Port lower plane, and the BLACK Band is prolonged to the rear by a black streamer.
    In order to indicate the most advanced position reached, the infantry alone will be prepared to light the flares, and will be on the lookout for the contact planes at ZERO plus one hour.

8. COMMUNICATIONS.
    (a) Before Zero hour:- All trenches can be used as IN and OUT trenches; troops proceeding to assembly having a prior right of way.
    (b) After Zero hour:-
        IN Trenches:- GENIE AVENUE - TRENCH 40 - THURSDAY AVENUE - FISH AVENUE.

        OUT Trenches:- SEAFORTH AVENUE - THURSDAY AVENUE - NEW TRENCH - FILATIERS AVENUE - GENIE AVENUE.

9. COLLECTION AND ESCORT OF PRISONERS
    Escorts will not exceed 10% of the prisoners in each batch, and, as far as possible, the lightly wounded should be employed for this duty. Prisoners will be escorted to the Collecting Post at the junction of GENIE and FILATIERS AVENUE (on LILLE Road), and escorts will then return for instructions to Brigade Headquarters. Captured Officers to be sent to Battalion Headquarters.

10. MEDICAL ARRANGEMENTS
    The Regimental Aid Post is opposite Brigade Headquarters at junction of THURSDAY AVENUE and FISH AVENUE (A.20.a.6.2.). All sick or wounded, who are able to walk, go to ANZIN.
    Wounded, either walking cases or stretcher cases, will not be allowed under any circumstances to use FISH TUNNEL.

11. CASUALTIES AND BURIALS.
    It must be impressed on all ranks that identity discs on the dead are not to be interfered with by any one but properly constituted burial parties.
    The upper disc known as "Disc, identity, No 1 green" will not be removed but will be buried with the body. The lower disc known as "Disc, identity, No 2 red" will be removed and disposed of as before.

12. REPORTS
    Every effort must be made by Company and Platoon Commanders to send back information regarding position, opposition, etc. Two runners must invariably be sent with messages, which should be prepared beforehand as far as possible.

13. EQUIPMENT etc.
    Instructions regarding equipment and clothing will be issued as soon as received from Brigade.

14. HEADQUARTERS
    Battalion Headquarters will be in "I" Work, FISH TUNNEL, and Brigade Headquarters will be at junction of FISH AVENUE and THURSDAY AVENUE (A.20.a.6.1.)

15. DUMPS
    (a) Rations, Water, Solidified Alcohol;) at Eastern entrance
        Grenades, S.A.A., and Flares   ) to FISH TUNNEL.

    (b) R.E. Material at Brigade Headquarters.

(signed) Jas. Dawson, Lieut Colonel,
Commanding 6th Gordon Highlanders

INSTRUCTIONS FOR OFFENSIVE OPERATIONS

FIGHTING KIT.

1. Fighting dress will be as follows :-

   (a) Clothing – as issued. Officers to be dressed as the men.
   Leather Jerkins will not be worn.
   Overcoats will be worn before action, but will be collected
   from Assembly Trenches under arrangements to be issued later.
   Steel Helmets which have a polished surface must be coated
   with mud.

   (b) Arms as issued.

   (c) Entrenching tool – as issued.

   (d) Accoutrements – as issued, except pack which will be carried
   by rifle-grenadiers of bombing squads only. Haversack on
   back except above mentioned.

   (e) Box Respirator in "Alert" position and P.H. Helmet.

   (f) Articles to be carried in Haversack:- Pair socks, oil-tin
   and cloth, iron ration, special breakfast ration, current day's
   ration, and tin of solidified alcohol, (as available).
   Waterproof-sheet to be carried on top of haversack under flap.
   Mess-tin to be slung outside haversack.

   (g) Rations – as above. One filled water-bottle.

   (h) Ammunition – 120 rounds except for Bombers, Signallers,
   Runners and Lewis Gunners who will carry only 50 rounds.

   (i) No. 5 Mills Grenades – Two carried by each man; one in each
   lower pocket of jacket.
   See below for Bombing Squads, "P" Bombers and Rifle Grenadiers.

   (j) Sandbags – Three each, rolled, tied round with string and
   fixed to equipment of every 3rd. line man.

   (k) Tools – 10 shovels and 5 picks per platoon detailed for 3rd.
   line.

   (l) Aeroplane flares – 12 per platoon detailed for 3rd. line.

   (m) Artillery Signals.
   Green and White Very Pistol ammunition – as available:
   To be kept in the hands of the Officer Commanding the Company.

   (n) Wire cutters and gloves – as issued.

   (o) Trench Equipment – per Company :- 2 Box, 4 Lifeguard and 16
   Vigilant Periscopes, 8 Very Pistols or as available.

   (p) 1. Bombing Squads.
   ```
   N.C.O.                         -  3 No. 5.
   1st. & 2nd. Bayonet men        -  3 "   " each.
   1st. & 2nd. Throwers           - 12 "   " each, (in
                                                   buckets.
   1st. & 2nd. Carriers           - 12 "   " and 2 "P"
                                           each, in buckets.
   1st. & 2nd. Rifle Grenadiers   3 No. 5 and 12 No.23
                                  each: No. 23's to be carried
                                  in pack.
   ```

   2. "P" Bombers. – 6 per platoon carry 2 each in sandbag
   pockets.

   3. Rifle Grenadiers – 2 per platoon carry 4 each in sandbag
   pockets.

   (q) Lewis Gun Drums – Each Lewis Gun Team will carry 32 Drums.

(Signed) J. Lawson, Lieut. Colonel,
Commanding

File Copy

IV

Headquarters,
152nd Infantry Brigade.

REPORT ON RECENT ENGAGEMENT

In the recent engagement, the German trench system allotted to this Battalion for capture consisted of three sets of trenches. In every case the objective was reached immediately the barrage lifted and the trenches quickly and effectively cleared. Isolated groups and snipers in front of each captured trench were stalked and killed before much damage was done to the succeeding waves. In the front line system, especially at the large traverses and in the neighbourhood of the two tunnels, access was got to the rear of the high parados, but this method of defence was rendered quite ineffective by the method adopted for clearing, viz:- from the top and from the rear. All arrangements were carried out both to the letter and in the spirit, and the only feature not anticipated was the blowing up of a minnenwerfer ammunition dump, which was probably occasioned by the bursting of a Mills bomb in the store. A good many casualties, probably 20, resulted from the explosion which formed a crater about 30 feet deep. The enemy resisted strongly at certain points; his casualties were relatively heavy, and probably about 100 prisoners were captured.

Items under heading (a) 152nd Infantry Brigade No S/660/50

i   No difficulty was experienced either in moving into or in leaving the assembly positions.

ii Overcoats were worn while waiting in the assembly trenches and this arrangement proved very satisfactory. No difficulty was experienced in collecting these and distributing to the men in the forward trenches. Various considerations point to the number of bombs, drums, etc., being sufficient and as many as can be carried. No reduction is suggested except "P" bombs, and, owing to weight, the number of Lewis Gun drums cannot be increased.

iii The Artillery and Stokes Mortar barrage is reported to have been very satisfactory, and no difficulty was experienced in getting at assaulting distance before it lifted.

iv The German trenches were very badly damaged by our Artillery and Trench Mortar fire. The wire cutting was perfectly performed.

v   The system of attack which was adopted proved very suitable, and the numbers were in every case sufficient to clear the trench.

vi All reports agree that the forming up was correctly done and that the moving off was at the exact time ordered.

vii The pace of the barrage, as far as the Black Line is concerned, seemed correct.

viii The method of ration and water supply was satisfactory, but one tin of water for 20 men is not sufficient.

ix Control, as far as can be learned, was maintained throughout the action in spite of heavy casualties in Officers and N.C.Os.

Page 2.

x   Communication by orderlies between Companies and Battalion Headquarters commenced soon after first objective was reached, and was kept up by this means as long as desired. By afternoon a wire was run out to the old BLACK LINE, and this remained intact. Orderlies were used between Battalion and Brigade Headquarters at periods when wire was broken.

xi   KLAXON Horn from aeroplane was heard about 15 minutes after we had occupied the NEW BLACK LINE (Z plus 1 hour). No lights were seen fired, and our flares were too damp to light. The men waved their helmets. The flare is very unsatisfactory as very little moisture seems to affect the lighting arrangement. Some other means of communication is required.

xii   Number 23 Grenades were used:-
        (a) against Southern Salient during barrage
        (b) to keep down snipers while waiting for the final rush on third line.
The distance in both cases, approximately 80 and (say) 40 yards, was a very suitable range for No 23, and unsuitable for both 5s and 20s. The Battalion Bombing Officer considers that in an advance and at short range (up to 90 yards) the No 23 is the only feasible grenade.

Jas Dawson   Lieut Colonel,
Commanding 6th Gordon Highlanders

14.4.17

War Diary   Copy No. 10.

6th. GORDON HIGHLANDERS.
BATTALION ORDER No. 146.

1. **MOVE.**
   The 6th. Battalion, Gordon Highlanders will move to Assembly Trenches in H. 16 b. to-night, 22nd. April, 1917.

2. **PARADE.**
   Companies will parade ready to move off at 7.15 p.m. Order of the march will be Headquarters, B, A, D and C Companies. Battalion will move by platoons at 100 paces interval, care being taken to maintain touch.

3. **MARCHING.**
   Route will be Railway Bridge over SCARPE at G. 25. a. 5. 65. (starting point) - Tow Path along North Bank of SCARPE to Path at H. 13. d. 4. 5. - HERVIN FARM. Head of the column will pass starting point at 7.30 p.m. Tea will be issued at HERVIN FARM. Battalion will leave HERVIN FARM in the same order at 10.30 p.m. and will proceed to Assembly Positions via RAILWAY BRIDGE at H. 14. a. 1. 25., and overland track commencing H. 14. a. 1. 5.

4. **TRANSPORT ETC.**
   Cookers with 2 cooks per Company and Lewis Gun Limbers will leave ARRAS at 2 p.m. and await Battalion at HERVIN FARM. Company Lewis Gun Instructors will accompany Limbers and distribute Lewis Gun Magazines at HERVIN FARM.

5. **BAGGAGE.**
   Packs, blankets and Officers' kits will be sent to Q.M. Stores by 6 p.m.

6. **DISCIPLINE.**
   No singing, noise or smoking will be allowed on the march. One latrine per platoon will be dug immediately Assembly Positions are reached.

7. **REPORTS.**
   Companies will report their arrival in Assembly Positions to Battalion Headquarters, H. 16. b. 7. 9.

                                   (Signed) D.Mackenzie, Lieut. & A/Adjutant,
                                            6th. Gordon Highlanders.

Copy No. 1   File
         2   H.Q. 153 Infantry Brigade.
       3 - 6 Companies.
         7.   Transport Officer.
         8   Quartermaster.
         9   R.Q. Mess.
        10.   Spare.

War Diary   II A

Instructions for Offensive Operations.

Reference - Sheet FAMPOUX 1/10,000.

1. **OBJECTIVE.**

   The Objective of the 6th Gordon Highlanders is the RED LINE, Line of German Trenches from I.20.b.7.5 to I.15.c.5.8 and HAUSA and DELBAR WOODS.

2. **ASSEMBLY.**

   The Battalion will assemble in the Old German Trenches in H.16.b.

   "A" Company in PORT TRENCH H.16.b.8.2. to H.16.b.9.5.
   "B"   "   " PORT TRENCH H.16.b.9.5. to H.16.b.9.85.
                                        (junction of Port and PRIM.)
   "C"   "   " PUDDING TRENCH H.16.b.7.2 to H.16.b.7.5.
   "D"   "   " PUDDING TRENCH H.16.b.7.5. to H.16.b.7.85
                                        (junction of PUDDING and PRIM.)

3. **ATTACK.**

   Companies will leave Assembly Trenches in Artillery Formation - each Company in two lines of half platoons in file at an approximate interval of 70 yards between half platoons. Distances between lines of half platoons will be 100 yards, distance between companies will be 200 yards. The left flank will direct.

   ∧ BLUE

   This formation will be maintained until the Battalion is clear of the CHEMICAL WORKS and, until leading right platoon of "A" Company reaches the LINE in the German Trench, I.14.c.0.6, when companies will form 2 extended waves - each of two ranks - A and B Companies the leading wave. C and D Companies the second wave - on a front directly facing their Objective. The direction of the leading waves will be given by the line - right flank of A Company as given above - WINDMILL at I.14.b.9.9.

   A and B Companies will conform closely with the movement of the BARRAGE, C and D Companies following at a distance of 200 yards.

   A and B Companies will capture the RED LINE from I.20.b.7.5. to I.15.c.5.8.

   C and D Companies will dig a support line 200 yards in rear of the RED LINE. When BARRAGE lifts off WOOD, one platoon of B Company will clear HAUSA WOOD and establish a Lewis Gun Post at I.15.c.4.0, and one platoon of C Company with a Lewis Gun Team of A Company attached, will clear DELBAR WOOD, establishing Posts at I.21.a.8.5 and I.21.a.3.4. One rifle section will be left in DELBAR WOOD in support of the two Lewis Gun Posts.

4. **TIME TABLE.**

   Battalion leaves Assembly Trenches   - ZERO + 1 hour
   Battalion moves from position near
        BROWN LINE   Z plus 3 Hours
   Barrage commences to move forward - Z plus 3 hours 12 minutes.
   Assault of RED LINE   - Z plus 3 hours 30 minutes.
   Assault of HAUSA and DELBAR WOODS   - Z plus 3 hours

5. **ACTION TO BE TAKEN ON CAPTURE OF OBJECTIVE.**

   Immediately objectives are captured, A and B Companies will consolidate the RED LINE, C and D Companies will dig the Support Line. The various Posts will be put into a state of defence.

   Consolidation and digging will be carried out by groups, and the Posts made will be subsequently joined up.

   During these operations, outposts and patrols will be pushed well forward from the front line.

6. **CO-OPERATION WITH AIRCRAFT.**

   On reaching Objective, Flares will be lit by troops in the RED LINE and Outposts, when called for by contact Aeroplane.

2.

7. COLLECTION AND ESCORT OF PRISONERS.

Prisoners will be sent back to Brigade Head Quarters in PUDDING TRENCH H.16.b.7.4. Slightly wounded men should be used as Escort.

8. CASUALTIES AND BURIALS.

It must be impressed on all ranks that Identity Discs on the dead are not to be interfered with by anyone but properly constituted burial parties.

The Upper Disc known as "Disc, Identity, No. 1 Green" will not be removed, but will be buried with the body. The lower Disc known as "Disc, Identity, No.2 Red" will be removed and disposed of as before.

9. REPORTS.

Every effort must be made by Company and Platoon Commanders to send back information regarding position, opposition, etc. Two runners must invariably be sent with messages, which should be prepared beforehand as far as possible.

10. Head Quarters.

Battalion Headquarters will be at H.16.b.7.9 until advance takes place, when it will move to German Trench in neighbourhood of I.14.c.0.5.

11. DUMPS.

Rations and water for Z plus 1 day can be drawn from Brigade Dump at H.17.c.3.5 - west end of FAMPOUX.

12. EQUIPMENT.

Dress and Equipment as already issued.

9 Rounds will be placed in the Magazine and 1 round in the Breech before leaving Assembly Trenches.

(Signed) D. MACKENZIE, Lieut. & A/Adj.

Page 2.

All tools, Bombs, S.A.A., Trench Equipment will be available for distribution at Orderly Room at 3.30 p.m. on 22nd. April, 1917.

(Signed) D.MacKenzie, Lieut. & A/Adjt.
6th. Gordon Highlanders.

Copy No. 1 File.
2-5 Companies
6. B.B.O.
7. Quartermaster.
8. R.S.M.
9. H.Q.Mess.
10 Spare.

Copy......... /C

INSTRUCTIONS FOR OFFENSIVE OPERATIONS.

Fighting Dress, Arms and Equipment.

(a) Clothing - as issued. Officers will be dressed as the men. Great coats will be worn looped up.

(b) Arms - as issued.

(c) Entrenching Tool - as issued.

(d) Accoutrements, as issued, - except pack. Haversack on back.

(e) Small Box Respirator in "Alert" position,& P.H. Helmet

(f) Articles to be carried in haversack :- Pair socks, oil-tin ad cloth, iron ration, special breakfast ration, current day's ration, and tin of solidified alcohol, (as available). Waterproof sheet to be carried on top of haversack under flap. Mess-tin to be slung outside haversack.

(g) Rations - as above. One filled water-bottle.

(h) Ammunition - 120 rounds except for bombers, signallers, runners and Lewis Gunners who will carry only 50 rounds. Every second man of the rifle sections will carry an extra bandolier.

(i) No. 5 Mills Grenade - 2 carried by each ALTERNATE man of all except bombing sections, 1 in each pocket of great coat. See below for bombing squads and rifle-grenadiers.

(j) Sandbags - 3 each, rolled, tied with string and fixed to equipment.

(k) Tools - each man of C and D Companies in the proportion of 1 pick to 2 shovels.
Each alternate man of A and B Companies in the same proportion.

(l) Aeroplane Flares - 20 per platoon of A and B Companies and No. 9 platoon of C Company.

(m) Artillery signals -
Red Very Pistol ammunition, 24 rounds per Company - to be kept by Officer Commanding Company.
White - 1 packet per pistol. Forward posts will carry 2 packets.

(n) Wire-cutters - A and B Company will each carry 32 pairs rifle- attachment wire-cutters.

(o) Trench equipment.

Periscopes - 2 Box   )
              4 Lifeguard) per Company.
              3 Vigilant)

1" Very Pistols - 2 per Company
                  1 per Lewis Gun Team.

(p) Bombing Squads -
N.C.O.   - 3 No. 5   (in greatcoat pocket.)
1st. & 2nd. Bayonet men - 3   - 3 No. 5 each   do
1st. & 2nd. Throwers   - 8 No. 5 each   (in buckets.)
1st. & 2nd. Carriers   - 8 No. 5 each   do
1st. & 2nd. Rifle- Grenadiers   - 3 No. 5 each   (in great coat pocket)
                                     10 No. 23 each   (in waistcoat carriers)

(q) Lewis Gun Drums - each Lewis Gun Team will carry 32 Drums.

ADDENDA to INSTRUCTIONS for OFFENSIVE OPERATIONS

S.O.S. Signal is 9 Red Lights fired in rapid succession.

Lengthen Range   Series of White Lights

"Tank Wanted"   Helmets placed on end of fixed bayonets and raised straight above head.

Tank to Infantry - Green Disc - Wire Cut

Do.   Red Disc - Wire Uncut.

2. BARRAGE

A Smoke Barrage will be placed on GREEN LAND HILL & ROEUX by our Artillery. Men will be warned that this is NOT enemy gas.

3. EXTENSIONS

Company Commanders will use their own discretion in extending before reaching BLUE LINE if circumstances demand it.

4. COMMAND

Company and Platoon Commanders will each move with one small column, and will not move from group to group unless in case of urgency.

5. DRESS

Kilt aprons will be worn.

6. SYNCHRONIZATION OF WATCHES

Each Company will send a representative to Battalion Headquarters after reaching assembly trenches to have watches synchronised.

(signed) D. MacKenzie, Lieut & A/Adj.
6th Gordon Highlanders

REPORT ON 6th. GORDON HIGHLANDERS' ACTION IN THE OPERATIONS ON
23rd April, 1917.

Map. FAMPOUX, Sheet 51B NW. 1/10,000

The work assigned to the 6th. Gordon Highlanders in the operation on the 23rd April was the capture of a German trench running from I.20.b.7.5. in a north westerly direction to I.14.d.5. and thence in a north easterly direction to I.15.c.55 (known as the RED LINE); the capture of HAUSA AND DELBAR WOODS and the digging of a support line about 200 yards on the British side of the German trench. The assault on the trench was to be delivered by two Companies in a wave of two ranks and the digging by two supporting companies.

The 153rd Brigade to which the 6th. Gordon Highlanders were temporarily attached were to act as follows: The 7th Black Watch on the right of the Brigade front with the 7th Gordon Highlanders on the left were to take the BLACK and BROWN lines. The 6th. Gordon Highlanders on the right and the 6th Black Watch on the left were to pass over the other two battalions; the 6th. Gordon Highlanders to take the objectives already mentioned and the 6th Black Watch to dig a line running roughly northward from the trench captured by the 6th. Gordon Highlanders.

An elaborate artillery barrage scheme had been prepared for dealing with all objectives.

The 6th. Gordon Highlanders were to jump off from the Assembly Trenches PUDDING and PORT. (H.10.b.)

The Commanding Officer intended to advance his Battalion in artillery formation of half platoons in an easterly direction keeping the trenches named HOPEFUL, HUMID and HUDDLE on his left flank and marching on a front of about 450 yards. It was expected that the battalion would reach the CHEMICAL WORKS (I.13.b and d.) before an extension would be needed, seeing that the BLACK and BLUE lines were to be taken by a preceeding battalion. When the railway culvert (I.14.d.44) had been reached by the left flank the battalion was to change direction half right and, following closely the artillery barrage, the trench was to be assaulted and three platoons pushed forward to take the woods and establish posts on the eastern outskirts at I.15.c.3. and I.21.a.74.

The battalion, on the 23rd April, reached the Assembly Trenches without mishap at 2 a.m. and took up its position, starting the advance at ZERO plus 1 (5.45 a.m.)

"A" Company on the right and "B" Company on the left were the assaulting companies and "C" Company followed by "A", and "D" Company "B" Company in support.

The battalion came under heavy shell-fire immediately on leaving the Assembly Trenches, but proceeded without great loss, except in the case of a platoon of "B" Company which was practically wiped out, until it came under violent machine gun fire, which made an extension necessary much earlier than was intended. This extension took place somewhere in H.18. a. and c. and the advance was continued with great difficulty as the front German trench was still untaken (BLACK line) and was held very strongly by the enemy. The delay occasioned by the taking of this line CHEMICAL WORKS and the succeeding line (BLUE) lost to the attack the advantage of the artillery barrage and the battalion suffered accordingly.

On the left one platoon of "B" Company managed to reach a position about I.13.a.94. but by this time three of the four Company officers had fallen. "A" Company on the right had also to extend early. In order to escape the edge of FAMPOUX at a point H.17.b.91. which was being very heavily shelled, it closed to the left and then worked round to the right. Part of the company reached a trench which the FAMPOUX - CHEMICAL WORKS road intersects immediately in front of the German front line and were here held up owing to the severity of the fire. By this time the confusion was very great. Platoons, Companies and Battalions were mixed and the accounts of the fighting are very confused. The men managed to advance only by the use of bits of trenches and shell holes. A Tank which came in response to a signal rendered great assistance at this stage of the attack. It attacked the German trench, cleared it and then proceeded to deal with the CHEMICAL WORKS.

About 6 a.m. when the advance had reached about H.18.b.32., Lieut. Colonel J. Dawson, D.S.O. had been severely wounded and the command had devolved on Captain Hutcheson.

When the Tank came on the scene Captain Hutcheson carried the advance forward until the CHEMICAL WORKS were reached.

About 9.30 a.m. Captain Hutcheson established his Headquarters at

REPORT ON THE 6th GORDON HIGHLANDERS ACTION IN THE OPERATIONS OF
23rd APRIL, 1917. (continued)
_____

I.13.c.99. and posts were thrown out round the CHEMICAL WORKS.
Urgent messages were despatched, by pigeons and runners, for reinforcements but none were forthcoming and as the enemy fire was very heavy and the number of casualties great, while the number of men at Captain Hutcheson's disposal was small, he decided to withdraw. This he did, at 12 noon, leaving a post at the QUARRY (H.13.a.23.) This post held its ground until a general advance later in the day, assisted by the 6th. Seaforth Highlanders, permitted a line to be dug 30 yards in front of the ROEUX - GAVRELLE ROAD. This advance took place at 8.30 p.m.

The 6th. Gordon Highlanders were withdrawn to the British Front line about 11.45 p.m. and there they remained during the night. They were relieved next day at 12 noon by the 25th. Northumberland Fusiliers, (103rd Brigade), and after a period of rest in the Assembly Trenches, were moved back the same night to bivouac in ST. NICHOLAS.

(Signed) J. W. Adams Major,
Commanding 6th Gordon Highlanders.

27.4.17.

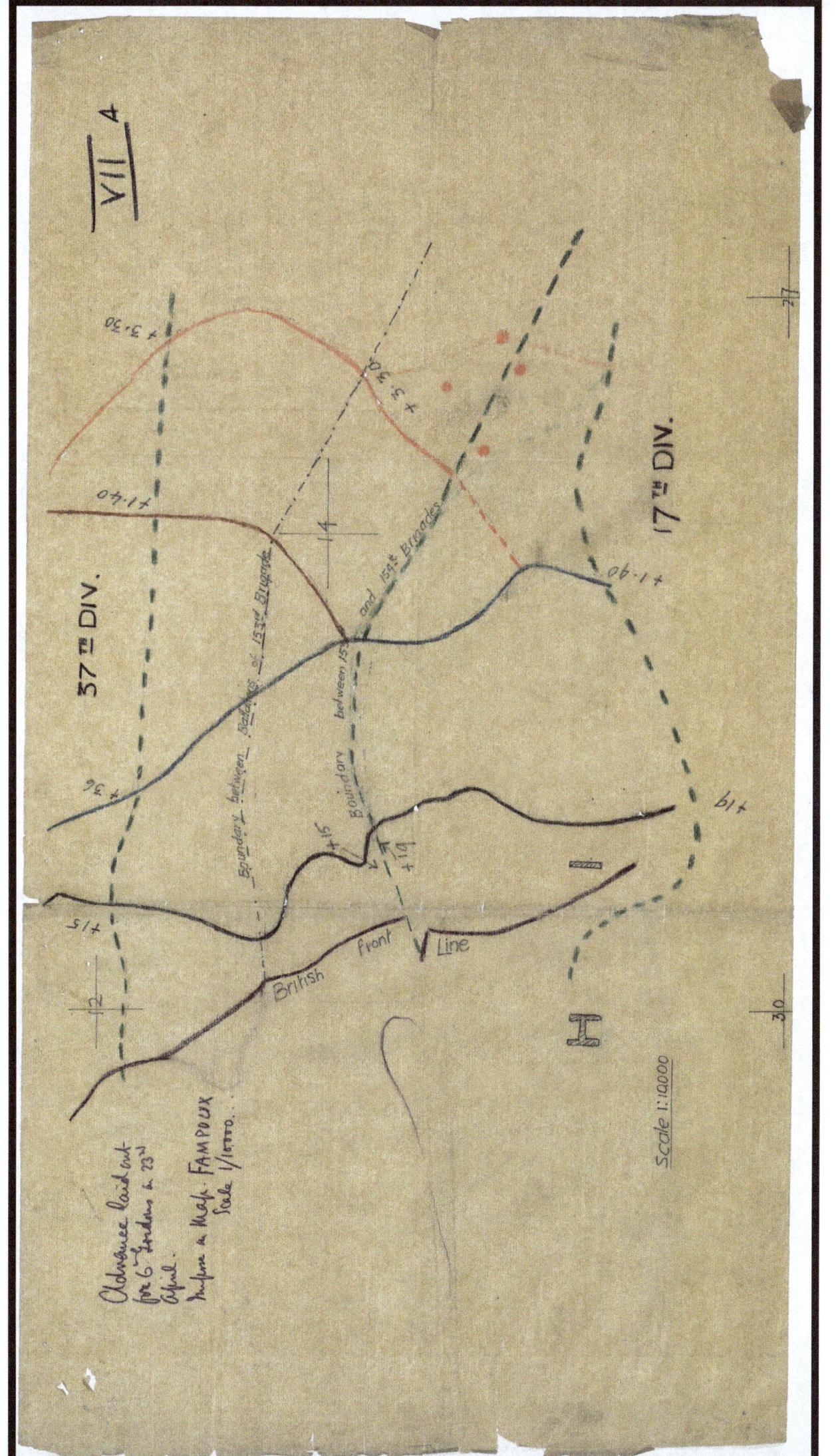

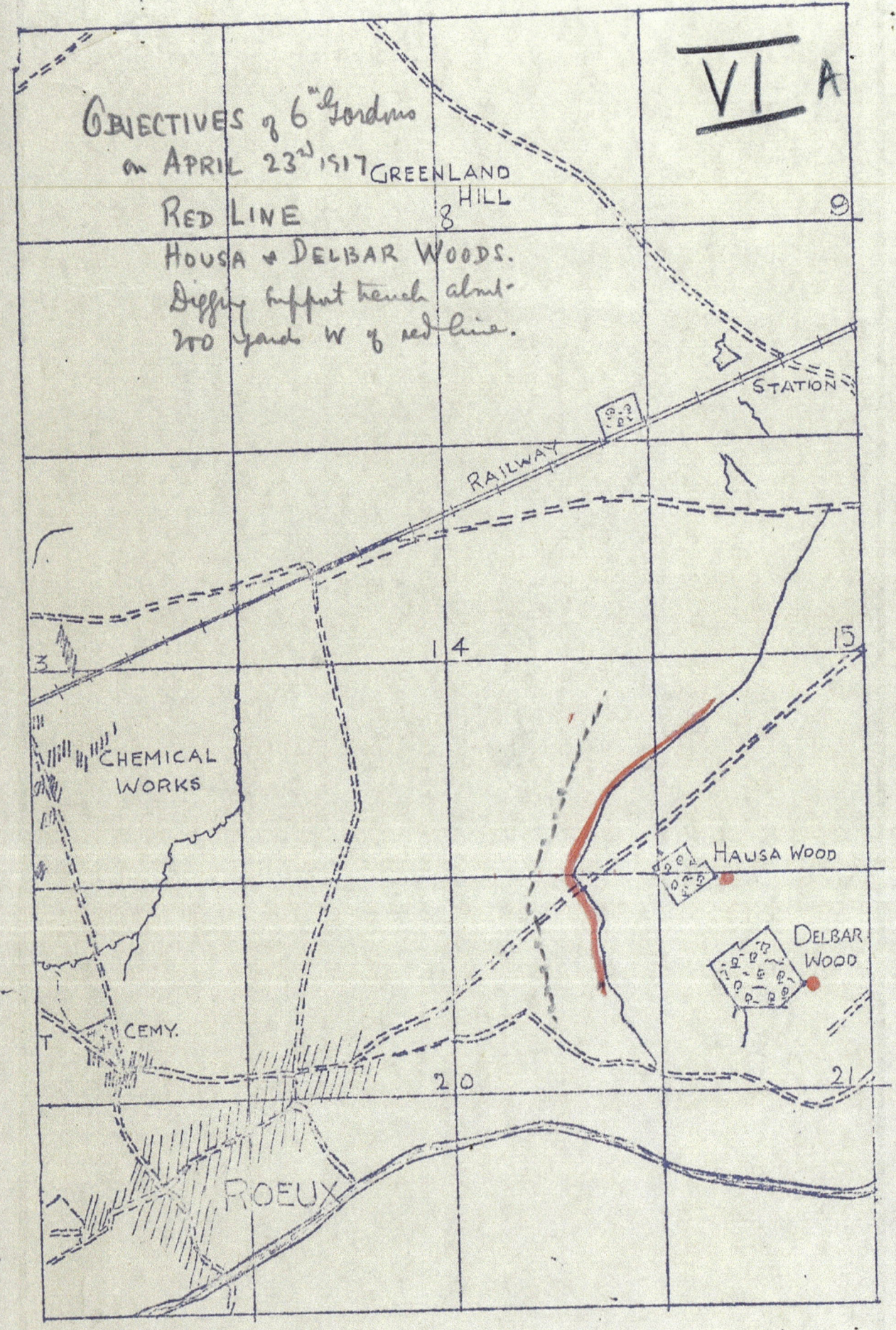

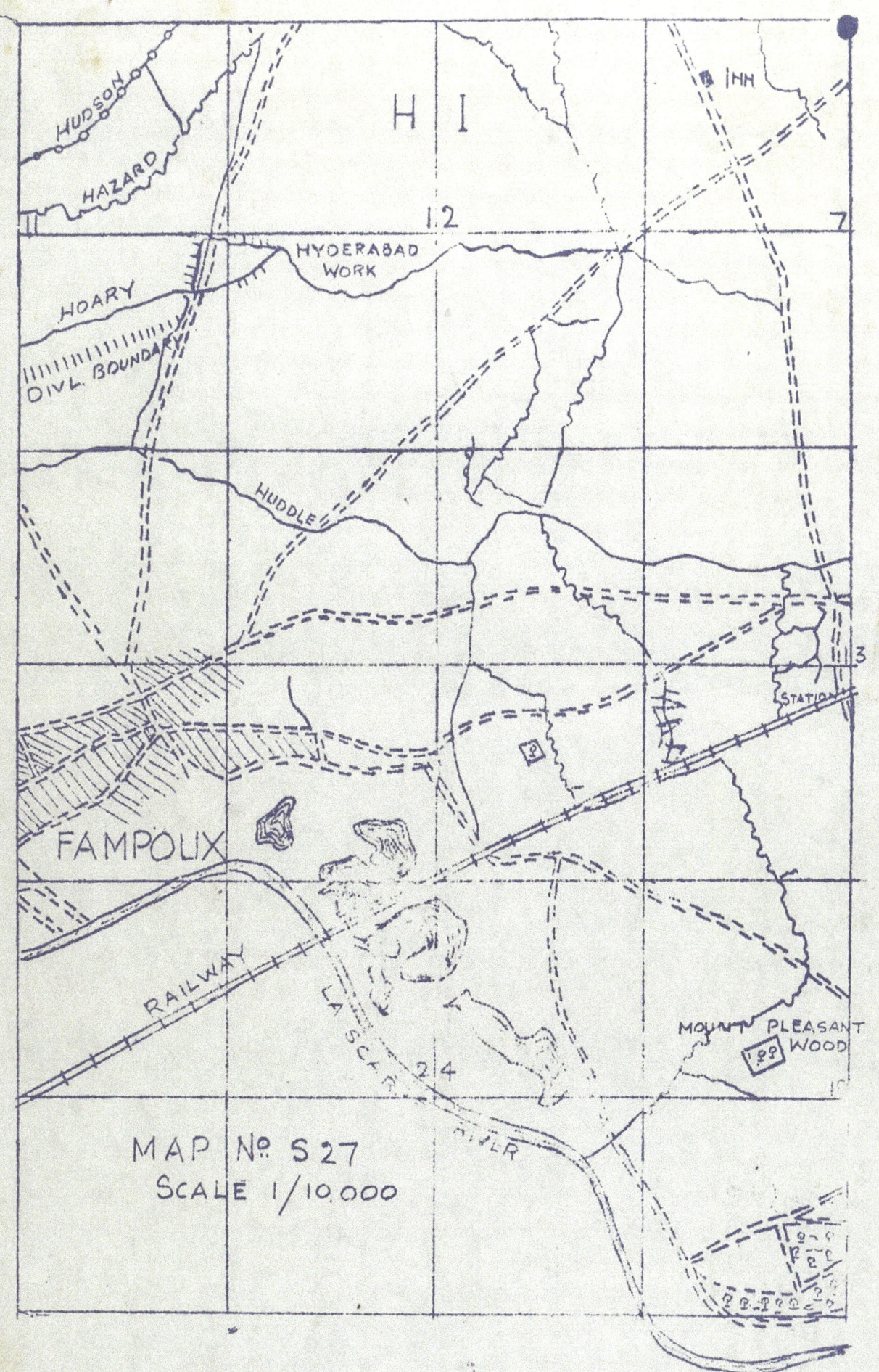

German Anti-Aircraft Gun — from description and sketch supplied by N.C.O. who destroyed gun and brought in a belt of ammunition Ã.

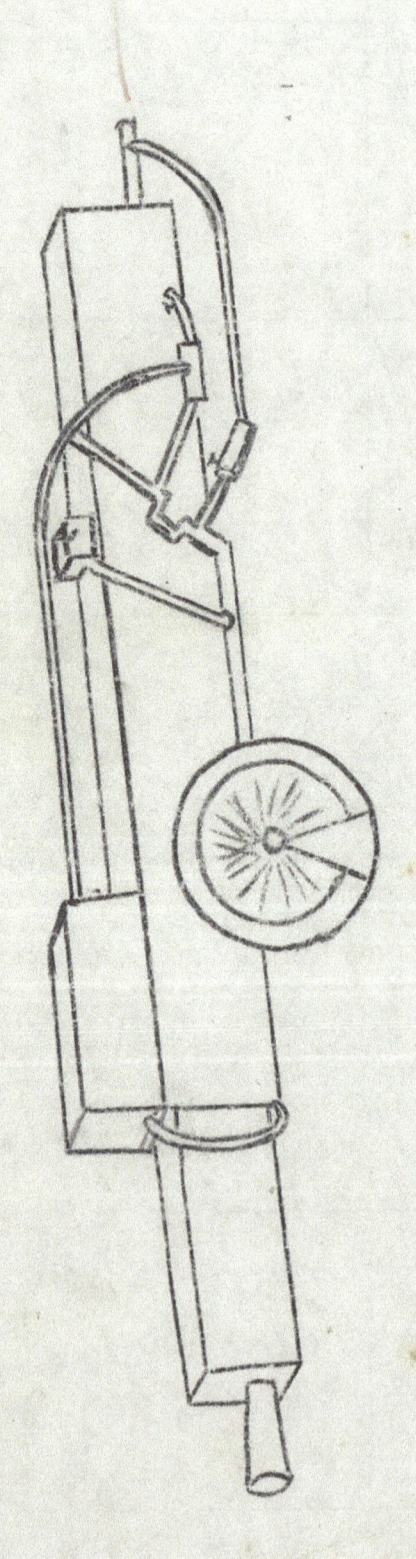

WAR DIARY

of

1/6th Bn. The GORDON HIGHLANDERS.

MAY, 1917.

Army Form C. 2118.

WAR DIARY
or
INTELLIGENCE SUMMARY.
(Erase heading not required.)

Instructions regarding War Diaries and Intelligence Summaries are contained in F. S. Regs., Part II. and the Staff Manual respectively. Title pages will be prepared in manuscript.

Place	Date	Hour	Summary of Events and Information	Remarks and references to Appendices
ROUY-EN-TERNOIS	May 1-9		In Billets. Training. Musketry Competition and Battalion Sports were held. Battalion did not prove strong in shooting.	
ARRAS	10		Battalion entrained at LIGNY ST. FLOCHEL and travelled to ARRAS where it went into Billets in RUE DES AUGUSTINES (XVIIth Corps area.)	
"	11		In Billets.	
BIVOUAC	12		Moved to BIVOUAC G.18.b. (ARRAS 1/10,000.) Orders came later the same night to move to the FAMPOUX - OPPY line, between BLANGY -- FAMPOUX Road and River SCARPE. This move was completed before dawn on the 13th May without incident.	REFERENCE MAPS ARRAS 1/10,000
TRENCHES	13 - 15		In FAMPOUX - OPPY line, PANSY TRENCH. At 11 p.m. on the 15th May orders were received to move to relieve the 1/5th Seaforth Highlanders in East end of ROEUX village and posts between junction of CEYLON and CORONA trenches and the river SCARPE, also the 1/8th Argyll & Sutherland Highlanders in COLUMBO from I.14.b.9.5. to I.20.a.5.3., and in CORONA from I.13.d.8.2. to junction of CORONA and CEYLON. The Battalion moved shortly after midnight, but were subjected to a heavy shelling of gas and H. E. shells which delayed the relief. By the time the bulk of the Battalion had reached the Headquarters of the 1/5th Seaforth Highlanders, in CRUMP trench, the Germans put down an extremely heavy artillery barrage in all the ground between the front line and the river SCARPE from point H.24.d.10.6. to the Railway, and an advance was made by their Infantry on both our flanks - the Railway and the village of ROEUX. Under these circumstances the Companies of the 6th Gordon Highlanders were unable to relieve the 1/5th Seaforth Highlanders and the 1/8th Argyll & Sutherland Highlanders; instead all Battalions and the 1/6th Seaforth Highlanders in addition had to turn to and repel the German attack. The battle proceeded all day and our troops were successful in completely defeating the enemy attempt. Towards evening the situation was as follows :-- Part of COLUMBO trench was held by our men. CORONA we held and the posts in the middle of the village of ROEUX. An enemy concentration at the Eastern end of ROEUX seemed to indicate the imminence of an attack from that direction. Our right flank was therefore strengthened, an artillery fire was directed on the enemy concentration. The attack did not develop. A detailed account of the operation is attached (Appendix I.)	FAMPOUX Trenches APPENDIX I. Report of Engagement of 16th May

Army Form C. 2118.

WAR DIARY
or
INTELLIGENCE SUMMARY.
(Erase heading not required.)

Instructions regarding War Diaries and Intelligence Summaries are contained in F. S. Regs., Part II. and the Staff Manual respectively. Title pages will be prepared in manuscript.

Place	Date	Hour	Summary of Events and Information	Remarks and references to Appendices

TRENCHES	May 13-15		On Appendix II is marked in red the approximate position of the British Troops on the evening of the 16th May. Our casualties were :-
			
			                  Officers Other Ranks.
			 Killed 2 18
			 Died of Wounds - 1
			 Wounded 8 65
			 Wounded, remaining at duty - 6
			 Unaccounted for - 17
			
			                  10 107
			
			 The names of the officers are :- Killed Wounded.
			                           2/Lieut. G. DONALDSON Capt. P. KYNOCH SHAND.
			                           " F. J. SMITH. 2/Lieut. J. M. McLEOD.
			                                                                " D. J. GARDEN.
			                                                                " A. GORDON.
			                                                                " W. K. LEGGAT.
			                                                                " J. S. B. WARD.
			                                                                " B. DOWNIE.
			                                                                " J. McMURTRIE. (gas.)
				APPENDIX II
				 TRENCH MAP showing position on 16th May.
				
				 APPENDICES: III, IV, V. Appreciation of the work done.

ARRAS	19-30		On the night of the 16/17th May the Battalion was withdrawn, the relieving Battalions being the 6th Black Watch and the 4th Seaforth Highlanders. The men were marched to a bivouac in G. 18.a.; where they rested for several hours and then were marched to Billets in RUE DES AUGUSTINES in ARRAS. In Billets. Training in Musketry, Arm Drill, Trench Digging etc. Special attention was devoted to the training of Non-commissioned officers under the Regimental Sergeant Major. The Battalion had lost very heavily in N.C.Os. and specialists and every effort was made to recover the lost ground thus lost.	
ARRAS	22-26		Orders were received for a working party of 400 men with complement of officers to dig a trench in the forward area. The trench was for buried cable to Battalion Headquart/ers	

A5834   Wt. W4973/M687   750,000   8/16   D. D. & L. Ltd.   Forms/C.2118/13.

Army Form C. 2118.

WAR DIARY
or
INTELLIGENCE SUMMARY.
(Erase heading not required.)

Instructions regarding War Diaries and Intelligence Summaries are contained in F. S. Regs., Part II. and the Staff Manual respectively. Title pages will be prepared in manuscript.

Place	Date	Hour	Summary of Events and Information	Remarks and references to Appendices
ARRAS	May 22-26		In the line and the work was to be carried out under the supervision of A. D. XVIIth Corps Signals. The detachment, consisting of 360 6th Gordon Highlanders and 40 men of the 152nd Trench Mortar Battery, left ARRAS under the command of Major J. W. ADAMS and proceeded to DINGWALL CAMP (H.23.a.2.5.r.f.) (H.13.d.4.5.) The work was carried out on the following four nights and the trench was dug from a point H.16.d.1.6 across the FAMPOUX Road to the South Western end of FAMPOUX (H.23.a.5.W.) thence on the other bank of the SCARPE to the Railway Embankment (H.23.b.4.2.) (trench marked Red on Appendix II) The nature of the soil varied. In the higher parts digging was mostly in chalk and a depth of 6 ft was reached. In the lower parts near the river a depth of 4½ ft., as an average, was reached owing to water. The width of the trench was 3 ft. at the top and 1 foot at the bottom. Every night the working party was subjected to more or less shelling, but it was specially severe on the second night (the 23/24th.) The men had to be withdrawn for a time from part of the trench, and the party suffered 5 other ranks casualties, (2 men of the 152nd Trench Mortar Battery and four 6th Gordon Highlanders, all slight.) on the 26th May the detachment was relieved by the 6th Seaforth Highlanders who carried on the work. About half past four on the morning of the relief, DINGWALL CAMP was heavily shelled by German Field Guns and 5 other ranks casualties were sustained. At intervals during the forenoon shells fell near the camp, and at 2 p.m. when the relieving Battalion arrived, it had to take refuge in the trenches owing to the unwelcome attention of the German guns. The detachment of the 6th Gordon Highlanders reached their Billets in ARRAS without further mishap. The casualties sustained by the working party were :—	

	24th May.	25th May.	Total
Other Ranks	1	5	11
	(2 T. M. B.)	5	

One of whom remained at duty.

Army Form C. 2118.

WAR DIARY
or
INTELLIGENCE SUMMARY.
(Erase heading not required.)

Instructions regarding War Diaries and Intelligence Summaries are contained in F. S. Regs., Part II. and the Staff Manual respectively. Title pages will be prepared in manuscript.

Place	Date	Hour	Summary of Events and Information	Remarks and references to Appendices
ARRAS	May 30		Strength at beginning of month	
			Officers. O.R.	
			29 687	
			Deduct Casualties:- Officers. O.R.	
			Killed in action 2 18	
			Wounded 8 73	
			Died of Wounds - 1	
			Missing - 17	
			Evacuated Sick - 43	
			10 152	
			19 535	
			Reinforcements:-	
			Drafts 1 183	
			Casuals 1 22	
			2 205	
			Strength at end of Month 21 740	
FOUFFLIN RICAMETZ	30		The Battalion moved out of ARRAS by busses to FOUFFLIN RICAMETZ and were billeted in the village.	
do.	31		In Billets. Training.	

27.5.17.

W. Green
Lieut. Colonel,
Commanding 6th Gordon Highlanders.

REPORT ON OPERATIONS OF
6th GORDON HIGHLANDERS
15th and 16th May, 1917.

About 11 p.m. May 15th a verbal message was received by telephone, ordering the 1/6th Battalion The Gordon Highlanders, then occupying FAMPOUX - OPPY line between the BLANGY - FAMPOUX road and river Scarpe, to take on trenches held by 152nd Infantry Brigade, as follows :-

From 1/5th Seaforth Highlanders in East end of ROEUX village, in posts between junction of CEYLON and CORONA and the river Scarpe.

From 1/8th Argyll & Sutherland Highlanders in COLUMBO from I.14.b.9.5. - I.20.a.5.3., and in CORONA from I.13.d.8.2. to junction of CORONA and CEYLON.

The move was complicated by extreme darkness, and further delay was caused by gas shells which fell among the Battalion as it was preparing to move, causing several casualties, and necessitating the adjustment of anti-gas helmets, which further increased the difficulties of movement over the rough ground.

At about 2.15 a.m. the first Companies arrived at H.Q. 1/5th Seaforth Highlanders and where guides were present from 1/5th Seaforth Highlanders and 1/8th Argyll and Sutherland Highlanders to conduct them to their allotted positions.

Shortly after this an intense barrage was opened by the enemy, which included all ground between the front line and the river Scarpe from point H.24.d.10.0. to the railway. It will be easier to follow the sequence of events from this point, by following the actions of the various Companies in detail.

"A" Company.

This Company was to relieve one Company of the Argyll & Sutherland Highlanders in COLUMBO, and two platoons of 1/5th Seaforth Highlanders in posts at Eastern end of ROEUX. Two platoons, under 2/Lieut. W. K. Leggat (Company Commander) proceeded across the open as far as road running North and South through centre/

centre of ROEUX. Lieut. LEGGAT, and the first platoon had g
forward to the East end of the village and one of the posts ha
been relieved, when the enemy barrage opened, and the enemy wer
seen advancing between the village and the river Scarpe. The
remainder of the platoon were then extended on either side of th
post and opened fire. There they remained for some time, and
subsequently occupied COLUMBO TRENCH, which was garrisoned by
men of the 8th Argyll & Sutherland Highlanders.

They afterwards retired from here, as it appeared fully
manned, and joined Captain CLARK in CORONA. The second platoon
was coming through ROEUX when the barrage opened. They were
extended through the village and Southwards towards the canal, and
subsequently retired on the posts held by 1/5th Seaforth Highlanders
in the centre of the village.

Two platoons under 2/Lieut. B.DOWNIE, proceeded up
CEYLON TRENCH and CORONA as far as the communication trench
commenced between CORONA and COLUMBO. This trench was only half
dug, and very shallow. At this moment the enemy barrage opened,
and the men occupied the communication trench. Shortly after,
the Germans were seen advancing from the railway, also from the
direction of ROEUX. From their position in the communication tren
trench fire was opened by these platoons, and the enemy were
driven back suffering casualties. A German officer entered the
communication trench, and suggested to our men that they should
surrender. He is still there. Later, these platoons occupied
CORONA, and came under the orders of Captain D. G. CLARK, on his
arrival in that trench.

"B" Company.

This Company was to relieve one Company of Argyll &
Sutherland Highlanders holding CORONA from junction of CEYLON
and CORONA Northwards with two platoons,

One Company of 1/5th Seaforth Highlanders between
junction of CEYLON and CORONA and the river Scarpe with two
platoons. This line consisted of a series of posts which ran in
front of the cemetery and through the centre of ROEUX.

Two/

Two platoons of this Company, under 2/Lieut. J. M. McLEOD proceeded up CEYLON TRENCH to relieve one Company of the ARGYLL & Sutherland Highlanders in CORONA. They had reached the junction of CEYLON and CAP when the enemy barrage opened, and shortly afterwards the Germans were seen advancing between CORONA and the CHEMICAL WORKS. Some men of these platoons occupied CAP, and went forward later with Captain D. G. CLARK when he advanced. The remainder, under 2/Lieut. J. M. McLEOD, occupied the trench between the South East corner of the CHEMICAL WORKS and CORONA, and opened fire. The enemy retired. Two platoons, under Captain CLARK, advanced along CRUMP and entered CUSP. The leading platoon was in CUSP, the rear platoon was still in front when the enemy barrage opened - also machine gun fire from the right bank of the river. Seeing that relief was impossible under these circumstances, Captain CLARK occupied CUSP and CRUMP with his two platoons.

"C" Company.

This Company, under Captain P. KYNOCH SHAND, had been more disorganised than the remainder by the gas shell attack, and was about 30 men short on arrival. (These men did not arrive until about 2 p.m. on the 16th instant, having been employed under orders of H.Q. 152nd Infantry Brigade all the morning to carry ammunition to the 5th ARgyll & Sutherland Highlanders North of railway.)

It proceeded to occupy CRUMP from junction of CEYLON and CRUMP Southwards.

"D" Company.

This Company was ordered to occupy CRETE with two platoons and CRUMP with two platoons, which it did.

Page 4.

At 7.30 a.m. the situation appeared to be as follows:-

The enemy were in the village of ROEUX behind the posts in the village held by us, and in the Eastern end. They had come through between the railway and the Northern ends of COLUMBO and CORONA, and had occupied the CHEMICAL WORKS.

No definite news was available of the position in COLUMBO and CORONA, and in posts in EAST of Cemetery, but it was certain that portions at least of all these positions were occupied by our troops.

Shortly before 8 a.m. a report arrived that the 6th Seaforth Highlanders had advanced from CORDITE, and were driving the enemy out of the CHEMICAL WORKS.

Captain CLARK was therefore put in command of a mixed force of 1/5th Seaforth Highlanders and 1/6th Gordon Highlanders who were in CAP, CARE and CUSP, with orders to advance from there and occupy the CORONA and the line of Posts in front of Cemetery, and to get touch with the posts through centre of ROEUX. At the same time a party advanced through the wood West of ROEUX to protect his left. Simultaneously, "D" Company, 6th Gordon Highlanders, were ordered to advance from CRETE and push forward to CORONA on Captain CLARK'S left. On arrival in CORONA they were to be under the orders of Captain CLARK. This operation was perfectly successful everywhere except in the wood West of ROEUX. Here the advance was carried out as far as the Western end of the village, where they were held up by heavy enemy barrage across the village between points I.19.d.4.5. and I.19.d.5.2., and they were unable to push forward to the posts in the centre of the village. The advance was further complicated by enemy machine guns from South bank of the Scarpe. At the same time CUSP was occupied by troops from CHUMP.

On arrival in CORONA Captain CLARK re-organised his line and thinned it out by sending as many men of 1/5th Seaforth Highlanders and 1/8th Argyll & Sutherland Highlanders back as possible.

He then endeavoured to clear up the situation in COLUMBO by means of an officer's patrol, but the ground between CORONA and/

and COLUMBO was swept with machine gun fire, and the officer wounded and the patrol retired.

He then decided that it would not be possible for him to advance to COLUMBO before dusk, but it appeared certain that our troops were still holding the kxxx trench.

Meanwhile CORUNA Support Trench had been occupied by men of 1/6th Seaforth Highlanders.

At about 3 p.m. reports were received that the enemy was massing between the Eastern portion of ROEUX and the river Scarpe, and it was decided to strengthen the right flank.

A part of "C" Company, 1/6th Gordon Highlanders, who were holding CRUMP, were therefore moved into position in a line across the wood West of ROEUX from point I.19.o.6.4. to I.19.o.5.o., their right flank being protected by a machine gun, and they were further reinforced by one more machine gun and three Lewis Guns. Two of these latter were, however, destroyed by hostile fire. At the same time field artillery were ordered to fire on enemy concentration. The enemy attack did not develop.

The intention was to push forward at dusk to clear up the situation in COLUMBO and in the Eastern end of ROEUX, but this move was eventually carried out by Battalions of another Brigade.

The operations on the right flank, i.e. in ROEUX and South of it were greatly hampered by hostile machine guns fire from the South bank of the Scarpe.

The operations of this Battalion were made exceedingly difficult by the following circumstances:-

1. The fact that the night was exceedingly dark and neither officers nor men knew the ground, there having been no opportunity for reconnaissance.
2. The bombardment with gas shells, which assailed the Battalion as it was moving from the FAMPOUX – OPPY line. This necessitated the adjustment of box respirators,/

respirators, and made it quite impossible to see at all. The difficulties of movement over bad ground under these circumstances cannot be exaggerated.

3. The intense barrage put down by the enemy before any portion of the two front lines had been relieved, Portions of Companies had proceeded by different routes towards the positions allotted to them, and it became impossible for Company Commanders to know where platoons of their Companies were.

Under these circumstances the relief could not be carried out.

II

S.G. 259/189.

Divisional H. Q.
18th May, 1917.

The Divisional Commander wishes to express his sincere appreciation of the resource and bravery shewn by all which led to the great defeat of the enemy on the 16th May.

He has great pleasure in communicating the following message from the Corps Commander.

G. O. C., 51st Division.
=================

"Heartiest congratulations to you all on fine work on 15th and 16th and especially to General BURN and 152nd Brigade whose tenacity and pluck saved an awkward situation aaa The Division may well be proud of their latest achievment".

CORPS COMMANDER.

(signed) LAURENCE CARR, Major, G.S.
for Lieut. Colonel,
51st (Highland) Division.

IV

SPECIAL ORDER.

I wish to place on record my high appreciation of the very gallant conduct of all ranks and all units of the Brigade on the 15th and 16th May, 1917, when the German attack on ROEUX and the CHEMICAL WORKS was driven off with very heavy losses to the enemy.

The hostile bombardment which preceded the attack, and which continued throughout the 15th May was heavier and of longer duration than any bombardment I have yet seen, and to have withstood this and then to have so thoroughly defeated the enemy is a performance which calls for the highest praise.

In an action where all did so well, it is invidious to mention any special unit or detachment, but I would make an exception in the case of the Headquarters of the 1/8th Argyll & Sutherland Highlanders, who, led by Lieut. Colonel CAMPBELL personally, vigorously attacked a party of the enemy who had broken through our lines and turned the flank of our position, killing some 25 of their number and capturing 50 others, thus restoring the situation.

My congratulations and thanks are due to all Commanders and men for their great gallantry in this battle.

H. P. R....

Brigadier General,
Commanding 152nd Infantry Brigade.

19th May, 1917.

Appended is copy of appreciation of the work done
by the 6th Gordon Highlanders on the 23rd and 24th
of April, by Brigadier General D. CAMPBELL, of the
153rd Infantry Brigade. (Marked V.)

War Diary

B. G. C.
152nd Infantry Brigade.

Please convey to the 6th Seaforth Highlanders and 6th Gordon Highlanders which battalions were attached to this Brigade on 23rd and 24th inst. my congratulations on the part they took in the operations. Both battalions did very well indeed. I deeply regret the heavy loss sustained by the 6th Gordon Highlanders and especially that of Lieut. Colonel Dawson who was severely wounded. The Battalion advanced magnificently and had the Black Line been taken as had been expected I have no doubt that the Brown Line would have been reached preparatory to an assault on the Red Line in accordance with the Divisional plan of attack. As it was the 6th Gordon Highlanders did most valuable work in reaching the Chemical Works in spite of heavy loss.

The 6th Seaforth Highlanders took over the line late in the day under very difficult circumstances the position having become obscure. They did very well indeed. Lt. Col. McDonald was indefatigable in his efforts to carry out his orders personally going round the line twice during the night in order to clear up the situation and get his battalion into the best position.

I am proud to have commanded these two fine battalions in action.

(Signed) D. Campbell, Brig. Genl.,
Commanding 153rd Infantry Brigade.

28.4.17.

S.G. 259/189.　　　　　　　　　　　　　　Divisional H.Q.
　　　　　　　　　　　　　　　　　　　　　　18th May, 1917.

　　　　　The Divisional Commander wishes to express his
sincere appreciation of the resource and bravery shewn by
all which led to the great defeat of the enemy on the
16th May.
　　　　　He has great pleasure in communicating the
following message from the Corps Commander.

G.O.C. 51st Division.
=====================

　　　　　"Heartiest congratulations to you all on fine
work on 15th and 16th and especially to General BURN
and 152nd Infantry Brigade whose tenacity and pluck
saved an awkward situation aaa The Division may well be
proud of their latest achievement".

　　　　　　　　　　　　　　　　　　CORPS COMMANDER.

　　　　　　　　　　　　　　(sd) LAURENCE CARR, Major, G.S.
　　　　　　　　　　　　　　for Lieut. Colonel,
　　　　　　　　　　　　　　51st (Highland) Division.

SPECIAL ORDER.

I wish to place on record my high appreciation of the very gallant conduct of all ranks and all units of the Brigade on the 15th and 16th May, 1917, when the German attack on ROEUX and the CHEMICAL WORKS was driven off with very heavy losses to the enemy.

The hostile bombardment which preceded the attack, and which continued throughout the 15th May was heavier and of longer duration than any bombardment I have yet seen, and to have withstood this and then to have so thoroughly defeated the enemy is a performance which calls for the highest praise.

In an action where all did so well, it is invidious to mention any special unit or detachment, but I would make an exception in the case of the Headquarters of the 1/8th Argyll & Sutherland Highlanders, who, led by Lieut. Colonel CAMPBELL personally, vigorously attacked a party of the enemy who had broken through our lines and turned the flank of our position, killing some 25 of their number and capturing 50 others, thus restoring the situation.

My congratulations and thanks are due to all Commanders and men for their great gallantry in this battle.

H. P. R...

Brigadier General,
Commanding 152nd Infantry Brigade.

19th May, 1917.

WAR   DIARY
of
1/6th Bn. The GORDON   HIGHLANDERS.

JUNE, 1917.

CONFIDENTIAL.

Army Form C. 2118.

WAR DIARY
or
INTELLIGENCE SUMMARY.

(Erase heading not required.)

Instructions regarding War Diaries and Intelligence Summaries are contained in F. S. Regs., Part II. and the Staff Manual respectively. Title pages will be prepared in manuscript.

Place	Date	Hour	Summary of Events and Information	Remarks and references to Appendices
FOUFFLIN RICAMETZ	June 1917 1-3		In Billets. Training.	Map Reference 1/100.000 HAZEBROUCK
HEUCHIN	4		In Billets. Training.	
DELETTE & COYECQUE	5-7		The Battalion less "A" Company billetted in DELETTE. "A" Company billetted in COYECQUE.	
ARQUES	8		In Billets.	
GANSPETTE ELO MA/SON	9-21		In Billets. Training. Special attention given to Musketry. The Battalion improved very much and won the Brigade Inter-Company Falling-Plate Competition	
BOONERHEM	22-30		In Billets Training.	

The following awards have been given during the month :-
MILITARY CROSS.
Captain D. McKELVEY, R.A.M.C., attached to 6th Gordon Highlanders.
2/Lieut. W. K. LEGGAT
2/Lieut. R. RISK.
BAR TO THE MILITARY CROSS.
Captain D. G. CLARK.
Lieut. D. MACKENZIE.

	Officers.	O.R.
Strength at beginning of month	20	309
Add:— Drafts	1	365
Casuals		82
	21	740
	21	374
	42	1114
Deduct:— Evacuations	1	82
To Base, P.B.		3
To R.E.		4
To Base, u/age		3
To Indian Army	1	-
	2	92
Strength at end of month	40	1022

A. Brown Lieut Colonel
Commanding 6th Gordon Highlanders.

30.6.17.

WAR DIARY
or
INTELLIGENCE SUMMARY.
(Erase heading not required.)

Army Form C. 2118.

1/5 1/6 Gordon H^{rs}
31/1
Vol 33

Place	Date	Hour	Summary of Events and Information	Remarks and references to Appendices
BOESEGHEM	July 1-2		In Billets training.	MAPS:- HAZEBROUCK 1/100.000 ST JULIEN 1/10.000 SHEET 28 N.W. 1/20.000
Camp "D" al A 30. Central	3-7		In Huts. Training continues.	
In the Line	7-8		Left Sub-Sector of Divisional Front where we relieved the 5th Seaforth Highlanders. "D" Company held the front line in posts with "C" Company in support. "A" & "B" Companies were in reserve on the Canal Bank – on the right the 9th Argyll & Sutherland Highlanders were stationed, and on the left the 4th Worcester Battalion of 39th Division. Our Battalion Headquarters were in LANCASTER FARM. The Battalion were subjected to heavy shell fire during its tour in the trenches, and suffered considerably. Ten men were killed and 21 wounded. On the night of the 9th/10th an exceptionally heavy bombardment of our positions in the support area took place. The Germans attempted a raid on the Battalion on our left, and put a barrage on our trenches. The raid was unsuccessful. Work in the line consisted mainly in keeping the trenches in good repair. On the night of 10/11th the 4th Seaforth Highlanders (154th Brigade) relieved us in the line.	
LEDERZEELE	11-23		In Billets training for the attack.	
ST JANSTER BIEZEN	23-29		In Camp – Huts and Canvas.	
Camp "B" al A 30. Central	29-30		In Huts – Battalion moved off at 7.30 p.m. on the 30th to Assembly Position preparatory to attack. The Battalion was distributed as follows :– To Front Line – "A" & "D" Companies. To Hardy's Trench – "C" Company and "B" Company (less one Platoon) To "X" Line – one Platoon of "B" Company.	
In the Line	30.1st		The night was quiet, and no difficulties were experienced from enemy shelling. All Companies had been reported in position by 1.30 a.m. Shortly before ZERO Hour (3.50 a.m.) the enemy shelled the Front Line and ground in rear of it, but not heavily. A few casualties were sustained by	

Army Form C. 2118.

WAR DIARY
or
INTELLIGENCE SUMMARY.
(Erase heading not required.)

Place	Date	Hour	Summary of Events and Information	Remarks and references to Appendices
In the Line	20-1		/by Companies in the Front Line.	

From 4.10 a.m. onwards, our Front Line was heavily shelled, and the trench very much knocked about, but Companies moved into No Man's Land, and thus avoided loss.

At 4.20 a.m. "A" & "D" Companies moved forward in three waves as per programme, and passed through the BLUE LINE (already captured by 1/5th SEAFORTH HIGHLANDERS).

At 4.20 a.m. two Platoons of "B" Company detailed for VON WERDER'S HOUSE and ADAM'S FARM moved from HARDY'S TRENCH, and overtook "A" & "D" Companies on the BLUE LINE.

The whole moved forward under the barrage at 5.13 a.m. and the BLACK LINE parties detailed for ASCOT COTTAGE, GATWICK HOUSE, NEWSON'S HOUSE and MINTY'S FARM occupied these points without resistance.

A Machine Gun in action between ASCOT COTTAGE and the BLACK LINE was dealt with by means of Rifle Grenades. About 12 of the enemy were killed or captured here.

The BLACK LINE was reached by "D" Company at 5.25 a.m. close under the barrage. At this time the BLACK LINE on the left of the Battalion Front had not been occupied. One Platoon of "D" Company was therefore pushed forward off to the left to get touch with the 1/6th SEAFORTH HIGHLANDERS. This Platoon captured a Machine Gun in this part of the BLACK LINE. Machine Guns were also active from MACDONALD'S WOOD, and effective fire was directed on these by this Platoon. These Machine Guns were finally destroyed by a Tank.

The two Platoons of "A" Company detailed for HURST WOOD, BUCHCASTEL and KITCHENER'S HOUSE, passed through the BLACK LINE immediately it had been captured, and reached their objectives under the barrage.

Of the Platoons of "B" Company detailed for ADAM'S FARM, half platoon/

Army Form C. 2118.

WAR DIARY
or
INTELLIGENCE SUMMARY.
(Erase heading not required.)

Instructions regarding War Diaries and Intelligence Summaries are contained in F.S. Regs., Part II. and the Staff Manual respectively. Title pages will be prepared in manuscript.

Place	Date	Hour	Summary of Events and Information	Remarks and references to Appendices
In the Line	30-7-		A half platoon pushed forward beyond KITCHENER'S WOOD and reached ADAM'S FARM. A hostile Machine Gun in action 200 yards in advance of this point was dealt with successfully. One and a half platoons pushed on to HURST WOOD, and assisted in dealing with two Machine Guns which were active at the North edge of the wood.	
			Two Officers and 30 men were captured at this point. Subsequently one section pushed on to VON WERDER'S HOUSE – the remainder lost direction, and, pushing out to the left, reached the neighbourhood of FRANÇOIS FARM – two hostile Machine Guns which were in action here were dealt with by this party, and one Officer and 50 men were captured.	
			The loss of direction was then discovered, and they proceeded to VON WERDER'S HOUSE, where they consolidated.	
			"C" Company (GREEN LINE Company) left HARDY'S TRENCH at ZERO plus 1 hour, and, filing up BOAR LANE, assembled in the Front Line Trenches.	
			Then it pushed forward to a point between the BLUE and BLACK LINES. As touch had not been obtained with the Battalion on the right (16th R.B.) the officer commanding the company pushed the right flank out as far as RACECOURSE FARM. A Machine Gun still active between that point and KITCHENER'S WOOD was dealt with by this company.	
			The advance was then continued to a position 500 yards in front of the BLACK LINE where the Company was re-organised preparatory to moving forward to the GREEN LINE under the barrage.	
			At 7:30 a.m. the advance was continued, and the GREEN LINE was reached at 7:50 a.m.	
			Consolidation was commenced about 250 yards South West of STEENBECK under observation by hostile aeroplanes. These presently retired, and the front line was moved forward about 100 yards, and the support line withdrawn an equal distance. This move was successful, as the enemy shelled the original position taken up, but failed to locate the new position.	
			Battalion Headquarters moved from the British Front Line /KITCHENER'S HOUSE/	

Army Form C. 2118.

WAR DIARY
or
INTELLIGENCE SUMMARY.

(Erase heading not required.)

Instructions regarding War Diaries and Intelligence
Summaries are contained in F. S. Regs., Part II.
and the Staff Manual respectively. Title pages
will be prepared in manuscript.

Place	Date	Hour	Summary of Events and Information	Remarks and references to Appendices
In the Line	20.12		Line to near KEMPTON PARK at 6.45 a.m.	
			The intention was to move thence to the BLACK LINE (MINTY'S HOUSE) as soon as possible, but hostile shelling did not admit of a telephone line being laid and maintained, until 12.30 p.m. As communication from the front was fairly satisfactory, Headquarters were not moved forward till that time.	

Lieut. Colonel,
Commanding 6th Gordon Highlanders.

SECRET.   Copy No. 11

6th GORDON HIGHLANDERS
INSTRUCTIONS FOR OFFENSIVE OPERATIONS.

Section I.   Orders for the Attack by the Infantry.

1.   At a date to be notified later the Fifth Army will attack the enemy lines, East and North-East of YPRES.   The 51st Division will attack with 152nd Infantry Brigade on the right and 153rd Infantry Brigade on the left.
      The 117th Brigade (39th Division) will attack on the right of the 152nd Infantry Brigade.
      The 154th Infantry Brigade will be in reserve.

2.   The 152nd Infantry Brigade will attack with four Battalions on a front of two Battalions.
      The Objectives of the Brigade will be :-

   1. Capture of BLUE Line.
   2. Capture of BLACK Line.
   3. Establishment of a defensive line (GREEN Line) on the South bank of the STEENBECK.
   4. The advance of one Company to North bank of STEENBECK to form a post at MAISON DU RASTA.

3.   Battalions are allotted to objectives as follows :-

   1st Objective   ...   ... (1/5th Seaforth Highlanders on the right.
                                  (1/8th Argyll & Sutherland Highlanders on the left.

   2nd & 3rd Objectives ...   (1/6th Gordon Highlanders on the right.
                                  (1/6th Seaforth Highlanders on the left.

   4th Objective   ...   ... (1/6th Seaforth Highlanders.

      The 16th Rifle Brigade (117th Brigade) will capture the BLACK & GREEN Lines on the right of the 1/6th Gordon Highlanders and will establish posts on the North bank of the STEENBECK at MAISON DU HIBOU, C.6.c.1.3. and at C.5.d.2.1.

4.   Battalions allotted to the first Objective will advance in three waves of 50 paces distance, starting at "O" Hour.
      Battalions allotted to the further Objectives will advance at O plus 30 minutes and O plus 1 hour as shown in Appendix A.

5.   The 1/6th Gordon Highlanders will advance as shown in Appendix A.

6.   ~~One Platoon of "B" Company with Yukon Packs will be located in "X" Line and will move forward.~~

6.   One Platoon of "B" Company will remain in reserve in HARDY'S Trench under 2/Lieut. J. L. Hay, and will ~~move forward~~ only move on receipt of orders from G.O.C. 152nd Infantry Brigade or O.C. 1/6th Gordon Highlanders.

7.   One Platoon of "B" Company with Yukon Packs will be located in "X" Line and will move forward under orders from O.C. 1/6th Gordon Highlanders.   They will draw loads as ordered from Brigade Dump in rear of HARDY'S Trench, C.20.b.2.3.   One N.C.O. and 10 men from this Platoon will report to Battalion Headquarters at O plus 10 minutes, with Yukon Packs.   They will be attached to the Section 152nd Stokes Mortar Battery which is attached to 1/6th Gordon Highlanders for the operation and will work under the orders of the Officer Commanding this Section.
      N.B.   As No. 24 Grenades have to be detonated by parties drawing same from Brigade Dump, C.20.b.2.3. - four men of Bombing Section of this Platoon will be told off for this duty.   (See Appendix "E").

Page 2.

8. The following points should be noted :—

    (I) The 39th Division are responsible for the whole of Kitchener WOOD.

    (II) That portion of the road running from point C.10.d.0.6. to bend in road at C.11.a.1.5. is inclusive to the 152nd Infantry Brigade.
        The houses on the North-West side of this road are in the 152nd Brigade Area, and on the South-East side of the road in the 16th R.B. (117th Brigade) Area.

    (III) The 16th R.B. (117th Brigade) are responsible for the buildings of REGINA CROSS and the small work at C.11.a.75.45.

9. Two Stokes Guns have been allotted to 1/6th Gordon Highlanders for the operation. They will move forward via CALENDAR LANE, CALENDAR AVENUE as far as the BLACK LINE. They will be at the disposal of O.C. "D" Company, both during advance to BLACK LINE and after. In default of instructions, the officer in charge of the Section will report to O.C. "D" Company on arrival in BLACK LINE.

10. In order to ensure close touch with Battalions on either flank during the advance, points of Liaison have been selected as shown in Appendix "B".

11. Strong points will be constructed as follows :—

    1. East of ENGLISH TREES about C.9.d.8.4. by 6th Seaforth Highlanders.
    2. North of VON WERDER HOUSE about C.10.b.35.60. by troops detailed for capture of VON WERDER HOUSE.
       R.E. have been detailed to assist with these posts but this does not absolve the Infantry from responsibility for their construction.

12. The Barrage will be of shrapnel and will move in accordance with the tracing showing lifts of the Barrage, already issued.

13. In addition to reserve mentioned in para. 6, it will be noted that troops that have reached their objectives up to the GREEN LINE will become reserves, each in its turn, to assist in the assault of further objectives, the Commander on the spot calling on them on his own initiative.

14. On reaching his objective it is the duty of every Commander to get touch with the troops on the flanks and if necessary energetically to attack from a flank any of the enemy who may be holding up his neighbours or separating him from them. Failure to do this can only result in the holding up of succeeding waves.

15. The following Appendices have already been issued :—

Section II. — Artillery and Trench Mortar Plan.
Section III. — Action of Massed Machine Guns.
Section V. — Co-operation with Aircraft (Contact Aeroplane).
Amendment to Section V. — Co-operation with Aircraft.
Section XI. — Fighting Kit.
Section XII. — Prisoners.

16. The following Appendices are attached :—

Appendix "A" — Time Table of Advance.
        "B" — Points of Liaison.
        "C" — Action of Tanks.
        "D" — Medical Arrangements.
        "E" — Location and Contents of Dumps.
        "F" — Information required.
        "G" — Position of Battalion Headquarters on "Z" Day.
        "I" — Chain of Responsibility.
        "H" — Communications.
        "J" — Cavalry.

17.   Watches will be synchronised by an officer from Battalion Headquarters under arrangements to be notified later.

18.   ACNOWLEDGE.

                              (signed) W. H. Newson, Capt. & Adj.
                                       6th Gordon Highlanders.

Copies to :-

    No. 1.   File.
      2 - 5. Companies.
        6.   Officer i/c H. Q. Details.
        7.   16th Rifle Brigade.
        8.   H.Q. 152nd Infantry Brigade.
        9.   1/6th Seaforth Highlanders.
        10. 152nd Trench Mortar Battery.
     11 - 15. Spare.

APPENDIX "A".

TIME TABLE OF ADVANCE.

WAVE	UNIT	OBJECTIVES	STARTING POINT	TIME.
1st Wave	"D" Company less 2 Platoons / 2 Platoons of "A" Coy.	BLACK LINE and Farms b-etween BLUE & BLACK LINES.	British Front Line.	O plus 30 mins
2nd Wave	2 Platoons of "D" Company	BALCK LINE	do.	50 yards in rear of first wave.
3rd Wave	"A" Company less 2 Platoons	BLACK OUTPOST LINE.	do.	50 yards in rear of 2nd wave.
4th Wave	"B" Company less 2 Platoons.	ADAMS & VON WERDER FARMS.	HARDY'S Tranch	O plus 30 mins
5th Wave	2 Platoons of "C" Company.	GREEN LINE.	HARDY'S Trench	O plus 1 hour.
6th Wave	2 Platoons of "C" Company.	do.	do.	O plus 1 hour 50 yards in rear of 5th Wave.

    The 4th Wave will advance steadily until it arrives within 50 yards of 3rd Wave, when it will regulate its advance by the Waves in front. Later, passing through the preceeding Waves, it will attack its objectives as soon as the Barrage lifts.

APPENDIX "B".

POINTS OF LIAISON (a) ON RIGHT FLANK
                           (b) ON LEFT FLANK.

(a)

OFFICER OR N.C.O. RESPONSIBLE.	POINT OF LIAISON.	WITH WHOM.
N.C.O. i/c ASCOT COTTAGE.	Pond, RACECOURSE FARM.	16th R.B.
OFFICER OR N.C.O. i/c BUCHCASTEL.	BUCHCASTEL and houses at C.10.b.6.9.	16th R.B.
OFFICER OR N.C.O. i/c ADAMS FARM.	ADAMS FARM.	16th R.B.
O.C. "C" COMPANY.	Pond North of REGINA CROSS.	16th R.B.
O.C. "C" COMPANY.	ROAD JUNCTION C.5.d.3.1.	16th R.B.

(b)

OFFICER OR N.C.O. i/c NEWSON'S HOUSE.	ENGLISH TREES	1/6th Seaforth Highlanders
O.C. "D" COMPANY.	BLACK LINE C.10.d.35.80.	1/6th Seaforth Highlanders.
OFFICER OR N.C.O. i/c HURST WOOD.	NORTH CORNER of HURST WOOD.	1/6th Seaforth Highlanders.
OFFICER OR N.C.O. i/c VON WERDERS HOUSE.	VON WERDERS HOUSE.	1/6th Seaforth Highlanders.
O.C. "C" COMPANY.	FERDINAND FARM.	1/6th Seaforth Highlanders.

APPENDIX "C".

ACTION OF TANKS.

1. Tanks are divided into two Echelons.

Of Echelon I, two Tanks are allotted to 152nd Brigade, one of which will operate on the front allotted to 1/6th Gordon Highlanders. Its line of advance will be via GATWICK COTTAGE, CLARK'S COTTAGE, VON WERDERS HOUSE to the GREEN LINE. Its duties will be to assist the advance of the Infantry by mopping up the BLACK LINE, if necessary, and lending aid in the reduction of any strong points.

In addition, one Tank attached to 117th Infantry Brigade, will visit BOCHCASTEL ESTAMINET, and will then, accompanied by a second Tank of the 117th Infantry Brigade, proceed round the North West side of KITCHENER'S WOOD.

2. The duties of Echelon 2 will be to operate on the far side of the STEENBECK.

Infantry are responsible for affording them any possible assistance in the crossing of this obstacle.

—o—o—o—o—o—o—o—o—o—o—

APPENDIX. "D".

MEDICAL ARRANGEMENTS.

At Zero hour the position of the AID-POST of the 1/6th Gordon Highlanders will be in HEADINGLY LANE, about C.20.a.8.8. This AID-POST is shared by the 1/8th Argyll & Sutherland Highlanders. It will probably remain at this point until after the capture of the BLACK OUTPOST LINE, when it will be moved forward as opportunity offers to the neighbourhood of road junction at C.15.b.3.4.

After the capture of the GREEN LINE the AID-POST will be moved forward to the neighbourhood of MINTY'S FARM.

The above moves will take place as circumstances permit and at the discretion of the Medical Officer.

—O—O—O—O—O—O—O—O—

APPENDIX "E".

LOCATION AND CONTENTS OF DUMPS.

The 152nd Infantry Brigade Main DUMP is situated in rear of HARDY'S TRENCH, C.20.b.2.3.

Its contents are as follows :-

    1.   RATIONS AND WATER.

    2.   SAA

            GRENADES ... ... (No. 5.
                                   (No. 23.
                                   (No. 24.

        STOKES BOMBS.

        VERY LIGHTS ... ... 1".
        " " ... ... $1\frac{1}{2}$".
        " " RED ... ... 1".
        " " GREEN ... ... 1"

        FLARES.

        WEBLEY PISTOL AMMUNITION.

Grenades numbers 5 & 23 will be detonated.

Grenades number 24 will be detonated by parties drawing same
    from the Dump.

A series of small dumps will also be established behind the
    front line.

APPENDIX "F".

INFORMATION REQUIRED.

1. Only weapons will be removed from prisoners, except in the case of officers, whose papers and documents will be removed and handed to the escort who will hand them over to the Divisional Intelligence Officer at the Prisoners Collecting Station.

2. Information will be required on the following points :-
    (a) Progress of Attack.
    (b) Action of the Enemy.
    (c) Enemy Movements.
    (d) Enemy Strength.
    (e) Disposition of the Enemy.
    (f) Reports on Roads, Rivers, Bridges, Crossings, etc.
    (g) Any destruction done by enemy to hinder our advance.

Reports should be accompanied by a map whenever possible.

—o—o—o—o—o—o—o—

APPENDIX "G".

POSITION OF BATTALION HEADQUARTERS ON "Z" DAY.

Map Reference - ST. JULIEN, 1/10,000.

1. BRITISH FRONT LINE, C.15.c.40.75. until BLACK LINE is captured.

2. ROAD JUNCTION near KEMPTON PARK on report of capture of BLACK LINE.

3. Near CLARK'S COTTAGE on report of capture of GREEN LINE.

APPENDIX "H".

COMMUNICATION.

1. Communication while the Battalion is in the Assembly Position will be maintained by Runner.

2. Before Battalion Headquarters moves forward to the vicinity of KEMPTON PARK, communication from the front with Battalion Headquarters can be obtained through the Brigade Visual Station on HIGH COMMAND REDOUBT, or, by using the Brigade Report Centre at KEMPTON PARK, if this is in signal communication with the rear. If this is not the case, the Company Runner is responsible for delivery of the message to the addressee.
The Brigade Stations move forward immediately behind the troops detailed for the capture of the BLUE LINE.

3. On the capture of the BLACK LINE, a Brigade Report Centre will be established at HURST PARK (to be used as described in para. 2), and Companies can also speak back to Battalion Headquarters at KEMPTON PARK as soon as the wire is laid.

4. When Battalion Headquarters moves to CLARK'S COTTAGE, "D" & "A" Companies will be connected up by wire with Battalion Headquarters direct, and "C" & "B" Companies through the Brigade Report Centre at C.10.b.45.85. (To be used as described in para. 2)

5. The fullest use possible is to be made of Visual Signalling.
All Company Signalling Sections will carry :-

   1 White Signalling Flag.
   1 Blue   "   "
   1 Small Signalling Panel.

In addition, "C" Company will take forward two pigeons to be released on capture of that line.
One Lucas Lamp will be sent forward to "C" Company with lineman laying their telephone line.

6. Full use will be made of walking wounded and foot orderlies will be used as sparingly as possible, messages being sent either by signal or telephone.

7. Messages conveying information which might be of use to the enemy must be in code, unless sent by Runner.
Units will always be referred to by their code names.

APPENDIX "I".

CHAIN OF RESPONSIBILITY.

"A" Company   Commanding   - 2/Lieut. A.E.Paterson.
               Second-in-Command -   P.H.Mitchell.

"B" Company.   Commanding   - 2/Lieut. C.A.Baird.
               Second-in-Command -   A. G. Godsman.

"C" Company.   Commanding   - Captain J. Hutcheson.
               Second-in-Comm.   - 2/Lieut. W. Weir.

"D" Company.   Commanding   - Captain I.G. Fleming.
               Second-in-Command - 2/Lieut. H. Wilson.

In case of Captain I. G. Fleming becoming a casualty the joint command of "D" & "A" Companies will devolve on 2/Lieut. A. E. Paterson.

—o—o—o—o—o—o—o—o—o—o—

APPENDIX "J".

Should opportunity permit, one Squadron of Cavalry, (attached to 51st Division) will push forward across the STEENBECK, and will carry out reconnaissances as far as the LANGEMARCK - GHELNVELT Line. These reconnaissances will be supported by Infantry, specially detailed for the purpose.

6th GORDON HIGHLANDERS.
INSTRUCTIONS FOR OFFENSIVE OPERATIONS.

Section II.   Artillery and Trench Mortar Plan.

1. ORGANISATION.
   The Field Artillery supporting the attack of the 152nd Infantry Brigade consists of :-
   256 Brigade, R.F.A.
   58 Brigade, R.F.A.
   282 Brigade, R.F.A.
   under the command of Lieut. Colonel Dyson, D.S.O. R.F.A.

   The following medium and Heavy Trench Mortars will be in action on the Divisional front :-
   2" Medium   8.
   6" Newton   2.
   9.45 Heavy   2.

2. PRELIMINARY BOMBARDMENT.
   The Attack will be preceeded by a 10 day's preliminary trench bombardment and by harassing fire on communications by 18 pdrs. especially at night.

3. WIRE-CUTTING.
   The wire-cutting will be carried out by 6" and 2" Trench Mortars, and by 4.5" Howitzers with "106" Fuses, supplemented, if necessary by 18 pdrs.
   The following policy will be to destroy the whole of the German front wire.

4. BARRAGE ON "Z" DAY.
   The 18 pdr. creeping barrage will be time shrapnel.   The standing or trench barrage will be formed by the 4.5" howitzers, which will never fire nearer than 200 yards from the creeping barrage, and by a proportion of 18 pdrs. sweeping up and down the lanes.   Beyond this trench barrage will be the fire of the 6" howitzers and 60 pounders.   The mean point of impact and the time at which the barrage leaves each time will be shown on the barrage map which will be issued down to Platoon Commanders.
   The rate of fire will generally be four rounds per minute.
   Under present arrangements the barrage opens on the German front line at ZERO, and lifts off this line at Z plus 6 minutes. It will then advance generally at the rate of 100 yards in four minutes.
   It will lift off the BLUE dotted line at Z plus 48 minutes, off the BLACK dotted line at Z plus 2 hours 10 minutes, and off the GREEN line at Z plus 4 hours, 5 minutes.
   Protective barrages will be put down 200 yards in advance of the BLUE and BLACK dotted lines and 500 yards in advance of the GREEN line.

5. LIAISON.
   An Officer of the 256 Brigade, R.F.A. will be at Battalion Headquarters and will act as Liaison between the Battalion and covering artillery.

ACKNOWLEDGE

Capt. & Adj.
6th Gordon Highlanders.

Copies to all Companies.

6th GORDON HIGHLANDERS
INSTRUCTIONS FOR OFFENSIVE OPERATIONS

Section III Action of Massed Machine Guns.

1. The massed machine guns available are:—
   - 51st (H) Division   48
   - 11th Division   48
   - **TOTAL   96**

2. These guns will be used as follows:—

   "A" Barrage   32 guns.
   H.Q. of Machine Gun Commander   FOCH FARM
   Position of Guns   X Line
   TASK   To cover the high ground between the BLUE and BLACK lines and ground about 100 yards beyond the BLACK Line.

   "B" Barrage   16 guns
   H.Q. of Machine Gun Commander   FOCH FARM
   Position of guns — These guns will take up a position on the high ground East of KEMPTON PARK as soon as the BLUE LINE has been captured.
   TASK   To cover the ground between BLACK and GREEN Lines, and prevent hostile guns retiring over the STEENBECK.

   "C" Barrage   16 guns.
   "M" Battery of 8 guns will cover the 152nd Infantry Brigade front. This battery will move into position on the high ground at CANNON TRENCH, East of HURST PARK.

   The Task of "M" Battery will be to cover the ground beyond the GREEN LINE and to put down a protective barrage covering the GREEN LINE against counter-attack.

3. GUNS FOR CONSOLIDATION.
   Two machine guns will be attached to the Battalion for consolidation, and will take up a position at VON WERDER HOUSE covering the GREEN LINE.

4. ACKNOWLEDGE.

                                    Capt. & Adj.
                                    6th Gordon Highlanders.

Copies to all Companies.

6th GORDON HIGHLANDERS
INSTRUCTIONS FOR OFFENSIVE OPERATIONS.

Section V - Co-operation with Aircraft (Contact Aeroplanes).

1. The 7th Squadron R.F.C. will provide contact aeroplanes during forthcoming operations.

Each contact aeroplane will be marked with two BLACK rectangular flags (2 feet by 1 foot 3 inches) attached to and projecting from the lower plane on each side of the fusilage.

2. SIGNALS FROM AEROPLANES.

The signal from the contact aeroplane for the Infantry to light flares will be as under :-

    (a) A series of white lights.

    (b) A succession of "A"s (Morse Code) on KLAXON HORN or Daylight Signalling Lamp.

3. FLARES.

Infantry will show their position to the contact aeroplane by lighting GREEN flares. As far as possible these flares should be lighted in bunches of three.

4. MARKINGS OF H.Qs. etc.

Each Brigade and Battalion H.Q. will be marked by ground sheets of authorised shape with the code letters of the unit laid out with white stripes alongside.

Signalling to aeroplanes will be done by panels.

5. A contact aeroplane will be in the air -

    (a) During the attack on each objective.

    (b) When asked for in order to clear up an obscure situation.

Troops are to be warned to be particularly on the lookout for calls from contact aeroplanes immediately after the arrival at each objective.

6. ACKNOWLEDGE.

(Signed) W. H. Newsom, Capt. & Adj.
6th Gordon Highlanders.

14.7.17.

Copies to :-
    All Companies.
    Signalling Officer.
    Intelligence Officer.

6th GORDON HIGHLANDERS
INSTRUCTIONS FOR OFFENSIVE OPERATIONS.

ADDENDA to Section IX - Signal Communications.

The following are the positions and calls of the Brigade Signalling Stations for the forthcoming operations:-

Brigade H.Q.	FOCH FARM	NAZ
Advance Stn.	KEMPTON PARK	NAZA
do.	HURST PARK	NAZB
Terminal Stn near	VANACKERT FARM	NAZC
Central visual Stations	HIGH COMMAND REDOUBT.	HC.

TANK CALLS.

GREEN disc — Wire cut.
RED Disc — Wire uncut.
RED & GREEN Disc — Have reached my objective.
RED, WHITE, RED disc — Enemy in dugouts.

Capt. & Adj.
6th Gordon Highlanders.

24.7.17.

Page 2.

(p) Lewis Guns.

Each Lewis Gun to have a sling.
Each Section to carry spare parts, as already detailed for offensive operations.
25 magazines to be carried as arranged.
Numbers I only to carry revolvers.

2. ACKNOWLEDGE.

[signature]
Capt. & Adj.
6th Gordon Highlanders.

14.7.17.

Copies to :-
    All Companies.
    Signalling Officer.
    Scout Officer.

6th GORDON HIGHLANDERS.
INSTRUCTIONS FOR OFFENSIVE OPERATIONS.

Section XII.   Prisoners.

1. Escorts should not exceed 10% of the prisoners in each batch. No more men than are absolutely necessary are to be sent back from the front line on escort duty.

2. Prisoners will be handed over to the A.P.M. or his representative at the Advanced Prisoners of War Collecting Station at C.25.a.5.6.

3. After obtaining receipts for the prisoners handed over, escorts will report as soon as possible to Brigade Headquarters for instructions.

4. ACKNOWLEDGE.

                                           Capt. & Adj.
                                     6th Gordon Highlanders.

17.7.17.

6th GORDON HIGHLANDERS.
INSTRUCTIONS FOR OFFENSIVE OPERATIONS.

Corrigendum to Section XVII - Positions of H.Q. on Z Day.

Machine Gun Company H.Q. will now be at BOAR LANE
C.20.d.30.80.

                                            [signature], Capt. & Adj.
                                              6th Gordon Highlanders.

24.7.17.

6th GORDON HIGHLANDERS.
INSTRUCTIONS FOR OFFENSIVE OPERATIONS.

Amendment to Section V - Co-operation with aircraft.

1. In para. 3 - Delete GREEN and substitute WHITE or RED. WHITE Flares only will be used until a change to RED is ordered.

2. ACKNOWLEDGE.

                                                        Capt. & Adj.
                                            6th Gordon Highlanders.

18.7.17.

6th GORDON HIGHLANDERS.
INSTRUCTIONS FOR OFFENSIVE OPERATIONS.

Section XI - Fighting Kit.

1. Fighting Dress will be as follows :-

    (a) Clothing as issued.
    (b) Arms as issued.
    (c) Entrenching tools will NOT be carried.
    (d) Accoutrements as issued, except pack. Haversack on back.
    (e) Box Respirator; P. H. Helmet.

    (f) The following articles will be carried in the haversack :- Spare pair of socks, spare oil-tin, iron ration; mess-tin and cover, will be slung outside the pack. Waterproof sheet will be carried on top of the haversack under the flap.

    (g) Great-coats and cardigans will be left with packs.

    (h) <u>Aeroplane Flares</u>.- 2 per man.

    (i) <u>Wire Cutters</u>. - 2 per Section other than Lewis Gun Sections.

    (j) <u>Very Pistols, 1"</u>. - 2 per Company.
        Very Pistol Ammunition - 48 rounds.

    (k) <u>S. A. A.</u>

        Riflemen   -   170 rounds.
        Lewis Gunners   -   50   "
        Rifle Grenadiers -   120   "
        Rifle Bombers   -   120   "
        Bombers   -   170   "
          (except Rifle Bombers)
        Runners   -   50   "
        Signallers   -   50   "
        Scouts   -   50   "

    (l) <u>Rations and Water</u>

        1 Iron Ration.
        1 complete day's ration.
        1 filled water-bottle.
        1 Tin Solidified alcohol.

    (m) <u>Sandbags</u>.
        3 per man.

    (n) <u>Spades and Picks</u>.
        Every other man will carry a tool in the proportion of 1 pick to 5 shovels.
        Men of the reserve platoons will carry tools.

    (o) <u>Bombs</u>.
        Rifle Grenadiers   -   10 No. 24s
          (2 per Rifle Section)

        Rifle Bombers   -   10 No. 23s
          (4 per Bombing Section)

        Remainder   -   1 No. 5 in bottom
                                  pocket of tunic.

    (p) <u>Lewis Guns</u>./

6th GORDON HIGHLANDERS.

INSTRUCTIONS FOR OFFENSIVE OPERATIONS.

Section XX - Maps to be carried.

1. In order to avoid any chance of information falling into the hands of the enemy, no documents, maps showing our trenches, secret maps or papers (including private letters), will be taken into action, with the exceptions noted below :-

    (a) ST. JULIEN, 1/10,000 5A or 6A (not showing our trenches).

    (b) PILCKEM, 1/10,000 - Ed. 1.

    (c) Barrage Map, 1/5,000 and 1/10,000 (issue to platoons).

    (d) Message forms, with map on back. (issue to platoons).

    (e) Pigeon message maps.

    (f) Oblique aeroplane photographs.

    (g) B.A.B. Code, Edition III (not to go beyond Battalion H.Q.).

    (h) Company, Platoon and Section Rolls.

    (i) A.B. 64.

    (j) "S" Corps Map of STEENBEEK River and Valley, 1/10,000.

2. With the exception of above, all papers will be collected and stored under Company arrangements previous to the attack.

3. Any maps and private papers belonging to men will be stored with packs.

    Officers' maps not required, and private papers will be packed in their valises.

    ACKNOWLEDGE.

Capt. & Adj.
6th Gordon Highlanders.

WAR DIARY
or
INTELLIGENCE SUMMARY.

Army Form C. 2118.

(Erase heading not required.)

Place	Date 1917	Hour	Summary of Events and Information	Remarks and references to Appendices
In the Line	Aug 1		STEENBECK. The Battalion remained in the positions which had been captured on July 31st., foremost positions being held by "C" Company under Captain J. HUTCHESON, M.C. 2/Lieut. J. R. CHRISTIE had arrived on the 31st July to take over command of "D" Company vice Captain I. A. FLEMING, M.C. who had been killed leading his Company in the attack on the morning of that day. The weather was bad, and under heavy rains the ground, which was a mass of enormous shell craters, was reduced to an indescribable condition. The positions which had been consolidated were from one to two feet deep in water; a message received from Captain HUTCHESON at this time well illustrated the spirit which animated the men. It ran as follows :- "Posts are all about two feet deep in water, but spirits high". On the night of August 1/2, the Battalion was relieved by the 1/9th Royal Scots, and, owing to the careful arrangements for guides, a very difficult relief was carried through without a hitch.	Reference Maps. ST. JULIEN. 28 N.W. 1/10,000 28 N.W. 1/20,000
A.30.Central	2nd		The first hours of August 2nd found the Battalion on its way back to Camp at A.30.Central. The roads were knee deep in mud, and heavy rain was still falling. A man of "A" Company fell into a shell hole filled with water – far from being discouraged, he immediately commenced to quack like a duck, and the remainder of his Platoon, following his example, quacked their way cheerfully back to Camp. On arrival, hot soup and rum punch were served out to the men, and these, together with a dry shirt and socks, enabled all to sleep soundly. The state of the Camp in which the Battalion now found itself was very bad. Tents pitched in a sea of slippery mud, which in many places was knee deep, made cleaning up and reorganising a matter of some difficulty. In addition, the continuous rain made it impossible to get their clothing dry. Major A. A. DUFF, C.I.E., M.V.O. arrived and took over the duties of second-in-command from Major J. W. ADAMS. A draft of 80 men joined the Battalion.	28 N.W. 1/10,000
	3rd 4th		Rain still falling, but the spirits of the men undamped. Orders/	

Page 2.

Army Form C. 2118.

WAR DIARY
or
INTELLIGENCE SUMMARY.
(Erase heading not required.)

Instructions regarding War Diaries and Intelligence
Summaries are contained in F. S. Regs., Part II.
and the Staff Manual respectively. Title pages
will be prepared in manuscript.

Place	Date 1917	Hour	Summary of Events and Information	Remarks and references to Appendices
A 30 Central	August 4th		Orders were received to proceed to SIEGE CAMP. This move was accordingly carried out. The new Camp was decidedly an improvement on the old, being situated in a grass field which had not been transformed into mud.	Reference map 28 N.W. 1/20,000 B.20.d.6.6.
Siege Camp	5th		A great improvement in the weather enabled the men to clean themselves and their clothing. For the first time since July 30th, all were dry. Church Parade was held by Companies.	
	6th		The reorganisation of the Battalion was carried on, and promotions to replace casualties decided on. An enemy aeroplane bombed the Camp at about 10.30 p.m. but no casualties were suffered by the Battalion. A draft of 39 men joined the Battalion.	
	7th		Training. The fact that most of the ground in the vicinity had been uncultivated for three years gave exceptional facilities, and the usual difficulties about crops were non-existent. Orders were received to proceed on the following day to SCHOOLS CAMP, ST. JANSTER BIEZEN.	
	8th		The Battalion proceeded by march route to ST. JANSTER BIEZEN where it was accommodated, partly in huts and partly under canvas. Camp muddy, and the accommodation not too good.	France & Belgium sheet 27 & 28 1/40,000
St Janster Biezen	9th		Training. Improved the Camp and got more tents.	
	10th		Training.	28 N.W. 1/20,000
	11th		Training.	
	12th		Church Parade.	
	13th		Training continued.	
	14th		do. do.	Training carried out:— Platoons in Attack. Companies in Attack. Choosing and consolidating positions. Musketry. Rifle Grenade. Squad and Arm Drill.

Army Form C. 2118.

Page 3.

WAR DIARY
or
INTELLIGENCE SUMMARY.
(Erase heading not required.)

Instructions regarding War Diaries and Intelligence Summaries are contained in F. S. Regs., Part II. and the Staff Manual respectively. Title pages will be prepared in manuscript.

Place	Date 1917	Hour	Summary of Events and Information	Remarks and references to Appendices
Camp Reigersburg	August 15th		Training. Final of Platoon Tug-o'-War. No. 12. - winners.	Reference Map France & Belgium Sheet 27 N.E. 1/40,000 28 N.W. 1/20,000
	16th		Training.	
	17th		do.	
	18th		do. Final of Battalion Section Football Competition.	
	19th		Church Parade. Battalion beaten by 2nd Grenadier Guards in Tug-o'-War.	
	20th		Training.	
	21st		do.	
	22nd		do. A draft of 32 other ranks joined Battalion.	
	23rd		do. A draft of 14 other ranks joined Battalion.	
	24th		do. A draft of 5 officers joined Battalion.	
	25th		do.	
	-		do.	
	26th		Church Parade.	
	27th		Training.	
	28th		do.	
	29th		A draft of 1 officer and 13 other ranks joined Battalion. On morning of this day the Battalion moved by train from POPERINGHE to REIGERSBURG en route for the line. Moved by route march from REIGERSBURG to CANAL BANK where Battalion remained for six hours. At dusk it proceeded to the line where it was to relieve	

Army Form C. 2118.

Page 4.
WAR DIARY
or
INTELLIGENCE SUMMARY.
(Erase heading not required.)

Instructions regarding War Diaries and Intelligence
Summaries are contained in F. S. Regs., Part II.
and the Staff Manual respectively. Title pages
will be prepared in manuscript.

Place	Date 1917	Hour	Summary of Events and Information	Remarks and references to Appendices
Line	August 29th		/relieve the 9th West Yorkshire Regiment. The night was dark, and the posts not easy to relieve; however, the relief was effected in a short time in spite of the dreadful state of the ground, with only one casualty. The front was held by "A" Company under Captain A. S. Fortune, "B" Company under Captain D. G. Clark, "C" Company under 2/Lieut. D. MacDuff in support at Headquarters and "D" Company in reserve at CANAL BANK under Captain J. R. Christie.	Reference Map POELCAPPELLE 1/10,000
	30th		A good deal of shelling at intervals, otherwise fairly quiet.	
	31st		Shelling rather heavier, and a few casualties in the Support Line. Battalion Headquarters shelled at intervals during the day One Boche prisoner. 2/Lieut. P. H. MITCHELL, M.C. wounded, (slight). and night.	

AWARDS to BATTALION during the MONTH

D. S. O.
Captain J. HUTCHESON, M.C.

MILITARY CROSS.
2/Lieut. P. H. MITCHELL.
" A. D. MILLER.

D. C. M.
265097 Sgt W. GLENNIE.
265621 Sgt G. DYCE.
266205 Pte A. RALPH.

MILITARY MEDAL.
265712 L/S ROBIE J. 265002 Sgt COLLIE J.
266326 L/C SMART G. 292465 Pte MOSELEY C.
266473 Pte TENNANT J. 265020 Sgt CRUICKSHANK W.
265114 Cpl SUTHERLAND J.C. 265615 Sgt WEST J.
43578 L/C McEACHREN P.
BAR to MILITARY MEDAL.
265762 Pte WOOD A.

265290 L/C THOMSON H.
266841 " REWSHEA P.E.
266870 Pte ALLAN R.M.
7168 Cpl ANDERSON G.

Lieut Colonel,
Commanding 6th Gordon Highlanders.

G.A. 657/275.
2nd Aug. 1917.

1. The Army Commander wishes to offer his heartiest congratulations to the troops under his command on the success gained by them on 31st July.

2. For a fortnight prior to the attack the enemy has maintained a heavy and continuous artillery fire including an unprecedented use of H.V. guns against back areas, and a new form of gas shell, all of which caused severe casualties. Despite this and the fact that the forward area was dominated by the enemy at all points, the necessary preparations for the battle were completed and the difficult forward march and assembly of nine Divisions successfully carried out and the assault launched. This alone constitutes a performance of which the Army may well be proud.

3. As a result of the battle the enemy has once again been driven by the 1st French Army and ourselves from the whole of his front system on a front of about 8 miles, and we are now firmly established in or beyond his second line on a front of 7 miles.

4. We have already captured 5448 prisoners, including 125 officers. Up to date the capture of 8 guns, 10 T.Ms. and 36 machine guns has been reported.

5. In addition we have inflicted extremely heavy casualties on the enemy. Owing to losses during our preliminary bombardment he was forced to bring up 6 fresh divisions. Since then 3 more divisions have been withdrawn shattered.

Thus in a fortnight, we have disposed of 7 or 8 divisions and severely handled 10 more, several of which must shortly be withdrawn.

6. The Second Army on our right and the 1st French Army on our left have been as successful as ourselves. The French captures to date number 157 prisoners and 3 guns. The Second Army have also taken 390 prisoners and several machine guns.

7. Despite the weather on the day of the battle we shot down 5 enemy machines and 1 balloon, losing only 1 machine ourselves.

sd/ R. T. COLLINS, Lt. Col.
for Major General, G.S.

(2)

Officer Commanding,
   5th Sea. Hrs.   6th Sea. Hrs.
   6th Gor. Hrs.   8th A.&S.Hs.
   152nd M.G.Co. 152nd T.M.By.

S.G.152.

Herewith copies of Fifth Army Letter No. G.A. 657/275 of 2nd August, for information.

Captain, Brigade Major,
152nd Infantry Brigade.

7th August, 1917.

1/6 Gordon H[ighlanders]
Army Form C. 2118.
VII 35

WAR DIARY
or
INTELLIGENCE SUMMARY.
(Erase heading not required.)

Place	Date	Hour	Summary of Events and Information	Remarks and references to Appendices
In the line	1917 1/1		Holding the line. Except for shelling, which in early morning was pretty heavy for one hour, the day was quiet.	Reference Maps. POELCAPELLE 1/10000. Sht. 28NW 1/20000
	2		The Battalion was relieved by the 6th Arg/ll & Sutherland Highlanders. The relief was completed without casualties, and the Battalion returned to quarters under the CANAL BANK where a hot meal and rum were provided for the men, as well as dry socks & shirts and blankets.	
Canal Bank	3 + 4		CANAL BANK - resting and cleaning up. Accommodation good; the Companies were in dugouts on East bank and Battalion Headquarters shared H.Q. Mess with 6th Seaforth Highlanders on West bank. Comfortable mess.	
	5		CANAL BANK. The West bank received several shells between 10 and 11 p.m. Physical Training.	
	6		Battalion moved by route march to Camp at DIRTY BUCKET CORNER (A.30.Central), in the afternoon, being relieved on the CANAL BANK by 7th Argyll & Sutherland Highlanders. We marched into a very heavy thunder storm just before arriving at the Camp, and everyone got wet through, the rain for about 10 minutes being very heavy and flooded the whole Camp; but, as the Battalion was billeted in huts, after a cup of hot tea, which was waiting for the men, they were soon comfortable. During night, so we were not disturbed by bombs.	
Dirty Bucket Camp	7		Improving Camp, Gas Drill, Physical Drill, Lecture to Officers and N.C.Os. Consolidating positions, platoons - Musketry, Bayonet exercises, Physical Drill. Some bombs were dropped round the Camp last night. One splinter of a bomb hit one of the officer's chargers.	
	8		Training. A letter was received from the Brigadier General announcing that the King had been graciously pleased to approve of the award of the VICTORIA CROSS	
			to/	

Army Form C. 2118.

WAR DIARY
or
INTELLIGENCE SUMMARY.
(Erase heading not required.)

Instructions regarding War Diaries and Intelligence Summaries are contained in F. S. Regs., Part II. and the Staff Manual respectively. Title pages will be prepared in manuscript.

Place	Date	Hour	Summary of Events and Information	Remarks and references to Appendices
Duty Line't Camps	1919 Sept 8		1/to 20579 Private GEORGE IMLAH McINTOSH, 1/6th (The Banff & Donside) Bn. Gordon Highlanders. For most conspicuous bravery when, during the consolidation of a position, his Company came under machine gun fire at close range. Private McINTOSH immediately rushed forward under heavy fire, and, reaching the emplacement, he threw a Mills' grenade into it, killing two of the enemy and wounding a third. Subsequently, entering the dugout, he found two light machine guns, which he carried back with him. His quick grasp of the situation and the utter fearlessness and rapidity with which he acted undoubtedly saved many of his comrades and enabled the consolidation to proceed unhindered by machine gun fire. Throughout the day the cheerfulness and courage of Private McINTOSH was indomitable, and to his fine example, in great measure was due the success which attended his Company. The Divisional Commander congratulates the recipient.	Reference Map PROVEN APRIL Wipers Sheet 28 N.W. 1/20,000
	9		Church Parade.	
	10		Usual training. Inter-Platoon Football Competition. Work in connection with protection of the huts from aerial bombs begun.	
	11		Training. Improving Camp.	
	12		Training. Improving Camp. Band and Instructors arrived from Echelon "B". Battalion furnishes work party of 400 men to-night.	
	13		Work party returned to Camp at 3 a.m. Camp was inspected by Brigadier General H.P. Parm, D.S.O., who expressed himself very pleased with the general cleanliness and tidiness of the Camp.	
	14		Usual Training. Lieut. P.K. MITCHELL, M.C. died at PROVEN Hospital from wounds received by a shell when in the line on 29th August.	

Army Form C. 2118.

WAR DIARY
or
INTELLIGENCE SUMMARY.
(Erase heading not required.)

Instructions regarding War Diaries and Intelligence Summaries are contained in F.S. Regs., Part II. and the Staff Manual respectively. Title pages will be prepared in manuscript.

Place	Date 1917	Hour	Summary of Events and Information	Remarks and references to Appendices
	Sept 15		Usual Training.	Reference Maps: POELCAPPELLE 1/1,000 Sheet 28 N.W. 1/20,000
			The Battalion had to supply another work party of 200 men. The Party left Camp at 4 a.m. and returned at 1.15 p.m. Usual training. "A" Company received musketry training on small range near Camp.	
	16		Church Parade.	
	17		"A" Company - firing at SIEGE RANGE. "C" & "D" Companies provided work party of 120 men for work on range.	
	18		"D" Company - firing on range at SIEGE CAMP. "B" Company, made up to required strength from "A" Company, furnished a working party of 150 men for Heavy Artillery, to remain with them for two or three days. "C" & "A" Company provided working party for work on range - 2 officers and 120 other ranks	
	19		"D" Company - Musketry at SIEGE RANGE in the morning, from 9 a.m. - 12.30 p.m. "B" Company - Working Party, 1 Officer and 100 other ranks strong. "A" Company - Musketry.	
	20		"A" & "D" Companies - Musketry on the Range at SIEGE CAMP. Lewis Gunners on BRIELEN RANGE.	
Canal Bank	21		"A" Company - Musketry on small range at A.30.Central. Orders received for the Battalion to be ready to move up to the line on 21st instant. Battalion left DIRTY BUCKET CAMP, (A.30.Central) at 8.30 a.m. and proceeded to the CANAL BANK by march route. "B" Company rejoined the Battalion at CANAL BANK, having sustained 16 casualties while being attached to the Heavy Artillery for carrying ammunition. Left CANAL BANK at 6.30 p.m. and marched up to the line. The disposition of the Battalion was as follows :-	
In the Line			"C" & "D" Companies relieved two Companies of the 8th Argyll & Sutherland Highlanders in the Support Line, and "A" & "B" Companies at MAISON BULGARE and MAISON DU RASTA respectively. The relief of "C" & "D" Companies was complete at 11 p.m. without casualties.	

Army Form C. 2118.

WAR DIARY
or
INTELLIGENCE SUMMARY.
(Erase heading not required.)

Instructions regarding War Diaries and Intelligence Summaries are contained in F.S. Regs., Part II. and the Staff Manual respectively. Title pages will be prepared in manuscript.

Place	Date	Hour	Summary of Events and Information	Remarks and references to Appendices
L. de Zone	Sept 21		Battalion Headquarters were at VON BULOW FARM.	Reference maps. POPERINGHE 1/40,000 Sheet 28 N.W. 1/20,000
	22		Front line quiet, but Battalion Headquarters shelled at intervals all night. "C" & "D" Companies improved and pushed forward their line in order to get further away from the old German line which the enemy was shelling at intervals. Orders received for "A" & "B" Companies to move up into the Support line to relieve the remaining two Companies of the 8th Argyll & Sutherland Highlanders after dark. This relief was completed at 1 p.m., without casualties, in spite of a good deal of shelling. Battalion Headquarters moved to SNIPE HOUSE. Battalion Headquarters at VON BULOW FARM bombed by enemy aircraft early in the morning.	
	23		No. 14 Platoon's Headquarters — a small "pill Box" — received a direct hit and 2/Lieut G.S. DUNCAN and his two Signallers were killed. "D" Company had 10 other casualties. With the other companies the casualties were slight. Very heavy barrage put up by us and a fairly heavy one by the enemy at 6.15 a.m. which lasted until 8 o'clock.	
	24		A very thick mist prevailed all night which lasted up to 12 noon, and all communication with the front line was cut off during this time. The Battalion to be relieved to-night by the 9th West Yorkshire Regiment.	
	25		The relief of the Battalion was completed by 11.30 p.m. with only two casualties, including 2/Lieut. D.J.T.M. Henry, wounded. The Battalion marched by Companies to SIEGE CAMP, arriving there between 1 a.m. and 2 a.m. Resting and cleaning kit.	
Siege Camp	26		Cleaning up the Camp. Saluting Drill.	
	27		Companies inspected in Full Marching Order. Squad Drill.	
	28		Training. Bombs dropped round the Camp last night.	
	29		Training.	

Army Form C. 2118.

WAR DIARY
or
INTELLIGENCE SUMMARY.
(Erase heading not required.)

Instructions regarding War Diaries and Intelligence
Summaries are contained in F. S. Regs., Part II.
and the Staff Manual respectively. Title pages
will be prepared in manuscript.

Place	Date	Hour	Summary of Events and Information	Remarks and references to Appendices
			Officers O.R.	
			Strength at beginning of month 41 944	
			INCREASE :- Drafts 4 138	
			Drafts of Casuals . 63	
			45 1145	
			Officers O.R.	
			DECREASE :- Killed 1 12	
			Died of Wounds 1 5	
			Wounded 1 56	
			Evacuated Sick . 55	
			To 152nd T.M.Battery 1 .	
			Transferred to U.K. 3 .	
			Wounded, Sick &c. . 2	
			To U.K. for Commission . 1	
			To Base - P.B. . .	
			7 131	
			Strength at end of month 38 1014	
			30.9.17.	
			[signature]	
			Lieut Colonel,	
			Commanding 6th Gordon Highlanders.	

6th GORDON HIGHLANDERS.

NOMINAL ROLL OF OFFICERS as at 30.9.17.

RANK	NAME		REMARKS.
Lieut. Col.	Fraser, Hon. W.	M.C.	Commanding Officer.
Major	Duff	A.A. C.I.E., M.V.O.	2nd in Command.
Captain	Newson	W.H. M.C.	Adjutant.
"	Hutcheson	J. D.S.O., M.C.	Company Commander.
"	McCombie	C.	Transport Officer.
"	Clark	D.G. M.C.	Company Commander.
a/Captain	Fortune	A.S.	Company Commander.
"	Christie	J.R.	Company Commander.
Lieutenant	Minty	G.	
"	Paterson	A.E.	
"	Cooper	D.C.	
Hon. Lieut	Findlay	F.W.	Quartermaster.
2/Lieut.	Risk	R. M.C.	
"	Archibald	J.	Assistant Adjutant.
"	MacDuff	D.	
"	Simmers	R.P.	
"	Carnie	A.J.W.	
"	Duffus	W.	
"	Cowie	C.A.	
"	MacKay	K.	
"	Hector	J.	
"	Allan	J.K.	
"	Raitt	J.L.	
"	Thomson	R.D.	
"	Hay	J.L.	
"	Miller	A.D. M.C.	
"	Blacklaws	C.G.	
"	Brown	E.J.	
"	Taylor	W.	
"	Wilson	N.J.	
"	Godsman	A.G.	
"	Ross	J.M.	
"	Riddell	J.S.	
"	Rutherford	G.	
"	Kydd	W.A.	
"	Crichton	R.R.	
Lieut	Simpson	R.F.	
Captain	McKelvey	D. M.C.	M.O. (R.A.M.C.) att. on Leave
Capt. & Rev.	Coulter	H.	Chaplain, att. On Leave.
Captain	Laing	A.C.	M.O. temporarily attached.

30.9.17.

6th GORDON HIGHLANDERS.

NOMINAL ROLL OF OFFICERS as at 15th 9.17.

RANK	NAME		REMARKS.
Lieut. Col.	Fraser, Hon. W.	M.C.	Commanding Officer.
Major	Duff	A.A.	C.I.E.,M.V.O. Second-in-Command.
Captain	Newson	W.H.	M.C. Adjutant.
"	Hutcheson	J.	D.S.O., M.C. Company Commander.
"	McCombie	C.	Transport Officer.
"	Clark	D.G.	M.C. Company Commander.
a/Captain	Fortune	A.S.	Company Commander.
"	Christie	J.R.	Company Commander.
Lieutenant	Minty	G.	
"	Paterson	A.E.	
"	Cooper	D.C.	
Hon. Lieut.	Findlay	F.W.	Quartermaster.
2/Lieut.	Risk	R.	M.C.
"	Archibald	J.	Assistant Adjutant.
"	MacDuff	D.	
"	Simmers	R.P.	
"	Carnie	A.J.W.	
"	Duncan	G.S.	
"	Duffus	W.	
"	Cowie	C.A.	
"	MacKay	K.	
"	Hector	J.	
"	Allan	J.K.	
"	Raitt	J.L.	
"	Thomson	T.D.	
"	Hay	J.L.	
"	Miller	A.D.	M.C.
"	Blacklaws	C.G.	
"	Brown	E.J.	
"	Taylor	W.	
"	Henry	D.J.L.M.	
"	Williamson	A.A.	
"	Wilson	N.J.	
"	Thom	W.	
"	Godsman	A.G.	
"	Ross	J.M.	
"	Riddell	J.S.	
"	Rutherford	G.	

Captain	McKelvey	D.	M.C. M.O. (R.A.M.C.) att. on Leave
Capt. & Rev.	Coulter	H.	Chaplain attached.
Captain	Laing	A.C.	M.O. temporarily attached.

15.9.17.

War Diary

October 1917

6th Bn Gordon Hrs.

WA 36

CONFIDENTIAL
No 31(A)
HIGHLAND DIVISION.

Army Form C. 2118.

Confidential.

WAR DIARY
or
INTELLIGENCE SUMMARY.
(Erase heading not required.)

Instructions regarding War Diaries and Intelligence Summaries are contained in F. S. Regs., Part II, and the Staff Manual respectively. Title pages will be prepared in manuscript.

Place	Date	Hour	Summary of Events and Information	Remarks and references to Appendices
	September 30		On the transfer of the 51st (Highland) Division from the XVIIIth Corps to the VIth Corps, the Battalion proceeded by rail en route for the ACHIET-le-PETIT area, entraining at HOPOUTRE at 10.45 a.m. our last night in Flanders at Siege Camp was the worst the Battalion experienced as regards bombing, as enemy aeroplanes started bombing the area at 8.15 p.m. and went flying over at intervals till 2 a.m. dropping bombs luckily no bombs fell in our camp, and there were only one Casualty in the Battalion.	1 100,000 HAZEBROUCK LENS
In the field	October 1		The Battalion arrived at RAPAUME after 4.20 hours journey from HOPOUTRE at 6 a.m. and marched to ACHIET-le-PETIT (about 7 kilometres) where the camp we occupied consisted of half tents and half Bivouacs - the latter very makeshift arrangements. The party furnished by the Battalion at HOPOUTRE under Captain J. MINTY for loading transport was specially mentioned for their work by the R.T.O. - having loaded a regimental transport in record time for that station. A.A.W	1/40,000 March 29.1.78 LENS 1/20,000 51.B.S.W.
Achiet-le-Petit	2		Improving Camp. A.W.	
Do	3		Training - "A" and "B" Companies - preliminary musketry - "C" and "D" Companies - drill. A.W.	
Do	4		Training - "A" and "B" Companies on Range - "C" and "D" Companies preliminary training. A.W.	
Do	5		Training - All Companies doing Field Practice on Field Practice Range. A good Range with good targets. A.W.	
Do	6		Training - "C" and "D" Companies on Range. "A" and "B" Companies drill. A.W.	
Durham Lines	7		The Battalion marched by route march to BOISLEUX AU MONT (about 7 kilometres) to a hut camp, which, if finished, would have been comfortable, but there is much to do to make the huts wind and water proof. Owing to state of the huts the men were very cold. A.W.	S.11.a
Do	8		Improving huts and duckboards etc. A.W.	
Do	9		Training and improvement of camp carried on; building walls around the huts which makes them much warmer. W.	
Do	10		Training - "A" and "B" Companies Range Practice. "C" and "D" Companies	

Page 2.

WAR DIARY
or
INTELLIGENCE SUMMARY.

(Erase heading not required.)

Army Form C. 2118.

Place	Date	Hour	Summary of Events and Information	Remarks and references to Appendices
Duchaumes	October 10		Arm drill, close order drill, and physical training. Improving Camp.	S.11.G.
Do	11		Training - All Companies Musketry and Bayonet Fighting.	
Do	12		Improvement of Camp carried on.	
Do	13		Usual Training was carried out. Night operations. Patrolling.	
Do	14		Usual training.	
			Church Parade, and cleaning up. A large amount of work has been done on this Camp by the Battalion, and the huts are now much more comfortable; good brick and mortar fireplaces built in the Officers' Messes by our pioneers.	
Do	15		The Battalion gave a Demonstration Attack before an American General and his Staff.	
Do	16		Left ROISIEUX AU MONT at 7.40 a.m. to take over the front line trenches just west of FOMPEUX NECroisolles as shown on attached map (Right Sector) from the 6th Black Watch, about 4½ miles march). The relief was completed at 12.45 p.m. without casualties.	HENINEL 1 GUEMAPPE 1/10000
			The line is held by posts our frontage being 1400 yards as shown by map and there was much work to do to improve the posts and trenches. The enemy's front line is about 300 yards from ours. "A" and "B" Companies were in front line posts commanded respectively by Lieut. Cooper and Capt. Clark. "C" and "D" Companies in support, commanded by Capt. Minty and Capt. Christie respectively. The work of repairing trenches was begun.	
In the trenches	17		The work of wiring of front line and repair of front trenches was carried out last night, and work which could be done by day, such as laying duckboards and improving and revetting posts was carried out during the day. The weather was fine. The evening was pretty quiet, except for occasional bursts of shell fire at intervals.	

Army Form C. 2118.

Page 3.

WAR DIARY
or
INTELLIGENCE SUMMARY.

(Erase heading not required.)

Instructions regarding War Diaries and Intelligence Summaries are contained in F. S. Regs., Part II. and the Staff Manual respectively. Title pages will be prepared in manuscript.

Place	Date	Hour	Summary of Events and Information	Remarks and references to Appendices
In the Trenches	October 18		Improving duckboards, work in trenches, and revetting posts by day. Wiring front and support lines, and improving trenches by night. Weather fine. Evening quiet. aeg	
do	19		An inter-Company relief took place. The work of improving the trenches and wire in front was carried on by night and day. Two casualties last night (both slight) aeg	
do	20		Work by night and day continued. The Mining Platoon, under Lieut P. MACKAY, which was formed a day or two ago and then disbanded, was reformed, and is working on dugouts aeg	
do	21		Work as usual. Divisional Races to-day, but this Battalion won no events. aeg	
do	22		The Battalion went into support trenches, being relieved in the front line by the 8th Argyll & Sutherland Highlanders. Relief was completed by 4 p.m. No casualties. aeg	
do	23		In support trenches. The Battalion supplied working parties for various work as well as carrying parties. aeg	
do	24		In support trenches. The usual working parties were supplied for day and night work. One casualty. aeg	
do	25		In support trenches. The Mining Platoon did very good work making dugouts. The usual wiring and repairs to trenches and communication trenches were carried out. aeg	
do	26		In support trenches. Very wet. Usual work being carried on. aeg	

Army Form C. 2118.

Page 4.

WAR DIARY
or
INTELLIGENCE SUMMARY.

(Erase heading not required.)

Place	Date	Hour	Summary of Events and Information	Remarks and references to Appendices
In the Trenches	October 27		In support trenches. The Battalion received orders that it would not be relieved till the 31st. and	
Do	28		In support trenches. and	
Do	29		In support trenches. Enemy artillery a bit more active, otherwise fairly quiet. Work continued as usual. The Mining Platoon, under Lieut F. MACKAY, have done good work and made two shafts to dugout 30 feet deep. and	
Do	30		In support trenches. and	
Dainville	31		The Battalion was relieved in the support trenches by the 9th Battalion Northumberland Fusiliers. The relief was completed by 12 noon. The Battalion entrained at HENIN on the light railway in three trains and proceeded to DAINVILLE two hours' journey, where it is billeted in fair billets, but somewhat scattered.	

Page 5.

Army Form C. 2118.

WAR DIARY
INTELLIGENCE SUMMARY.
(Erase heading not required.)

Summary of Events and Information

Strength at end of last month

	Officers	Other Ranks
	38	1014
Increase – Drafts	6	60
Casuals	–	–
	44	1074

	Offrs	O.R.
Decrease – Killed	–	2
Died of Wounds	–	3
Wounded	–	53
Evacuated Sick	1	–
To 7th Gordon Hrs.	1	–
To U.K. for Commission	–	3
To Base as T.B. Offr.	1	–
To H.K. sick	2	–
	4	61
	40	1013

Honours and Rewards.   Military Medal.

One Other Rank.

W. Smith
Lieut.Colonel,
Commanding 6th Gordon Highlanders.

SECRET.   6th GORDON HIGHLANDERS.

OPERATION ORDERS NO. 139.

27th, September, 1917.

Reference Maps :-
   1/100,000 HAZEBROUCK.
   1/100,000 LENS.
   1/ 40,000 Sheets 27 & 28.

1. The 51st (Highland) Division will be transferred from the XVlllth Corps to the Vlth Corps, and be accommodated in the ACHIET-LE-PETIT Area.

2. The Battalion will proceed by rail on the 30th instant in accordance with attached Table "A".

3. INSTRUCTIONS FOR MARCH TO ENTRAINING STATION.
   (a)   "A" COMPANY.
               TIME   ...   ...   3.30 a.m.
               STARTING POINT   SIEGE JUNCTION
               ROUTE   HOSPITAL FARM - DROMORE CORNER -
                                    Main ELVERDINGHE ROAD to
                                    POPERINGHE - Main POPERINGHE STEEN-
                                    VOORDE Road to Road Junction in
                                    L.17.b.20.Sheet 27.

   (b)   REMAINDER OF BATTALION.
               TIME   ...   ...   7.20 a.m.
               Starting Point   SIEGE JUNCTION.
               ROUTE   ...   ...   As above.
               ORDER OF MARCH   H.Q., B., C., D., Companies.
               INTERVAL BETWEEN
               COMPANIES   100 yards.

4. Transport will move under orders of the Transport Officer to the Entraining Station.

5. BAGGAGE.
    Officers' valises, baggage, Mess kit, etc., will be ready for loading at 5.45 a.m.
    The above will be dumped at the Q.M. Store by that hour.

6. Breast Ropes for horse trucks will be provided by the Transport Officer; ropes for lashing vechicles are provided by the Railway.

7. Supply and Baggage Wagons will accompany the Battalion.

8. "C" Company will detail a loading party of two platoons, each 1 Officer and 50 Other Ranks strong. 2/Lieut. D. MacDuff's Platoon will be one of these.
    This party will report to the R.T.O., HoPoutre at 12.30 p.m. on 28th instant. It will work in two reliefs.
    Rations for 29th and 30th insts. will be taken.
    This party will travel by Train No.23 on 30th instant.
    Lieut. G. Minty will be in charge of the whole party.
    The Transport Officer will detail one G.S. Wagon for the blankets and baggage of the above party to report to O.C., "C" Company at 10 a.m. on 28th instant.

9. Lieut. A. E. Paterson is detailed as Brigade Entraining Officer at Hopoutre. He will report to the R.T.O. at Hopoutre at 16.5 hours on 29th September, 1917, and will remain on duty until the whole Brigade Group has moved.

10. The Company Cooker and Company Commander's Horse will travel with "A" Company in Train No. 21.

11. Special care must be taken to see that Camp and surroundings are properly cleaned up before leaving.
The usual Certificates will be rendered.

12. Details as regards the carriage of blankets will be issued later.

13. Cookers, except "A" Company's which leaves at 2.30 a.m., will have to leave Camp at 6.15 a.m. Breakfasts must be arranged accordingly.

ACKNOWLEDGE.

        (Signed) W.H. Newson, Capt. & Adj.
           6th Gordon Highlanders.

Copies to :-

No.	Recipient
1	File
2	H.Q. 152nd Infantry Brigade.
3 - 6	Companies.
7	Transport Officer.
8	Quartermaster.
9	H.Q. Details.
10	Entraining Officer.
11	H.Q. Mess.
12 & 13	War Diary.

SECRET.   6th GORDON HIGHLANDERS.

OPERATION ORDERS NO. 140.

5th October, 1917.

Reference Maps :-
    LENS 11   1/100,000.
    51 B. S.W.   1/ 20,000.

1. The 6th Gordon Highlanders will move by march route to DURHAM LINES, S. 11.a. on 6th October 1917.

2.   STARTING POINT   East entrance to present Camp.

    TIME   8.55 a.m.

    ORDER OF MARCH   H.Q., A. B. C. & D Companies.

    INTERVAL BETWEEN COMPANIES   200 yards

    Band will march with their Companies.

3. The transport will follow 200 yards in rear of last Company to Road Junction, S.11.a.7.0., when it will move under orders of Transport Officer to new lines at M.10.d.7.2.

4. Officers' Quartermaster's valises and Mess kit will be stacked at Q.M. Store by 8.15 a.m.
Blankets will be conveyed to new camp by motor lorry. They will be stacked, ready for loading at east entrance to Camp. Blankets will be loaded by Companies under supervision of Quartermaster by 8 a.m.

5. Billeting Party, Lieut. F. MacKay and 5 Headquarters Runners, will report to Staff Captain at M.30c.0.1. at 2.45 p.m. on 5th. They will meet Battalion at Road Junction, S.11.a.7.0. Bicycles will be taken by this party.

6. Breakfast will be at 7 a.m.

7. The Camp will be left scrupulously clean.
The usual certificates will be rendered to Adjutant before leaving.

8. ACKNOWLEDGE.

    (Signed) J. Archibald, Lieut & A/Adj.
    6th Gordon Highlanders.

Copies to :-
    No. 1   File
    2   H.Q.,152nd Infantry Brigade.
    3-6   Companies
    7   Transport Officer
    8   Quartermaster
    9   H. Q. Details
    10   H. Q. Mess
    11 & 12   War Diary.

SECRET.

N A S A L

OPERATION ORDERS NO. 142

18th October, 1917.

1. An inter-company relief will be carried out tomorrow (19th instant) as under :-

    "C" Company will relieve "A" Company in Right Sub-Sector.
    "D" Company will relieve "B" Company in Left Sub-Sector.

    Relief will be complete by 10 a.m.

2. "C" Company will relieve via FIRST AVENUE.
   "D" Company will relieve via PIONEER.

3. All details of relief will be arranged direct between Officers Commanding Companies concerned.

4. All Trench Stores will be taken and handed over on relief and details of stores taken and handed over forwarded to this office by all Companies.

5. Completion of relief will be notified to Battalion Head Quarters by Runner.

6. ACKNOWLEDGE.

                                (Signed) J. Archibald, Lieut. & A/Adj.
                                         N A S A L.

Copies to :-

   No. 1   File
      2-5 Companies
      6-7 War Diary.

SECRET.   6TH GORDON HIGHLANDERS.

OPERATION ORDERS NO. 143.

21st October, 1917.
--oo--oo--oo--oo--oo--oo--

1. The 6th Battalion The Gordon Highlanders will be relieved in its present position by 8th Battalion, Argyll & Sutherland Highlanders on 22nd instant.
   On rel--ief the Battalion will move into support in the HINDENBURG LINE.

2. Relief will be carried out as per attached Table A.

3. Guides as below will report at Headquarters, 6th Gordon Highlanders one hour and an half before the relief is timed to commence.

   Battalion Headquarters   -   1 Guide
   "A" Company ....   -   1 Guide per Platoon.
   "B" Company ....   -   1 Guide per Platoon.
)1 Guide per Post in Front Line.
)1 Guide per Platoon in WOOD TRENCH.
   "C" Company-)1 Guide for Platoon in Brown Trench.
)1 Guide per Lewis Gun Section
)1 Guide for Company Headquarters.

   Guides from "D" Company as follows, will report at Head Quarters of "C" Company, 8th Argyll & Sutherland Highlanders at the NEST half an hour before the relief is timed to commence. They will be under an officer :-
       1 Guide per Lewis Gun Section.
       1 Guide per Post in Front Line.
       1 Guide per Platoon in SWIFT SUPPORT.
       1 Guide for Company Head Quarters.

   All Guides will reconnoitre the routes to be used by 5 p.m. to-day, 21st instant.

4. Parties working on Posts under R.E. supervision (as per Table A. of my 755 of 18.10.17) will be found from 6th Gordon Highlanders tomorrow, and will rejoin their Companies in their new locations after completion of task.
   Night parties will be found by 8th Argyll & Sutherland Highlanders.

5. The Mining Platoon will move to the HINDENBURG LINE.
   Work will not be interupted on account of change of location.

6. The following will be handed over on relief :-
   (a) Trench Maps taken over from 6th Black Watch.
   (b) Aeroplane Photographs.
   (c) Details of work in progress and Working Parties.
   (d) Trench Stores.

   A list of all Trench Stores handed over will be forwarded to this office by 8 p.m. tomorrow.
   For purposes of handing over, PELICAN DUMP will be in charge of O.C., B. Company.

7. Billetting Parties as under will report at this H.Q. at 10 a.m. to-morrow :-
       1 N.C.O. from A. B. & C Companies.
       1 O.R. from Battalion Headquarters.

   This party will be in charge of Lieut. D. MacDuff who will report to this office at the same hour.
       1 N.C.O. from "D" Company will report at H.Q., "C" Company, 8th Argyll & Sutherland Highlanders at 9.30 a.m.

Page 2. (Contd.).

7. Billetting Parties will meet their Companies at junction of CONCRETE RESERVE and HINDENBURG LINE.

8½. Battalion Head Quarters will move to Billet No. 48 in HINDENBURG LINE on completion of Relief.

9. Officers Commanding Companies will be responsible that all trenches and dugouts in their area are handed over in a thoroughly clean and sanitary condition, and a certificate to this effect will be forwarded to this office with report of completion of relief.

10. Completion of relief will be reported to this office by Runner.

11. ACKNOWLEDGE.

(Signed) J. ARCHIBALD, Lieut. & A/Adj,
6th Gordon Highlanders.

Copy No. 1   File
        2   H.Q, 152nd Inf. Brigade.
    3 - 6   Companies.
        7   O.C., 8th Argyll & Suthd. Hrs.
        9   Transport Officer.
  10 & 11   War Diary.

Table A.

Company & Present location	Relieved by	Destination of Company after Relief	Route for Relief: Incoming	Route for Relief: Outgoing	Time of commencement	Remarks
"D" Coy. (6th G.H.) (Left Sub-Sector)	"C" Coy 8th A. & S. H.	The Rest	Foster Av. Anchor Res. Boreas Alley	Lark Lane Bluff Support Boreas Alley Anchor Reserve Foster Avenue	10 a.m.	Relief to be complete by 1.30 p.m.
"C" Coy. (6th G.H.) (Right Sub-Sector)	"A" Coy 8th A. & S. H.	Hindenburg Line	Concrete Res. First Av. – Tank Trench – Front Line	First Avenue Concrete Reserve	1.30 p.m.	Relief to be complete by 5.30 p.m.
"B" Coy. (6th G.H.) (Lantern Road) (Anchor Res.) (The Rookery)	"B" Coy 8th A. & S. H.	do.	Concrete Res. First Avenue Anchor Passage	Anchor Passage First Avenue Concrete Res.	1.30 p.m.	do.
"A" Coy. (6th G.H.) (Concrete Res.)	"D" Coy 8th A. & S. H.	do.	Concrete Res.	Concrete Res.	1.30 p.m.	do.
Battn. H.Q. (First Aven.)	Battn. H.Q. (8th A. & S. H.)	do.	Concrete Res. & First Avenue	First Avenue Concrete Res.	1.30 p.m.	do.

SECRET.   6th GORDON HIGHLANDERS.

OPERATION ORDERS NO. 144.

30th October 1917.

Reference Maps:-
    LENS 11   1/100,000
    51B.S.W.   1/20,000
    HENINEL)
    GUEMAPPE) 1/10,000

1. ...The 6th Gordon Highlanders will be relieved by the 9th Northumberland Fusiliers on 31st instant and will move by train to DAINVILLE.

2. Guides, as follows, will meet incoming Unit at N.34a.7.7.
      "A", "B", and "C" Companies   -   1 Guide each
      Battalion Headquarters   -   1 Guide.

    They will be under command of Lieutenant D. C. Cooper, and will report to him at Battalion Headquarters at 9 a.m.
    Lieut. Cooper will report to the Adjutant before moving off.

    One Guide per Platoon from "D" Company, under Lieut. J. Hector, will meet "D" Company 9th Northumberland Fusiliers at Henin Cross Roads (N.32.d.3.1.) at 10 a.m.

3. Mid-day meal will consist of a dry ration. Dinners will be served on arrival in billets.
    Cooks and Cooking Utensils will be at the Crucifix at 9.30 a.m. where a limber will be in readiness to convey them to the transport lines.

4. Lewis Guns and Drums will be carried to HENIN, and will be taken by train to DAINVILLE.
    Lewis Gun limbers will meet the Battalion at detraining point where they will be loaded up.

5. All mess and officers' kits, and Battalion Stores will be at Crucifix at 10 a.m. where a limber will be in readiness for their further conveyance.
    Loading Party will rejoin their Companies and will NOT proceed with limber.

6. The following will be handed over on relief:-
    (a) All trench maps, air photographs, and defence scheme.
    (b) Statement of work in progress, and proposed work.
    (c) All trench stores.
    (d) All special maps issued to facilitate handing over.
    Attention is directed to this office No. re Lists of Trench Stores.

7. On completion of relief Companies will proceed to entraining point (S.W. of HENIN), T.2.b.4.0.) by march route.
    An interval of 200 yards between Platoons will be preserved during march.
    Companies in HINDENBURG LINE will move off in following order:-
      "A", "B", "C".

8. Four trains available for conveyance of the Battalion are allotted as follows:-

    1st Train - 1 p.m.   "A" Company
                              Battalion Headquarters.
    2nd Train - 1.15 p.m. "B" Company
    3rd Train - 1.30 p.m. "C" Company.
    4th Train - 1.45 p.m. "D" Company.

On arrival at entraining point each party will halt 50 yards from the entraining point, and the officer in charge will report to the officer superintending the entraining etc.., who will give the necessary instructions for entraining. Permission to quit the train will only be given by the Officer Commanding Train, who will be the Senior officer travelling with it.

Entrainment will take place quietly and without loss of time.

9. On arrival at DAINVILLE Officers commanding companies will report to Officer in charge of detraining point for instructions before detraining their men.

10. Completion of relief will be reported to Battalion Headquarters by Code Word "YES" or by runner.

Officers commanding companies will report arrival in billets at DAINVILLE.

11. ACKNOWLEDGE.

                              (Signed) J. Archibald, Lieut. & A/Adj,
                                        6th Gordon Highlanders.

Copies to:-
    No. 1   File
        2   H.Q., 152nd Infantry Brigade.
      3/6   Companies.
        7   Transport Officer.
        8   R.Q.M.S.
        9   O i/c H.Q. Details.
       10   O/C 9th Northumberland Fusiliers.
  11 & 12   War Diary.

152nd Brigade.

51st Division.

1/6th BATTALION

GORDON HIGHLANDERS

NOVEMBER 1917.

Report on Operations.
Operation Orders etc.

WAR DIARY
or
INTELLIGENCE SUMMARY.
(Erase heading not required.)

Army Form C. 2118.

6/ Gordon H/Q

Place	Date	Hour	Summary of Events and Information	Remarks and references to Appendices
DAINVILLE	Nov. 1st		The Battalion was occupied in cleaning up after a tour of fifteen days in the Trenches. Billets where they required it, were repaired and made more comfortable. The Training Area is good and a good range is available about 2 kilometres away.	Reference Maps /ENS.II./16400
"	2nd		Training commenced with Physical Training, Squad and Arm Drill. Captain A.S. FORTUNE developed dyphtheria. (O.C. "A" Company).	
"	3rd		Parades for Drill and Musketry were carried out. Two teams of the best players played a match with a view to selecting a team to represent the Battalion in a Brigade Football Competition. Two Tug o' War teams competed for the same reason. An Inter-Company Football Competition was started on the League System.	
"	4th		Battalion paraded for Church Parade. Lieut. D.C. COOPER, "A" Company developed dyphtheria. Results of Inter-Company Football Competition played to-day :- "A" Coy. beat "B" Company, 3 Goals to Nil. "C" Company drew with "D" Company, 1 Goal each.	
"	5th		Physical Training, Close Order drill and Wire-cutting were carried out according to programme. Tug o' War Competitions - "A" and "B" Companies, Winners "A" Company. Transport beat "D" Company.	
"	6th		Companies carried out attack practice as per programme. Weather good, dry and cold. In the Football Matches played to-day "A" Company beat "C" Company, 4 Goals to 3. "D" Company beat "B" Company, 1 Goal to Nil.	
"	7th		Battalion paraded for Battalion Drill and then carried out a Battalion Attack. The weather broke and rain fell heavily the whole day.	
"	8th		Training in Musketry and Attack Formations was carried on. A Battalion Cross-Country Run took place in the afternoon. Out of 97 starters, 90 runners finished. The time of the first man home was 17½ minutes. This was very good as going was heavy. Order of finishing of Companies :- "D" Coy, 1st; "B" Coy, 2nd; "C" Coy, 3rd; and "A" Coy, last. A prize of 100 francs was given to "D" Company, and a prize of 5 francs each was given runners finishing in the first 10 places.	
			Tug o' War/	

Army Form C. 2118.

WAR DIARY
or
INTELLIGENCE SUMMARY.
(Erase heading not required.)

Instructions regarding War Diaries and Intelligence Summaries are contained in F.S. Regs., Part II. and the Staff Manual respectively. Title pages will be prepared in manuscript.

Place	Date	Hour	Summary of Events and Information	Remarks and references to Appendices
DAINVILLE	Nov. 8th		Tug o' War was pulled off after race with the following results :- "A" Coy. pulled "C" Coy; "B" Coy. pulled "D" Coy; "A" Coy. pulled "D" Coy; and "C" Coy. pulled "B" Coy. Weather was very cold.	
"	9th		The Battalion marched to WAILLY to carry out a Brigade Attack practice in conjunction with Tank Corps. Left billets at 7.45 a.m., had Dinners on the Field, and returned 3.30 p.m.	
"	10th		A Battalion parade was held and was followed by an Attack practice. A relay race was won by "A" Company. In a Tug o' War against R.A.M.C., the Battalion won by two pulls.	
"	11th		Battalion paraded for Church Parade. All Officers and Sergeants attended a Lecture by the R.G.C. on forthcoming operations. The results of Inter-Company Football league are as follows :- "A" Coy, 4 points; "D" Coy. 3 points, "C" Coy. 1 point; and "B" Coy. nil.	
"	12th		Training according to programme. "D" Company on Range. Remainder of Battalion on Attack practice.	
"	13th		This being the anniversary of BEATMONT HAMEL the day was celebrated by a general holiday throughout the Brigade. Football matches were played within the Battalion with the following results:- "B" Coy. beat "C" Coy, 2 goals to 1 goal; "A" and "D" Companies drew with 2 goals each. Dinners at mid-day consisted of Soup, Roast Beef, Pudding, Beer and Cigarettes. Semi-final of the Tug o' War against the 5th Battalion Seaforth Highlanders was won by this Battalion by two pulls at the Brigade Sports which were held in the afternoon. In the final the Battalion was beaten by the 8th Battalion Argyll & Sutherland Highlanders, after three pulls. A successful day was brought to a close by a Battalion Concert.	
"	14th		Physical Drill, Musketry and Attack practices were carried out by all Companies. Two Companies spent the afternoon studying the model which had been made of the ground over which forthcoming operations were to be carried out. The weather was fine.	

Companies/

Army Form C. 2118.

WAR DIARY
or
INTELLIGENCE SUMMARY.

(Erase heading not required.)

*Instructions regarding War Diaries and Intelligence Summaries are contained in F. S. Regs., Part II. and the Staff Manual respectively. Title pages will be prepared in manuscript.

Place	Date	Hour	Summary of Events and Information	Remarks and references to Appendices
DAINVILLE	Nov. 15th		Companies went to Baths and then spent alternate hours in Training and at the Model. Weather good.	
"	16th		Battalion practised the attack. Men's packs were collected and were sent along with surplus stores to SAVY.	
"	17th		At 5.20 a.m. the Battalion paraded and then proceeded by route march to BEAUMETZ-LES-LOGES and entrained there for BAPAUME. On detraining the Battalion then marched to ROCQUIGNY, a distance of about six miles, and was billeted in huts erected amongst the ruins of the village. The Transport which left DAINVILLE on the night of 15th arrived at ROCQUIGNY at 4 a.m. on 17th. The weather was misty and very suitable for the move.	See O.O. No.145
ROCQUIGNY	18th		To prevent enemy aircraft from observing the fact that an unusual concentration of troops was taking place in this new area, men were not allowed to leave their huts and transport was camouflaged. At 4.20 p.m. the Battalion marched to the village of METZ and on arrival there at 8.5 p.m. was billeted in the ruins of the village. Billets were quite comfortable and were chiefly elephant shelters. The men had tea and then turned in. No lights or fires were allowed.	See O.O. No.147
METZ	19th		All men with the exception of special parties detailed to draw stores were kept under cover in billets. The greater part of the day was fully occupied in issuing stores and special equipment and in making final preparations for coming operations. The Commanding Officer accompanied by the Company Commanders spent the forenoon in reconnoitring the various assembly positions of the companies.	
"	20th	3.30 a.m.	At 3.30 a.m. the Battalion moved off by Companies to assembly positions in rear of the British Front Line. The cookers were brought up to a prearranged point and the men had a good hot breakfast at 6 a.m., just before the commencement of the attack. The/	See O.O. No.146

Army Form C. 2118.

WAR DIARY
or
INTELLIGENCE SUMMARY.
(Erase heading not required.)

Place	Date	Hour	Summary of Events and Information	Remarks and references to Appendices
BRITISH FRONT LINE	NOVR 20th	6.20am	The Battalion was reported in its Assembly Positions. ZERO hour. At this hour the assaulting troops (5th Seaforth Highlanders) advanced to the capture of the enemy's first system of defences up to and including the railway, K.24.a.5.0.- L.25.a.4.o. This advance was preceded by tanks, which left their assembly position a short time before Zero. This assembly position roughly corresponded to that of "B" Company. Enemy retaliation to our barrage was very weak; a few rounds fell in the vicinity of Battalion Headquarters but no damage was sustained.	See Report on Operation of 20-21/11/17. Reference Maps: MARCOING 1/10.000
"	"	7.50am 8 am	At this hour the leading waves of the Battalion, "B" Company on right, began to move forward to the attack, followed at an interval of ten minutes by the second waves, composed of "C" and "D" Companies. The advance from this point was carried out in section columns and the formations were admirably kept. The men were very keen.	
"	"	8.27am	At this stage it was found necessary for the leading waves to halt in order to allow the troops ahead to complete their task and to avoid the chance of their becoming involved in any fighting before their time. Reports being received from scouts that all was clear in front, the leading waves moved forward. On reaching the line of the railway (K.24.a.5.0.- L.25.a.4.o.) the correct number of tanks (six) were seen pushing forward on the battalion front, and the first wave extended. The whole advance up to the SUNKEN ROAD (K.24.d.10.90.- L.10.C.5.0.) was carried out in a very excellent manner, and without a single casualty. The tanks were going well and the first wave was following their advance at about two hundred yards distance in readiness to capture their objective. On the tanks appearing over the skyline in front of the HINDENBURG SUPPORT LINE, an enemy battery came into action at a point blank range and succeeded in putting out of action every tank on the battalion front. Owing to the configuration and the irregular shape of the enemy's wire, it seemed to those in charge of the leading wave that the tanks had managed to pass over the wire before becoming casualties, and so they went on. Too late they discovered the real situation and as they neared the belt of enfanglement, they came under very heavy machine gun fire from the direction of FLESQUIERES WOOD which was on the left flank. This fire the leading waves were held up and here the first casualties occurred.	
"	"	9.30am	Orders were received at this hour for the reserve companies, "C" and "A" to move forward from assembly positions, and their advance was carried out in excellent formation	

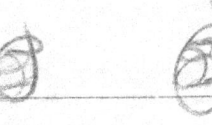

Army Form C. 2118.

WAR DIARY
or
INTELLIGENCE SUMMARY.
(Erase heading not required.)

Instructions regarding War Diaries and Intelligence Summaries are contained in F. S. Regs., Part II. and the Staff Manual respectively. Title pages will be prepared in manuscript.

Place	Date	Hour	Summary of Events and Information	Remarks and references to Appendices
	Nov 19 20th	10.15am	Formation and at 10.15 a.m. crossed our front system. On receiving	
	"	10.20am	Battalion Headquarters moved to WEST HOUSE, RIBECOURT.	
			On receiving information that the leading waves had failed to gain their	
	"	11.50am	objective the reserve companies took up a position in SUNKEN ROAD (F.24.d.10.00.- L.10.b.5.c.). Meanwhile the leading wave, finding it impossible to force an entry to its objective, had withdrawn into STATION ALLEY and part of SUNKEN ROAD with the intention of working along HINDENBURG SUPPORT to the left flank.	
	"	12.15pm	All this was found impracticable, a defensive flank was formed in STATION ALLEY facing FLESQUIERES, with one strong post at the dead end at top of STATION ALLEY. Touch was obtained on the right flank with 11th Battalion Essex Regiment.	
	"	12.5/pm	Casualties at this time were estimated at 4 Subalterns and 60 Other Ranks.	
	21st	2 am 3.30 am	Orders were received from Brigade Headquarters for an attack on FLESQUIERES and were issued to companies at 3.30 a.m. as far as they concerned the battalion. The objective being the BROWN LINE.	
	"	6.15am	ZERO hour. At this hour "A" and "C" Companies attacked, the first wave being extended, and the second following in section columns. No tanks were available for this attack.	
	"	7am 7.30am	A message was received from "C" Company that they had passed FLESQUIERES and at 7.30 a.m. reports were received that objectives had been gained and that fresh troops (8th Argyll & Sutherl and Highlanders) were passing through to continue the attack. A few casualties were sustained and a small number of prisoners were captured.	
	"	12.15pm	The HINDENBURG SUPPORT LINE was now consolidated and Battalion Headquarters moved to top of STATION ALLEY.	
	"	5.30pm	The position which the battalion established about this time runs as follows:- In front of FLESQUIERES TRENCH - L.10.b.o.5. - L.10.b.70.65. - L.10.b.5.0. - L.13. d.4.1. - L.13.d.2.5. - L.13.d.7.0. Touch was obtained with 11th Essex on right and 6th Seaforth Highlanders on left.	
	"	6pm	Orders were issued to companies to obtain as much rest as possible and to re-organise and re-equip. Men were given a hot meal and dry socks were issued.	
	"	11pm	Battalion spent the day in resting and completing re-organisation. Orders/	

Army Form C. 2118.

WAR DIARY
or
INTELLIGENCE SUMMARY.
(Erase heading not required.)

Instructions regarding War Diaries and Intelligence Summaries are contained in F. S. Regs., Part II and the Staff Manual respectively. Title pages will be prepared in manuscript.

Place	Date	Hour	Summary of Events and Information	Remarks and references to Appendices
	NOVR 22nd	11 p.m.	Orders were received from Brigade that the Brigade was to retake the village of FONTAINE NOTRE DAME, which had been lost by the 154th Infantry Brigade. Orders and details of the part to be played by the battalion in the attack issued to company commanders. The leading wave was to consist of "C" Company on left and "A" Company on right with "B" and "D" Companies forming a second wave.	
	23rd.	12 p.m.		See O.O. No. 17-19
		3.30 am	The battalion, including Battalion Headquarters, moved off to assembly position in SUNKEN ROAD, running from L.1. central to Cross Roads L.1.d.10.40., and was in position at dawn (6.15 a.m.).	
	"	10.30 am	ZERO hour. The leading waves advanced to the attack following tanks, and suffered some casualties from enemy barrage, the second waves coming on at two hundred yards distance.	See Report on operations of 23.11.17.
	"	10.45 am 1.35 pm	Battalion Headquarters moved up to CANTAING MILL. Information was received that the leading waves ("A" and "C" Companies) were held up by heavy machine gun fire from LA FOLIE WOOD and ridge N.E. of FONTAINE. At this point Captain G. MINTY, commanding "C" Company was killed. A heavy enemy counter attack developed from the north east of FONTAINE but failed to materialise owing to the fire brought to bear on it by Vickers and Lewis Guns. Tanks had to retire from village.	
	"	6.30 pm	When it was found impossible to advance a line was consolidated astride SUNKEN ROAD from a small copse, F.21.d.5.4., to join up with the right Company ("A" Company) at F.21.central. "B" Company on the left got touch with 6th Seaforth Highlanders. "D" Company on right was in touch with 9th Royal Scots.	Reference Major BOURLON 1/10,000
	"	7 pm	Information was received at this time that the 6th Seaforths were retiring from the N.W. end of FONTAINE village and that the 40th Division were also falling back from BOURLON WOOD. Steps were taken by "B" Company to ensure the safety of the left flank.	
	"	8.30 pm	Orders were received that the Brigade was to be relieved and arrangements were made for guides. A complete list of casualties is appended.	
	24th.	3 am	The battalion was relieved by the Irish Guards, without incident or casualty and marched back to area round FLESQUIERES. The men were very exhausted. A good hot meal and a rum ration was waiting the battalion when it marched in. The men rested in the shelters which they had built the previous day and at 3.30 p.m. moved back to METZ. A halt was made near HAVRINCOURT WOOD for teas, after which the march to/	MARCOING 1/10,000 57C. 1/40,000

Army Form C. 2118.

WAR DIARY
or
INTELLIGENCE SUMMARY.
(Erase heading not required.)

Instructions regarding War Diaries and Intelligence Summaries are contained in F.S. Regs., Part II. and the Staff Manual respectively. Title pages will be prepared in manuscript.

Place	Date	Hour	Summary of Events and Information	Remarks and references to Appendices
YPRES	Nov.R. 24th	3.30 p.m.	to METZ was resumed. Buses were supposed to meet the battalion there and convey it to YPRES. They failed to appear, with the result that YPRES had to be reached by route march. This was done in pouring rain and the men were absolutely exhausted on reaching the entraining point. In spite of the hardships they had undergone, not a man fell out. No train was available owing to an accident on the line, and a most miserable night was spent at the station where there was no cover from the hurricane of wind and rain.	Reference Maps: LENS 11. 1/100,000
"	25th	6 a.m.	Fortunately dixies had been carried and it was possible to give the men tea, which cheered them up a little. The train turned up and after a very cold journey the battalion detrained at	
MILLENCOURT	"	10.30 a.m. 2.30 p.m. 4 p.m.	AVELUY at 2.30 p.m. and marched to MILLENCOURT. Here the men were billeted in poor billets and got a hot meal. The grit shown by the men was magnificent and in spite of their condition they marched well. They then turned in to rest.	LENS 11. 1/100,000
"	26th		The day was spent in rest.	
"	27th		Resting and cleaning up.	
"	28th		Battalion went to Baths at SENLIS.	
"	29th		N.C.O.s Class on Musketry. Recent drafts paraded for squad drill. Remainder of battalion occupied in cleaning up and fitting of clothing &c.	
"	30th		Companies commence training. War material captured by the battalion during operations of 20th to 23rd is as follows :- Two 5.9 Guns; three 4.2 Hows; 5 Machine Guns.	

Army Form C. 2118.

WAR DIARY
or
INTELLIGENCE SUMMARY.
(Erase heading not required.)

Instructions regarding War Diaries and Intelligence Summaries are contained in F.S. Regs., Part II. and the Staff Manual respectively. Title pages will be prepared in manuscript.

Place	Date	Hour	Summary of Events and Information	Remarks and references to Appendices
MILLENCOURT	Novr 30th		Strength at end of last month ... ... Officers. 40 Other Ranks. 1013	
			INCREASE :- Drafts 4 95	[initials]
			Casuals 51	
			44 1159	
			DECREASE :- Officers. Other Rank.	
			Killed 2 30	
			Died of Wounds ... 1 2	
			Wounded 8 166	
			Evacuated Sick 50	
			To Base 1 1	
			To R.F.C.	
			12 250	[initials]
			Strength at end of month 32 900	
			HONOURS & AWARDS.	
			NIL.	
			[signature]	
			Lieut Colonel,	
			Commanding 6th Gordon Highlanders.	

REPORT on OPERATIONS carried out by
6th Battalion The Gordon Highlanders
on November 20th and 21st, 1917.

1. **Assembly**   The assembly was carried out without incident, the Battalion being formed up as follows:-
       "D" Company ... BEAUCAMP RESERVE (between
                                 SHAFTESBURY AVENUE and SUNKEN Rd)
       "B" Company ... In rear of STAFFORD RESERVE
       "A" & "C" Companies ... BROKEN TRENCH
       Battalion Headquarters   BEAUCAMP SUPPORT

           Cookers were brought up forward of BROKEN TRENCH, and hot tea and sausages served to all ranks before the attack commenced.

2.   Zero Hour was at 6.20 a.m., and the 5th Seaforth Highlanders advanced to the capture of the enemy positions up to and including the Railway, K.24.d.5.0 - L.25.a.4.9. The Tanks, which had gone forward before Zero, pushed on without casualties and did excellent work, and the whole operation was a complete success.

3.   At 7.50 a.m. the leading Companies ("B" on the left; "D" on the right) left their assembly positions and advanced in artillery formation (lines of sections). The extension was excellent, and the men were in great spirits.
           The advance got within distance of the six Tanks which had been detailed to precede it, immediately after crossing the railway, and the first wave (two platoons of each Company) extended and pushed on - followed at a distance of 200 yards by the second wave still in section columns.

4.   The Tanks on arriving in front of the wire protecting the HINDENBURG SUPPORT LINE, came into view from the far side of the crest, and were destroyed in succession by a battery of enemy field guns in action at point blank range (about 500 yards away at L.14.c.k.1. and L.13.d.7.2.)

5.   Owing to the formation of the enemy wire the Officers Commanding "B" and "D" Companies did not realise that the Tanks had not got through, and continued the advance. On reaching the wire, however, it became apparent that all had been knocked out before penetrating it. The infantry came under a very intense machine gun fire from Eastern edge of FLESQUIERES, and began to suffer casualties. ("B" Company lost 20 men and "D" Company 40 from this fire in a very few minutes).

6.   Both Companies were withdrawn into STATION ALLEY and the SUNKEN ROAD (between RIBECOURT and FLESQUIERES), and an advance was made up STATION ALLEY with the intention of working into and along the HINDENBURG SUPPORT LINE. It was found that STATION ALLEY did not join up with the HINDENBURG SUPPORT LINE which necessitated another advance over the open from the head of STATION ALLEY. This was carried out by one platoon.

Page 2.

7. This platoon on reaching the HINDENBURG SUPPORT LINE found that it was not dug throughout its length, and that to advance along it in daylight under machine gun fire from FLESQUIERES was not possible.

8. At about 10.15 a.m. the Reserve Companies ("A" and "C") had been moved forward and were about the original German outpost line. They continued their advance as far as the SUNKEN ROAD South of the Railway where they halted on learning the situation in front of them.

Shortly afterwards they continued their advance as far as the RIBECOURT - FLESQUIERES ROAD.

9. About 11.30 a.m. the situation was as follows:-

"D" Company holding STATION ALLEY from L.19.c.9.6 to L.19.d.3.9½ with one platoon in HINDENBURG SUPPORT LINE at L.19.b.4.1.

"B" Company in STATION ALLEY from RIBECOURT - FLESQUIERES ROAD to L.19.c.9.6. with some men in the road itself.

"A" and "C" Companies in SUNKEN ROAD and in small lengths of enemy trench behind it.

Lewis Guns from HINDENBURG SUPPORT LINE had silenced the enemy field guns (L.13.c. and L.14.d), but no more Tanks were now available to continue the advance, and it was still impossible to pass the wire in front of HINDENBURG SUPPORT LINE in face of machine gun fire from FLESQUIERES.

10. It became apparent that there were too many men forward and the Battalion was therefore disposed as follows:-

"D" Company to occupy HINDENBURG SUPPORT LINE and STATION ALLEY between that line and RIBECOURT - FLESQUIERES ROAD.

"B" Company to occupy trench L.19.c.3.3. with some men, the remainder to dig in in depth in this vicinity facing Eastern edge of FLESQUIERES.

"A" and "C" Companies to occupy STATION ALLEY between RIBECOURT and the Railway, with some men dug in in fresh positions in rear of Railway.

These last named Companies were not required from the point of view of consolidation. The intention was to keep them as safe and fresh as possible for further advance.

11. Battalion Headquarters was established in RIBECOURT, K.30.b.10.1½.

12. It was thought feasible to move the two Reserve Companies round in rear of the 18th Brigade on the right who were holding a line PREMY CHAPEL HILL - F.19.b.6.4., and advancing towards the BEETROOT FACTORY to turn the flank of the defenders of FLESQUIERES.

Liaison/

12. (Contd.) Liaison with the 18th Brigade on the right was established with this end in view — but it was evident that co-operation from the direction of the FLESQUIERES — GRAINCOURT ROAD would be required, and owing to the difficulty of communication the suggestion could not be got back in time for action before dark.

13. At 1.15 a.m. orders were received to advance on the BROWN LINE (F.20.a.2.9. — F.13.d.4.6.) at the same time pushing some troops along in a Westerly direction between the HINDENBURG SUPPORT LINE and FLESQUIERES TRENCH to join up with the 6th Seaforth Highlanders on the left.

14. "A" and "C" Companies were detailed to advance to the BROWN LINE, and owing to the difficulty of the uncut wire in front of HINDENBURG SUPPORT on the front of this Battalion, arrangements were made with the 11th Battalion The Essex Regiment to vacate a portion of the HINDENBURG SUPPORT LINE, F.19.b.5.0. — F.19.b.8.½ to allow room for these Companies to form up. Guides were provided by the Officer Commanding 11th Essex Regt. to lead Companies to their assembly positions.

One platoon of "D" Company was detailed to effect junction with 6th Seaforth Highlanders in HINDENBURG SUPPORT and FLESQUIERES TRENCH.

15. At 5 a.m. "A" and "C" Companies were formed up on Railway about F.25.a.5.8., and the guides led them direct to assembly position in HINDENBURG SUPPORT LINE. Bearings had been taken off the map from assembly position to point where right of "A" Company and left of "C" Company should rest on BROWN LINE ("A" Company was on the right; "C" Company on the left.), and the right and left sections of these Companies respectively were to advance on compass bearing. The advance was in two waves opening out fan-wise during advance until on reaching the objective the right frontage was gained. The first wave advanced in extended order, the second in section columns.

16. The attack took place under a thin barrage at 6.15 a.m., and was carried out without a hitch, which was to the credit of Officers Commanding Companies concerned, as it was by no means an easy manoeuvre to effect in the almost darkness of the dawn.

At the same time the platoon of "D" Company advanced towards FLESQUIERES — one section dealing with the HINDENBURG SUPPORT and one with FLESQUIERES TRENCH, the remaining two being extended between these lines.

17. After the advance it was found that "C" Company had extended too far to the left and occupied a line L.13.d.1.9 — L.13.d.6.4., while "A" Company was holding from L.13.d.6.4. to L.20.a.1.8. Two 5.9 guns were captured by "C" Company about F.13.b. and the two 4.2 guns, the teams of which had been dealt with on the previous day by "D" Company, were captured by "A" Company in L.13.c. and L.14.d.

18. Consolidation   "A" and "C" Companies were then ordered to consolidate in depth on the front they held — contact having been established on both flanks and the leading waves of 5th Seaforth Highlanders, who were advancing with the SUNKEN ROAD South of the CANTAING LINE as their objective, having gone forward.

"D" Company was moved forward and consolidated a line F.19.b.7.4. - F.13.c.8.2.

"B" Company passed into Battalion Reserv and was accommodated in the HINDENBURG SUPPORT LINE.

19. Later on the occupation of CANTAING by the 154th Infantry Brigade was reported, and the supporting platoons of "A" and "C" Companies were accommod:ated in gun pits near their position, while "D" Company was mostly withdrawn to dugouts about F.19.b.7.4. "B" Company remained in the HINDENBURG SUPPORT LINE where the men had made themselves very comfortable with corrugated iron shelters.

20. The men were tired but very keen and pleased that the advance which had been held up the previous day had eventually been accomplished.

21. Throughout the operation the liaison with the 11th Battalion The Essex Regiment was excellent, and kindness of their Commanding Officer in providing an assembly position and guides to assist in its occupation contributed largely to the success of the attack.

(signed) W. Fraser   Lieut Colonel,
Commanding 6th Gordon Highlanders.

27.11.1917.

Report on the Operation carried out
by the 6th Battalion, The Gordon Highlanders.
November 23rd., 1917.

--oo--oo--oo--oo--oo--oo--oo--oo--oo--

1. At 11 p.m. on November 22nd., information was received that 152nd Infantry Brigade had been ordered to recapture the village of FONTAINE NOTRE DAME.

    At the same time orders were received that the 6th Battalion, The Gordon Highlanders would attack the village on the right of the 6th Seaforth Highlanders.

2. Company Commanders were assembled at Battalion Headquarters at 12 midnight and the orders for the attack were issued and all details discussed.

    The attack was to be carried out by "A" & "C" Companies, "A" Company on the right and "C" Company on the left, supported by "D" Company on the right and "B" Company on the left.

    The advance was to be carried out in artillery formation (lines of sections), each company being in two waves on a two platoon frontage.

    The leading wave was to extend on nearing the objective.

3. The attack was of a most difficult nature as the right flank was entirely exposed from LA FOLIE WOOD and the high ground to the North and East of FONTAINE NOTRE DAME. As no attack was to be carried out against LA FOLIE WOOD, a request was made that a smoke barrage should be put down between this wood and the village, with a view to protecting the advance from enfilade fire from this wood. This barrage was not forthcoming.

4. At 6.30 a.m. the Battalion was formed up in the Assembly Position (the SUNKEN ROAD between L.1.d.2.8. and L.2.c.3.4.).

5. Zero Hour was fixed for 10.30 a.m. and at 10.10 a.m. the Tanks which were to precede the Infantry advance moved forward.

6. Just before Zero Hour the enemy commenced to shell the Assembly Position and several casualties occurred before the Battalion moved off.

7. At 10.30 a.m. the Infantry moved forward in excellent formation. A fairly intense hostile barrage commenced just before Zero Hour on the ground which had to be traversed between the Assembly Position and our front line - but the casualties sustained during this part of the operation were light.

8. As soon as the supporting companies had gone forward, Battalion Headquarters moved to CANTAING MILL.

9. The leading waves of the attack extended about our own front line and pushed forward towards FONTAINE.

    Before reaching the village it was necessary to cross a deep valley, both slopes of which were swept by machine gun fire, from LA FOLIE WOOD and the ground to the North of it. During the earlier part of the day this valley was also swept by machine gun fire from the left flank (BOURLON WOOD).

    In addition, every house on the Southern front of the village itself appeared to contain more than one machine gun, and these had not been dealt with by the Tanks, which attacked the village from both flanks but not from the front.

    Several efforts were made to push forward across this valley, but it was continually found to be impossible. Some portions of "C" Company had indeed pushed forward and/

Page 2.

/and dug themselves in quite close to the village, but later they had to be withdrawn to the main line which was being consolidated about 500 yards Southwards.

10. The Tanks which had occupied the village were compelled to withdraw owing to the exhaustion of ammunition, and the very heavy fire with armour-piercing bullets to which they were subjected.

11. At about 1.30 p.m., news was received that an enemy attack was developing in four waves from the East and North East of FONTAINE NOTRE DAME. This attack came under our fire from the SUNKEN ROAD at F.21.c, and suffered considerable casualties. It did not develop, the enemy contenting himself with re-occupying his original line in front of the village, which had been evacuated on the advance of the Tanks.

12. The position of the Battalion at about 2 p.m. was as follows :-
"B" & "C" Companies in and astride the SUNKEN ROAD, F.21.c.
"A" Company dug in on a line facing the Eastern edge of FONTAINE NOTRE DAME and FOLIE WOOD, F.21.d.
"D" Company in rear of "A" Company.
Two companies of the 8th Argyll & Sutherland Highlanders were in position in rear of the Battalion and across the whole front.

13. About 2 p.m. orders were received to the effect that a fresh attack would be launched against FONTAINE NOTRE DAME from the Eastern edge of BOURLON WOOD. The attack was to be carried out by two companies of the 5th Seaforth Highlanders preceded by Tanks, and 100 rifles from each of 6th Gordon Highlanders and 8th Argyll & Sutherland Highlanders were to co-operate as soon as the attack developed.

14. The force required was assembled in the SUNKEN ROAD, and placed under the command of Captain D. G. CLARK, but strict orders were given to this officer not to move until the attacking troops, preceded by Tanks, had approached the Western edge of the village.
In event the attack did not develop, and Captain CLARK remained in his original position.

15. At about 3.30 p.m. a considerable body of the enemy was seen about F.22.Central. These were engaged with machine gun fire and scattered.

16. At dusk it was apparent that no further advance would be possible. Contact had been obtained on both flanks of the Battalion, and a line was selected for consolidation from F.21.d.10.3. to F.21.c.1.4.
This line was then held as follows :-
"A" Company on the right supported by "D" Company, "B" & "C" Companies which had become inter-mingled on the left under command of Captain CLARK.
The reserve line was held by Companies of the 8th Argyll & Sutherland Highlanders.

17. The Battalion was relieved on the night of November 23rd/24th, the relief commencing about 1 a.m. It was effected without incident and completed about 3 a.m. when the Battalion retired to vicinity of FLESQUIERES.

18. Considerable casualties had been sustained, more especially in officers, and Captain G. MINTY had been killed.
All ranks were very tired and a little depressed that the operation had not been attended with greater success.

19/

19. It is considered that the ill-success which attended this attack was due to the fact that insufficient time was available for preparation, in consequence of which, no reconnaissance was possible before the plan of attack was formed. In addition the necessary number of shells and more especially of smoke shells were not forthcoming.

The attack was launched with the right flank entirely exposed, and it was in great part machine gun fire from this flank which held up the advance.

A holding attack against the Southern flank of the village by one company and a strong attack launched from the Eastern edge of BOURLON WOOD after the troops on the left had got forward, would possibly have resulted in the capture of the objective. The success of the operation appeared to depend upon the enemy retiring without fighting - in the face of stubborn resistance it was doomed to failure.

Lieut Colonel,
Commanding 6th Gordon Highlanders.

28th November, 1917.

6TH GORDON HIGHLANDERS.

Nominal Roll of Officers who remained with Echelon "A"
During Operations 20th - 23rd November, 1917.

    Major A.A. Duff, C.I.E., M.V.O.
    Lieut. R. Risk, M.C.
       . A.E. Paterson.
       . W. Duffus.
       . J. F. Allan

Nominal Roll of Officers who remained with Echelon "B"
During Operations 20th - 23rd November, 1917.

    Captain Sir J.H. Seton, Bart.
    Lieut. R. F. Simpson.
    2/Lieut. J.S. Riddell.
       . N.J. Wilson.
       . J.L. Hay.

LIST OF OFFICERS OF 6TH BATTALION GORDON HIGHLANDERS, WHO TOOK PART IN THE OPERATIONS 20TH - 23RD NOVEMBER, 1917.

RANK.	NAME.			REMARKS.
Lieut. Colonel	Fraser, Hon. W.		M.C.	Commanding Officer.
Captain	Clark	D.G.	M.C.	Company Commander.
a/Captain	Christie	J.R.		Company Commander.
"	Minty	G.		Company Commander.
"	Archibald	J.		Acting Adjutant.
Lieutenant	Carnie	A.J.W.		
"	Duffus	W.		
"	McKay	K.		Company Commander.
"	Hector	J.		
2/Lieutenant	Raitt	J.L.		Signalling Officer.
"	Thomson	T.D.		
"	Miller	A.D.	M.C.	
"	Taylor	W.		
"	~~Wilson N.~~			
"	Rutherford	G.		
"	Robson	R.M.		
"	Robinson	A.E.T.		
"	Hastings	G.G.		
"	Watson	J.A.		
"	Crichton	R.R.		
"	Reid	W.J.		
Captain	McKelvey	D.	M.C.	R.A.M.C. (Attached).

- - - - - - - - - - - - - - - - - - -

RANK.	NAME.			REMARKS.
Lieut. Colonel	Fraser, Hon. W.		M.C.	Commanding Officer.

APPENDIX.

BATTLE CASUALTIES.

OFFICERS.

KILLED.

    Captain G. Minty   (C)   23.11.17.
    2/Lieut. R. R. Crichton (D)   20.11.17.

WOUNDED.

2/Lieut.	Thomson	T.D.	(A)	23.11.17.
"	Robinson	A.H.T.	(A)	23.11.17.
"	Watson	J.A.	(B)	20.11.17.
"	Caldwell	G.I.	(B)	23.11.17.
"	Robson	R.W.	(C)	.
* "	Reid	W.J.	(C)	.
"	Hastings	G.O.	(D)	20.11.17.
Lieut.	Duffus	T.	(D)	23.11.17.
"	Hector	J.	(D)	.

*check if wounds

OTHER RANKS.

KILLED.

40923	L/C Jackson	J.	(A)	23.11.17.
267807	Pte King	J.	(A)	.
S/41496	" Reid	J.	(A)	.
266290	" Reid	G.	(B)	20.11.17.
201778	L/C Fraser	J.	.	.
266375	Pte Petrie	G.	.	.
265608	L/C Nicol	W.	.	.
S/14368	Pte Norman	W.	.	.
288029	" Marshall	A.B.	.	.
202950	" Hunter	W.	.	.
202045	" Dalrymple	R.	.	23.11.17.
266530	L/C Gordon	T.	(C)	.
266286	" Smith	R.	(C)	.
17744	Pte Gregson	R.	.	.
17408	" Hadden	J.	.	.
202406	" Gerrie	B.	.	.
265165	" Johnstone	J.G.	(D)	20.11.17.
202572	L/C Goodall	W.	.	.
265368	Pte Duncan	D.	.	.
14976	" Coutts	J.	.	.
266264	" Innes	A.	.	.
265674	" Alexander	J.	.	.
15370	" Martin	M.	.	.
17057	" Stephen	W.	.	.
11305	" Nelson	J.	.	.
285088	" Grieve	W.	.	.
17022	" Yeats	H.	.	.
17689	" Tait	J.	.	.
290126	" Pirie	J.	.	23.11.17.

WOUNDED.

265700	Sgt Phimister	J.	(A)	23.11.17.
265795	Cpl Garden	D.D.	.	.
266063	" Weir	D.	.	.
240382	L/C Davidson	J.	.	.
241373	" Findlay	J.	.	.
202078	" Hunter	A.	.	.
12718	" Lewis	T.	.	.
1404	" Lines	R.	.	.
12881	" Mitchell	A.	.	.
292167	Pte Murison	.	.	.
288048	" Steedman	G.	.	.
13151	L/C Syme	F.	.	.
265260	" Thomson	A.	.	.
17322	Pte Aitken	J.	.	.
266610	" Bowell	J.	.	.
288219	" Bremner	G.	.	.
288618	" Booth	R.	.	.
17683/				

Page 2.

WOUNDED (continued)

17682	Pte	Cameron	K.	(A)	23.11.17.
266032	"	Christie	T.	"	"
292420	"	Cathey	G.	"	"
17256	"	Donald	C.	"	"
240235	"	Dunbar	A.	"	"
265291	"	Davie	T.	"	"
266006	"	Flanagan	J.	"	"
13356	"	Fulton	D.	"	"
17712	"	Hadden	G.	"	"
285063	"	Hunter	A.	"	"
17974	"	Jack	J.	"	"
265771	"	Johnstone	J.	"	"
265686	L/C	Finnison	K.M.	"	"
266877	Pte	Lamont	J.	"	"
285064	"	Langslow	O.	"	"
202993	"	Lashie	W.	"	"
17268	"	Morgan	C.	"	"
266786	"	Myles	J.	"	"
17683	"	McKay	J.	"	"
263286	"	McLaren	E.D.	"	"
266052	"	McKinnie	B.	"	"
266906	"	McGregor	G.	"	"
15795	"	O'Shaughnessy	P.	"	"
14040	"	Paterson	A.	"	"
266968	"	Skinner	W.C.	"	"
13732	"	Swan	L.	"	"
10815	"	Stalker	D.	"	"
7795	"	Thomson	H.	"	"
266311	"	Taylor	G.A.	"	"
240370	"	Taylor	J.	"	"
266865	"	Wiseman	H.	"	"
17272	"	Watson	F.	"	"
11168	"	Welsh	P.	"	"
266856	"	Watson	G.	"	"
265562	C.S.M.	Forbes	J.	"	"
265046	Pte	Cormack	A.	"	"
285040	"	Hamilton	J.	"	"
240503	"	Jaffray	C.	"	"
18196	"	Smurthwaite	A.	"	"
415604	Pte	Stoddart	J.	(B)	20.11.17.
265744	Sgt	Chisholm	J.	"	"
4650	Pte	Blakeman	J.	"	" (shell shock)
266986	L/C	Massie	M.	"	"
11305	Pte	Roberston	W.	"	"
201148	"	Thomson	O.	"	"
291963	"	Leighton	A.M.	"	"
266639	"	Craven	J.	"	"
6996	Cpl	Reid	M.	"	"
266273	"	Ross	W.	"	"
295237	Pte	Morrison	W.	"	"
10002	"	Marshall	J.	"	"
265338	"	Caesar		"	"
265748	Cpl	Dawson	J.	"	23.11.17.
266412	Pte	Baudison	I.	"	"
265290	Cpl	Thomson	H.	"	"
14085	Pte	McDonald	J.	"	"
240985	"	Munro	J.A.	"	"
15151	L/C	Nolan	C.	"	"
266140	"	Burnett	J.	"	"
285024	Pte	Riddell	D.	"	"
265620	Sgt	Smith	J.D.	(C)	21.11.17.
265704	"	Chalmers	H.	(C)	23.11.17.
265395	"	Ross	J.	"	"
s/14355	L/C	Thomson	W.	"	"
265650	"	Thow	W.G.	"	"
202466	"	Simpson	J.	"	"
265266	"	Lowe	F.	"	"
266095	"	Hutcheon	G.	"	"
201603	"	Howell	G.	"	"
266102	"	Johnstone	W.	"	"
266064/					

Page 3.

Wounded (continued)

266064	L/C.	Pickford	P.	(D)	23.11.17.
285065	"	Quinny	A.	"	"
40201	Pte.	Clark	A.G.	"	"
316278	"	McKay	A.	"	"
266903	"	Milne	W.S.	"	"
S/40915	"	Gavin	P.	"	"
285126	"	Wilson	J.W.	"	"
S/18881	"	Hutchison	W.	"	"
17014	"	Greig	A.	"	"
285076	"	Finnimore	L.	"	"
S/17400	"	Hassie	A.	"	"
242008	"	Guy	W.S.	"	"
288018	"	Carson	J.	"	"
S/18848	"	Henzie	P.	"	"
266999	"	Wood	R.	"	"
265500	"	Grant	J.	"	"
202957	"	McNaughton	W.	"	"
41183	"	Maxwell	W.	"	"
285086	"	Sweeney	J.	"	"
285002	"	Corrigan	J.A.	"	"
S/15927	"	Wilson	J.A.	"	"
203004	"	Robertson	G.S.	"	"
S/41186	"	Hogan	G.	"	21.11.17.
6206	"	McDonald	P.	"	23.11.17.
S/17316	"	Gunn	W.	"	"
28800S	"	Radden	W.	"	"
241876	"	Gallacher	P.	"	"
285055	"	Steele	A.	"	"
43252	"	Rambling	W.	"	"
265040	"	Munro	W.	"	"
43637	L/C.	Gibb	J.	"	"
S/17484	Pte.	Anderson	A.	"	"
70808	Pte.	Simons	P.	(D)	20.11.17.
285050	"	Swanson	J.	"	"
40062	"	Stirling	R.	"	"
285000	"	Marshall	R.	"	"
40623	"	Young	J.	"	"
265171	L/C.	Morrison	W.	"	"
290172	Pte.	Silver	F.	"	"
6287	"	Leiper	P.	"	"
266236	L/C.	Ross	W.	"	"
201975	"	Minnie	J.	"	"
11025	Pte.	Walker	W.	"	"
43590	"	Drummond	M.	"	"
6200	"	Young	J.	"	"
17656	"	Felman	J.	"	"
285057	"	Hope	J.	"	"
285135	"	Spence	J.	"	"
288058	"	Kelly	H.	"	"
20410	L/C.	Christie	W.	"	"
285894	"	McKay	A.	"	"
292017	Pte	Bowie	W.	"	"
267024	"	Thomson	W.S.	"	"
266070	"	Ingram	J.	"	"
242020	"	Munro	W.	"	"
235425	"	West	A.	"	"
11077	"	Lyon	R.	"	"
266482	"	Medley	W.T.	"	"
288067	"	McIntosh	A.	"	23.11.17.
265270	"	Sutherland	W.	"	"
266978	L/C	Davidson	A.	"	"
288066	Pte	McKillan	W.	"	"
14851	L/C	Kerr	J.	"	"
17510	Pte	McLeod	W.	"	"
17714	"	Donald	F.	"	"
3643	"	Cliffe	I.	"	"
265063	L/C	Beans	J.	"	"
41454	Pte	Gillespie	J.	"	"
10143	"	Powell	J.	"	"
288037	"	Johnstone	W.	"	"
17304	"	Ewen	A.	"	"
267025/					

Page 4.

WOUNDED (continued).

267025	Cpl Stewart	J.	(D)	20.11.17. (Enemy barbed wire).
15933	L/C Murray	J.	(D)	20.11.17 admitted 22.11.17
10730	Pte McNeill	J.	.	23.11.17.
298035	. Black	A.	.	20.11.17.
240867	. Smith	E.C.	.	23.11.17.

WOUNDED - REMAINING AT DUTY.

266960	Pte Thom	A.A.	(C)	G.S.W. knee (r)	23.11.17.
295193	. McClelland	D.	(D)	G.S.W. knee	23.11.17.
41167	. Duncan	J.	(A)	G.S.W. arm	23.11.17.

DIED OF WOUNDS.

41185	Pte Muirhead	J.	(D)	20.11.17.

UNACCOUNTED FOR.

241145	Pte Clark	R.	(A)	23.11.17.
3774	. Malloch	G.	(A)	.
266455	L/C Watt	G.R.	(A)	.
S/40264	Pte Way	H.	(A)	.
403950	. Duncan	W.	(D)	20.11.17.
285117	. Conley	T.	(D)	23.11.17.
266562	. Henderson	W.J.	(D)	.

-o-o-o-o-o-o-o-o-o-

SECRET.   Copy No. 10

6th Bn. Gordon Highlanders.
OPERATION ORDERS NO. 145.
16th November 1917.

Reference Maps :-   51 C.
                     Lens 11.

1. The 51st (H) Division will concentrate in IVth Corps area.

2. The Battalion, less Transport and Echelon "B", will move by rail to ACQUINCY tomorrow 17th Novr. 1917.

3.   Entraining Station   -   BEAUMETZ - les - LOGES.

       Detraining Station   -   BAPAUME.

4. Instructions for march to Entraining Station :-

       Time   -   5.20 a.m.

       Starting Point -   L.34.b.3.8.

       Route   -   Station DAINVILLE, Main ARRAS-
                                                 BOULOGNE Road - BEAUMETZ -
                                                 les - LOGES.

       Interval   -   200 Yards between Companies.

   An officer will march in rear of each Company.

5. Transport will move under orders of Transport Officer on 16/17th Novr. 1917 according to Brigade Instructions.

6. Echelon "B" will move by march route to "Y" Huts under Capt. Sir J. E. Seton Bart., according to Instructions issued separately.

7. Officers' Valises and Mess Kit will be at various Messes ready for collection by 5 p.m. today.
   Officers may retain a limited personal and mess kit, which will travel with Blanket Lorries. These should be sent to Store along with mens' blankets.

8. One Blanket per man will be carried on the man. The remainder will be rolled in bundles and sent to store by Echelon "B" party by 9 a.m.
   Lorries will report at Head Quarters at 9 a.m. for transport of these.
   R.Q.M.S. REID will arrange for billeting party of 4, who will travel with lorries.
   Lorries must not start before 3 p.m.

9. Cooking utensils will be retained. These will be carried to new area.
   Fresh meat for tomorrow's dinners will be boiled today and issued cold to men tonight.

10. Breakfasts will be at 4 a.m.

11. Billeting party of 2/Lieut. C.G. MACPHERSON and 1 N.C.O. per Company will report to Captain MACDONALD at the station BEAUMETZ les - LOGES at 6.30 a.m.
    Lieut. Y

2.

11.   Lieut. MACLEAN will be prepared to give exact number of personnel entraining and assist in allotment of trucks.
    They will report to Staff Captain on arrival at BEAULIEU JUNCTION.
    N.C.Os will report to Lieut. MACLEAN at orderly room at 5 a.m.

12.   Acknowledge.

                    (Signed) J. ARCHIBALD Capt. & A/Adjt.

                        6th Gordon Highlanders.

Copy No. 1   File.
        2.   H.Q. 152nd Inf. Brigade.
        3-6   Companies.
        7   Transport Officer.
        8   H.Q.M.Lgt.
        9   O. i/c H.Q. Details.
        10.   H.Q. Mess.

SECRET.   Copy No. 9

6th Gordon Highlanders

OPERATION ORDERS   No. 146.

16th November 1917.

1. (a) On a date and at an hour to be notified later, the 51st Division, with the 62nd Division on its left and the 6th Division on its right, will attack the enemy's positions, as shown on Maps already issued.
    The 51st Division will attack with :-
    152nd Infantry Brigade on the right,
    153rd Infantry Brigade on the left,
    154th Infantry Brigade in reserve.

    (b) 152nd Infantry Brigade will attack as follows:-

    Blue Line - 1st objective (i.e. ground up to and including Railway) will be captured by the 5th Seaforth High-
    -landers on the right, and the 8th Argyll & Sutherland Highlanders on the left.

    Brown Line - 2nd objective (i.e. ground up to and including FLESQUIERES Trench) will be captured by 6th Gordon Highlanders on the right, and the 6th Seaforth High-
    -landers on the left.
    These latter Battalions will be prepared to occupy later the line of the road I.9.d.2.0 - I.2.c.7.2 (Red dotted Line) upon receipt of orders to do so.

2. The 6th Gordon Highlanders will attack as follows:-
    (a) "B" Company will capture the HINDENBURG SUPPORT LINE from I.19.b.5.0. (approximate) to I.19.b.6.2. (approx.) with two platoons, and FLESQUIERES Trench from I.19.b.9.4. (approximate) to I.19.b.2.5. (approximate) with two platoons. "D" Company will capture the HINDENBURG SUPPORT LINE from I.19.b.6.2. (approximate) - I.19.a.4.3. (approx) with two platoons, and FLESQUIERES Trench I.19.b.2.5. (approximate) - I.19.a.7.6. (approximate) with two platoons.
    On capture of these objectives, an outpost line will be pushed forward beyond FLESQUIERES Trench. The exact distance cannot be laid down, but the object will be to obtain observation down Northern slopes of FLESQUIERES Ridge.
    (b) "A" and "C" Companies will be in reserve. They will move forward on receipt of orders from Battalion Headquarters to the neighbourhood of the GRAND RAVINE, and will be in readiness to advance and occupy the Red Dotted Line (I.9.d.2.0. - I.2.c.9.0.) on receipt of orders to that effect.
    In this case "B" and "D" Companies will be prepared to move forward in rear of "A" and "C" Companies, if so ordered.

3. The attack will be carried out under a barrage, and the advance of the infantry will be preceded by Tanks.
    Six Tanks have been specially detailed for capture of second objective on the Battalion front, but these will be reinforced by all Tanks surviving from capture of First Objective.
    The leading waves of infantry will advance about 200 yards in rear of the general line of tanks.

2.

4.   Details of the attack are as follows:-
The artillery barrage will open on the enemy front line at ZERO. At this hour the leading wave of Tanks will be moving forward from their positions of assembly.
The attack will be carried through to BOLD Trench without pause, after which there will be a pause of one hour to enable troops on the right to deal with village of AIRECOURT.
During this hour any resistance on this side of GRAND RAVINE will be dealt with.
The attack on second objective will commence at ZERO plus 120, irrespective of situations in villages of AIRECOURT and RAVALCOURT, and will be initiated by the advance of one Company of each of 5th Seaforth Highlanders and 8th Argyll & Sutherland Highlanders to line of the railway.
After capture of BROWN LINE, one Company of Tanks will be speedily re-organised and will move forward to capture any guns that may be in valleys beyond.

5.   Companies of the 6th Gordon Highlanders detailed for capture of second objective ("B" and "D" Companies) will move forward from their positions of assembly as follows:-
First Wave at ZERO plus 90
Second Wave at ZERO plus 100.
This should allow a distance of approximately 300 yards between waves.

6.   Officers Commanding Companies will be responsible for maintaining touch with troops on their flanks throughout the advance, and special parties will be detailed for this purpose on the capture of each objective.
Troops on flanks will be as follows:-
On the left throughout the advance - 6th Seaforth Highlanders
On the right, up to and including BROWN LINE, -
On the right beyond BROWN LINE - 9th Norfolk Regiment.

7.   Companies will be formed up for the attack as follows:-
"D" Company - Behind parados of BEAUCAMP Reserve on either side of SHAFTESBURY AVENUE.
"B" Company - West of SHAFTESBURY AVENUE about Q.11.b.3.3.
"A" Company - HACKSAW Trench, East of SHAFTESBURY AVENUE.
"C" Company - West of SHAFTESBURY AVENUE about Q.11.c.5.6. (opposite junction of BROKEN Trench and SHAFTESBURY AVENUE).

Should there be no hostile shelling after ZERO officers Commanding "B" and "D" Companies will be prepared to move forward to our front line on receipt of orders to do so.

8.   The attack of 152nd Infantry Brigade will be covered by:-
256th Brigade R.F.A.
70th Brigade R.F.A.
4th Brigade R.H.A.
The whole essence of the operation being surprise, there will be no preliminary bombardment.
A proper centage of the guns will be used to form a smoke barrage on the FLESQUIERES RIDGE during initial stages of the attack.

9./

Page. 3.

9. Two men per platoon in the two leading Companies will carry red flags to mark crossing places for Tanks over the German trenches. One man will place his flag where previous Tank has crossed, while the other man will proceed to guide succeeding Tanks to that place.

Immediately a trench is cleared of the enemy, and touch obtained on either flank, platoon Commanders will take steps to fill in the trench where the red flag has been posted, by having the spoil forming the parados shovelled back into the trench. At each crossing place work must continue until the trench is filled in up to the ground level, and a track suitable for all arms has been formed.

As opportunity permits lanes will be cut in the German wire opposite these crossing places.

10. The use of "P" Bombs is to be restricted as much as possible so that we may not be deprived of the use of German dugouts.

11. The following will be marked by flags, as shown:-
  Brigade Headquarters - Red Pennant
  Bn. H.Q. 5th Sea. Hrs- Regt. Badge (Gold)
          Green Flag.
   do. 6th Sea.Hrs.- Regt. Badge (Red)
          Blue Flag.
          (2 Red Stripes)
   do. 6th Gor. Hrs- Yellow Flag.
   do. 8th A & S.Hrs - A. & S Tartan
          3'6" x 2' with four
          red stripes on it.

  Dumps - Brigade) Blue Flag with Red "D"
   do - Battalion)

  Regt. Aid Post at Q.10.b.8.2. - Red Cross

12. The position of Battalion Headquarters at ZERO hour will be in REDOUBT SUPPORT Q.12.a.4.7. It will move forward (probably after capture of second objective) along line of communication trench which forms approximate right boundary of Battalion during advance.

13 acknowledge.

    (Signed) J. Archibald Capt. &Adj.
      6th Gordon Highlanders.

Copies to:-
 No 1 File
  2 H.Q. 152nd Inf. Brigade
 3 - 6 Companies
  7 O. I/c H.Q. Details.
 9 - 12 Spare
  8 Major A.a Duff

S E C R E T

APPENDIX I
Subject - S.O.S. Signals.

1. The S.O.S. signals to be used in the coming operations will be as follows:-

   (a) IVth Corps   Rifle Grenade bursting into two RED and two WHITE

   (b) III Corps   (on our right) Rifle Grenade bursting into two GREEN and two WHITE.

   (c) VIth Corps   (on our left) Rifle Grenade bursting into two RED and two GREEN.

   (d) DIVISION   GREEN - 1" Very Light

2. In an emergency two RED and two WHITE Very Lights may be used as an S.O.S. Signal by 51st Division.

(signed) J. Archibald Capt. & A/Adjt.
6th Gordon Highlanders.

SECRET.

APPENDIX II.

Subject – Intelligence Arrangements.

1. **Prisoners of War.**

    Prisoners of war will be sent under escort to Collecting Post at TRESCAULT Q.10.a.4.4, where A.P.M. will take them over.

    Officer prisoners should be searched for documents on capture, and their documents sent to Forward Collecting Post in charge of escort.

    N.C.Os. and Men should NOT be searched for documents until they arrive at the Corps Cage, where arrangements will be made for this. Weapons only will be removed.

2. **Captured Documents.**

    Coys. will arrange for special parties to search dugouts and H.Q.s for documents. Documents and one-half of the Identity Disc should be taken from German dead, (the other half should be left on the body). All such documents and discs collected are to be forwarded immediately to Bn. H.Q.,

3. **Maps to be carried.**

    In order to avoid any chance of information falling into the hands of the enemy, no documents, maps shewing our trenches, secret maps or papers (including private letters) will be taken into action, with the following exceptions :-
    - (a) Beaucamp Sheet – 1/10,000.
    - (b) Demicourt   "   –   do.
    - (c) Marcoing   "   –   do.
    - (d) Bourbon   "   –   do.
    - (e) Flesquieres (Message Maps).
    - (f) Ribecourt   (do.   )
    - (g) Mierquies   – 1/20,000.
    - (h) Gouzeaucourt   –   do.
    - (i) Moeuvres   –   do.
    - (j) Valenciennes   – 1/100,000.

4. **Bab Code.**

    The Bab Code will not be taken into action. Copies will be returned to Bn. H.Q., for safe custody on "Y" day.

(Signed) J. ARCHIBALD. Capt. & A/Adj.

6th Gordon Highlanders.

SECRET.

APPENDIX III.

Subject - Contact Patrol and Flares
- - - - - - - - - - - - - - - - - -

1.　　　No 15 Squadron R.F.C. are detailing Contact Aeroplanes to take flare signals on "Z" day at times to be notified later.

2.　　　Each Contact Aeroplane will be marked with a black rectangular sign 6ak 16' x 1" on the rear edge of the lower plane on each side, and will fly along the line some 300 yards in rear of our foremost posts, sounding a KLAXON horn.
　　　The KLAXON horn is the signal to get ready to light flares. No flares will be lit till the Airman fires a rocket or rockets which is the signal to light WHITE flares.

3.　　　It is of great importance that flares should be lit whenever called for as above whether the time happens to be that ordered or not.

4.　　　As it is of vital importance to the success of the operations that immediate information of our position after the capture of the second objective is available, Commanding Officers will ensure that the lighting of flares at this period has the special attention of all officers.

　　　　　　　　　　　　(signed) J. Archibald, Capt. & A/Adj.
　　　　　　　　　　　　　　　　6th Gordon Highlanders.

B.B.C.M.R.

APPENDIX IV

SUBJECT – LOCATION OF, and DISTRIBUTION OF STORES in DUMPS

1. The Location, Designation and Contents of Dumps are as follows; they will be denoted by a Blue Flag with a Red "D" in the centre.

	"A" Dump "CLAY TRENCH" Q.11.a.8.9.	"B" Dump where "STAFFORD DUGOUT" Trench cuts Sunken Rd. Q.11.b.9.7.	"C" Dump At junction of HASU LANE with front line Q.5.d.8.5.
Stokes Bombs Rds.	500	250	250
S.A.A. Rds.	50,000	50,000	50,000
S.O.B. Grenades Rds.	100	75	75
Rifle Grenades No 23.	.	250	250
do. 24	500	500	500
"P" Bombs	.	200	200
Mills Grenades No 5	.	250	250
Very Lights			
1" White	200	500	500
1" Red	100	50	50
1" Green	100	50	50
Ground Flares	200	500	500
Watley Pistol Amn. Rds.	.	276	276
Tins of Water	.	50	50
Sandbags	500	250	250
Lewis Gun Drums filled	64	.	.
Yukon Packs	.	30	30

In addition to the above 3000 Iron Rations and 300 tins of water will be stored at Brigade Headquarters Q.10.d.2.8. ready to go forward by pack animals under Brigade arrangements.

The foregoing will be formed before "Z" day, and the following will be formed probably about noon on "Z" day; the stores being taken forward by pack transport.

	Advanced dump A.S.D.R...	Rainbow dump 100 yards south of main road junction in P.O.W.?
A...	...	10000	30 ...
Very Lights:			
1" white		4 boxes	
Rifle Grenades No 3		10 boxes	
Rifle Grenades No 23		10 boxes	
do. 24		10 boxes	
Tins of water		30	10

All No 3 and No 23 Grenades will be detonated by the dump personnel.
Grenades No 24 will be detonated by parties drawing same from dump.

6. Each unit on the Brigade front is carrying for the use of the Infantry:-
2 boxes ......
1 box "D" bombs
10 P.H. Bag..... filled.

(Signed) F. Macdonald. Capt, a/Adjt,
6th Gordon Highlanders.

SECRET

APPENDIX V

KIT — BOMB.

1. **Fighting Dress** — Fighting Order with jerkins

2. Picks and shovels will be carried in the ratio of one pick to one shovel. 50% of the men will carry these.

3. Each man will carry 170 rounds S.A.A. except the following, who will carry 50 rounds:-
    Scouts
    Runners
    Signallers
    Lewis Gunners.

4. **Bombing Sections** will carry:-
    12 No 5 Mills Grenades
    12 No 23 Rifle Grenades
    2 "P" Bombs

5. **Rifle Section**
    Two men of each Rifle Section will carry —
        6 No 24 Rifle Grenades
    Four men of each Rifle Section will carry —
        1 No 5 Mills Grenade

6. Two men per platoon S.O.S. Rockets, Pistols and Lights as usual.

7. Every second man will carry a Ground Flare.

8. A complete preserved ration in addition to the Iron Ration will be carried.

9. In accordance with above seven picks and seven shovels per platoon will be issued along with grenades, "P" Bombs, Very Lights, S.O.S. Rockets, and rations at UNIT

(signed) J. Archibald, Capt. & A/ADJ.
6th Gordon Highlanders.

Acknowledge.

SECRET   Copy No. 10

6th Gordon Highlanders
Addendum to
OPERATION ORDER No. 145.
17th November, 1917.

1.   Should the attack be successful in its earlier stages, the advance of "A" & "C" Companies will not be limited by the SUNKEN ROAD (L.9.c.) but will, in all probability be continued to enemy line, L.3.d.4.3. - L.10.d.6.7. (MIUS WOOD - BOURLON ;Inc). This advance will however be dependant on the situation on the flanks.

   Any advance beyond this line will be undertaken by fresh troops.

2.   The advance beyond FLESQUIERES TRENCH will be initiated by Tanks, if these are available, but it will not be dependant on Tanks. Provided that the flanks are secure, Companies will push forward by their own power if the Tanks fail. The most suitable formation will in all probability be section columns, covered by Scouts, who should push forward about 200 yards in front of their Platoons.

3.   ACKNOWLEDGE.

                    (Signed) J. ARCHIBALD, Capt. & A/Adjt.
                              6th Gordon Highlanders.

Copies to :-

   No 1   File.
      2   H.Q. 152nd Infantry Brigade.
    3 - 6 Companies.
      7   O.C. Headquarters Details.
      8   Major A. A. DUFF.
    9 -12 Spare.

SECRET

ANNEXE VII.

SUBJECT :- SIGNAL COMMUNICATIONS.

Communications within the Battalion and to Brigade will be maintained as follows :-
(1) Runners.
(2) Visual.
(3) Pigeons.
(4) Wire.

1. **RUNNERS.**

Runners will form the most important part of the signal organisation during operations.

Each Runner must know the position of the Headquarters of the next higher formation, i.e. Platoon Runners to know Company Headquarters, etc.

Full use should be made of the Brigade Signal Stations at F.36.a.2.2. and I.19.a.2.0. where messages may be handed in for transmission to Battalion Headquarters. In case of these Stations not being through, Runners must understand that messages must be delivered personally at Battalion Headquarters.

2. **VISUAL.**

Full advantage will be taken of this method from the FLOUGISTEED RIDGE to the rear, and also from the final objective to the FLOUGISTEED RIDGE from which no answer must be expected however.

3. **PIGEONS.**

Two birds are allotted to each Company and two to Battalion Headquarters.

These birds will be let off by "B" & "D" Companies when they have taken their objective, with a message to that effect.

"A" & "C" Companies must keep their birds until they reach their final objective. If possible the same two birds should carry the messages for both "B" & "D" Companies or "A" & "C" Companies as the case may be.

4. **WIRE.**

Lines will be run out to Companies as soon as circumstances permit, from Battalion Headquarters by H.Q. Signals, after Companies get settled in their final objectives.

5. Acknowledge

(Signed) J. ARMSTRONG, Capt. & A/Adj.
5th Gordon Highlanders.

SECRET.

6TH GORDON HIGHLANDERS.

OPERATION ORDERS No. 147.

18th November, 1917.

- - - - - - - - - - - - - - - -

Reference Maps :-
    VALENCIENNES 12.
    LENS 11.
    57 C. 1/40?000.

1.   The Battalion will move by route march to METZ to-night, 18th November, 1917.

    STARTING POINT   -   O.27.b.8.0.

    TIME   -   4.27 p.m.

    ORDER OF MARCH   -   H.Q., D., C., B., A. Coys.

    ROUTE   -   BUS - YTRES - Cross Roads
                  P.22.d.0.6. Road Junction
                  P.28.b.5.9. - METZ.

    INTERVAL BETWEEN
        COMPANIES -   10 Yards.

2.   Transport will move under orders of Transport Officer.

      Cookers will accompany Battalion; the horses will return to NEUVILLE to-night. Transport Officer will arrange to send on baggage wagons, Mess Carts and Lewis Gun Limbers immediately on arrival in NEUVILLE. These will be met at entrance to METZ and guided to Battalion Area.

3.   Officers' baggage and Mess Kits will be loaded on wagons by 4 p.m.

4.   One blanket will be carried on the men.
      The remainder will be dumped in one Billet per Company, ready for loading. Quartermaster will supervise loading, for which purpose Companies will detail two men each to be left behind and travel with lorries. 2/Lieut. C. G. BLACKLAWS will arrange for guide to collect two lorries from road in front of Camp Commandant's Office at 3 p.m.

5.   ACKNOWLEDGE.

                            (signed) J. ARCHIBALD, Capt. & Adj.
                                    6th Gordon Highlanders.

6TH GORDON HIGHLANDERS.

OPERATION ORDERS — NO. 149.

23rd November, 1917.

✱
The attack will be
carried out by the
6th Sea. H⁰ˢ on the left;
and the 6th Gor. H⁰ˢ on
the right; the 8th A&SH
will form a defensive
flank, and the 5th S.H
will be in Brigade
Reserve.

1. At an hour to be notified later the 152nd Infantry Brigade will capture and consolidate high ground north of FONTAINE NOTRE DAME, at same time forming a defensive flank ✱ to right. The final of and boundaries of attack will be as shown to O.S.C., Companies, on the Map.

2. The attack by the 6th Gordon Highlanders will be carried out as follows :-

1st Objective, (Railway Line North of FONTAINE NOTRE DAME from F.16.a.8.5. - F. 15. b.c.7.) will be captured by "A" Coy. on the right and "C" Coy. on the left. These Companies will advance in two waves, two platoons in each wave, at a distance of one hundred yards between each wave.

2nd Objective, will be captured by "D" Company on the right and "B" Company on the left. These Companies will advance in two waves leading wave two hundred yards in rear of last wave of two front Companies; one hundred yards between ~~in~~ each wave in the Company.

All waves will advance in columns of sections in single file with the exception of leading wave, which will be extended in single rank, but in this wave too, sections will keep well together during the advance through the village.

The rear platoons of leading Companies must push forward quickly on entering Village, and assist leading platoons in its capture.

When Companies for 1st Objective reach the Railway they will consolidate in depth, and Companies for 2nd Objective will pass through.

3. The attack will be preceded by Tanks.

4. The Battalion will form up on PREMY CHAPEL - GRAINCOURT ROAD, between the points L.1.d.10.50. and L.1.d.o.8. by 6.30 a.m.

No movement at all will be permitted in the assembly position in order to avoid being seen by low flying enemy aircraft.

5. Artillery/

5. Artillery barrage and Smoke screen will be notified later.

6. Ground Flares and S.O.S. Grenades will be issued in Assembly position.

7. Cookers will remain where they are at present. Capt. McCombie will keep in touch with movements of Battalion and push forward Cookers at his own descretion when feasible. Every endeavour must be made to give the men a hot meal in the evening after the operation.

Water Carts with horses will stand by and move forward under orders of Transport Officer.

(signed) J. ARCHIBALD   Capt. & A/Adj,
6th Gordon Highlanders.

6TH GORDON HIGHLANDERS.

OPERATION ORDERS NO. 150.

24th November, 1917.

Reference Maps:-
   57C 1/40,000.
   LENS 11.

1. The Battalion will move from present Area and proceed to SENLIS to-day, 24th current, by route march, bus, and train, in accordance with Table as under :-

STARTING POINT	Battalion Headquarters.
TIME	3.30 p.m.
ORDER OF MARCH	H.Q., B, D, A, C.
INTERVAL BETWEEN COMPANIES	200 Yards.
EMBUSSING POINT	METZ Q.19.b.0.5.
TIME	8 p.m.
ENTRAINING STATION	YPRES.
TIME	10 p.m.
DETRAINING STATION	AVELUY.

2. Special attention will be paid to discipline on the march and at embussing and debussing, entraining and detraining points.

3. Leather Jerkins will be worn, and Greatcoats carried bandolier fashion.

4. Battalion will halt at Quarry in HAVRINCOURT WOOD near foot of SHAFTESBURY AVENUE, when teas will be served.

5. All Battalion Stores which have not already been handed in will be carried to New Area.

6. Immediately on arrival at entraining point one N.C.O. per Company will report to 2/Lieut. C.G. BLACKLAWS, who will report to Lieut. CUMMING, Brigade Headquarters, at Station.

7. ACKNOWLEDGE.

(signed) J. ARCHIBALD Capt. & A/Adj,
6th Gordon Highlanders.

6th GORDON HIGHLANDERS.

SUPPLEMENTARY ORDERS FOR DEMONSTRATION ATTACK.

1. Objectives to be captured will be as follows, and not as stated in original order.

   <u>FIRST OBJECTIVE</u> — Enemy Front Line.
   <u>SECOND OBJECTIVE</u> — Enemy Second Line (about 500 yards beyond Front Line).

2. Enemy Front Line will be captured by "A" Company on a front of 4 Platoons, and advancing in one wave.

   Enemy Second Line will be captured by "C" & "D" Companies as in original order.

   "B" Company will be in reserve, and will move forward to vicinity of original enemy front line as soon as final objective has been reached. It will form the local reserve for counter-attack.

3. The barrage will lift 50 yards in two minutes, not 100 yards in 4 minutes as in original order.

4. Signallers will be with their Companies, and a Battalion Headquarters will be established in our front to which messages will be sent. Visual will be used from final objective

5. Parties will be detailed from troops capturing each objective, to establish communication with imaginary troops on the flanks. All officers must realise the importance of securing their flanks.

6. There will be a practice attack to-morrow (14th instant) at 3 p.m.

   DRESS: Rifles and waist-belts.

7. The Commanding Officer will conduct Company Commanders over the ground at 9.30 a.m. to-morrow (14th inst.). There will be a lecture for all officers at 11 a.m. in connection with the attack.

13th October, 1917.

Lieut. & A/Adj.
6th Gordon Highlanders.

6th GORDON HIGHLANDERS

ORDERS for DEMONSTRATION ATTACK.

1. INTENTION

The Battalion will carry out a demonstration attack before General EDWARDS, United States Army, on Monday 15th instant.

2. INSTRUCTION

The attack will be carried out on a frontage of two companies, each on a front of two platoons.

3. OBJECTIVES

The objectives to be captured are as follows:-
Enemy front and support line, distant 200 yards and 300 yards respectively from assembly trench.
Enemy reserve line distant about 400 yards from enemy support line.
Frontage of attack — about 300 yards.

4. DETAIL OF TROOPS

The enemy front and support lines will be captured by "A" and "B" Companies — "A" Company on the right, "B" Company on the left.
The reserve line will be captured by "C" and "D" Companies, "C" Company on the right, "D" Company on the left.

5. CONSOLIDATION

Each position captured will be consolidated in depth without delay.
In the case of "C" and "D" Companies, where there is only one line to capture, the second wave will pass through the first wave and consolidate 100/150 yards in front of it

6. FORMATION

The attack will be carried out in the usual attack formation practised in the Division — 50 yards between waves and 30 yards between lines in a wave.
Machine Gun Emplacements encountered between objectives/

Page 2.

6. FORMATION
   (continued) objectives must be dealt with without hesitation by the troops to whom they are opposed.

   The necessity of rapid action when held up in this manner, in order to avoid losing the barrage, must be impressed upon all ranks.

7. FLANKS

   It may be assumed that other troops are attacking on the flanks and gain their objectives.

   Flanks will be denoted by flags, both in assembly position and in all objectives.

8. BARRAGE

   The attack will be carried out by a barrage represented by flags.

   The barrage will be organised in two lines. It will open on enemy front line at ZERO hour, and will lift 100 yards every four minutes.

   After capture of final objective the barrage will lift to a line 250 yards in front, and will remain as a protective barrage for 30 minutes after which it will cease.

9. ASSEMBLY

   The Battalion will assemble in our front line trench, "A" and "B" Companies in the trench, "C" and "D" Companies behind the parados.

10. GRENADES

    Rifle Grenades will be carried as follows:-
       Rifle Sections - 12 Nos. 24
       Rifle Grenade
             Sections - 12 Nos. 23

11. DRESS

    Dress:- Fighting Order. Tools will be carried by every other man in rifle and rifle bombing sections in the proportion of one pick to three shovels.

12. STRENGTHS/

Page 3.

12. STRENGTH   Platoons will parade at least 36 strong, including Platoon Headquarters.

13. ZERO HOUR   The Battalion will be in its assembly position half-an-hour before ZERO.   ZERO HOUR will be notified later.

J.L.R.
DSO.

Battalion
after capture and
consolidation of
positions.

Enemy Second Line

Enemy Front Line

British Front Line

Battalion
before attack.

1 Platoon A Coy — ———
1 Platoon D   — ———
1 Platoon C   — ———
1 Platoon B   — ———

O.i.c. O.B.S. Coffin
at the
Base

C. R. Gordon Str

WM 38

Army Form C. 2118.

Instructions regarding War Diaries and Intelligence
Summaries are contained in F. S. Regs., Part II.
and the Staff Manual respectively. Title pages
will be prepared in manuscript.

WAR DIARY
or
INTELLIGENCE SUMMARY.
(Erase heading not required.)

Place	Date 1917	Hour	Summary of Events and Information	Remarks and references to Appendices
MILLENCOURT BARASTRE	Nov. 30th Dec 1st	6.30 p.m 5.15 a.m	The battalion marched to ALBERT and entrained for BAPAUME. Detrained there and marched to BARASTRE which was reached about 5.15 a.m. on 1st December. Inspections were held by Company Commanders during the afternoon. W.R.	O.O.151. Reference Maps LENS 11. FRANCE 57C 1/40.000
FREMICOURT	2nd		Orders were received to move and the battalion marched at 10.30 a.m. for FREMICOURT. On arrival "A" and "B" companies were accommodated in tents, the remainder of the battalion going into huts. The surroundings of the huts and tents were cleaned up. Weather clear and frosty. Enemy aircraft dropped bombs in neighbourhood of village about midnight. W.R.	O.O.152.
	3rd		Companies carried out Close Order and Gas Drill. "A" and "B" companies moved into huts.	
	4th		Orders were received that the 152nd Infantry Brigade was to take over from the 152nd Infantry Brigade in the line, and preparations were made accordingly. The battalion moved off to the trenches at 6.30 p.m.; Companies moved at intervals of 200 yards. Guides for the Companies were picked up at Battalion Headquarters and they proceeded to relieve the 6th Battalion Black Watch. Relief was reported complete at 12.30 a.m. and was carried out without incident or casualty. The dispositions of the battalion in the line were as follows :- "C" Company, LEFT FRONT; "B" Company, RIGHT FRONT; "D" Company, SUPPORT; and "A" Company, IN RESERVE. Battalion sector from left to right runs :- D.21.d.7.3. to D.20.a.3.7. A.J.	O.O.153.
IN TRENCHES	5th		Battalion in the line. The front line system trenches are bad, being very narrow and in some parts shallow. The wire entanglement along the battalion front is fair and considerably above the average. Work was commenced on the parts which were most likely to cause trouble in event of a thaw but this was slow and difficult on account of the frost having penetrated so deep. Cookhouses were built by Companies in their sectors so that hot meals were assured. The neighbourhood of Right Company sector was lightly shelled, resulting in two slight casualties. The night passed quietly.	Reference Map (Special Sheet) MOEUVRES 1/20.000
	6th		Repair of trenches continued. A daylight work party commenced work on a new support line which had been started during the night of 5th/6th. The necessity of having	

Army Form C. 2118.

WAR DIARY
or
INTELLIGENCE SUMMARY.
(Erase heading not required.)

Instructions regarding War Diaries and Intelligence Summaries are contained in F. S. Regs., Part II. and the Staff Manual respectively. Title pages will be prepared in manuscript.

Place	Date	Hour	Summary of Events and Information	Remarks and references to Appendices
IN TRENCHES	DEC. 6th		having deep and wide trenches seems to have been realised at last and the new Support Line will make a good trench. The day passed fairly quiet and frost still holds.	
	7th		Work continued on trenches. Enemy artillery more active during the d.w. Wind South Westerly and fresh. Frost slackened and there is every sign of a thaw.	OO.155
	8th		Usual work continued. Thaw commenced and wind freshening from S.W. An inter-company relief took place at 5 p.m., "A" Company relieving "B" Company, and "D" Company relieving "C" Company. Relief was reported complete at 10.30 p.m. The day passed quietly.	OO.156
	9th		Laying duckboards in new Support line and finishing off sides of trench. Weather fresh and fine.	Reference Map Sheet 57C 1/40.000.
	10th		Enemy artillery showed increased activity throughout the day. The battalion was relieved in the line by the 6th Battalion Black Watch, and on relief marched to FREMICOURT. Relief was reported complete at 10.20 p.m. The total casualties during the tour were two men slightly wounded. The men were in wonderfully good spirits during the whole spell.	
	11th		The day was spent in resting. This battalion is in huts in LOCH CAMP but these huts are very scattered and ground is very wet underfoot.	
FREMICOURT	12th		Kit inspections were carried out by companies. Weather is good but cold.	
	13th		Companies went to baths. Thaw still continues. Improvements on Camp started.	
	14th		Parades for Physical, Close Order and Arm Drill. Special wiring parties commenced under R.E. supervision. Frost has again set in.	
	15th		Parades as on 14th, one Company "A" commenced Range Practice. Frost very intense.	
	16th		Church Parade. Companies/	

Army Form C. 2118.

WAR DIARY
or
INTELLIGENCE SUMMARY.
(Erase heading not required.)

Instructions regarding War Diaries and Intelligence Summaries are contained in F. S. Regs., Part II. and the Staff Manual respectively. Title pages will be prepared in manuscript.

Place	Date	Hour	Summary of Events and Information	Remarks and references to Appendices
FREMICOURT	DEC. 17th		Companies were issued digging practice on specimen trenches. A Lewis Gun Class was commenced under Lewis Gun Officer.	Programme attached
	18th		Digging parades continued. "A" Company on range. Frost continues severe.	(1st)
	19th		Weather so cold that all parades except digging were cancelled.	(2nd)
	20th		Digging continued by Companies. One Company on range.	(3rd)
	21st		Orders were received from Brigade that Companies all battalions were to concentrate on those subdivision, the reason being that all ranks must get a correct impression of how a trench should be dug, and what it looks like when finished. A standard type of trench seems to have been arrived at at last.	(4th)
	22nd		As battalion relieves 7th Battalion Argyll & Sutherland Highlanders, 154th Infantry Brigade, in the line, on the right sector of the Divisional Front, routes were reconnoitred and preparations made. The battalion moved off from LOCH CAMP at 2.45 p.m. marching by platoons at 100 yards interval. Guides were met at Battalion Headquarters and the relief was carried out without a hitch and was reported complete at 7.30 p.m. The night passed quietly, there being little hostile artillery or machine gun fire.	O.O. "P." ADDENDA. Reference MAP Sheet 57c M.C. 000.
IN TRENCHES	23rd	7.30 p.m.	The weather is clear and frosty. A few shells fell about the centre of the battalion front from J.6.2.3. (left) to K.7.c.10.90. (Right), are a great improvement on those of the left sector which the battalion held during its previous tour. The wire is pretty good along the whole front, but as usual there are points where it is weak and has been put out without any system. All cooking is done by companies in their own sectors, water being sent up with rations at night. There are several Store Tanks for water in the Battalion area but these are all frozen. The day passed quietly. A few shells fell about the centre of the battalion front about mid-day, doing no damage. An enemy working party was dispersed by Lewis Gun fire on the main CAMBRAI ROAD. The dispositions of the battalion are as follows :- "B" Company, RIGHT FRONT; "D"	Reference Map DEMICOURT.

Army Form C. 2118.

WAR DIARY
or
INTELLIGENCE SUMMARY.
(Erase heading not required.)

Instructions regarding War Diaries and Intelligence Summaries are contained in F. S. Regs., Part II. and the Staff Manual respectively. Title pages will be prepared in manuscript.

Place	Date	Hour	Summary of Events and Information	Remarks and references to Appendices
IN TRENCHES	DEC. 23/24		"D" Company, LEFT FRONT: "C" Company in SUPPORT, and "A" Company in RESERVE. The reserve company supplies wiring party and mining platoon. Enemy showed no activity during the night. Work was commenced on continuing SETAGHON SUPPORT.	
	24th		The morning being foggy work was continued on Support line and the opportunity taken to make a thorough inspection of the wire along the front. When mist lifted, enemy artillery became rather active and the left centre of the front received a considerable amount of attention about noon and again at 2 p.m. One man in "D" Company was wounded. A fine drizzling rain fell towards dusk, but later it commenced to freeze. The night passed quietly.	
	25th		Christmas Day – In the trenches! Enemy artillery was inactive at different periods during the day especially on left front, where one man was killed in a cubby hole. A freshening wind brought a partial thaw, and some parts of the trenches fell in. Snow fell towards dusk and continued at intervals for an hour or two.	
	26th		The ground is covered with snow to the depth of several inches. There was little artillery activity on either side but increased activity was shown by aircraft. On receipt of orders that Brigade was to remain in the line for two days more, an inter-company relief was carried out and was completed at 7.15 p.m. "A" Company relieved "D" Company, and "C" Company relieved "B" Company.	OO.159
	27th		Enemy artillery was active on whole battalion area throughout the day. Battalion Headquarters received a considerable amount of attention, 5 men being wounded as a result. Weather continues cold. Men are in wonderful spirits. Work on Support Line, deep dug-outs, and wiring carried on.	
	28th		Enemy quiet all day with the exception of a few bursts of fire near Battalion Headquarters. The usual working parties carried on in Support line and dug-outs.	
	29th		Work commenced on Cubby Holes in Front line. The day passed quietly.	
	30th		Enemy artillery more active during the night, tracks to the front line being shelled.	

Army Form C. 2118.

WAR DIARY
or
INTELLIGENCE SUMMARY.

(Erase heading not required.)

Instructions regarding War Diaries and Intelligence Summaries are contained in F. S. Regs., Part II. and the Staff Manual respectively. Title pages will be prepared in manuscript.

Place	Date	Hour	Summary of Events and Information	Remarks and references to Appendices
IN TRENCHES	Dec. 30th		Shelled. The battalion was relieved by the 7th Battalion Argyll & Sutherland Highlanders, 154th Infantry Brigade, and on relief marched back to LYNDOP CAMP, FREMICOURT.	OO.160
FREMICOURT	31st		Day spent in resting and cleaning up.	
			The following awards have been made during the month :-	
			The MILITARY CROSS.	

			Lieut. A. J. W. Cairnie.
			    Lieut. J. Hector.
			    2/Lieut. G. Rutherford.	

			The D.C.M.	

			265305 Sgt. James Ross.
			    266546 L/C. Ppeter McLean.
			    S/14067 James Alexander MacGregor.
			    266064 Pte. George Runcie.	

			Bar to MILITARY MEDAL.	
			266326 Cpl. Sword G.	
			The MILITARY MEDAL.	

			17711 Pte. Stephen C.H.
			    S/15151 L/C Nolan C.
			    265940 Pte. Brown J.
			    265454 Sgt. Macpherson J.
			    266571 L/C. Donald J.
			    265776 Davidson G.
			    201082 Pte. Smith R.N.
			    291378 Grant J.
			    266604 L/C. Rencroft H.G.
			    263054 Cpl. Imray J.
			    266267 Pte. Oldman J.
			    295037 L/C. Torrie L.
			    267025 Cpl. Stewart J.
			    292099 Pte. Millar D.H.
			    265101 Harper D.
			    265573 Pte. Gauld J.
			    40531 Cameron J.
			    10743 Cpl. Sword G.	

Army Form C. 2118.

WAR DIARY
or
INTELLIGENCE SUMMARY.

(Erase heading not required.)

Instructions regarding War Diaries and Intelligence Summaries are contained in F. S. Regs., Part II. and the Staff Manual respectively. Title pages will be prepared in manuscript.

Place	Date	Hour	Summary of Events and Information	Remarks and references to Appendices
FREMICOURT	DEC 31/17			

	Officers.	Other Ranks
STRENGTH at end of last month ...	32	900
INCREASE :— Drafts ...	11	63
Casuals ...	.	46
	43	1009

	O.	O.R.
DECREASE :— Killed ...	.	1
Died of Wounds ...	.	-
Wounded ...	.	8
Evacuated Sick ...	.	62
To Labour Corps ...	.	4
To U.K. for Commission ...	3	2
To U.K. Sick ...	.	.
	3	77

| STRENGTH at end of present month ... | 40 | 932 |

[signature]
Major,
Commanding 6th Gordon Highlanders.

31st December, 1917.

Vol 39

– Confidential –

War Diary
of
6th Bn. Gordon Highrs.

From 1st to 31st Jan., 1918.

WAR DIARY
or
INTELLIGENCE SUMMARY.
(Erase heading not required.)

Army Form C. 2118.

Instructions regarding War Diaries and Intelligence Summaries are contained in F. S. Regs., Part II. and the Staff Manual respectively. Title pages will be prepared in manuscript.

Place	Date	Hour	Summary of Events and Information	Remarks and references to Appendices
FREMICOURT	Jany 1st		Holiday, except for a short parade at 12.15 p.m. when the Commanding Officer gave out the Certificates of Congratulation for Acts of Gallantry during recent operations, which were sent by Major General Sir G. MONTAGUE HARPER, K.C.B., D.S.O., Commanding 51st (Highland) Division. The men had a very good dinner - soup, beef, plum pudding, besides other delicacies sent by their friends at home, and of tea they all had haggis.	Reference Maps Rows 11 -1/1/0000 Sheet 57C 1/40000.
do.	2nd		Baths. Inspection of Box Respirators, and improving Camp and digging slits. "A" and "C" Companies moved to some other huts about 1,000 yards away, which gave more room for everyone.	
do	3rd		The Battalion began work on a Corps line which is being due, 500 yards being allotted to each Battalion of the Brigade. The Battalion had 400 yards to do yesterday, 240 men working from 8 a.m. to 12.30 p.m., this party being furnished by "B" and "D" Companies, and 240 men were working from 12.30 p.m. to 4 p.m., being supplied by "A" and "C" Companies. The men were taken up to their work in 'buses and returned in 'buses. Our line rather exceeded 400 yards - being nearer 500 yards- so was not quite completed but where completed was very well done. Both parties had their dinners from the Cookers at BEAUMETZ Village. It was a very cold day and this was the best way the men could have been employed. The frost had got 6 inches into the ground which made the work much harder.	
do	4th		The Battalion was again employed on Corps line. "A" and "C" Companies should have started in 'buses at 7.30 a.m. but the 'buses did not turn up, so it was 10 a.m. before the men started work, the result being that this Unit was unable to finish its bit of the line to-day. Very severe frost last night and the ground frozen to a depth of about 1 foot.	
do	5th		Battalion training.- Close Order Drill, Physical Training and Musketry. Improving Camp in the afternoon.	
do	6th		Still very cold and hard frost last night. Battalion Training - Physical Training, Close Order Drill, Musketry, and Gas Helmet Drill. "C" Company furnished Wiring Party of 100 men under R.E. Owing to the frozen state of the ground, the digging of slit shelters in Camp was very slow and hard work.	

Army Form C. 2118.

WAR DIARY
or
INTELLIGENCE SUMMARY.
(Erase heading not required.)

Instructions regarding War Diaries and Intelligence Summaries are contained in F. S. Regs., Part II. and the Staff Manual respectively. Title pages will be prepared in manuscript.

Place	Date	Hour	Summary of Events and Information	Remarks and references to Appendices
FREMICOURT	Jany 6th		"D" Company was allotted the Range for the day.	
LEBUCQUIERE	7th		The Battalion moved up to LEBUCQUIERE - 2½ miles march, and is Reserve Battalion of Brigade, being relieved at FREMICOURT by 7th Argyll & Sutherland Highlanders and relieving the 5th Seaforth Highlanders at LEBUCQUIERE. "B", "C" and "D" Companies furnished Mining platoons of 1 Officer and 36 Other Ranks and were accommodated in the line. Echelon "B" accompanied the Battalion to LEBUCQUIERE. Thaw set in with heavy rain.	
do	8th		Weather changed in the night to frost and the whole country was a sheet of ice. The Battalion furnished a Working party of 2 Officers, 2 Sergeants, and 120 Other Ranks ("A" Company) to dig a Support Trench. The party left at 2.30 p.m., started work at 4.30 p.m., and did not return to Camp till 2 a.m. Echelon "B" training - Physical Training, Close Order Drill, and Musketry. A very cold day - a regular blizzard in the morning.	
do	9th		The Battalion supplied the following Working parties :- (1) "B" and "C" Coys., 60 men each with 2 Officers and 2 Sergeants digging Support trench, (2) "D" Coy. - 2 parties of 1 Officer, 1 Sergeant, and 40 men laying duckboards, (3) "A" Company - 1 Officer, 2 Sergeants, and 120 men to complete trench. Echelon "B" training - Physical Training and Musketry. It was too cold to use the Range allotted. Very cold wind and snow in the afternoon.	
do	10th		Usual Working parties furnished for work in Front and Support lines. 1 Officer and 120 men supplied by "B" and "D" Companies. Two parties of 1 Officer and 40 men supplied by "C" Company and H.Q. Details for wiring. Thaw set in and it rained most of the night. The country was a morass and digging trenches, slow work.	
do	11th		Still thawing hard. Usual Working parties. "A" and "B" Companies, 2 Officers and 120 men. "C" Company - wiring. "D" Company on Corps line to finish the old Boche part of it, which comes in to our line, and which owing to the hard frost before was almost impossible to work on; firesteps were also put in. All the Battalion had Baths to-day. Echelon "B" - Usual training.	

One/

Army Form C. 2118.

WAR DIARY
or
INTELLIGENCE SUMMARY.
(Erase heading not required.)

Instructions regarding War Diaries and Intelligence Summaries are contained in F. S. Regs., Part II. and the Staff Manual respectively. Title pages will be prepared in manuscript.

Place	Date	Hour	Summary of Events and Information	Remarks and references to Appendices
LERUCQUIERE	11th		One casualty in the Transport last night and two horses killed taking up rations – the two best Horses which took 1st Prize at the Divisional Transport Show last summer.	
do	12th		Working parties were supplied as on the 11th instant. "D" Company also working on Corps line. Echelon "R" working on Corps Line.	
do	13th		Working parties the same as on the 12th instant. Snow and frost again.	
do	14th		Working parties for work on the front line the same as for 13th. Snow and rain.	
do	15th		Working parties on Front and Support Lines the same as on 14th.	
do	16th		The Mining Platoons rejoined their Companies. A party of 150 men were employed in wiring Corps Line. No other parties working.	
do	17th		The Battalion was relieved at LERUCQUIERE at mid-day by the 9th Norfold Regiment, and proceeded by route march to Ruchanan Camp near ACHEIT–LE–GRAND – 11 miles. No men fell out during the march. This Camp is in a hollow and a sea of mud – not complete – six Huts still to go up. No Cookhouses, latrines, ablution benches, or beds for the officers, and very few duckboards; 4 Huts without stoves – not an ideal place to rest men who have been in the front line for practically two months. This is no fault of the Division who do all they can to make us comfortable. Weather dull and showery.	
ACHIET-LE-PETIT	18th		Resting and cleaning up – the latter not so easy as there is no place for the men to wash in the camp. Good parade Ground, and the Range, when repaired, will be good. Wet day.	
do	19th		Started training. Saluting Drill, Physical Drill, Close Order and Arm Drill. All newly joined Officers and N.C.Os. paraded under the Sergeant Major in the afternoon. The new draft paraded under Sergeant SUTTON. Weather fine. Lewis Gun, Signalling and Scouting Classes started. Dull day – rain in the afternoon.	

Army Form C. 2118.

WAR DIARY
or
INTELLIGENCE SUMMARY.
(Erase heading not required.)

Instructions regarding War Diaries and Intelligence Summaries are contained in F.S. Regs., Part II. and the Staff Manual respectively. Title pages will be prepared in manuscript.

Place	Date	Hour	Summary of Events and Information	Remarks and references to Appendices
ACHIET-LE-PETIT	20th		Church Parade.	
do	21st		The Battalion moved from Buchanan Camp to "A" Camp – quarters of a mile nearer ACHIET-LE-PETIT – a much better Camp, well laid out, and everything ready except the ablution benches. The Huts are well built and all have got stoves. Everyone was glad to get out of the bog we were in before. The day was spent in settling down in Camp and improving the Camp, mounting Lewis Guns &c. Laid out two quite good football grounds.	
do	22nd		The Battalion training. Physical Training, Close Order and Arm Drill, Saluting Drill, Preliminary Musketry, Platoon Football Matches.	
do	23rd		The Battalion training. Physical Training, Drill by Section Commanders, Platoon in Attack, Preliminary Musketry. Lewis Gun, Signalling, Scout and Runner Classes. Platoon Football Matches.	
do	24th		The Battalion training. "A" Company Firing on Range, remaining Companies – Physical Training, Preliminary Musketry, Platoon in the Attack. The Battalion played the 5th Argyll & Sutherland Highlanders at Football and were beaten by 4 goals to 3. Classes as usual.	
do	25th		The Battalion training. Physical Training, Platoon in Attack and Company in Attack, Preliminary Musketry. Classes as usual.	
do	26th		Physical Training, Company Drill, Musketry, Rifle Grenade Work. The Battalion and Transport were inspected in the afternoon by the Acting Brigadier who expressed himself as very pleased with all he saw.	
do	27th		Church Parade.	
do	28th		"A" and "C" Companies at Baths. "B" Company on Range. Training :- Bayonet Fighting, Rifle Grenade Practice, Company in Attack. Football match in Brigade Competition. The Battalion played 404th Field Company R.E's. who were far too good for us and beat us by 7 goals to 1. "A"/	

Army Form C. 2118.

WAR DIARY
or
INTELLIGENCE SUMMARY.
(Erase heading not required.)

Place	Date	Hour	Summary of Events and Information	Remarks and references to Appendices
ACHIET-LE-PETIT	29th		"A" and "B" Companies did a Field Practice on the Range. "B" Company were much the better. The best platoon is to enter for the Brigade Competition. "C" and "D" Companies did Physical Training, Company in Attack, and Rifle Grenade Practice. First lovely day.	
do.	30th		Additional Range was allotted to the Battalion, so "A" and "C" Companies were both shooting on the Range to-day. The shooting is improving very much, which is due mainly to each Company having done 12 hours preliminary Musketry, which before, we so seldom had time to do thoroughly. Weather frosty and fine. "B" and "D" Companies – usual training.	
do.	31st		A Tactical Exercise – Capture of a Wood – was carried out by the Battalion in the morning.	

HONOURS AND AWARDS.

    Lieut. Colonel Hon. W. FRASER, M.C.   D.S.O.

                  M.C.

    Captain C. McCOMBIE.
    Hon. Lieut. F. W. FINDLAY.

MENTIONED IN DESPATCHES.
    Lt.Col. FRASER Hon. W. D.S.O., M.C.
    Capt. J. HUTCHESON, D.S.O., M.C.
    265123 Sgt. W. FORSYTH.
    265407 Sgt. A. PHILIP.
    265817 Sgt. M. DALGARNO.
    265839 Sgt. C. MITCHELL.

STRENGTH/

Army Form C. 2118.

WAR DIARY
or
INTELLIGENCE SUMMARY.
(Erase heading not required.)

Instructions regarding War Diaries and Intelligence Summaries are contained in F. S. Regs., Part II. and the Staff Manual respectively. Title pages will be prepared in manuscript.

Place	Date	Hour	Summary of Events and Information	Remarks and references to Appendices
ACHIET-LE-PETIT	31/1			

		Officers.	Other Ranks.
STRENGTH at end of last month		40	932
ADD	Drafts	4	49
	Casuals	1	29
		45	1010
DEDUCT		Officers.	Other Ranks.
Wounded			4
Evacuations			56
To Base, P.B.			4
To Base, Underage			1
To U.K. for Commission		1	1
To R.F.C.		1	
To M.G.C., GRANTHAM.			
		2	66
STRENGTH at end of this month		43	944

31st January, 1918.

R. Rorell
Major,
Commanding 6th Gordon Highlanders.

Army Form C. 2118.

WAR DIARY
or
INTELLIGENCE SUMMARY.
(Erase heading not required.)

1/6 Gordon H's
Vol 40

Place	Date	Hour	Summary of Events and Information	Remarks and references to Appendices
ACHIET-LE-PETIT	Feby 1st		The Battalion practised attacking a wood and consolidating the same. A thick mist made this operation somewhat difficult but proved the value of training scouts in the use of the compass, as correct direction was maintained throughout.	Reference map 57c. 1/40,000
	2nd		"C" & "D" Companies spent the forenoon on Field Firing Range. "A" & "B" Coys, on the 30 yards Range and H.Q. Details on the 100 yards Range. The Battalion Tug-'o-War' Team were beaten by the 6th Seaforth Highlanders by 2 pulls in the Brigade competition.	
	3rd		The whole Battalion went through the Divisional Gas Chamber, and then went to Baths. Each Company then had an inspection parade in view of the probable inspection by the Commander-in-Chief. Weather very fine.	
	4th		The Battalion lined the main road opposite the camp (Rienquerel Camp) to give the 8th Argyll & Sutherland Highlanders a send off as they were leaving this 152nd Infantry Brigade. They, the 8th Argyll & Sutherland Highlanders, were to have started in 'busses at 10 a.m., but as the 'buses did not turn up till 12.30 p.m., the whole forenoon was wasted. Rifle Grenade shooting was carried out in the afternoon by Companies. The Brigade Cross-Country Run in the afternoon was won by the 9th Royal Scots, Cpl. Moray of this Battalion coming in fifth. There were 60 starters but the going was heavy.	
	5th		Companies did one hour Physical Training and were then engaged in digging trenches under the floors of their huts as protection against hostile aircraft raids.	
	6th		Brigade Sports were held and the Battalion won the following events:- 1. The Best Turned-Out Squad of 1 Sergeant, 1 Corporal, 1 Lance Corporal and 1 Man. 2. The Best Drilled Platoon. 3. Rifle Grenade Competition. (No. 24's). 4. 1st & 2nd places in Transport Race.	
	7th		Battalion did a short parade for physical training and close order drill and then went to Baths. Weather very fine and mild.	

Army Form C. 2118.

WAR DIARY
or
INTELLIGENCE SUMMARY.
(Erase heading not required.)

Instructions regarding War Diaries and Intelligence Summaries are contained in F. S. Regs., Part II. and the Staff Manual respectively. Title pages will be prepared in manuscript.

Place	Date	Hour	Summary of Events and Information	Remarks and references to Appendices
ACHIET-LE-PETIT	Sept 8th		Companies took turns on the Field Firing Range and practised getting up to assembly positions by dribbling forward from a covered position behind. This method of assembly is carried out by the Germans and would prove very useful under certain circumstances, as this method offers no very good target to Machine Guns.	Reference Map SYC. 1/40000.
	9th		The Battalion marched out to LOGEAST WOOD to practise counter-attack. formations and a very profitable morning was spent, in spite of the difficulties of skirmishing a Counter-Attack.	
	10th		Sunday. Church Parades were held for the various denominations.	OO.165
	11th		Companies did half an hour's Physical training in the morning. At 2.10 p.m. the Battalion paraded and proceeded by route march to LEBUCQUIERE in accordance with orders. On arrival the Battalion was accommodated in CINEMA CAMP for the night.	OO.166
LEBUCQUIERE	12th		The forenoon was spent in preparing for going into the line. The Battalion moved off from camp at 4.50 p.m., Platoons moving at 1 minute's interval. Guides were met at the South end of DOIGNIES, and the relief of the 9th Norfolks was carried out. "B" Company sustained 5 casualties on the way up to the line. The Battalion occupies the Right Sector which runs from left to right from F.7.a.00.10. to F.8.a.00.50.; and is held :- "B" Company - Right Front Company; "D" Company left Front Company; "A" Company in Support and "C" Company in Reserve. The night passed quietly.	
IN TRENCHES	13th		Weather dull. Protective Patrols which were out during the night saw nothing. Work was commenced in trenches - clearing the bottoms and berm where necessary possible and preparations were made for wiring of front line to be started at night.	
	14th		Work continued on AUBREY & BETTY ALLEYS and front line. Wiring of Front line carried on. Three officers attended a Tank Demonstration at BRAY.	
	15th		Usual work and wiring continued. C.O.C. visited the Battalion Sector. New dugouts commenced in WALSH SUPPORT.	
	16th		Weather very fine. Visibility good. Work on trenches continued. An inter Company relief was carried out in the afternoon.	OO.167

Army Form C. 2118.

WAR DIARY
or
INTELLIGENCE SUMMARY.
(Erase heading not required.)

Instructions regarding War Diaries and Intelligence Summaries are contained in F. S. Regs., Part II. and the Staff Manual respectively. Title pages will be prepared in manuscript.

Place	Date	Hour	Summary of Events and Information	Remarks and references to Appendices
IN TRENCHES	Feb 16th		"A" Company relieved "D" Company and "C" Company relieved "A" Company. Relief commenced at 3 p.m. and was completed at 6 p.m.	
	17th		Work on JANKREY and PHILP Communication Trenches continued. Good progress was made the previous night with the wiring of the Front Line. A considerable amount of enemy movement was observed during the day, which was very hazy & clear.	
	18th		Wiring of front line continued during night. Enemy put down a light barrage along our front line at dawn. Observation being very good there was great activity in the air. The Army Commander visited the battalion sector.	
	19th		The usual working parties on communication trenches, Front Line &c. carried on. Orders for relief received.	OO.168
	20th		A quiet day. The battalion was relieved by 4th Seaforth Highlanders, and on relief marched back to LINDUP CAMP, FREMICOURT.	
FREMICOURT	21st		Day spent resting and cleaning up.	
	22nd		Battalion supplied 250 men for work on a cable trench under Divisional Signals.	
	23rd		Same work parties supplied. Commanding Officer inspected "D" Company. Lewis Gun Class commenced.	
	24th		Work parties on cable trench. Church Parades.	
	25th		Work parties on cable trench. Lewis Gunners at Range Practice.	
	26th		"A" Company inspected by Commanding Officer. "C" Company inspected by Commanding Officer.	
	27th		Work Parties as on previous days. "D" Company inspected by Commanding Officer. Companies Paraded for Baths when available.	

WAR DIARY
or
INTELLIGENCE SUMMARY.

(Erase heading not required.)

Army Form C. 2118.

Place	Date	Hour	Summary of Events and Information	Remarks and references to Appendices
FREMICOURT	Feby 28		Battalion supplied a working party of 2 officers and 100 men for work in FREMICOURT. Remainder of companies at disposal of Company Commanders.	
	28th		HONOURS & AWARDS. BELGIAN CROIX DE GUERRE. 265084 C.S.M. Peter EWING MITTON. (D) 265028 Lt. John MacPHERSON. (A)	

Instructions regarding War Diaries and Intelligence Summaries are contained in F. S. Regs., Part II. and the Staff Manual respectively. Title pages will be prepared in manuscript.

Army Form C. 2118.

WAR DIARY
or
INTELLIGENCE SUMMARY.

(Erase heading not required.)

Place	Date	Hour	Summary of Events and Information			Remarks and references to Appendices
FREMICOURT	Feb 28th					

Strength at end of last month ... ... Officers 43 Other Ranks 944

ADD :-
Drafts 1 128
Casuals 1 15
Lieut Colonel J.G. Thom, D.S.O., M.C. joined
Battalion to command, 21.2.18. 1 -

                                              45 1087

                                              OFF. O.R.
DEDUCT :-
Wounded ... ...   -   43
Evacuations   1   1
To U.K. for Commission   1   -
Died in hospital   -   1
(2/Lieut. W.D. Latto)
Left Battalion to command 1   -
18th Corps School
Lt. Col. Hon. W. Fraser, D.S.O., M.C.
To 152nd T.M.B. for duty   -   7
To 252nd M.G.C. for duty   -   5
To 245 Divl. Employment. Coy 1 2
To U.K. for 6 months
substitution :-   3   75
(a/Capt. D. Macduff)

Strength at end of this month 42 1012

[signature] Lieut Colonel,
Commanding 6th Gordon Highlanders.

51st Division.
152nd Infantry Brigade.

WAR DIARY

1/6th BATTALION

GORDON HIGHLANDERS

MARCH 1 9 1 8

Appendices attached :-
Report on Operations 21st-26th March

Vol 41

Confidential

War Diary
of
16th London Rgt

March, 1916

157/5/1

WAR DIARY or INTELLIGENCE SUMMARY.

Army Form C. 2118.

Place	Date	Hour	Summary of Events and Information	Remarks and references to Appendices
FREMICOURT	March 1st		Companies at the disposal of Company Commanders for inspection of trench kit, and preparing for the line. Battalion moved off from camp at 7.45 p.m. 100 yards interval between platoons. Guides were met at post 20 (t.10.a.3.3.) and the relief of the 4th Gordon Highlanders commenced and was completed at 12.30 a.m. The Battalion occupies the Brigade Centre Section left Sub. Section, running from D.29.c.8.4. left to t.6.a.5.2. right. "D" Company LEFT front, "B" Company RIGHT front, "C" Company SUPPORT, and "A" Company RESERVE. Battalion Headquarters at J.10.b.0.7.	Reference Map 57c. 1/40,000 O.O.169
In Trenches	2nd		Forenoon spent reconnoitring Front line and Defensive posts. Work of wiring Sunken Road, t.4.3.b.1. - t.5.c.0.3. arranged for when dark. 2 officers and 100 men employed. Weather very cold with intermittent snow showers. 450 yards of wire put up in afternoon. The work of cleaning and repairing Front and Support lines went on all day. Enemy very quiet all day and night. Thickening front wire.	
	3rd		A dull morning and slight rain. Wiring of Sunken Road. Construction and improvement of fire bays in front and support lines. 800 yards of wiring done on Sunken Road and RUBBIES. The night passed quietly.	
	4th		Dull, damp, cold morning. Quiet night. Owing to the mist it was possible to wire the reserve line all day and 1100 yards were completed as well as part thickened by "C" Company. "D" Company thickened up wire opposite No.20 Post. A party was also working clearing the berm of FISH AVENUE and making fire-steps.	
	5th		Cold dull morning turned into a fine drying day. The wiring of the reserve line completed in the morning. Work on duckboards in support line. Revetting firesteps in front and support line. Digging and enlarging Post 21. also improving Posts 1F & 10. Quiet night.	
	6th		Frost at night. Fine day but hazy and visibility bad. Usual work on trenches, repairing and making firesteps. Enlarging Post 21 and digging firesteps between Posts 10 & 20. Wiring and improving trenches. Battalion to be relieved to-morrow by the 6th Seaforth Highlanders.	

Army Form C. 2118.

WAR DIARY
or
INTELLIGENCE SUMMARY.
(Erase heading not required.)

Instructions regarding War Diaries and Intelligence Summaries are contained in F.S. Regs., Part II. and the Staff Manual respectively. Title pages will be prepared in manuscript.

Place	Date	Hour	Summary of Events and Information	Remarks and references to Appendices
In Trenches	7th		The usual work. General ALEXANDER of the U.S. Army was taken round our trenches and shown everything this morning. Owing to a haze the relief took place during daylight between 4p.m. and 6 p.m. We had two casualties coming out and it was very lucky we had not more as an eight" shell burst on the CAMBRAI - RAPAUME Road amongst a section and only two men were wounded. The Battalion is in huts at O'SHEA CAMP in Brigade Reserve.	O.O.170
O'SHEA CAMP	8th		O'SHEA CAMP. Cleaning up and improving camp. Company Commanders reconnoitring routes and positions in Reserve line.	
	9th		Battalion at Baths all day.	
	10th		Church Parade.	
	11th		"A" & "C" Companies inspected by Commanding Officer. All Respirators inspected. Reconnoitring Front line.	
	12th		All Companies inspected by Commanding Officer. Officers reconnoitring line.	
	13th		The Battalion moved off to the line, the first Company moving off at 12.30 p.m. 300 yards between sections. The Battalion took over Centre Battalion Sector from 5th Seaforth Highlanders. "A" Company - Front line, "C" Company - Support, "B" Company - Intermediate and "D" Company - Reserve line.	O.O.171
	14th		All available men in support and Intermediate lines working 8 hours per day on wiring and general trench repair.	
	15th		Weather very fine. Same work as yesterday. Party of 75 men carrying bomb. bombs to No Man's Land.	
	16th		Work as above, enemy quiet.	
	17th		Work as above, enemy quiet.	
	18th		Work as above. Enemy registering on batteries and DOIGNIES and DOIGNIES - DEMICOURT Road.	

WAR DIARY
or
INTELLIGENCE SUMMARY.
(Erase heading not required.)

Army Form C. 2118.

Place	Date	Hour	Summary of Events and Information	Remarks and references to Appendices
In Trenches	March 19th		Inter-Company relief. "C" Company relieved "A" Company in Front Line. "B" company relieved "C" company. "A" Company came back to Intermediate Line. Working parties suspended on account of relief.	O.O.172
do.	20th		During day men rested. At night all available men on working parties digging new reserve line from C.5.c.1.0. to BOURSIES - DOIGNIES Road. Battalion worked in two shifts. First from 7.15 p.m. to 11.30 p.m., second 11.45 p.m. to 3 a.m. Trench completed.	
	21st to 26th		For report on operations from 21st March to 26th March, 1918 see Appendix attached hereto.	
NEUVILLETTE	27th		The Battalion were to entrain from PAS to NEUVILLETTE, but owing to the uncertainty of the arrival of the 'buses we were given the option of marching about 8 miles which we did. Starting at 10.45 a.m., having dinners en route from the Cookers at POMMERA and arriving at NEUVILLETTE at 4.30 p.m. where the Battalion was billeted in comforta[ble] billets. Indents for kit had already gone in.	
	28th		The Battalion resting and cleaning up. Some of the fighting equipment indented for arrived.	
	29th		Orders were received to march to FREVENT and then to entrain for the LILLERS area at 1 p.m. The Battalion left at 10.15 a.m. Cookers were sent on and the men had their dinners in a field near the station. While resting after their dinners the King's car was seen coming along the road and the Battalion received him with tremendous cheering. Whereupon His Majesty stopped his car and spoke to several officers and N.C.Os. Then the Battalion was marched past the King and His Majesty expressed his admiration for the appearance of the Battalion and his pleasure at having seen them. The train left FREVENT at 3.30 p.m. and arrived at LAPUGNOY at 6 p.m. The Battalion was billeted at LABEUVRIERE quite close to the station in good billets.	O.O.173 O.O.174
LABEUVRIERE	30th		Battalion resting at LABEUVRIERE.	
	31st		Battalion cleaning up. More equipment arrived from the Ordnance.	

Army Form C. 2118.

WAR DIARY
or
INTELLIGENCE SUMMARY.
(Erase heading not required.)

Instructions regarding War Diaries and Intelligence Summaries are contained in F. S. Regs., Part II. and the Staff Manual respectively. Title pages will be prepared in manuscript.

Place	Date	Hour	Summary of Events and Information	Remarks and references to Appendices
LABEUVRIERE	March 31st			

HONOURS & AWARDS
Nil.

	Off.	O.R.	Officers	O.R.
Strength at end of last month	...	...	42	1012
ADD:-				
Drafts	...	46		
Casuals	...	15		
Officers joined during month	2	...	2	61
			44	1073
DEDUCT:-				
Evacuations	...	98		
To United Kingdom for Commission	...	2		
To Base – Tradesmen	...	2		
To U.K. – Officers' Substitution Scheme.	2	0		
To 51st (H) Battn. M.G.C.	...	...		
Casualties :-				
Killed	2	35		
Wounded } as per	11	150		
Unaccounted for } Appendix	3	74		
Died of wounds	...	6		
			18	365
			20	336
Strength at end of this month	...	...	26	708

[signature] Major,
Commanding 6th Gordon Highlanders.

1/6th Gordons Diary
"March 1918"
22nd March, line 2.
"D.29.c." is a mistake for
"J.20.c."

HRDavies

23.7.25.

ACCOUNT OF OPERATIONS commencing near
BOURSIES on 21st March, 1918, and
lasting till 26th March, 1918.

21st March, 1918.

4.45 a.m. Intense bombardment of British lines, Front, Support, and Intermediate lines all being included. Barrage consisted of 8", 5.9" and gas shells.

The QUARRY was barraged and a large number of gas shells fell in and around it.

9.15 a.m. Enemy seen bombing along STURGEON SUPPORT Trench from direction of BOURSIES. What men were left in Front line were withdrawn to Support line and a block was formed in the trench and the enemy held up.

A platoon from the QUARRY had been moved up and manned STURGEON AVENUE between Sunk Road and STURGEON SUPPORT.

10.15 a.m. The troops in STURGEON SUPPORT were driven out. Enemy were now in STURGEON AVENUE and tried to bomb down towards BOURSIES - CRUCIFIX Road. A block was made in STURGEON AVENUE and enemy held up.

11 a.m. Bombs ran short and block was forced down STURGEON AVENUE a short distance.

11.30 a.m. Enemy in great numbers seen coming from BOURSIES and trying to get down BOURSIES - DOIGNIES Road. Three Lewis Guns and all rifles in STURGEON AVENUE opened fire on them inflicting many casualties. The garrison by this time was forced down STURGEON AVENUE some eighty yards south of BOURSIES - CRUCIFIX Road and a block established there. More bombs and rifle grenades arrived from Battalion Headquarters and enemy were again held up for about an hour.

1.30 p.m. Owing to increasing enemy pressure from front and left flank the block in STURGEON had again to fall back about seventy yards below the QUARRY. This position was held till orders were received to withdraw at 1.30 a.m. on 22nd March, 1918.

The platoon at J.5.c.1.0. on CAMBRAI Road were nearly all taken prisoners. They held their position till nearly surrounded and then only the officer and four men got away down the BOURSIES - DOIGNIES Road to the Intermediate line.

"A" Company and two platoons of "D" Company in the Intermediate line were heavily shelled and gassed. When enemy were seen coming out of BOURSIES they were ordered to counter-attack, but, owing to the heavy machine gun fire from the hedge in front of the Reserve line the attack was held up. After this "A" Company lost touch on their left flank and withdrew and formed a defensive flank South of DOIGNIES which was shortly afterwards occupied by the enemy. This line was held till 1.30 a.m.

The remaining two platoons of "D" Company who were in reserve at LEBUCQUIERE held a part of the BEAUMETZ - MORCHIES line South of the BAPAUME - CAMBRAI Road till 2 a.m. on the 23rd March, 1918.

22nd March, 1918.

At 1.30 a.m. the battalion was ordered to take up a position along the Plank Road in J.19. and D.20.c. and remained there till 1.30 p.m. when orders were received to hold a line on the North side of the BAPAUME - CAMBRAI Road covering BEUGNY.

At/

2.

At 3 p.m. orders were received to proceed to MIDDLESEX CAMP where the battalion had a hot meal.

At 5.30 p.m. the battalion was ordered to form a line along the railway 1500 yards North of FREMICOURT facing BEUGNATRE.

23rd March, 1918.

At 1 a.m. the battalion was withdrawn to MIDDLESEX CAMP when a hot meal was provided for the men and where Echelon B joined the battalion.

At 12 noon orders were received to take up a position on a line 200 yards North and South of MILL CROSS facing LEBUCQUIERE; the line North of MILL CROSS was astride the FREMICOURT - LEBUCQUIERE Road. This line was 600 yards from the Green line. The orders were to reinforce Green line if necessary and hold our line. The line was held in section posts - "B" and "C" Companies in Front line, "A" and "D" Companies in support. This position was intermittently shelled during the afternoon and evening.

At 4 p.m. orders were received that the battalion was attached to the 50th Brigade and under orders of the Officer Commanding, 8th North Stafford Regiment.

24th March, 1918.

At 8 a.m. the position held by the battalion was shelled continuously.

At 9 a.m. orders were received from the Division that the battalion was to be relieved immediately by the N. & W. Division, and at 9.20 a.m. an officer reported to me with same orders I had received, informing me that he had his battalion at BARCOURT and was ready to carry out the relief. I reported to O.C., 8th North Stafford Regiment and the relief was carried out by 10.30 a.m. On the way out of the position, the battalion did not return to Headquarters owing to the heavy shelling of the Valley in front of the Headquarters, but came out by the road South of BARCOURT and proceeded to REINCOURT where I halted and reported to the Brigade that the relief was complete and asked for orders, as the only orders I had received were from the Division.

While awaiting orders the B.G.C., 154th Infantry Brigade, came up to me and gave me orders to take the battalion across the BAPAUME - PERONNE Road and act as a reserve to his Brigade.

At 12 noon the B.G.C. came up and issued orders to form a line in front of BEUGNENCOURT extending each side of the BAPAUME - PERONNE Road to cover the withdrawal of the 17th Division. The whole Battalion were in the line, in two lines - "A" and "B" Companies North of the Road, "C" and "D" Companies, South - the Front line in shell holes and the Support line in an old trench and in shell holes, the 6th Brigade on our right and the 6th Seaforth Highlanders on our left.

About 4.30 p.m. the 17th Division were reported to be falling back but not fighting, and half an hour after they came through the line on our left and the troops of our line withdrew with them. Our left flank was left in the air and "A" Company came back in good order, having been under heavy machine gun fire and fire from a field gun in LE TRANSLOY. At the time they with-
:drew the enemy was within 250 yards of them coming from the direction of VILLERS-AU-FLOS. There were also enemy troops in a small wood on their front and along the huts North of the Main road. In the meantime "B" Company was under machine gun fire from three guns but could not see the enemy advancing owing to the huts on their half right front which was where the enemy were assembling, but saw large forces of the enemy in LE TRANSLOY and also a field gun brought up which fired on our lines and on BEUGNENCOURT.
"A"/

3.

"A" Company having withdrawn, "B" Company went, when the enemy were within 400 yards in front of them and only 200 yards on their right, among the huts.

O.C. "C" Company states as follows :-

"At about 5 p.m. I received a message from O.C. "B" Company that the enemy were advancing up the main road from LE TRANSLOY and to watch it. On receipt of this I put another Lewis Gun on the main road (I had one there before) and shortly after I saw the enemy coming down the main road in fours about 800 to 1,000 yards away. These two Lewis Guns fired about 30 drums which held up the enemy on the road. Half an hour afterwards I saw the enemy coming down the slope in front of LE TRANSLOY and they were fired at and held up, and sent up Very lights to the artillery. I then went to my right flank to find out what the situation was and found a General and a Brigadier in a trench in which was a red and white flag. I asked them what the situation on the right was and the General said that it was alright, and that he would on till 9 p.m. Shortly after, the Brigadier came along and said that he was outflanked as the enemy was coming down the valley on our right, and that he was withdrawing. I sent a message to O.C. "B" Company informing him of this. After waiting till the messenger returned from "B" Company I withdrew my company. The enemy was then only on the outskirts of LE TRANSLOY on my front".

I had left my headquarters and was collecting the men of this Division whom I saw retiring, and formed a line with them in the Water-Pipe Trench 500 yards in rear of BEAULENCOURT and south of the main road, but when my battalion withdrew this trench was so crowded that I formed another line on the ridge 600 yards in rear, with the left flank well back parallel to the road. By this time the general retirement was stopped and I got in touch with O.C. 4th Seaforth Highlanders and O.C. 4th Gordon Highlanders and they got their men together and I reported the situation to Brigade. I extended the 4th Seaforth Highlanders along the main road as the enemy was showing lights on our flank the other side of the road. About 7.30 p.m. orders were received from the Brigade to proceed to LOUPART WOOD. The battal-ion assembled at THILOY WOOD and reached WARLENCOURT at 10.20 p.m. when our new position was explained. The disposition was as follows :-
Our left flank was 200 yards south of LOUPART WOOD, next the 6th Seaforth Highlanders and ran south just behind the sunken road to where it joined the 154th Infantry Brigade on the sunken road leading to WARLENCOURT. "A", "C" & "D" Companies in front, "B" Company in support, the whole in shell holes.

The night was quiet.

25th March, 1918.

Orders were received that the 19th Division were to withdraw through our front. Except for a slight shelling the morning was quiet and at mid-day the enemy could be seen on the skyline two miles away. About this time orders were received that the 62nd Division was on its way up to reinforce our line and that we must hold out till it arrived.

At 12.45 p.m. O.C. 7th Argyll & Sutherland Highlanders asked me if I could hang on and I informed him that there was nothing on my front to prevent my staying there. At 1 p.m. O.C. 7th Argyll & Sutherland Highlanders came to me and informed me that he must withdraw as the enemy were in great numbers on his right flank. I informed my right company - "A" Company - to try and keep in touch with 7th Argyll & Sutherland Highlanders, but they came back so quickly that he could not and withdrew.
"C"/

4.

"C" & "D" Companies remained in their positions for another quarter of an hour and engaged the enemy on their left front at about 600 yards, then they withdrew through "B" Company and suffered many casualties during this withdrawal. "B" Company remained till "C" & "D" Companies had gone across the ravine behind and then withdrew being engaged with the enemy who were in the Sunken road on our front.

I tried to form a line with my battalion on the high ground East of IRLES and "B", "C" & "D" Companies got into position but the other troops would not remain, so the whole line came back to IRLES.

Ammunition was getting short at about 5 p.m., and, shortly afterwards, a general retirement took place to COLIN CAMPS. This battalion was engaged with the enemy at the time of the withdrawal. A mixed force, including "B" and some of "A" company and four officers of this battalion, got in touch with the 62nd Division and held a line to the right of the railway by FUSIEUX till orders were received to withdraw at midnight.

When the 152nd Infantry Brigade got to SAILLY-AU-BOIS, there were only 2 officers and 120 men. This party bivouaced in FRONTVILLERS and got a hot meal at 4 a.m. from the cookers.

26th March, 1918.

At 5 a.m. orders were received to put out outposts South of SAILLY-AU-BOIS, 6th Seaforth Highlanders and 153rd Infantry Brigade on my left.

At 9 a.m. orders were received to withdraw in the formation in which we were, with the main party on the road SAILLY-AU-BOIS — BAYENCOURT — SOUASTRE, 500 yards from the village of SOUASTRE the battalion took up a line across the road, 4 platoons on the right of the road and four platoons on the left, with the right flank well back covering the valley in front. At 1 p.m. the battalion was relieved by an Australian battalion, had a hot meal at SOUASTRE and moved to PAS where it bivouaced the night.

During these operations the men had undergone a severe strain --
(i) From the enemy's bombardment on the 21st March and the subsequent fighting, and
(ii) From the exposure to cold nights without greatcoats or any adequate means of keeping warm which was unavoidable as their coats were all left in the trenches on the 21st March, 1918. Owing to the severe cold at nights they got no real rest.

Owing to the excellent arrangements of the Staff Captain, a hot meal was provided on four days and on the 23rd March, besides a hot meal, this battalion got hot tea at night.

The absence of any artillery support was noticeable on the morning of the 21st March when masses of the enemy troops were seen to be assembling in LOUVERVAL WOOD all day and not a shell was fired at it. There were not many of our aeroplanes about the front line on the morning of the 21st March which may account for the artillery not taking advantage of some good targets.

On the night of the 22nd March there was much traffic on the BAPAUME — CAMBRAI Road which was not taken on by our artillery.

There/

5.

There was also a noticeable absence of artillery support in the operations of the 23rd., 24th & 25th March.

The absence of any defensive line behind the BEAUMETZ - MORCHIES line no doubt increased our casualties and added to the already great strain on the men by having to dig hurried positions wherever they were ordered under shell fire.

Our aeroplanes after the first day appeared to have complete command of our front.

A special feature during the retirement from IRLES to COLIN CAMPS when the troops were somewhat disorganised, was the escort formed by our aeroplanes who guarded the column the whole way and never gave an enemy aeroplane a chance of coming near the column as it withdrew.

Lewis Guns, when in a good position and well manned, proved over and over again how important this weapon is in inflicting casualties on the enemy and holding them up.

The control of rifle fire is part of the training of men which requires special attention. A few instances of a good rifle section under fire control proved how important this is.

Rifle Grenades. None were used by this battalion after the 21st March. Owing to the enemy bombardment the supply on the 21st March was inadequate in the front and support lines as all the recesses were buried or blown up. The same applies to bombs but fresh supplies of these were sent up from the Intermediate line.

                                                 Major,
Commanding 6th Gordon Highlanders.

31st March, 1918.

51st Division.
152nd Infantry Brigade.

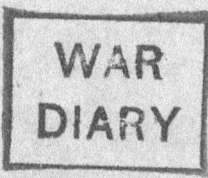

1/6th BATTALION

THE GORDON HIGHLANDERS

APRIL 1 9 1 8

Attached :- Reports on Operations
Operation Orders.

Vol 4 2

War Diary

of

16th Battn Gordon Highlanders

From 1st April 1918 to 30th April 1918.

Confidential

Army Form C. 2118.

WAR DIARY
or
INTELLIGENCE SUMMARY.
(Erase heading not required.)

Instructions regarding War Diaries and Intelligence Summaries are contained in F. S. Regs., Part II. and the Staff Manual respectively. Title pages will be prepared in manuscript.

Place	Date	Hour	Summary of Events and Information	Remarks and references to Appendices
	April			Reference Maps:-
Labeuvrie	1		Companies at disposal of Company Commanders. Inspection of Rifles and Small Box Respirators. Four Officers reconnoitred the Reserve Line on the Front.	Bethune 1/40.000. Hazebrouck S.A. 1/100.000. 36 A 1/40.000. 36 A.S.E. do.
Do.	2		Orders were received at mid-day that the Battalion was to move to OBLINGHEM. They proceeded there by route march of 4½ miles, and were billeted in good billets.	
Oblinghem.	3		"A" and "B" Companies were inspected by the Commanding Officer - remaining Companies carrying out training, Close Order Drill, Arm Drill, Saluting Drill, and Box Respirator Drill.	
Lapugnoy.	4		Orders were received to go to LAPUGNOY, and the Battalion proceeded there by route march in the morning. The Battalion was billeted in good billets.	
Do.	5		Training :- Lewis Gun, Scouts & Runners, and Signallers' Classes. Companies at disposal of Company Commanders. Most of the equipment indented for arrived. A great difficulty was experienced in getting cleaning material and Barbers' Tools, as all these were lost with the men's kits on the 21st March 1918. At 12.30 p.m. orders were received that the Battalion had to be clear of present billets by 2.30 p.m. and to proceed to HAM-EN-ARTOIS. The Battalion marched off at 3.30 p.m., arriving there at 6.30 p.m. - a distance of 8 miles. The billets for the men were somewhat scattered, and Officers' Billets were none too plentiful.	
Ham-en-Artois	6		Inspection of "C" and "D" Companies and Headquarters Details by Commanding Officer. Brigade Gas N.C.O. inspected Box Respirators. There were not many facilities for training purposes here.	
Do.	7		Companies at disposal of Company Commanders. Barbers and Tailors allotted to Companies. Half an hour's Box Respirator Drill.	
			Training/	

WAR DIARY
or
INTELLIGENCE SUMMARY.
(Erase heading not required.)

Army Form C. 2118.

Place	Date	Hour	Summary of Events and Information	Remarks and references to Appendices
Ham-en-Artois	8		Training :- Preliminary Musketry. Squad Drill. Classes for Lewis Gunners, Scouts & Runners, and signallers. Training hampered greatly on account of the poor training area, and on account of available ground being limited. Brig.-General H. P. BURN, D.S.O. left for the United Kingdom yesterday, and, Brig.-General W. DICK-CUNYNGHAM, took over command of the 152nd Infantry Brigade.	
Do.	9		Orders were received at 5.35 a.m. to "stand To", following which came orders that the Battalion would proceed by route march to BUSNES CHURCH. The Battalion left HAM-EN-ARTOIS at 8 a.m., and embussed at 10.30 a.m. for subsequent days see Appendix No. 1 - "Account of Operations near ZELOBES commencing on 9th April 1918 and lasting to 13th April 1918", and Notes thereon (Appendix 2) attached hereto.	
Busnes.	14		The one company of this Battalion in the Composite Battalion of 152nd Infantry Brigade was in Reserve. Company Officers reconnoitred the line.	
Do.	15		The composite Battalion still in reserve.	
Witternesse	16		Marched by route march to WITTERNESSE (about 8 miles). The Battalion had dinners at HAM-EN-ARTOIS enroute, and were billeted here. The Billets were only fair, as the village was full of refugees.	
Do.	17		The re-organisation of the Battalion was commenced. A draft of 76 Other Ranks arrived.	
Do.	18		Re-organisation continued. Two Companies at Baths. Draft of 40 Other Ranks arrived.	
Do.	19		Training :- Preliminary Musketry, Arm Drill, Box Respirator Drill. One Company on Range, and two Companies at Baths. Classes for Lewis Gunners, Scouts and Runners, and signallers, were commenced.	

Army Form C. 2118.

WAR DIARY
or
INTELLIGENCE SUMMARY.
(Erase heading not required.)

III.

Instructions regarding War Diaries and Intelligence Summaries are contained in F.S. Regs., Part II. and the Staff Manual respectively. Title pages will be prepared in manuscript.

Place	Date	Hour	Summary of Events and Information	Remarks and references to Appendices
Witternesse	20		Training :- Musketry on 100 yards Range for "C" and "D" Companies. Saluting Drill. Arm Drill. Box Respirator Drill. Classes as usual.	
Do.	21		'Church Parade. "C" and "D" Companies left for a five day's Musketry Course at First Army Musketry Camp, MATRINGHEM.	
Do.	22		Five officers joined Battalion. Training as usual.	
Do.	23		The Corps Commander inspected the Battalion this morning. "A" and "B" Companies practised the attack, and carried out Musketry Training.	
Do.	24		"A" and "B" Companies practised the attack. The Commanding officer visited "C" and "D" Companies at First Army Musketry Camp. The men had long hours of parade, but were well housed and fed, and were well reported on by the Chief Instructor.	
Do.	25		Training as usual. Draft of 25 Other Ranks joined. Lecture to officers. and senior N.C.Os. by Corps Commander. Brig.-General E.T. de S. THORPE, D.S.O., gave a lecture to officers and N.C.Os. on "Outpost Duty".	
Do.	26		Training as usual. Lecture by Commandant, 1st Army School on "Open Warfare".	
Do.	27		"A" and "B" Companies left at 8 a.m. for a six day's course at First Army Musketry Camp, MATRINGHEM. "C" and "D" Companies returned from this School.	
Do.	28		'Church Parade.	
Do.	29		"C" and "D" Companies training - Attack, and Arm Drill. Classes in Lewis Gun, Scouts, and Runners, and Signallers as usual. Musketry for N.C.Os. and R.S.M's.	

Army Form C. 2118.

WAR DIARY
or
INTELLIGENCE SUMMARY.
(Erase heading not required.)

IV

Place	Date	Hour	Summary of Events and Information	Remarks and references to Appendices
Willerval	29		R.S.M's Class daily.	
Do.	30		"C" and "D" Companies Training – Bayonet Fighting, Companies in Attack, Arm Drill and Box Respirator Drill.	

With reference to the Operations from 9th to 13th April 1918, the following Appendices are also attached hereto:—

Appendix 3. Further Notes on operations near ZELORES – 9 – 13th April 1918.
4. Extracts from Account of Operations near ZELORES – 9th – 13th April 1918, as regards "A" Company, 6th Gordon Highlanders.
5. Extracts from Report on VIEILLE CHAPELLE etc. Action by Lieut. Col. L. JAMES, Commanding 1st King Edward's Horse.
6. Statement of Casualties sustained during period 9th – 13th April 1918.
7. Copies of Operation Orders for month of April 1918.
8. Nominal Rolls of officers with Battalion as 15th and 30th April 1918.
9. Copies of Operation Orders for month of June 1916.

"HONOURS AND AWARDS" during the month of April 1918.

OFFICERS............................ Nil.
OTHER RANKS.....MILITARY MEDALS.... 14

STRENGTH/

WAR DIARY
or
INTELLIGENCE SUMMARY.
(Erase heading not required.)

Army Form C. 2118.

Summary of Events and Information

	Officers.	Other Ranks.
STRENGTH at end of last month	26	688
(INCREASE).		
Drafts joined	18	306
Casuals rejoined		51
	44	1045

	Officers.	Other Ranks.
(DECREASE).		
Casualties for period 9th to 13th April 1918 :—		
KILLED	1	15
WOUNDED	7	140
MISSING	3	185
DIED OF WOUNDS	1	6
Evacuations	—	57
Transferred to 152nd T.M. Battery.	—	6
	12	409

STRENGTH at end of this month................ 32   636

[signature]
Lieut. Colonel,
Commanding 6th Gordon Highlanders,

30th April 1918.

Appendix No. I.

Account of Operations near ZELOBES commencing on 9th April 1918 and lasting to 13th April 1918.

9th April 1918.

Map Reference 36 A SE.

The Battalion was in Billets training at Ham-en-Artois. At 5.35 a.m. orders were received from the Brigade to "stand to" at once, and at 6 a.m. orders were received to proceed to BUSNES and embus at 9 a.m. The Battalion had a hot breakfast, and arrived at BUSNES (a march of 5 kilometres) and embussed, and left there at 10.30 a.m. with orders to proceed to LES LOBES. Owing to the roads being heavily shelled the Lorries were stopped at R.25.b.2.8. and the Battalion got out of the Lorries and took up a position on each side of the road in R.25.a. A and C Companies in Artillery formation in depth to the North of the road in support of the 5th Seaforth Highrs, and D and B Companies on the South of the road in the same formation in support of the 6th Seaforth Highlanders

Commanding officers then proceeded to Brigade Head Quarters which was at R.26.a.7.5. My orders were to take up the Battalion in rear of ZELOBES to act as a reserve for the 5th and 6th Battalions Seaforth Highrs. The Battalion advanced in the formation it was in, and took up the following position :- A and C Companies 150 yards in rear of the LESTREM-LOCON Road, which was being heavily shelled, in depth, and B and D Companies in the same formation 100 yards behind the road which runs from R.26. central south through R.26.c. This road was also being heavily shelled at intervals. The Battalion was in position there at 1 p.m. My Head Quarters at the Farm at R.26.c.2.4. C Company had 10 Casualties from shells, and there were a few more casualties in the other companies, the whole area being heavily shelled between 7p.m. and 8 p.m. At 4.20 p.m. orders were received to send a company to VIEILLE CHAPELLE to defend the bridgehead there, and to report to the Commanding Officer of the KING EDWARD'S HORSE. If senior to him he was to be under him, and if not, he was to take command. "A" Company under Captain J.R. Christie was sent to VIEILLE CHAPELLE with orders to hold on to the bridgehead at all costs. He reported his dispositions that night as follows :- One platoon in the village of VIEILLE CHAPELLE and three platoons across the River LA LAWE covering the approaches to the bridgehead, dug in in section posts, and in touch with King Edward's Horse on his left and 6th Seaforth Highlanders on his right. A subsequent message was received stating that VIEILLE CHAPELLE came under orders of Col. S. Macdonald, D.S.O. 6th Seaforth Highlanders. At 7 p.m. I was sent for by the Brigadier, and got orders to form a line from R.25.b.3.2 to R.31.c.4.1. It was very dark before I got the Companies in position to dig in in section posts to make this line - C and D Companies in front and B company 400 yards in rear. In spite of the darkness this line was very well formed, and touch was maintained with 6th Black Watch on the left, but no touch was got on the right till dawn. When I inspected the line at daylight, the way it was done reflected great credit on the Officers, N.C.Os and section Commanders. I had moved my head quarters to Cottage at Q.30.d.8.8. The Brigade Head Quarters which was last situated at R.25.b.2.2. had moved to PACAUT.

The Cookers were got up at last night, and all companies except "A" Company had a hot meal. Rations were got up to "A" Company but not the Cooker. I also sent "A" Company 10 Boxes S.A.A. as the Ammunition Dump of S.A.A. arranged by the Brigade at ZELOBES POST had been partially destroyed by shell fire.

10th/

10th April 1918.

At daylight when I went round the line dug during the night, I found the men none too comfortable, as, after digging three feet down there was water, and most of them were up to their ankles in mud and water. There was intermittent shelling all the morning.

I heard at midday from Officer Commanding "A" Company acknowledging receipt of S.A.A. and Rations, and also that the village of VIEILLE CHAPELLE was being heavily shelled at intervals, but not the posts.

At 2.5 p.m. orders were received from the Brigade for a company to be ready to be sent up at a moment's notice to 6th Seaforth Highlanders. At 2.20 p.m. I got orders to send up a company to report to O.C. 6th Seaforth Highrs. to counter attack Cottages at X.3.a.2.0 and X.3.a.1.5, the counter attack to take place at 4.30 p.m. at which time the guns ✗ on the footbridge at X.3.a.3.1 would lift to the other side of the River. O.C. "D" Company detailed for this attack at once went up and placed himself under the orders of O.C. 6th Seaforth Highlanders. "D" Company formed up behind the farm at R.33.a.2.3 for the attack - one platoon to take the first farm, two platoons to go through the first objective and capture the second farm at X.3.a.2.4, the fourth platoon in reserve. While these platoons were crossing the open from the place of assembly to first objective, they came under a heavy machine gun barrage from the farm at X.3.a.2.4 and also from the houses just south of the River LAWE, and suffered many casualties. The first objective was taken and the farm found unoccupied. There is a second house (not shewn on the map) 50 yards further on, which was also unoccupied. When the two platoons for the second objective formed up and tried to rush their objective, they were stopped in the open by machine gun fire before they got there, the machine gun fire coming from the flanks and their objective. While lying out there they were attacked by a party of 50 or 60 of the enemy, who came from behind the farm, but they beat them off with ease. By this time there were only some 20 men left, and they withdrew to second farm, got two Lewis Guns in position and beat off another attack of the enemy. At dusk they withdrew, - 15 men only being left out of the 97 who took part in the counter attack.

They reassembled at the farm, where they assembled before, at R.33.a.2.3, and, with the platoon in reserve, dug in on a line about 500 yards North of the River LAWE. They were unable to get in touch with any troops on their flanks. The 6th Seaforth Highlanders were in support in the farm and along the stream behind them. They were heavily fired at by machine guns all the night, and were short of ammunition, and in the early morning withdrew when the 6th Seaforth Highlanders withdrew, and took up a line along the road LES LOBES running N.W.

At 10.45 p.m. a message was received that the enemy were moving down the road in R.27.a from the North to LES LOBES. "He must be stopped by you at all costs and driven back to the Canal". At 10.50 p.m. orders were received to move my two companies via LES LOBES and XX LOBES to XX LOBES POSTS, one company to garrison XX LOBES POSTS and one company to hold the road, running from XX LOBES POSTS to R.26.central. I issued necessary orders for this. I put my companies about 70 yards in advance of road mentioned in orders and in front of XX LOBES POSTS, - Three platoons of each company in front in section posts occupying about 500 yards of front, and one platoon of each company in rear as reserve. "B" Company were ordered to patrol the road running North and get in touch with 5th Seaforth Highlanders on his flank, "C" Coy. to get in touch with troops on his right. The Companies were in position at 2.35 A.m. I also ordered the two Machine Guns, which were at R.33.a.6.7, to support these companies and cover road.

Both these companies had a hot meal at 8 p.m. and also "D" Company. I moved my head quarters to cottage at R.26.c.10.1.

✗ firing

3.

11th April 1918.

Just as I got to my Head Quarters the sentry reported Very Lights dropping on the road on which my Head Quarters were, on my right, and coming from over main road on my right. I went out and saw these Lights myself. I got my Head Quarters Details out and made a line across the road and went off to R.25.b.2.2 where the Brigade Head Quarters had been, and where there was a telephone, and reported this to Brigade and also to O.C. 6th Seaforth Highlanders. The latter assured me his position was all right, and that he was patrolling the main road. I then met O.C. 5th Seaforth Highlanders who informed me that the enemy had got through and were behind his line about R.19.central, so we decided that he should join up with my company at R.26.central and continue my line. He gave these orders and went away shortly after to see how the line went, and almost walked into the enemy. In the meantime my companies, especially "C" Company, in front of ZELOBES POSTS were engaged with the enemy and inflicted many casualties on them in the wire in front, over 40 or 50 dead being left there. They also captured 11 prisoners and two machine guns. "C" Company was also attacked on its right flank and machine gunned from its right rear. "B" Company could not get in touch with any troops on its left, and saw our troops on its left rear withdrawing so went back and suffered heavy casualties in doing so. When I heard that these companies had come back, I put them in a line of posts which I dug on the night of the 9th, brought the left flank back and extended the line from R.25.c.5.5 to farm R.25.a.1.9, putting all troops that were withdrawing into this line. The left of this line hung on well, and engaged and stopped the enemy, but the troops on the right somewhere from LES LOBES direction came back and took my right with it, and the whole line was mixed up and out of hand. There were very few officers or N.C.Os in any Unit, and the Units were mixed. The O.C. 5th Seaforth Highlanders was with me now, and we managed to stop the line and formed a line again about the road at Q.29.d.5.5 through Q.36.central to X.1.a, and (some 8th Royal Scots were in touch on my left) with a support line some 250 yards in rear. O.C. 5th Seaforth Highlanders and I made our Head Quarters at Q.34.b.5.5. The night was quiet.

No sign of "A" Company at VIEILLE CHAPELLE. I received three messages from Captain J. R. Christie commanding this company, about 8 a.m., two timed 6.35 a.m. and one 7.45 a.m. I was unable to answer these. The first said that his left flank was being heavily pressed and that he could not get in touch with 5th Seaforth Highlanders on his left, but had been in touch with "C" Company of this Battalion and that he was withdrawing a platoon across the River LAWE to protect his left flank.

The second message said he was being very heavily shelled and in a very awkward position.

The third - "It is becoming almost unbearable. Can you give me any instructions?".

His instructions were to hold out at all costs, which he carried out.

12th April 1918.

At 5 a.m. the Brigade rang up and asked how things were, and were reported quiet. After going out I saw Very Lights being sent up from edge of wood behind our Head Quarters which looked awkward for the Brigade whose Head Quarters were at Q.27.a.5.7, so O.C. 5th Seaforth Highrs. rang up and informed them of this, and that is the last I heard of them.

I at once in consultation with Colonel Scott formed a line with our Head Quarters Details and odds and ends of Units who were found by the Cross Roads, running from Q.34.b.2.5 to Q.35.a.8.3 to cover Cross Roads. An enemy machine gun was in one of the houses in Q.28.d but when this line/

4.

line opened fire later the Machine Gun withdrew.

I visited the support line and went to 6th Seaforth Highlanders' Headquarters. There was a good deal of machine gun fire coming from my left but the guns seemed some way off.

COL. SCOTT and I then moved our Headquarters to FORT WINGES, and the line held till mid-day, when troops on the right began to fall back and most of the line came back. By this time there were practically no officers left and the men under no control. I reported to the Brigadier General of the 154th Infantry Brigade and he gave me orders to collect what men I could of 152nd Infantry Brigade and assemble them at LE CAUROY, W.S. central, leaving guides at the cross roads in WINGES to direct stragglers.

At mid-night orders were received to proceed to BUSNES where the units were billeted.

13th April 1918.

I received orders to take over command of Composite Battalion, one battalion of each 6th Gordon Highlanders, 5th and 6th Seaforth Highlanders, and got each unit made up into a company of about 150 strong.

I sent Company officers to reconnoitre Divisional Front and reconnoitred it myself.

Appendix II

Notes on operations near ZELOBES commencing on 9th April 1918 and lasting till 13th April 1918.

The most satisfactory part of these operations struck me as being the way the positions were taken up on the first day. There was very little opportunity for reconnoitring but the orders issued from the Brigade were very clear and the geographical features such as the River LAWE and roads facilitated this, but in spite of this whether during the day or night, mostly at night, when positions had to be taken up, they were carried out rapidly and without any confusion, which showed good training and grasp of situation for all Company Commanders and their subordinates.

Formations.

As far as this Battalion was concerned, it showed that when moving a battalion over open country which is being shelled, moving in artillery formation in depth over the country and avoiding roads, is a very good formation for taking up a position.

The supply of S.A.A. under arrangements of the Brigade was very good and worked very well.

The arrangements also for bringing up the cookers and rations every night under the Staff Captain of the Brigade were excellent, and the men got a hot meal every night.

The absence of any Trench Mortars was much felt. When "D" Company of this battalion had to counter-attack the houses on this side of the River LAWE, I asked for Trench Mortars or Stokes Mortars and could get neither. They would have been invaluable for crumping the cottages both on this side and the other side of the River and putting a barrage up on the footbridge and approaches to it. These places could not be dealt with by our guns as the infantry were too close, and when my company had to counter-attack they did so with practically no artillery support which was promised in the order to attack.

Ammunition for Mortars could easily have been brought up.

With regard to training the men, it was noticeable how dependent the men are on their Officers and N.C.Os., and I think every effort should be made to get platoon commanders to explain to their section commanders what the orders to be carried out are and the general situation. I feel sure much as one tries to get it done, it is not done enough, and if each man knew the situation it would help very much and I think men are left too much in ignorance of what is going on and what troops are behind them, etc. Company Commanders are told the situation and it should be impressed on them to let their platoon commanders and through them the section commanders know the situation.

Another important point which is hard to impress on men is that they are much safer lying in the open than in a trench which is marked on the map. I don't think too much stress can be laid on this.

Fire control of sections is most important. There is too much wild firing altogether.

The Lewis Gun Teams worked very well and did very good work in many cases.

The mixing up of units should be avoided as mu[ch] on 6th Seaforth Highlanders' front on the night [of] April 1918, there were the following units oppo[site] footbridge on right :- 7th Argyll & Sutherland ; a company of 4th Gordon Highlanders, then a comp[any] Gordon Highlanders, then 6th Seaforth Highlander[s] e.g. one company 4th Gordon Highlanders and a co[mpany] Gordon Highlanders being put in between the 7th Sutherland/

Sutherland Highlanders and 6th Seaforth Highlanders.

When the troops withdrew on the 12th April 1918. I think it was mainly because there were practically no officers or N.C.Os. left and there was no command at all. If there had been I don't think there would have been any withdrawal in spite of the mixture of units as in certain parts of the line which were commanded, the troops remained for several hours after the troops on their flanks had gone.
As is already known the new draft of 18½ year old boys had only been with this battalion two days so could not be expected to know their officers or N.C.Os., and after two sleepless nights and strain of the first two days, they were very highly tried, but in spite of this there were a few who showed very good spirit and endurance.

Patrolling and outpost duty is a part of training which owing to trench warfare has been entirely left out of the present training, and in my opinion every opportunity should be made to train every man in both duties.

The enemy artillery was at times was terrific on the front line. Our Field Artillery on the 12th April were splendid, and stopped the enemy's first attack at dawn, and during the rest of the day, were excellent, and from information from the front of my line that held on the left and who were engaged with the enemy, I was able to give the gunners some good targets, which they took full advantage of.

Very few enemy aeroplanes were seen over our lines and numbers of ours were about all day in all weathers during the operations.

The use the enemy made of Very Lights was very ingenious. As far as I can gather he sent two or three men forward with Very Lights, 100 or 200 yards in front of hisline. These men threw up lights and lit up the ground, and if they saw nothing the line behind them came forward, and the Very Light men were sent on again, and so on. He also lit fires at various places, presumably for guiding lights or taking bearings.

The 11 prisoners we took were all of them miserable specimens of humanity.

A good dug position in rear would hold the enemy up better than any other line as the men have got so accustomed to trenches and I think it is advisable that such a position should always be dug; to ensure this a dump of shovels should be made in rear.

I had 200 shovels dumped at my Headquarters at Q.30.b.8.8. which were most valuable in making a line afterwards.

There is too much movement and lack of concealment when positions are dug in section posts. It should be impressed on all ranks that when once dug in there should be no movement as it only gives the position away.

The arrangements for the evacuation of the wounded worked splendidly.

a.a.o.ff. Lt Col
Major,
Commanding 6th Gordon Highlanders.

17th April, 1918.

appendix no III.

Further NOTES ON OPERATIONS near ZELOBES
commencing on 9th April 1918 and
lasting to 15th April 1918.

DISPOSITIONS. In open country which is being shelled advancing in artillery formation in depth and keeping off roads showed itself on two occasions during the recent operations a very good formation for taking up positions.

Taking up a new defensive line was very badly done. All ranks seemed to consider it necessary to have a long continuous line, sited right in the middle of the area, to be defended. Very frequently a position could /have been defended with fewer casualties and better results by a few well selected posts. The rest of the available men could then be disposed of in depth.

COMMUNICATION. During the first two days of the operations communication on flanks was well maintained but after that when troops were moving in the open this was not the case, and I consider not enough use was made of visual signalling.

RIFLE GRENADE. There were few opportunities for good use of rifle grenades as far as my battalion was concerned.

LEWIS GUNS. The Lewis Gunners proved very good. Lack of control of rifle fire was most noticeable.. There were a few individual cases were good control of fire proved how important it is. I don't think too much reliance was placed on the Lewis Gunners but not enough use was made of the rifle especially where there was a machine gun barrage, the men in many cases keeping down and not firing although the barrage may not have been close to them.

TRENCH MORTARS. The want of Light Trench Mortars was certainly felt as they would have been most useful in dealing with houses, in which the enemy had mounted machine guns along the River LAWE. The supply of ammunition would not have been difficult. Cookers and limbers with S.A.A. went up every night along the road from LES LOBES to ZELOBES. Trench Mortars could have got within effective range of all the houses on the River LAWE.

The method of advancing by the enemy appeared to be to rush a machine gun up and then the infantry dribbled up under covering fire of this machine gun. At night it was done with Very Lights. Two or three men went ahead with Very Lights, sent up a light and lit up the ground, and when they saw no movement, signalled to parties in rear who came up, and then the Very Light party went ahead and repeated this operation. Several fires appeared to be lit by the enemy evidently as Guiding Lights or to take bearings on.

PATROLLING AND OUTPOSTS. The importance of training troops in the method of patrolling and outpost duty is most necessary, this part of training having dropped out entirely during trench warfare.

Throwing out Advance Guards and Rear Guards should also be practiced.

17th April 1918.

Major,
Commanding 6th Gordon Highlanders.

Appendix No. IV

6TH GORDON HIGHLANDERS.

EXTRACTS from ACCOUNT OF OPERATIONS near
ZELOBES, commencing on 9th April, 1918, and
lasting to 13th April, 1918, as regards "A"
Company of this Battalion.

Map Reference 36A. S.E.

9th April, 1918.

At 4.20 p.m. orders were received to send a Company to VIEILLE CHAPELLE to defend the Bridgehead there, and to report to the Officer Commanding, King Edward's Horse. If senior to him he was to be under him, and if not, he was to take command. "A" Company under Captain J.R. CHRISTIE was sent to VIEILLE CHAPELLE with orders to hold on to the Bridgehead at all costs. He reported his dispositions that night as follows :- One platoon in the Village of VIEILLE CHAPELLE and three platoons across the River LAWE covering the approaches to the Bridgehead, dug in in section posts, and in touch with King Edward's Horse on his left and 6th Seaforth Highlanders on his right. A subsequent message was received stating that VIEILLE CHAPELLE came under orders of Col. S. McDONALD, D.S.O., 6th Seaforth Highlanders.

The cookers were got up at night and all companies except "A" Company had a hot meal. Rations were got up to "A" Company but not the cooker. I also sent "A" Company 10 Boxes S.A.A., as the Ammunition Dump of S.A.A. arranged for by the Brigade at ZELOBES POST had been partially destroyed by shell fire.

10th April, 1918.

I heard at mid-day from Officer Commanding "A" Company acknowledging receipt of S.A.A. and Rations, and also that the Village of VIEILLE CHAPELLE was being heavily shelled at intervals, but not the posts.

11th April, 1918.

No sign of "A" Company at VIEILLE CHAPELLE. I received three messages from Captain J.R. CHRISTIE, commanding this company, about 6 a.m., two timed 6.35 a.m. and one 7.45 a.m. I was unable to answer these. The first said that his left flank was being heavily pressed and that he could not get in touch with 5th Seaforth Highlanders on his left, but had been in touch with "C" Company of this battalion, and that he was withdrawing a platoon across the River LAWE to protect his left flank.

The second message said he was being very heavily shelled and in a very awkward position.

The third - "It is becoming almost unbearable. Can you give me any instructions?".

His instructions were to hold out at all costs, which he carried out.

The following messages were received by Officer Commanding, 6th Gordon Highlanders, relative to the above :-

152nd Infantry Brigade Message No. B.M.101 dated 9/4/18 in reply to K.E.H. 572 :-

"1 Coy. of 6th Gordon Hrs. is being sent up to reinforce your VIEILLE CHAPELLE post and will come under your ordersaaa There is no question of RELIEF on the hostile front and all troops will remain in their present positions aaa VIEILLE CHAPELLE bridgehead must be held at all costs aaa Dispositions of 6th Seaforth Highlanders on your right are - Distributed in 3 lines in depth front line immediately W. of LAWE R. and extending from Bridge X.3.a.1.2. to VIEILLE CHAPELLE aaa Touch has been obtained with 55 Div. on/

"on right aaa Addressed K.E.H. repeated 6th Gordon
Highlanders aaa 152nd Infantry Brigade, 4.20 p.m. (signed)
R. BIRNEY FICKLIN, Capt. Brigade Major".

152nd Infantry Brigade Message No. B.M.116 dated 9/4/18 :-

"If O.C. 6th Seaforth Highlanders considers that VIEILLE
CHAPELLE can be held with fewer men company of 6th
Gordon Highlanders sent up there this afternoon will be
sent back to Brigade Headquarters aaa Addressed 6th
Seaforth Highlanders repeated 6th Gordon Highlanders aaa
152nd Infantry Brigade, 9.10 p.m. (signed) R. BIRNEY
FICKLIN, Capt. B.M.".

R.S. 1 dated 10/4/18 :-

"I am O.C. "B" Sqdn. K.E.H. attached to your /K/ Company at
VIEILLE CHAPELLE Bridgehead aaa It has been reported to me
that "A" and "C" Sqdns. K.E.H. who were at FOSSE Bridgehead
have been relieved aaa Would you please ask the Brigade if
I am being relieved to-day and if so by whom? aaa The
position is such that it would require two strong platoons
to relieve my squadron aaa (signed) Ian R. B. STIEN, Lt.
"B" Sqdn. K.E.H., R.34.a.7.9., 4.10 p.m.".

6th Gordon Highlanders Message No. J.R. 15 dated 9/4/18 to
NAII :-
"The following message has been sent me aaa Have you any
instructions aaa Begins ..... above R.S. 1 Message
.... ends, NASAI, (signed) J. R. RAITT".

152nd Infantry Brigade Message No. B.M. 177 dated 10/4/18 in
reply to number J.R. 15 :-
"K.E.H. holding VIEILLE CHAPELLE will not be relieved till
further orders aaa Of K.E.H. who were relieved from FOSSE
only sufficient numbers to look after horses were sent back
and remainder are still under orders of 5th Seaforth
Highlanders aaa 152nd Infantry Brigade, 6.10 p.m.

SECRET.   Appendix No V.   XI Corps G.A. 221.

First Army.

    I forward herewith the Report of Lt. Col. L. JAMES, Commdg 1st King Edward's Horse, on the VIEILLE CHAPELLE & MAISONS FOSSE Bridgeheads' action - April 9th, 1918.
    I think it was a very fine ~~soldier~~ performance.

        sd/ R. HAKING, Lt. Gen.

        Commdg. XI Corps.

15.4.18.

Copy to 51st Division.

-2-

S.G. 715/23.

152nd Infantry Brigade.

    The G. O. C. directs me to say that he has great pleasure in forwarding the attached report to be passed to the 5th Seaforth Highlanders.

        sd/ F. W. BEWSHER, Major, G.S.
          for Colonel,
          General Staff,
        51st (Highland) Division.

18th April, 1918

H 1.

The Officer Commanding,
   5th Bn. Seaforth Highlanders.

2.   Attached is forwarded in accordance with Minute

    Well done 5th Seaforth Highlanders !

        sd/ E. T. THORPE,
          Br. Genr.
        Commanding 152nd Infy. Brigade.

18th April, 1918.

EXTRACTS/

EXTRACTS from Report on VIEILLE CHAPELLE, HUITS MAISONS, FOSSE Bridgeheads, - Action - April 9th 1918 (Map 36A. S.E. 1/20,000), of Lt. Col. L. JAMES, Commanding 1st King Edward's Horse.

S E C R E T.
No. K.E.H. 365/18.

2.15 p.m. I received a message from 152nd Infantry Brigade that a company of 6th Gordon Highlanders had been sent to VIEILLE CHAPELLE under Capt. CHRISTIE and had been placed under my command. I sent a message to Lt. STEIN of my regiment to that effect and the same orders "Hold On". I sent a similar message to my left sector. My independent patrol having lost its commander killed and one missing now reported that BOUT DEVILLE was full of enemy with machine guns, and that there had been hand to hand fighting in the left of my left sector in which I had had two officers and several men killed.

The situation on my immediate front now became menacing. The enemy appeared to be massing in BOUT DEVILLE, uncertain about FOSSE and refusing it, to be working round my left towards LE MARAIS. At 1500 yards we could see successive waves of extended infantry moving west through R.17.central. We opened on these at long range but I had to husband my Hotchkiss ammunition. These enemy were very gallantly engaged by the Durham L.I. post in LE MARAIS FARM and although the enemy continued to build up in front of LE MARAIS we were not troubled by them until later in the evening.

3 p.m. Col. SCOTT withdrew has H.Q. to R.21.c. I remained at FOSSE Bridgehead. 3.30 p.m. Lieut. FINCKLEY of my regiment came in front VIEILLE CHAPELLE with a verbal message from Capt. CHRISTIE asking if I would let them withdraw. As I had received orders from the G. O. C., 152nd Infantry Brigade that the two Bridgeheads must be held at all costs I reiterated my previous orders.

Shortly after 4 p.m. I heard that the enemy had forced the Durhams out of LE MARAIS and we had practical demonstration as a machine gun now brought long range fire actually on the FOSSE BRIDGE. Col SCOTT had given me 30 Highlanders and they were put out as a left defensive flank along the MARAIS ROAD. The enemy were still refusing a direct attack upon the FOSSE BRIDGEHEAD.

8.15 p.m. I received an order from G.O.C., 152nd Inf. Bde. that he had divided his front into two sectors and all troops in the left sector would be under Col. SCOTT and all troops in the right sector would be under Col. McDonald. These orders divided VIEILLE CHAPELLE from the FOSSE command. I immediately reported to Col. SCOTT and placed myself and men at his disposal. Before I reported Lt. FINCKLEY again came in from VIEILLE CHAPELLE and said that Capt. CHRISTIE was still holding VIEILLE CHAPELLE POST proper but that the situation was desperate. I told this officer the new situation and where to report and gave him a last order to fall back if pressed to the shorter Bridgehead at VIEILLE CHAPELLE and to hold that to the end. This order I am proud to say was carried out and the last message from this bridgehead still held by the Highlanders, and my men was sent off at 8 a.m. on April 11th, 36 hours later.

From this point forward I was under Col. SCOTT'S command until I received orders to withdraw all my men except 40 at 10 a.m. on the following morning.
I would bring to the notice of the G.O.C., XITH Corps all my officers. All ranks quitted themselves like men. It would be impossible for men to speak temporately of Capt. CHRISTIE, Gordons, Lt. STEIN, FINCKLEY, and LAURINSON of my regiment. Unfortunately/

unfortunately I do not know the names of Capt. CHRISTIE's other officers. Major FURZE, who is an officer of the highest fighting quality assures me that he did magnificent execution with all his arms in the defence of 8 MAISONS and specially calls to my attention Capt. SUTHERLAND of the 5th Seaforths, Lt. ADDISON and Lt. RICH of my own regiment.
I may add that the reconnaissances of the positions which I was ordered to make previous to the operation proved of the utmost value and materially added to the defence of the position

          sd/ LIONEL JAMES, Lt. Col.
                 1st K. E. H.

14.4.18.

Appendix No. VI.

6TH GORDON HIGHLANDERS.

CASUALTIES SUSTAINED 9th – 13th April 1918.

OFFICERS.

KILLED.
    2/Lieut. J. Drysdale   11.4.18.

WOUNDED.
    Lieut. W. Dawson   12.4.18.
        "   R. S. Henderson   11.4.18.
        "   J. K. Allan   12.4.18.
    2/Lieut. J. S. Riddell   9.4.18.
        "   G. E. Wilkins   10.4.18.
        "   J. M. Ross   10.4.18.
        "   I. O. Morison   10.4.18.

DIED OF WOUNDS.
    Capt. D. G. Clark, M.C.   13.4.18.

MISSING.
    Capt. J. R. Christie   11.4.18.
    Lieut. P. W. Lyon   11.4.18.
    2/Lieut. A. D. Miller, M.C.   11.4.18.

OTHER RANKS.

KILLED	15
WOUNDED	140
Unaccounted For	185
DIED OF WOUNDS	6

	OFFICERS.	OTHER RANKS.
TOTAL CASUALTIES	12	346

Appendix No. VII
Copy No. 6

6TH GORDON HIGHLANDERS.

Operation Orders No. 181.

27th April, 1918.

REFERENCE MAP:—
HAZEBROUCK (1/40,000).

1. O.C. "A" Company with 2 Officers and 60 Other Ranks will proceed by route march to First Army Musketry Camp, MARTINQUES, to-morrow.

2. Orders for march:—

    Starting Point — Church, WITTERNESSE.

    Time — 7.30 a.m.

    Transport — Lewis Gun Limber will proceed with Company to MARTINQUES. & Cooker
    ~~Cooker will be left at WITTERNESSE.~~
    Lewis Gun Limber will carry five guns and usual complement of magazines, S.A.A. and carriers.

    Route — LINGHEM – GUARBECQUE – BEAURETZ – LES AMUSOIRES.

    Dress — Marching order.

3. Baggage. Blankets rolled in bundles by sections and officers' valises will be dumped at Church, WITTERNESSE, at 7 a.m. A reliable N.C.O. will be left in charge. Arrangements for collection and conveyance to MARTINQUES as early as possible to-morrow will be made by Adjutant. Rations for tomorrow will be taken with party. Yes subsequent

4. Rations. day rations will be drawn at Refilling Point each day commencing to-morrow and forwarded to MARTINQUES.

5. Company Quartermaster Sergeant and Sanitary Men will proceed with party. Men who are present isolated will be left at WITTERNESSE. Lewis Gun Instructor and sufficient Lewis Gunners in Beginners' Class to reduce numbers to 60 Other Ranks will be left at WITTERNESSE. One Senior N.C.O. to act as Quartermaster Sergeant for party at WITTERNESSE will be left behind.

6. Billets will be left scrupulously clean and a certificate that this has been done will be rendered to Orderly Room before moving off.

7. ACKNOWLEDGE.

                    sd/ R. KING, Capt. & Adjt.,
                    6th Gordon Highlanders.

Copies to:—

    No. 1   File.
    2   H.Q., 152nd Infy. Bde.
    3   O.C., "A" Company.
    4   Q.M.
    5   T.O.
    6   War Diary.

SECRET.

6th GORDON HIGHLANDERS.

Copy No. 10

Operation Orders No. 180.

26th April, 1918.

REFERENCE MAP :- HAZEBROUCK (1/40,000).

1. "C" and "D" Companies will return by route march from First Army Musketry Camp, HARDINGHEM, to-morrow, 27th instant. They will march off in time to arrive in billets by 12 noon and will have dinners on arrival.

2. "B" Company will proceed to First Army Musketry Camp, HARDINGHEM, by route march to-morrow, 27th instant.

3. Orders for March for "B" Company :-

   Starting Point ... ... Church, WITTERNESSE.

   Time ... ... 1 p.m.

   Transport ... ... Cooker, Watercart, and Lewis Gun limber will proceed with Company to HARDINGHEM and will march in rear. Lewis gun limber will carry 5 guns and usual complement of magazines, S.A.A. and Carriers.

   Route ... ... LINGHEM - GUARBECQUE - BEAUMONT-LES-AIRE -

   Dress ... ... Marching Order.

4. BAGGAGE.
   "B" Company's blankets, rolled in bundles by sections, and officers' valises will be dumped at Church, WITTERNESSE ready for collection by 9.30 a.m. They will be collected and taken to HARDINGHEM by lorry. On arrival at HARDINGHEM, the same lorry will collect and bring to WITTERNESSE blankets and valises of "C" & "D" Companies.

5. ADVANCE PARTY.
   "B" Company will detail one N.C.O. to proceed with baggage lorry. This N.C.O. will be under the orders of an officer to be detailed by 5th Seaforth Highlanders under whose orders he will arrange billets for his Company at HARDINGHEM.

6. RATIONS.
   "B", "C" & "D" Companies will carry rations for to-morrow, 27th instant. Rations for "B" Company will be deducted at Refilling Point each day and forwarded to HARDINGHEM.

7. Companies will proceed complete and will include Instructors, Quartermaster-Sergeants, Sanitary Men, &c. Men attached to Headquarters will NOT proceed with "B" Company.

8. Billets will be left scrupulously clean and a certificate that this has been done will be rendered to Orderly Room before moving off.

9. "C" & "D" Companies will report arrival in billets at WITTERNESSE to Orderly Room in writing.

10. ACKNOWLEDGE.

SO/ R. KERR, Capt. & Adjt.
6th Gordon Highlanders.

SECRET.   Copy No. 8

6TH GORDON HIGHLANDERS.
Operation Orders No. 179.
20th April, 1918.

Reference Map :- HAZEBROUCK (1/40,000.).

1. "C" and "D" Companies will proceed to the First Army Musketry Camp, MATRINGHEM, by route march, to-morrow 21st instant for a course of Musketry.

2. Orders for March :-

    Starting Point   —   Church, WITTERNESSE.

    Time ... ...   —   8 a.m.

    Order of March   —   "C" Company, "D" Company. Companies will march in column of route. "C" and "D" Companies' Cookers and Lewis Gun Limbers and one Watercart will accompany Companies." Lewis Gun Limbers will carry five Company Lewis Guns and usual complement of Magazines, Carriers, and S.A.A.

    " & will march in rear

    Route   —   LINGHEM - OUHEM - BEAUMETZ-LESAIRE

    Dress   —   Marching Order.

3. **Baggage.** Blankets rolled in bundles by sections, and Officers' Valises, will be dumped outside No. 10 Billet ready for collection by 8.15 a.m.

4. **Advance Party.** 2/Lieut. WATT and 1 N.C.O. per Company will proceed with lorry detailed for baggage and will report to the Commandant, 1st Army Musketry Camp, MATRINGHEM for billets.

5. **Rations.** Companies will carry rations for to-morrow. Quartermaster will send a representative to Refilling Point daily at 8 a.m. to deduct the rations for "C" & "D" Companies and see them loaded on to a lorry which will convey them to the Musketry Camp. Necessary forage will be deducted and sent at the same time.

6. Companies will proceed complete and will include Instructors Quartermaster-Sergeants, Sanitary Men &c. Men attached to Headquarters will NOT proceed with Companies.

7. Billets will be left scrupulously clean and a certificate that this has been done will be rendered to Orderly Room before moving off.

8. Companies will render Parade States to Orderly Room before their departure.

9. The strictest march discipline will be observed. O.C. "D" Company will detail a Rear Party under a responsible N.C.O.

10. ACKNOWLEDGE.

                                                        Sd/ R. RIDD, Capt. & Adj.
                                                        6th Gordon Highlanders.

Copies to :-
No. 1	File	No. 5	Sgt. LOGIE.
2	H.Q. 152nd Infantry Brigade.	6	Q.M.
3	O.C. "C" Company.	7	T.O.
4	O.C. "D" Company.	8	War Diary.

[War Diary]

6TH GORDON HIGHLANDERS.

Copy No......11....

Operation Orders No. 178.

9th April, 1918.

Reference Map :-
    SDA 1/40,000.

1. The Battalion will proceed by route march to BUSNES CHURCH where it will embus and proceed to position between LES HUGO and BELGIAN R.TE. where battalion will be distributed in depth for defence.

2. Orders for march :-

    Starting Point   —   Railway Station, R.W.

    Time   —   8 a.m.

    Order of march   —   H.Q., A., B., C., & D.

    Dress   —   Fighting Order. Coats rolled.

Lewis Gun limbers will march in rear of respective companies.

3. All employed men, and all instructors will be left at Transport Lines.

4. Breakfasts will be finished before moving off.
    Blankets will be rolled in bundles and left with packs in charge of party remaining behind.

5. APPENDICES.

                        (Sd/ R. BEST, Lieut. & A/Adj.,
                            6th Gordon Highlanders.

Copies to :-
    1   —   File.
    2   —   H.Q. 152nd I.F. Bde.
    3 – 6 — Companies.
    7   —   Q.M.
    8   —   T.O.
    9. —   O. i/c H.Q. Details.
    10. —   H.Q. Mess.
    11. —   War Diary.
    12. —   Spare.

SECRET-   Copy No.........

6TH GORDON HIGHLANDERS.

Operation Orders No. 177.

5th April, 1918.

–o–o–o–o–o–o–o–o–o–o–o–o–o–o–o–o–o–o–o–o–o–o–o–oeo–o–

1. **MOVE.**
In continuation of Warning Order of to-day, the 6th Gordon Highlanders will proceed by route march to-day to MANQUEVILLE.

2. **ORDERS FOR MARCH.**

    Starting Point   –   D.21.a.1.9.

    Time   –   3.18 p.m.

    Order of March   –   H.Q., D. A. B. C. Companies.
                                    Transport will march in rear of Battalion.

    Interval between Companies – 100 yards.

    Interval between rear Coy.
      and Transport   –   100 yards.

    Dress   –   As in warning order. Blankets will be carried on the man. All men who have not kilts will march as a party 300 yards in rear of Battalion.

    Route   –   D.21.a.1.9. – ALLOUAGNE – LILLERS – MANQUEVILLE.

3. **BILLETS.**
Billets will be left scrupulously clean, and a certificate that this has been done rendered to Orderly Room before moving off.

4. **ARRIVAL.**
Companies will report immediately on arrival in new billets.

5. **ALARM POSTS.**
Alarm Posts will be selected by Companies and H.Q. Details in new area and shown to men before they are dismissed.

6. **ACKNOWLEDGE.**

                                                 sd/ R. RISK, Capt. & Adj.,
                                                      6th Gordon Highlanders.

SECRET.   6TH GORDON HIGHLANDERS.   Copy No........

Operation Orders No. 176.

4th April, 1918.

-o-o-o-o-o-o-o-o-o-o-o-o-o-o-o-o-o-o-o-o-o-o-o-o-o-o-

Reference Map :-
    BETHUNE 1/40,000.

1. **MOVE.**
    The 6th Gordon Highlanders will move to LAPUGNOY by route march to-day.

2. **ORDERS FOR MARCH.**

Starting Point	-	Road Junction, W.19.d.4.6.
Time	-	10.50 a.m.
Route	-	CHOCQUES - LAPUGNOY.
Order of March	-	H.Q., C. D. A. B. Transport will march in rear of Battln.
Interval	-	500 yards between Battalions. 100 yards between Companies. 100 yards between Battalion and Transport.
Dress	-	Marching Order. One blanket per man will be carried on the man.

3. **ALARM POSTS.**
    On arrival in new area all companies and H.Q. Details will be given an Alarm Post and these Alarm Posts will be pointed out to all Ranks before they are dismissed.

4. **BAGGAGE.**
    All baggage will be ready for collection by 9.40 a.m. Officers valises and mess kits will be dumped either at Battalion H.Q. or at Road Junction W.20.c.4.0. (near Church Army Hut).

5. **BILLITING.**
    One N.C.O. and three men per company and two men from H.Q. Details will report to Lieut. C. A. Cowie at Orderly Room at 6.30 a.m. Party will then proceed to HENDIN-LES-BETHUNE, reporting to the Staff Captain at W.27.c.1.4. (Church) at 7.15 a.m.
    Lieut. C. A. COWIE will report to Adjutant before moving off.

6. **BILLETS.**
    Billets will be left scrupulously clean and a certificate that this has been done will be delivered at H.Q. before moving off.

7. **ARRIVAL.**
    Companies will report to H.Q. in writing on arrival in new billets.

8. **ACKNOWLEDGE.**

                                             sd/ R. RISK, Lieut. & A/Adj.,
                                                  6th Gordon Highlanders.

SECRET. COPY No........

6TH GORDON HIGHLANDERS.

Operation Orders No. 175.

2nd April, 1918.

1. In continuance of Warning Order of to-day, following orders are issued for the move of the battalion.

   The battalion will march in column of route.

   Starting Point   -   D.11.d.9.2. (Road Junction East of Brigade H.Q.).

   Time   -   2.15 p.m.

   Order of march   -   H.Q., B, C, D, & A.

   Dress   -   Marching Order. Blankets will be carried on the man.

   Route   -   ~~Road Junction~~ ANNEZIN – VENDEN – OBLINGHEM.

2. Transport will move under orders of Transport Officer. Cookers will march in rear of Battalion.

3. Billets will be left scrupulously clean, and a certificate that this has been done rendered to Orderly Room.

4. Companies will report immediately they are in billets.

5. ACKNOWLEDGE.

                                    sd/ R. RISK, Lieut. & A/Adj.,
                                         6th Gordon Highlanders.

Confidential.

Vol 43

War Diary

of

1/6th Bn Gordon Highrs.

to May, 1918.

Army Form C. 2118.

confidential.

1.

WAR DIARY
or
INTELLIGENCE SUMMARY.

(Erase heading not required.)

Instructions regarding War Diaries and Intelligence Summaries are contained in F. S. Regs. Part II. and the Staff Manual respectively. Title pages will be prepared in manuscript.

Place	Date	Hour	Summary of Events and Information	Remarks and references to Appendices
WITTERNESSE	1.5.18		General Programme of Training for C and D Coys. Specialists classes for:- Lewis Gunners, Scouts & Runners, Signallers. A and B Coys at First Army School of Musketry MATRINGHEM.	MAP REFERENCE HAZEBROUCK 5A-1/100000
	2.5.18		General Programme of training for C and D Coys. Captain D. McKelvey, M.C. proceeded for duty to the 2/1st Highland Field Ambulance, and Captain R.H. Jamieson, A.A.M.C., took over the duties of Medical Officer to the Battalion.	
	3.5.18		General Programme of training for C and D Coys, and Classes for Specialists. A and B Coys returned by route march from 1st Army School of Musketry at MATRINGHEM.	
	4.5.18		Battalion training (All Companies) (General programme) All Specialists with their companies. In the afternoon all companies marched to ECOHINGHIE for baths. Draft of 36 Other Ranks joined. Transport proceeded by road to ECURIE to reach there on night of 5th inst.	LENS 11 O.O.182
	5.5.18		The Battalion marched to AIRE Station, parading at 7.30 a.m. and entrained at 10 a.m. and detrained at ACQ at 4.30 p.m. Thereafter the Battalion marched to NEUVILLE ST VAAST where billets were in huts. Wet weather made the roads heavy and marching difficult.	
NEUVILLE ST VAAST	6.5.18		The morning was spent in preparing for the line. The Battalion marched off at 5 p.m. by platoons at 50 yards interval to ROCLINCOURT. After a rest and teas the Battalion marched up to the line, and took over the Sector occupied by the 50th Canadian Infantry Battalion on a front from R.17.c.0.2 to R.29.a.0.6. B, C, and D companies from right to left in the Front Line, and A Company in support. 16 officers and 387 Other Ranks with the Battalion (being roughly half the strength of the 50th Canadian Infantry Battalion in these trenches. A very good "hand over" was given the Battalion by the 50th Canadian Infantry Battalion./	MAP REFERENCE MAREQUIL 1/20,000 O.O.183

Army Form C. 2118.

WAR DIARY
or
INTELLIGENCE SUMMARY.
(Erase heading not required.)

Place	Date	Hour	Summary of Events and Information	Remarks and references to Appendices
IN THE LINE	7/5/18		Battalion, and the relief was accomplished without casualties, although rendered difficult by wet weather and a very dark night.	
	8/5/18		Wet weather continued. Enemy quiet. Communication Trenches bad, but owing to width of front held by the Battalion (2000 yards) and weakness in numbers, no labour available to drain them.	
	9/5/18		Owing to the adjustments of the line, this Battalion is now left front Battalion with 6th Seaforth Highlanders on the Right and 5th Seaforth Highlanders in support. A quiet day.	
	10/5/18		Battalion front shortened. Brigade on our left taking over south to R.27.a.7.8 and 6th Seaforth Highlanders relieving us of 150 yards on R Company's Right. Weather improved. Much movements on enemy front furnished good targets for the Field and Heavy Artillery.	
	11/5/18		Movement seen yesterday afternoon and evening having been thought to be an enemy concentration with a view to attack, preparations were made to disorganise the assembly of enemy troops, but the Artillery dispersed concentration and no attack materialised. Remainder of day quiet.	
			Our Artillery fairly active. Enemy's quiet. Nothing to record.	
	12/5/18		The day was uneventful. At night this Battalion was relieved by the 5th Sea--forth Highlanders, and moved back into support. The relief was accomplished smoothly and without casualties. Casualties for the tour of 6 days :- killed Other Ranks - 2 wounded do. - 7	O.O.194
	13/5/18		The Companies were widely scattered in the support area, and the day was spent in organising the defences. At night the Battalion provided a working party of 12 officers and 350 men to dig a new trench in front of present front line between TOWY ALLEY and THAMES ALLEY.	MAP REFERENCE MAREQUIL 1/20000

D. Durine,

Army Form C. 2118.

WAR DIARY
or
INTELLIGENCE SUMMARY.
(Erase heading not required.)

Place	Date	Hour	Summary of Events and Information	Remarks and references to Appendices
	14.5.18		During the day the Battalion continued improving defence positions, and at night again provided a party of 12 officers and 350 men for work on a new front line Trench.	
	15.5.18		Nothing to report. Working party again dug on new front line trench.	
	16.5.18		Enemy Artillery more active on Battery areas chiefly. Battalion working party for new front line again provided.	
	17.5.18		Enemy shelling again heavy around Support company and Head quarter areas. The day otherwise uneventful. At 10 p.m. the Battalion was relieved by 7th Bn Gordon Highlanders, and marched back to ECURIE CAMP, where billets were good. The relief was effected without incident or casualties. Casualties for the 5 days in support area :- 1 Other Rank wounded.	
	18.5.18		The day was spent resting and cleaning up. A draft of 143 other Ranks joined the Battalion, and companies were reorganised into three platoons of four Sections each.	
	19.5.18		The Battalion had Baths and change of clothing. Church Services were held.	
	20.5.18		A full programme of training was carried out in the forenoon, special attention being devoted to Lewis Gun Classes. The Battalion provided two working parties - each of 6 officers and 200 men for work on the POST LINE just EAST of BAILLEUL.	
	21.5.18		No forenoon parades with the exception of Specialist classes. Saluting drill in the afternoon and lecture to officers and N.C.Os by Corps Gas officer and Commanding Officer. Lieut. J. Black joined Battalion from England.	
	22.5.18		Battalion marched to BRAY Rifle Range to see demonstration arranged by Brigade in effect of rapid harassing fire by a platoon (20 rifles) rifle	

WAR DIARY
or
INTELLIGENCE SUMMARY.
(Erase heading not required.)

Army Form C. 2118.

Place	Date	Hour	Summary of Events and Information	Remarks and references to Appendices
	22.5.18		Thereafter B Company carried out Musketry practices – Grouping at 100 yards, Application and Rapid at 200 yards. A Company was accompanied by its Cooker, and after dinners carried out Grouping at 100 yards and Application at 200 yards. Specialist classes during forenoon in Camp.	
	23.5.18		All Companies went to baths during forenoon. Company Commanders went up to Front line to arrange relief with respective Company Commanders of 4th Gordon Highlanders. The Battalion relieved 4th An Gordon Highlanders in the left section of the OPPY Sector – i.e. from the left Divisional Boundary – TIRED ALLEY – to BOW TRENCH and SUGAR FACTORY. The relief was carried out by daylight 2 – 7.30 p.m. Dispositions :- Right Front Coy - B Coy. - BOW TRENCH. Left " " " - D " - PIMPLE. Support " " - C " - POST LINE. Reserve " " - A " - LONG WOOD. Bn Head Quarters = in Railway Cutting near LONG WOOD. All four Companies are organised in three platoons of four sections each.	MAP REFERENCE MAREOUIL
	24.5.18		"STAND TO" 3.15 a.m. Night without event. Some shelling. Wind W.N.W. Cold, and day broke wet. Rain most of the day on account of which the usual night working parties were cancelled by Brigade Orders. The number of Officers with the Battalion in the line being limited by order to 4 per Company and 6 at Head Qrs., those in excess of this returned to "Echelon B" at ECOIVRES. Rations for the Brigade in the line coming by light Railway from ECOIVRES due here at 10 p.m. only reached the Battalion at 12.45 a.m. on Saturday 25th inst., 6 hours for 10 miles – a naturally wrathful crew of Quarter Master and Company Quarter Master Sergeants having helped to push the Train some of the way.	
	25.5.18		Wind N.N.W. Day fair – warmer. Conference of Commanding Officers and 2nds in command at Brigade Head Quarters at 11.30 a.m.	

Army Form C. 2118.

WAR DIARY
or
INTELLIGENCE SUMMARY.
(Erase heading not required.)

Instructions regarding War Diaries and Intelligence
Summaries are contained in F. S. Regs., Part II
and the Staff Manual respectively. Title pages
will be prepared in manuscript.

Place	Date	Hour	Summary of Events and Information	Remarks and references to Appendices
	25.5.18		Day passed with quiet on all the front. The Commanding Officer, Lieut. Col. A. A. Duff, C.I.E., M.V.O., left during the afternoon to go to Divisional Head Quarters for a few days. B and D Companies relieved their platoons in front line tonight.	
	26.5.18.		Enemy Artillery more active. Began shelling front and support lines on our extreme Right and along 6th Seaforth Highlanders on our right, about 3 a.m., and continued till 1 p.m. We had no casualties and very little damage done. The Brigadier General came round our front and support lines in afternoon. Rations arrived 11.30 p.m. last night, and 10.10 p.m. tonight. Weather - fair, cool. Wind - N. by W.	
	27.5.18.		Enemy Bombardment began 2 a.m. along 25 miles front. Battalion front suffered little, but certain amount of phosgene gas shells about, and men were taken into the dugouts and curtains let down. Bombardment lasted about 3 hours. R Company had a patrol out 500 yards during night and found no sign of enemy. Work carried out by all companies as usual before bombardment began. Day quiet. Weather - fair. Wind - N. by E. Owing to actual or probable presence of mustard gas in soil, no digging parties were allowed to work tonight. Some wiring done by R and D Companies. News tonight - Enemy attacking between RHEIMS and SOISSONS on a 40 kilometre front.	
	28.5.18.		When relieving a listening post between 10 and 11 p.m. last night, 2nd Lieut. H.G. WATT and 3 Other Ranks of D Company were hit by an aerial dart (Trench Mortar missile). One of the Other Ranks seriously injured. Night and today passed quietly. Work - clearing dugouts - fitting antigas curtains. Carrying wire &c. Weather - fair. Wind - N. by W. Musketry being carried out in all companies and at Head Quarters, - 5 rounds per man fired daily at marks in or outside Trench. Rations come by train arriving now between 10 and 10.30 p.m.	
	29.5.18		Last night and today very quiet. C and A Companies relieved R and D Companies respectively in front line. Owing to work done by parties last night, this was carried out between 2 and 4 p.m. One platoon of D Company in PITMER extension excepted. This front line Trench is exposed to enemy view, is still too shallow	

WAR DIARY
or
INTELLIGENCE SUMMARY.
(Erase heading not required.)

Army Form C. 2118.

Place	Date	Hour	Summary of Events and Information	Remarks and references to Appendices
	29/5/18		for movement in daytime. Lieut. Colonel A.A. Duff returned to Battalion. The following Honours are published in Divisional Routine Orders of dates 24th May 1918 and 27th May 1918 :— **Bar to Military Cross.** T/Captain D. McPelvey, M.B. M.C. (R.A.M.C. attached.) **Military Cross.** Barff and Bonside Battalion (Gordon Highrs. T.F. **Distinguished Conduct Medal.** 10743 Cpl (A/Sgt) J. Shand M.M. 265982 L/C W.S. McIntosh. 265728 Private I. Fraser. **XXX. The Military Medal.** 265592 Private (A/Cpl) D. Main. 265601 " " A. Flett. 266071 " " A.C. Ramsay. 265800 " " T. Macdonald. 2944 L/Cpl. S. Wilson. 200237 Private G. Anderson. 10544 " " J.N. Murray.	
	30/5/18		Battalion working parties on PLUMER EXTENSION and new communication trench, — PLUMER to ROW, delayed by an operation by the Battalion of 52nd Division on our left, and little more than an hour's work done. Patrol went out under Intelligence officer 2nd Lieut. I.O. Morison to try and discover position of an enemy Trench Mortar. This, however, was not firing last night. Day — quiet. Musketry carried out on 30 yards Range constructed at Reserve Company, with fixed and disappearing targets. New Gas proof Aid Post made near junction of TIRED ALLEY and Railway cutting. Weather — fair — wind — N.E.	
	31/5/18		Working parties not interfered with last night. Two Officers and 50 other Ranks continued work on PLUMER EXTENSION and new communication trench, — PLUMER to ROW.— small day parties on other work — as construction of "CURVE HOLES" in PLUMER EXTENSION.	

Army Form C. 2118.

WAR DIARY
or
INTELLIGENCE SUMMARY.

(Erase heading not required.)

Instructions regarding War Diaries and Intelligence Summaries are contained in F. S. Regs., Part II. and the Staff Manual respectively. Title pages will be prepared in manuscript.

Place	Date	Hour	Summary of Events and Information	Remarks and references to Appendices

Strength at end of last Month

	Officers.	Other Ranks
	32	636

Increases.

	Officers	–	Other Ranks.
Drafts.	11		223
Casuals rejoined.	.		16
Reinforcements in Divisional Wing at end of Month.	1		69
	12		308
	44		944

Decreases.

Killed in action.	.	2
Wounded.	1	12
Evacuated sick.	.	54
To U. K. for commission.	.	1
Transferred to Lovat Scouts.	.	1
	1	70

Strength at end of this Month

| | 43 | 874. |

R. Duff Lieut. Colonel,
Commanding 6th Bn. The Gordon Highlanders.

In the Field,
31st May 1918.

6th Bn. The Gordon Highlanders.

Nominal Roll of Officers.

Rank	Name	Initials	Honours	Role
Lieut. Colonel	Duff	A.A.	C.I.E. M.V.O.	Commanding Officer.
Major	Cranstoun	C.J.H.		2nd in Command.
Captain	McCombie	C.	M.C.	Bde. Transport Off.
"	McCall	W.	M.C.	Coy Commander.
Lieutenant	Petrie-Hay	A.K.		
"	Cooper	D.C.		
"	Paterson	J.B.		
"	Semple	J.H.		Coy Commander.
"	Cowie	C.A.		Lewis Gun Officer.
"	Gray	H.		
"	Black	J.		11th R.H. attached.
2nd Lieut.	Ruyars	G.A.		Instructor at Divnl. Wing.
"	Milne	H.J.		Company Commander.
"	Raitt	J.L.		Signalling Officer.
"	Hay	J.L.		
"	Blacklaws	C.G.		In Hospital sick.
"	Wilson	N.J.		14th Corps Gas School
"	Caldwell	C.L.		
"	Riddell	J.S.	M.C.	Company Commander.
"	Alexander	F.P.W.		1st Army Musketry Course.
"	Mitchell	R.W.		In Hospital sick.
"	Morison	I.O.		Intelligence Officer.
"	Henry	R.		Divnl. Dg. School
"	Reid	A.		
"	Rhind	A.		17th Corps Infantry Course.
"	Proctor	W.F.		Divnl. Musketry School.
"	Watt	G.R.		
"	~~Watt~~	~~S.G.~~		
"	Conlon	G.W.R.		
"	Grant	P.W.		17th Corps Infantry Course.
"	Grosert	A.R.		
"	Burns	J.S.		
"	Archibald	H.J.		G.H.Q. P.& R.F. Course.
"	Boyd	F.A.N.		On Leave.
"	Beveridge	J.D.		
"	Thornton	A.		
"	Philip	A.		
"	Reid	H.		
"	Craig	J.W.		

Captain	Risk	R.	M.C.	Adjutant.
Lieutenant	Collier	F.		Assistant Adjutant.
Hon. Captain	Findlay	F.W.	M.C.	Quarter Master.

| Captain | Jamieson | W.H. | (A.A.M.C.) | Medical Officer attached |

C.E.C.

confidential.   WAR DIARY   Army Form C. 2118.
INTELLIGENCE SUMMARY.   1/6 Gordon Hfrs

Place	Date	Hour	Summary of Events and Information	Remarks and references to Appendices
June 1918. In the Line	1		Patrol of C Company out last night went out to MACHINE GUN TRENCH. Found it unoccupied, but heard sounds of hammering and voices from N. Patrol Commander – 2nd Lieut. J. W. CRAIG. Working parties carried on uninterruptedly. New Defence Scheme on Divisional front. Conference of Commanding Officers at Brigade Head Quarters at 5.30 p.m. and of Company Commanders at Battalion Head Qrs. at 8 p.m. Two instead of three Battalions to be on Brigade front – remaining Battalion to be in Brigade Reserve. Change to take place tomorrow. Weather remains very fine. Wind N.E.	Maps:— Mapsheit 1/ Bailleul (55,000) Willemare 1/ Printed on map C.L.C.
Do.	2		Evening shelling considerable. Railway broken at several places and Ration Train delayed. Heavy firing heard in distance to Northward tonight. Enemy shelled the Railway Cutting here at LONGWOOD at 2 a.m. with Field Guns and some heavy. Smell pungent, and Gas Alarm was given, and men came into dugouts or put on Gas Masks. Brigade Head Quarters suffered similarly, but our Companies in Front and Support Lines were not troubled. Casualties – 3 wounded. In accordance with new Defence Scheme 6th Gordon Highlanders took over Front and RED LINE from 6th Seaforth Highlanders up to and including TOMMY ALLEY, our Right Front Company taking over the extra front up to TOMMY ALLEY inclusive, which is the Battalion Boundary. C Company in ROW and RED LINE, and our Reserve Company ('D) taking over extra portion of the POST TRENCH including the SUGAR FACTORY. Relief carried out during afternoon and completed by 6 p.m.. Working parties carried on last night	C.L.C
Do.	3		Patrol of 1 officer (2/Lt. A. THORNTON) and 14 O.R. out last night over 500 yards in front of our new section of FRONT LINE; saw and heard nothing. Working parties as usual. Night quiet, and there was not the usual dawn "strafe". G.O.C. Corps came round Front Line in a.m. Orders for the relief tomorrow received. O. C. 7th Gordon Highrs. (relieving RN) came to H.Q., lunch, to arrange the take-over – Lieut. Col. MENZIES. Little shelling today. In evening railway and our Head Quarters in Railway cutting shelled vigorously between 10 and 10.30. Rations delayed. Weather fair. Cooler and some cloud. Wind N.E.	C.L.C
Do.	4		Night quiet. Our Divisional R. A. shelled Roche Front Line trenches for a few	

Minutes/m.

Army Form C. 2118.

WAR DIARY
or
INTELLIGENCE SUMMARY.
(Erase heading not required.)

Place	Date	Hour	Summary of Events and Information	Remarks and references to Appendices
In the line	4		minutes at morning "stand To". Working parties carried on last night, and all available men working. The Battalion was relieved by 7th Gordon Highlanders. Relief carried out during afternoon very smoothly, and was completed by 6.30 p.m. As platoons were relieved, they marched back by PLANY ROAD to ECURIE WOOD CAMP. This camp has been handed over in very good order by 7th G.H. Weather fine. Wind N.E.	CLC
Ecurie Wood Camp	5		Inspection of companies by Company Commanders in a.m. Arms, Box Respirators &c., in p.m. All companies paid today. A, B and C Coys went to Baths. Lieut. Col. A.A. Duff, C.I.E., M.V.O., having been detailed as a member of a F.G.C.M. was away during the day. R.C. Chaplain to the 152nd Bde - Capt. & Revd. T.T. O'Connor joined the Bn Head Qrs yesterday. The Battalion Canteen has been kept going while up in the Line, and has been opened here in Camp, but there is great difficulty in getting any kind of food stuffs. Weather very fine. Wind N.E.	CLC
Do.	6		Full morning's work for A, B & C Coys. D Coy went to Baths 8.30-10 a.m. and then came on parade. Parade 2.30 p.m. for all officers and N.C.Os. for saluting and Arm Drill. A train runs each p.m. from ECURIE to ECOIVRES to enable men to go to performance of "The Balmorals' Play "Turnip Tops" - 30 from this Battalion. The Commanding officer away during day at F.G.C.M. after taking Orderly Room at 8.30 a.m. Weather fine. Wind N.E. 7 awards of the Military Medal and 3 of the D.C.M. are published in orders. Also Bar to the Military Cross - T/Capt. D. McFelvey (attached) R.A.M.C.	CLC
Do.	7		Morning's work. Coys under Commanders. Specialists Classes &c. 8.30 a.m. to 12.30 p.m. Pioneers engaged on work in camp in construction of field ovens and other improvements. The Battalion furnished working party of 400 tonight - being at the rendezvous detailed at 10 p.m. The Commanding officer engaged on the F.G.C.M. during the day. Weather fair. Wind S.W.	CLC
Do.	8		Working parties returning during early a.m. Orderly Room 12 noon. Parades 1.30 - 2.30 p.m. A & C Coys 2.30 - 3.30 p.m. B & D Coys - wiring demonstration and instruction. Specialists/	

Army Form C. 2118.

WAR DIARY
or
INTELLIGENCE SUMMARY.
(Erase heading not required.)

Instructions regarding War Diaries and Intelligence Summaries are contained in F. S. Regs., Part II. and the Staff Manual respectively. Title pages will be prepared in manuscript.

Place	Date	Hour	Summary of Events and Information	Remarks and references to Appendices
Lattre St Ave Ecurie (Wood Camp)	8		Specialists parades 9 a.m.–12.30 p.m. Lewis Gun class for beginners and Refresher Class marched to BRAY RANGE for firing practice. Brigadier General Laing inspected Transport (2 Limbers and Water Cart) of each Battalion of the Bde. Officers of the Battalion gave a concert 8 to 9 p.m. in the Y.M.C.A. Hut. Weather fair. Wind S.W.	ccc
Do.	9		Church Parades during a.m. L.G. Classes worked in a.m. Orders for relief – 7th A.& S. Highrs. in left subsection of GAVRELLE Sector (Right Bde.) 2nd in command and Adjutant went up line to arrange details of relief with O.C. 7th A.& S. Highrs. Conference commanding Officer and Coy. Comdrs. at 7 p.m.	ccc
Do.	10		Lieut. Col. Buff as member of F.G.C.M. which is still sitting, is detained, and unable to take Battalion into the line. 9.30–11.30 a.m. – Inspection of Coys by 2nd in command. Camp handed over to 4th Gordon Highrs. The Battalion relieved 7th A.& S. Highrs. in the left Battn. Sector of the Right Brigade Section of the 51st Divnl. Front. The Battalion began moving off by platoons – 300 yards distance between platoons – at 1 p.m. and relief completed by 6 p.m. Dispositions:– Right front Coy. – R Coy. – Captain W. McCall. M.C. Left " – D " – " J.H. Semple. Right Support " – C " – " H.R. Milne. Left " – A " – " J.S. Riddell. M.C. Coys organised in 3 platoons of 4 sections. Battalion front runs from a point about due East of BAILLEUL about 1500 yards on a S.S.W. direction. 6th Seaforth Highrs. on right of Rn. 153rd Brigade on left. At 1 a.m. today 4300 cylinders of gas were released at points immediately North of this Battalion Front. Wind westerly. From OPPY WOOD Northwards, as far as eye can see from here – about 3 miles grass has been bleached by it. Enemy artillery very quiet all day	ccc
Do Do Line	11		Night passed quietly. Rations in this sector come by limber and then pack animal. Work by Battalion wiring in front of Front Line – making of firesteps – improving of firebays &c. A new trench is in course of making in front of existing Front Line, work being done.	

WAR DIARY
or
INTELLIGENCE SUMMARY.

(Erase heading not required.)

Army Form C. 2118.

Place	Date	Hour	Summary of Events and Information	Remarks and references to Appendices
In the Line	11		done by Battalion in Reserve. Conference with front line Coy Commanders 12 noon. Enemy artillery very quiet. Weather fine.	CEE
Do.	12		Patrol of D Coy (2/Lt. A.R. GROSERT) out last night located enemy Machine Gun in N. TYNE ALLEY. Working parties on wiring and new trench front line, which now done by Front Line Battalions. Reserve Battalion supplying wiring parties for trenches in rear. Enemy artillery quiet. Enemy aeroplane over Battalion Sector between 9 and 10 a.m. G.S.O 1 51st Division visited Battalion Head Qrs in afternoon — Lieut. Col. McClintock. Weather fair. Battalion Canteen drawings for 11th and 12th up in the line — Fr. 861. Supplies of eatables scarce.	CEE
Do.	13		Patrol out NORTH TYNE ALLEY under 2nd Lieut. H.A. ANDERSON, D Coy. last night. B Coy patrol cancelled because Reserve Battalion (5th Seaforth Highrs) sending one out on B Coy Front.	
Do.	13		Working parties wiring and on new trench front line. Enemy artillery more active. Shelled road near Battalion Hd Qrs 9.30 a.m. and 10.30 p.m. Sneezing gas — causing sore nose for a short time, and apparently no ill after effect. Two Officers affected by the Influenza Fever — 2/Lts. REID and GROSERT. Last Battalion had 7 officers ill. Hon. Capt. & Qr. Mr. F.W. Findlay comes up each night. Rations working smoothly. Rabbit for meat ration today. All coys have cook-houses. Weather fair. Wind W.S.W.	CEE
Do.	14		Patrol from D Coy. last night obtained no fresh information. Working parties — all available men by night. One of 40 as carrying party at 7 a.m. necessitated employing 30 of Right Front Coy. Lieut. Col. J.M. Scott of 5th Seaforth Highrs. commanding Brigade in absence of G.O.C. visited our Sector this a.m. Some shelling on our support front coy & Support Line last night. Day quiet. Patrol of 6th Seaforth Highrs. on our right met enemy patrol of 7 in No Man's Land last night and made prisoners of the whole. Our patrol arranged for tonight from B Coy cancelled for third night in succession on account of operation by 153rd Brigade on our left. Weather fair. Wind W.S.W.	
Do.	15		Operations on our left last night had no useful result. Our work and patrols in front and No Man's Land prevented, and again tonight on account of an operation	CEE

WAR DIARY
or
INTELLIGENCE SUMMARY.
(Erase heading not required.)

Army Form C. 2118.

5.

Place	Date	Hour	Summary of Events and Information	Remarks and references to Appendices
9.th Russ	15		on our Right which eventually did not take place. Work parties fully employed within our lines. Our Artillery active. In p.m. we shelled with 4.5. Hows. the Railway Cutting about TYNE ALLEY – the object of our patrol reconnaissances. Day fair. Wind W.S.W.	cee
Do.	16		Quiet day. Work on improvement of our section which badly needed. Enemy artillery very quiet. Day fair but for shower in afternoon. Company relief carried out 2 to 5 p.m. C & A Coys relieving B & D Coys in Front Line as Right and Left Companies respectively. Patrol from R Coy.-2/Lt. W.F. Proctor and 12 O.R. goes out tonight to recomnoitre Railway Cutting on TYNE ALLEY.	cee
Do.	17		"Our patrol reconnoitred enemy post at the Cutting last night. 2/Lt. Proctor and 5192 & Pte J. Grant on south side of the cutting and 240241 Cpl. A.E. McLeod and 43337 L/Cpl Middleton on North side getting to within 30 yards of the post and locating defences - 3 machine guns and a rifle section. They were fired on by rifles and machine guns, and lay for an hour, and then returned to our lines. Our own Divisional R.A. relieved 15th Division R.A. in this Divisional front last night, and were very active to day. Enemy artillery very quiet. Working parties as usual." Day fair. Wind W. to N.N.W. Intelligence Officer 2/Lt. I.O. Morison sent to Hospital today with this strange malady - feverish influenza. Draft of 78 O.R. came up tonight and were allotted to companies.	cee
Do.	18		"Our patrol - 2/Lt. W.T. Archibald A COY.- discovered last night strong enemy working party digging out in front of the position in the railway cutting and TYNE ALLEY. Were not discovered. Our working parties as usual." Lieut. B. Downie and 2/Lt J.S. Burns sent down to Hospital today with the malady. Our Battalion Scouts under Corporal GAULD are keeping a particularly good observation on all artillery and ground movement. Day fair - more sunny. Wind W.S.W.	cee
Do.	19		Patrol reported no working or other parties in front of Railway Cutting and TYNE ALLEY. Sending another there tonight and one from Right Front Company to patrol in TYNE ALLEY. A good deal of rain today has impressed on all working parties as usual.	

Army Form C. 2118.

WAR DIARY
or
INTELLIGENCE SUMMARY.

(Erase heading not required.)

Instructions regarding War Diaries and Intelligence Summaries are contained in F. S. Regs., Part II. and the Staff Manual respectively. Title pages will be prepared in manuscript.

Place	Date	Hour	Summary of Events and Information	Remarks and references to Appendices
Arthur Line	19		the need of getting on with improvement of trenches and of duckboards. Enemy artillery pretty quiet on our sector. His aeroplanes more active than they were. Weather warm. Good deal of rain and cloud. Wind S. by E. to S.W.	C 35
Do.	20		Right Front Company (C) patrol out and found no enemy in No Man's Land. Left Front Coy (A) 2/Lt. ROYD. - reconnoitred Railway Cutting and N. TYNE ALLEY. Left patrol - no fresh information. Working parties today and last night as usual. Marked improvement in rate and quality of digging, and to some extent in wiring. Weather cloudy at times and some rain.	C 33
Do.	21		Right Coy. patrol up to enemy posts and wire S. of TYNE ALLEY - Lieut. BLACK. Left Coy patrol - 2/Lt ROYD and 4 O.R. up to enemy wire and posts at end of N. TYNE ALLEY. Fire opened on patrol, and 2/Lt. ROYD got hit in ankle, but managed to get back with rest of patrol. 15th Division on our right carried out successful raid. Our divisional Artillery co-operated - 3 a.m. Good work by working parties last night. Our plans for small raid on N. TYNE ALLEY and Railway Cutting delayed by failure of last night's patrol to exactly locate wire. G.O.C. Division visited Bn. Head Qrs. today. We are short of officers - 4 gone down sick and 1 wounded. We had 1 man wounded last night - L/Cpl McFarlane A Coy. bullet through arm. Day fair - clouding at night. Wind S.W. 2/Lt. PROCTOR and 5 O.R. out tonight to locate enemy working parties, if any, about OUSE ALLEY.	C 33
Ecurie Wood Camp	22		Patrol went out last night and observed enemy line N. and S. of OUSE ALLEY - no working parties out there. Our working parties as usual. The Battalion was relieved this afternoon by the 7th Black Watch (153 Brigade). Relief complete by 5.30 p.m. Battalion marched back to Ecurie Wood Camp by platoons. Lieut. Col. A.A. Duff returned to Battalion on completion of F.G.C.M. 4 Bn Scouts reconnoitred N. TYNE ALLEY post at 8 a.m. Day fair. High S.W. Wind. in camouflage suits, getting close up and reporting enemy sentry's uniform. They saw no wire showing above the grass.	
Do.	23		Two companies went to Baths at ECURIE in morning - two to Baths at ROCLIN-court in afternoon. Coys paid. Commanding Officer held conference of all 'Officers'	C 33

Army Form C. 2118.

7.

WAR DIARY
or
INTELLIGENCE SUMMARY.

(Erase heading not required.)

Place	Date	Hour	Summary of Events and Information	Remarks and references to Appendices
Ecurie Camp	23		Officers at 12 noon - Subjects :- discipline, training, and various. Football Match between 6th and 5th Gordon Highrs in p.m. Result 2-1 in our favour. No Church Parade, but R.C. and C. of E. voluntary. Conference of commanding officers at Bde. Head Qrs 5 - 7 p.m.	see
Do	24		Two Coys. C and D at Musketry, each 5 hours on range. A and B Coys half morning at disposal of Coy Commanders; half - saluting and arm drill. Officers and N.C.Os. 2.30 - 3.30 p.m. Communication Drill. Inspection of drafts which joined Bn. 5th, 10th and 16th insts. numbering 20, 30 and 81 respectively by Comdg officer at 2.30 p.m. Field ovens now in use at 3 Coy cookhouses - remaining coy oven under construction. Good deal of rain in the afternoon.	see
Do	25		A Coy on Range - grouping, application and rapid practices. B, C & D Coys training and each inspected by Comdg officer during a.m. Draft which joined 24th inspected by Comdg officer at 2.30 p.m. Officers and N.C.Os. parade 2.30 p.m. Football Match versus 5th Seaforth Highrs in p.m. won by 6th Gordon Highrs 3-0.	see
Do	26		Presentation of Medal Ribbons by Army Commander (General Horne) to 152nd Inf. Brigade on Camp parade ground in morning. March past after the presentation. Training in wiring in squads from all four companies. Officers and N.C.Os. 2.30 p.m. In evening whole Battalion on working party in and about Support Line.	see
Do	27		Battalion being on working party during night, there were no parades. Weather fine.	see
In the Line	28		The Battalion relieved 7th A.& S. Highrs. in Brigade Reserve-in Left Brigade Sector (Oppy Sector) of 51st Divisional Front. Daylight relief carried out and completed between 3 and 6 p.m. Coys from right to left :- C, D, A, B. Bn Hd Qrs and all Coy Hd. Qrs about Railway Embankment between Railway C.T. and TIRED ALLEY. Each Coy with 1 Nucleus platoon Garrison in BROWN LINE. O.R. Lieut. Col. Duff Strength 21 Officers (including M.O.) 579 O.R. about/	see

Army Form C. 2118.

WAR DIARY
or
INTELLIGENCE SUMMARY.
(Erase heading not required.)

Instructions regarding War Diaries and Intelligence Summaries are contained in F. S. Regs., Part II. and the Staff Manual respectively. Title pages will be prepared in manuscript.

Place	Date	Hour	Summary of Events and Information	Remarks and references to Appendices
Willekins.	28		about to proceed on leave did not come with the Battalion.	
Do.	29		Work parties carried on – spoiling for new deep dugouts – digging new support trench to post Trench. Tonight work parties, except 100 men on burying cable, cancelled on account of a raid carried out 11.10 p.m. by Right Brigade. Conference on Defence Scheme and other points with coy commanders 4.30 to 5.30 p.m. Sick parade – a dozen or so cases of "FLU". Lieut. GRAY up from Divisional L. G. Class tonight will take over command of D'Coy at present commanded by 2/Lt G. A. Ruyers.	
Do.	30		Work parties on new Trench, burying cable, and spoiling at new deep dugouts, and also making concertina wire. Weather fair. Little enemy shelling. 2/Lt J.L. Hay takes over Works officer from Lieut. J. Black going on a course.	

Strength at end of last month

Increases

	Officers	Other Ranks
	43	874
Drafts.	1	140
Casuals.		24
Reinforcements in Divisional Wing.		20
	44	1058

Decreases

Evacuations		
Wounded.		63.
		12
To U.K. on duty.(Lieut. B. Downie)	1	.
To U.K. under 6 months scheme (Capt. McCombie)	1	.
To Base underage.		1
	3	76

Strength at end of this month. 41 . 982.

(signed) C.E. Cruickshank Major for Lieut. Colonel, Commanding 6th Bn Gordon Highlanders"

152nd Brigade.

51st (Highland) Division

1/6th BATTN. GORDON HIGHLANDERS

JULY, 1918.

Headquarters,
    152nd Infantry Brigade.

Herewith War Diary for month of July. Please acknowledge receipt.

Lieut. Colonel,
Commanding 6th Gordon Highlanders.

13th August, 1918.

Army Form C. 2118.

WAR DIARY
or
INTELLIGENCE SUMMARY.
(Erase heading not required.)

1/6 Gordon Hrs

Vol 4 5

No. 195

Place	Date	Hour	Summary of Events and Information	Remarks and references to Appendices
Vimy	July 1		Work parties uninterrupted last night. Slight shelling to-day. Conference of company commanders at 4.30 p.m. Business chiefly reorganisation of a special patrol body consisting of 2 officers, 4 N.C.Os. and 24 men. Officers selected - 2/Lieut. W.F.PROCTOR and R.F. ARCHIBALD. 1 N.C.O. and 6 other ranks from each company. Weather fine and hot. Patrol of 1 officer and 10 O.Rs. to go out to-night. Captain O'CONNOR - R.C. Chaplain joined Battn. H.Q. from Rear H.Q.	
	2.		Work parties last night uninterrupted. Patrol of 1 officer /2/Lieut. W.F. PROCTOR) and 10 other ranks did a good reconnaissance of road cutting between MACHINE GUN TRENCH and TOMMY ALLEY. A daylight reconnaissance was carried out of same place and also one of junction of OUSE ALLEY and VISCOUNT STREET. These were made by both :allion scouts, privates MURRAY and KEENE, and privates SHARP and GRAY respectively. Day quiet, weather hot and fine. 2/Lieut. W.F. PROCTOR and patrol go out to-night to try to cut out post at road cutting (sunken road) next day.	
	3.		Patrol returned at 2 a.m. It does not seem to have gone to the spot planned and to have blundered into enemy, who opened fire with rifles and bombs. 2/Lieut. W.F. PROCTOR was hit at first discharge after firing two or three shots with his revolver. One man was hit. 2/Lieut. R.F. ARCHIBALD brought patrol back after failing to find 2/Lieut. PROCTOR. Conference of commanding officers at Brigade Headquarters at 10 a.m. to 1 p.m. - on defence schemes and patrols. Work parties as usual. Very quiet.	
	4.		The battalion relieved 1/5th Seaforth Highlanders in right battalion sector of Brigade front. Relief carried out between 3 p.m. and 6 p.m. Dispositions - "D" Company - Right Front Company. "A" " - Left " " "C" " - Support "B" " - Reserve 9.30 p.m. 2/Lieut. W. F. PROCTOR whom we had reported missing this afternoon came into our lines - at ROW TRENCH after being out since Tuesday night and having crawled all the way with a bullet hole through left thigh. Flesh wound. Would not have been serious but had become infected, hoped not badly. He was still strong and gave good account of patrol. He is positive he shot the machine gunner. (In FENT ROAD)	

(A7092). Wt. W12839/M1293. 75,000. 1/17. D. D. & L., Ltd. Forms/C.2118.14.

Army Form C. 2118.

WAR DIARY
or
INTELLIGENCE SUMMARY.
(Erase heading not required.)

Instructions regarding War Diaries and Intelligence Summaries are contained in F.S. Regs., Part II. and the Staff Manual respectively. Title pages will be prepared in manuscript.

Place	Date	Hour	Summary of Events and Information	Remarks and references to Appendices
Hulluch	4		ROAD beyond the sunken road). Day quiet, weather fine.	
	5		Did not send out patrol last night. Battalion patrol party under 2/Lieut. ARCHIBALD carried out night training near Battalion Headquarters. Work parties carried on. Conference at Brigade Headquarters. Subject – A special minor enterprise. Party from "A" and from "C" had first practice to-night, in conjunction with 5th Seaforth Highlanders – 10 p.m. – 12 midnight on ground behind our support line.	
	6		R.Q.C. round our front and support lines this a.m. Work parties as usual. Patrol of two battalion scouts out to enemy posts near end of TOMMY ALLEY in afternoon. Good report on g. end of Sunken Road. Fired on by enemy sentries, though in camouflage suits. During afternoon Captain W.T. MILNE and Sgt. P. GRIFFITHS proceeded to VACCINE GUN TRENCH to reconnoitre ground about proposed raid – assembly point. They came on a German post and Sgt. GRIFFITHS seems to have got among the enemy before seeing them and has not returned. Captain MILNE had grenades thrown near him but was not hit and returned. Patrol under 2/Lieut. ARCHIBALD out to-night. Lying out to wait for Sgt. GRIFFITHS. Practice 10 p.m. to 12m/n to-night of raiding parties carried out last night.	
	7		Sgt. GRIFFITHS not come in. Patrol under 2/Lieut. ARCHIBALD last night saw no enemy. Conference with R.Q.C. of commanding officers concerned 11 a.m. – 1 p.m. Work parties as usual.	
	8		Last arrangements made for night raid taking place to-night. Zero 12.30 a.m. Party composed of 7 sections of 6th Gordon Highlanders and 6 sections of 6th Seaforth Highlanders. 2/Lieut. W. REID, "R" Company, being the officer of this Battalion party. Gordon party divided into A party – 3 sections of "C" company, and B " – 4 " " "R" company.	
	9		Working parties of last night and to-day as usual. 6th Gordon Highlanders pipe Band was 1st in the competition (of 25 Bands entered) held on Saturday and are to go to PARIS for the 14th July procession.	
	9		Raid last night – Sharp storm of thunder and vivid lightning and heavy rain as party/	

Army Form C. 2118.

WAR DIARY
or
INTELLIGENCE SUMMARY.
(Erase heading not required.)

Instructions regarding War Diaries and Intelligence Summaries are contained in F. S. Regs., Part II. and the Staff Manual respectively. Title pages will be prepared in manuscript.

Place	Date	Hour	Summary of Events and Information	Remarks and references to Appendices
Vimy	9.		as party moved to rendezvous and assembly points. All punctually and smoothly carried out. Barrage of Stokes and of artillery at Zero at 12.30 a.m. which was signal for advance to begin. Wire in front of KEMP ROAD – the objective was a serious obstacle and the maximum intense darkness added. caused some delay and confusion. Seaforth party got across our party's front. Few enemy were seen and none captured or even dead. No identification obtained. One of the stretcher bearers was wounded, arm and shoulder, by shrapnel, and three other men slightly wounded by splinters, or cut in the barbed wire. The men left their kits and went in the shirts or shorts with jackets and equipment. All in by 2.30 a.m. Some enemy engaged Seaforth party at junction of MACHINE GUN TRENCH and KEMP ROAD and they had eight casualties. Corps refused sanction of an issue of rum for the men when they came out, but a good breakfast and a whiskey ration was provided by the battalion. Orders for relief to-morrow. Canadian Division relieve the 51st in this sector. Work parties reduced or cancelled during last night except spoiling parties.	(S.C. (S.C.
Vimy &	10.		Patrol lay out last night for enemy patrol but encountered none. Work parties as usual. Relief – Battalion guides down to 40th Bn. Canadian Infantry 10 a.m. Canadian Advance party arrived in line at 8.30 a.m. Battalion relieved by 40th Canadians during p.m. Relief complete 6 p.m. Battalion marched back to ECURIE WOOD CAMP. Officers and details from Divisional Wing rejoined – Bde –	00.19 (S.C.
ECURIE WOOD CAMP			going into Divn/y area to-morrow.	
do	11.		A.M. – Companies at disposal of Company Commanders. Battalion entrained at 2.45 p.m. in five trains (light Railway) at ECURIE, and detrained at 5.30 p.m. at MONCHY-BRETON, whence it marched into billets at or near ST. MICHEL. Marching in strength – 32 officers and 862 other Ranks.	20.199 (S.C.
ST. MICHEL	12.		Day of heavy showers, sun in between. Companies at disposal of Company Commanders. Clean up, inspection, rest, and Pay.	
	13.		Battalion route marched through VAISNIL – SOUFFLIN-BICAMPS – RUITZ over in a.m. with Band. Lieut Colonel J.J. TROW, D.S.O., M.C. rejoined battalion and took over command. G.O.C. Brigade B.G., and later B.G., visited the battalion. morning/	

WAR DIARY
or
INTELLIGENCE SUMMARY.

(Erase heading not required.)

Army Form C. 2118.

Place	Date	Hour	Summary of Events and Information	Remarks and references to Appendices
Rt. Aubert	13.		Warning order for move received to-night. Lewis guns and ammunition loaded up.	C.O. D.S.O. C.S.C
En Train	14.		Orders for move to unknown destination in accordance with which battalion marched at 0.15 p.m. from ST. VITTEN to PERNES. "D" company left at ST. VITTEN following by a train 6 hours later than rest of battalion. Billeting preceded battalion. Transport marched to PERNES earlier in p.m. and entrained in same train as H.Q. and "A", "B", and "C" companies. Entrained at 3 a.m.	C.S.C
"	16		Left PERNES 4.20 a.m. In train all day. No long halts. Cookers on open trucks kept fires in and tea served. Dinners – fresh meat cooked on the way. Wash and some bathing during 40 minutes stop at RISORES. Passed PARIS about m/n.	C.S.C
Romilly sur Seine	16.		Detrained at ROMILLY-sur-SEINE about mid-day. Kept waiting some hours at the station till siding clear of another battalion. Marched to the poplar wood by Canal Ranks on N. side of the town and bivouaced. Day very hot but bivouac is shady and canal running through wood affords bathing to all ranks. The French are arranging this move and battalion is at present out of touch with Bde. or rest of Division and is also without "D" company, and the billeting party which preceded the battalion under 2/Lieut. J.T. WAY. The Germans attacked on a wide front early yesterday morning and except at a section about 2½ kilometres west of RETIMS, are reported to have been decidedly checked, and held.	C.S.C
"	17.		French motor transport came at 9 a.m. and took battalion to WERNIL-sur-COEN whence march 4 kilometres up the bluff to village of GIONGES. Billets in the village – H.Q. and officers quarters in chateau. Billeting and "C" company rejoined. Transport is following and should reach SEZANNE to-night. Distance from ROMILLY to GIONGES about 40 kilometres. Brigade now at IGSNTI-sur-COER. Rations were taken for 16th and 17th. No rations have been received for to-morrow. News:– Reported that enemy success was against the Italian troops holding line of R. MARNE in section 15.F. west of EPERNAY and that French counter-attacked this morning with six Divisions and drove him back across the River. Heavy gun fire audible here from N.W. Weather very hot. Heavy thunder storm by night.	C.S.C

Army Form C. 2118.

WAR DIARY
or
INTELLIGENCE SUMMARY.
(Erase heading not required.)

Instructions regarding War Diaries and Intelligence Summaries are contained in F. S. Regs., Part II. and the Staff Manual respectively. Title pages will be prepared in manuscript.

Place	Date	Hour	Summary of Events and Information	Remarks and references to Appendices
GIONGES			No rations. Brigade authorisation received to consume emergency ration. Parades under company commanders for inspection of arms etc. The battalion transport joined up, arriving 10.30 p.m. Rations for to-morrow arrived 11 p.m.	C.G.C.
CHAMPILLON SUR MARNE			Orders to move received in early morning and battalion marched with transport at 6 a.m. Two hour halt at OGER for breakfast. Route by OTRY - EPERNAY where River MARNE was crossed, and thence through DIZY, up the stiff hill to destination, CHAVILLON, which was reached about 5 p.m. Distance 11 to 12 miles. Weather very hot. Men marched well and very few fell out. The 152nd Bde. assembled here. At 8.15 p.m. orders received for move and the battalion marched this 1st at 10 p.m. to a point in the BOIS de ST. QUENTIN, about 4 kilos. N.W. of CHAMPION, with all transport, leaving Echelon B under Second-in-Command at CHAMPION.	C.G.C.
S. de Yard 20/17			As per Account of Operations S.T. of EVIENS, attached.	

	OFFRS.	O.Rs.
STRENGTH at end of last month	41	902
DECREASE -		
Casualties	OFFRS.	O.Rs.
Killed	3	34
Wounded	10	266
Missing	-	23
Died of wounds	-	8
	13	331
Evacuations	1	111
	14	442
	28	520
INCREASE -		
Drafts	2	60
Casuals	-	11
	2	71
	20	591
STRENGTH at end of this month		

13th August, 1918.

D. Muir Lieut. Colonel,
Commanding 6th Gordon Highlanders.

War Diary

ACCOUNT OF OPERATIONS
OF
6TH GORDON HIGHLANDERS
S.W. OF RHEIMS FROM 20th - 31st July, 1918.

On July 20th the battalion was located in the BOIS DE
ST. QUENTIN, where the 152nd Infantry Brigade Group in
Divisional Reserve had assembled the previous night. On the
morning of the 20th, the 153rd and 154th Brigades attacked,
and, on the afternoon of the same day, the 6th Gordon Highrs.
moved with the 5th Seaforth Highlanders to the woods S.W. of
NANTEUIL, where they bivouaced for the night.

Early the following morning orders were received to move
to the BOIS DE COURTON. This move was carried out, and at
5.30 a.m. the B.G.C. 152nd Brigade conferred with officers
commanding 5th Seaforth Highlanders and 6th Gordon Highlanders,
and explained the operation order for an attack which was to
be launched by the brigade in conjunction with the French on
the left at 8 a.m. 6th Gordon Highlanders were to form up
on the ride in the wood running from LES HAYES to LA NEUVILLE.
They were to clear the wood of the enemy. 5th Seaforth
Highlanders were to be in support, and were to leap-frog the *through*
6th Gordon Highlanders on ×this objective. A hot meal was
provided for the troops, and the battalion moved off towards
the assembly position about 6.45 a.m. On reaching the track
×*the road running along the N.W. edge of the wood*
which runs through the g in the BOIS DE COURTON to PARIDIS, it
was found that the ground beyond was in the hands of the enemy,
who could be seen in large numbers on the tracks and rides in
the wood. The battalion therefore deployed along the track
which was roughly parallel to the anxxx prescribed assembly
line, - but about 700 yards behind it. The advancing troops
did not benefit by the barrage. Stout opposition was
encountered in the wood where the enemy had many machine guns
and trench mortars - 7 of which were captured. On the left,
the attacking companies were in touch with the French but on
this flank the advance was definitely held up after it had
progressed about 500 yards. On the right progress was maxxx
further and more rapid. The line on this flank reached to within
200 yards of the N.W. edge of the wood, where the enemy were
holding a line in strong force and met our troops with bombs,
machine guns, trench mortar and rifle fire. The enemy also *found*
attempted to filter through the gaps to our lines and xxxxxx our
right flank which was unprotected. Our line, to avoid being
cut off, had therefore to return to a position 50 yards from
the track on which the battalion deployed. It was here
reinforced by one company and half of the 5th Seaforth Highrs.,
which filled up the gaps in the line. This line was
consolidated. During the course of the action many casualties
were inflicted on the enemy. Several German officers who
were riding about the tracks through the wood on horseback,
were shot. Several trench mortars and machine guns were
captured. The night of the 21st /22nd passed off fairly
quietly. Our patrols were active and reported having
encountered and driven back parties of the enemy.

On the afternoon of the 22nd the 6th Gordon Highlanders
came under the orders of the 153rd Infantry Brigade, and were
ordered to advance their left flank and conform with units of
153rd Brigade, who, in conjunction with the French, were
attacking in the direction of PARIDIS, at 5 p.m. As this
attack proved abortive, the battalion maintained its original
position.

At 7.30 p.m. orders were received from 153rd Infantry
Brigade that the 8th Royal Scots (Pioneer battalion) would
relieve the battalion, which, on relief, would proceed to the
assembly position of 152nd Infantry Brigade which was to
attack N.E. of the BOIS DE COURTON, on the morning of the 23rd.
Later, orders were received from 152nd Infantry Brigade
directing that the 6th Gordon Highlanders would form up, on
relief, on the left of the 5th Seaforth Highlanders, and would
take part in the advance over the ground between the BOIS DE
COURTON/

-2-

OUVETON and the River ANDON. The objective of the 6th Gordon
Highlanders was BUZANCY and the slopes beyond the village.

Owing to a confusion of orders received from 153rd Brigade
by 4.30 a.m. on 23rd only three companies of this battalion were
relieved. These three companies alone took part in the attack
which was launched at 6.10 a.m. At zero, the barrage of French
.75s fell on the assembly position of the battalion which therefore suffered many casualties, including all the officers of
one company, before the line began to advance. Nevertheless
the troops advanced with great gallantry in the face of an
extremely heavy enemy artillery barrage and machine gun fire.
The sunken road running from cross roads 300 metres east of
BUZANCY to N.E. side of BOIS DE L'ARBRET (reference map -
JAUCOURT - ARCIS-VESLE), was reached and it was found impossible
to continue over the slope into BUZANCY owing to a murderous
machine gun fire coming from the edge of the BOIS DE OUVETON on
the left. The 7th Argyll & Sutherland Highlanders, who were on
the left of the 152nd Brigade, and who were to advance through
the wood, were unable to get forward.

By this time, "C" Company of the 6th Gordon Highlanders,
which had at last been relieved, arrived, & were pushed in to
strengthen the line and protect the left flank of the battalion.
During the day several attempts to carry the line forward were
made - without success - owing to the continuous machine gun
fire from the BOIS DE OUVETON and from the village of NAPPES.
On the right of the sunken road at 21.9.2 26.5.9 (JAUCOURT map)
the battalion was in touch with the 6th Seaforth Highlanders.
The line of the sunken road was continued to the edge of the
wood and consolidated. Out-posts were pushed out 200 yards in
front at dusk. These posts were eventually withdrawn as orders
were received that an attack was to be launched from the line of
the sunken road on the 24th.

Late in the afternoon of the 23rd, orders were received from
51st (H) Division for surplus personnel of battalions of 152nd
Brigade at CHANTILLON to join their battalions. The composite
company organised in four platoons under Captain W.J. WEIR.
and four officers, platoon commanders, accordingly marched from
CHANTILLON and joined the battalion during night of 23rd/24th.

An attack was planned for evening of 24th, but during the
day orders were received cancelling the attack, and ordering the
battalion, which was holding the left of the Brigade front,
immediately to the north of the BOIS DE OUVETON, to organise
defensive position in depth. This was done during the 24th,
the fresh troops of the composite company under Captain WEIR
holding the front line and advance posts.

On 25th, the battalion remained in the position thus
organised. By Brigade order 100 of the most exhausted men
were withdrawn that night to BUZANCY under 2/Lieut. A. HENRY.

At 10 p.m. a patrol of 7th Argyll & Sutherland Highlanders
on our left came in contact with enemy, and fire was opened on
both sides. S.O.S. signals were sent up by the enemy, and
happened to be the same as our own S.O.S. Both enemy and our
own barrages were promptly put down, and heavy machine gun fire
opened. The enemy barrage for most part fell in the hollow
behind our battalion positions. The limbers were up with
rations and the ration parties assembled, but fortunately there
were only a few slight casualties. No shelling earlier in the
day there were some casualties in the front line. Movement
between rear and front was reduced as far as possible during
day time, the intervening ground being under enemy observation
from the high ground west of NAPPES and from the heights of the
BOIS DE BUZANCY FERMES on north of the ARDON valley.

During the following day, Friday, July 26th, the battalion
remained in the same positions. At nightfall the 154th Brigade
on the left in the BOIS DE OUVETON, was relieved by the 153rd
were withdrawn to the rear positions, their place being taken
by a battalion of the 187th Infantry Brigade of the 62nd Div.,
who/

who were to attack the following morning.

At 6 a.m. on Saturday, 27th, our artillery barrage opened according to plan and the 154th Brigade advanced on left in conjunction with 127th Brigade in centre, and the 5th Seaforth Highlanders (152nd Brigade) on the right. Little or no opposition was met with, and the attacking battalions cleared the BOIS DE COURTON and reached CHAMERY.

Early in the afternoon, 6th Gordon Highlanders and 6th Seaforth Highlanders were ordered to advance and occupy a line west of CHAMERY, covering that place. The battalion accordingly moved about 2 p.m. Between 3 p.m. and 4 p.m., its leading patrols pushed through the ruins of the village of CHAMERY (which was still being shelled by French artillery from the east while the enemy shelled it from the west), and established a line of posts about the ridge 500 yards west of the village. The battalion was then in touch with a battalion of the 62nd Divn. on its left, while the 6th Seaforth Highlanders held from the ARDRE River to the North side of the village. Weather was wet, and for the second night the men had to lie out in soaking rain in shellholes and such places as they could dig.

Patrols of Australian Light Horse were in touch with the enemy on the battalion front about MIRY and the MARFAUX de MIRY.

Rations came up in the limbers between 11 p.m. and 12 m/n.

On following morning, 28th July, the battalion was ordered to occupy the old French "ARS" line on west side of the height of the BOIS des ECLISSES, and moved accordingly to the left and through the wood to avoid the enemy shell fire which was now considerable.

In the wood the line ordered was held throughout the day from LA CHAPELLE northwards with touch on the right with 6th Seaforth Highlanders and on left by patrols with the 153rd Brigade. The battalion was relieved at 11 p.m. by two companies of the 4th Seaforth Highlanders. The wood was very heavily shelled by all calibres from about 8 p.m. till 10.30 p.m. but the shelling ceased almost entirely just before the arrival of the relieving companies and the relief was carried out without incident. The battalion then returned to the bank north east of the BOIS de COURTON, which had formed our assembly position prior to the attack on the morning of the 23rd. There the men were served with a hot meal, after which they lay down under what cover they could find.

On the evening of 31st, the battalion was ordered to move to woods S.E. of NANTEUIL where it bivouaced for the night.

6TH GORDON HIGHLANDERS.

Notes on Operations S.W.
of RHEIMS - 20th-28.7.18.

Throughout the fighting the machine gun fire and Lewis gun fire played a most important part. On several occasions, enemy machine guns were ousted by Lewis gun fire. It was obvious, however, that the tactical training of the Lewis gunners had not received the attention its importance demands. The possibility of outmanoeuvring the enemy machine gun with the more mobile Lewis gun was especially evident in these operations. When the country was wooded, it was possible to change position and move forward under cover very readily.

Throughout the operations the enemy's artillery fire was particularly harassing. Any position taken up by our troops during the advance was quickly spotted and heavily shelled.

sd. J.G.Yken., Lieut. Colonel,
Commanding 6th Gordon Highlanders.

5th August, 1918.

CONFIDENTIAL. W 46

War Diary

of

6th Battalion, The Gordon Highlanders

Col. Ferrant

19 August 1918   31 August 1918

Volume 46

Army Form C. 2118.

WAR DIARY
or
INTELLIGENCE SUMMARY.

(Erase heading not required.)

Place	Date	Hour	Summary of Events and Information	Remarks and references to Appendices
NANTEUIL/ OIRY	1918 August 1.		The Brigade marched from OIRY NANTEUIL to OIRY and PLIVOT at 6.20 a.m. The battalion went to OIRY arriving about 11 a.m., and bivouaced in the west end of the village. The day was very hot, and the men bathed.	
do.	2.		Good deal of rain. Battalion rested.	
do. AVIZE	3.		Battalion marched from OIRY to AVIZE at 1.30 a.m. "B" Company, as Brigade unloading party, preceded battalion, going by early afternoon train yesterday as also did Battalion billeting party under 2/Lieut. I.O. MORISON. Train left AVIZE 7 a.m. Route - Northern outskirts of PARIS and up the OISE valley.	B.O. 902
CAUCOURT	4.		Reached COMBLAIN - CHATELAIN at 1.30 p.m. where Battalion detrained and was conveyed in motor lorries to CAUCOURT, where it is in billets, (about 7 p.m. 5 p.m.	
do.	5.		Cleaning up. Pay. Orderly Room at 10 a.m. Battalion at Baths 12 noon to 5 p.m.	

do.	6.		Battalion rested. Baths again available. Companies at disposal of company commanders.
			Company Commanders at present :-
			  "A" Company - Captain W. J. C. FLEMING.
			  "B" " - " W. McCALL, M.C.
			  "C" " - Lieut. J. BLACK.
			  "D" " - " J. GRAY.
			Brig.General R. LAING leaves the Brigade. Lt.Col. W.H.E. SEYGRAVE, D.S.O. appointed to command.	

do.	7.		Sick parade - 9 a.m. Orderly Room - 10 a.m. Companies and Headquarters Details carried out Arm Drill and Close order Drill under own arrangements. All companies inspected by the commanding officer.	
do.	8.		Companies and Headquarters Details on parade - 9 a.m. to 12 noon. Specialists same hours on Transport Field. N.C.Os. Class - 2 p.m. - 3 p.m. Commanding/	

Army Form C. 2118.

WAR DIARY
or
INTELLIGENCE SUMMARY.
(Erase heading not required.)

Instructions regarding War Diaries and Intelligence
Summaries are contained in F. S. Regs., Part II.
and the Staff Manual respectively. Title pages
will be prepared in manuscript.

Place	Date	Hour	Summary of Events and Information	Remarks and references to Appendices
BAVINCOURT	August 8		Commanding officer inspected all huts and billets. Several new officers joined us - some of these are Argyll & Sutherl. Highrs. and Cameron Highrs. Draft of 205 other Ranks joined Battalion and were posted to companies.	
do.	9.		Orderly Room - 12.30 p.m. Company parades - 8.30 a.m. - 12 noon. "B" Company on the Rifle Range, 8.30 a.m, & "C" Company during the afternoon. Fired practices 5 rounds grouping at 100 yards and 10 rounds application at 200 yards. Draft of 205 other Ranks inspected by commanding officer.	
do.	10.		Orderly Room - 2.30 p.m. "A" and "D" Companies on Rifle Range during forenoon. Physical Training. Arm Drill, close order drill, etc. carried out at company parades from 8.30 a.m. to 12.30 p.m. All men of drafts, in France for first time, paraded under C.S.M. J. W. CHALMERS, M.C., D.C.M., (Acting R.S.M.) from 8.30 a.m. to 12.30 p.m. Friendly match on football field with 5th Seaforth Highlanders this afternoon. Result - Battalion lost - 1 goal to nil.	
do.	11.		Sick parade - 9.30 a.m. Church parades. Weather remains hot. An enemy aeroplane with 3 men fell close to our parade ground last night. Draft of 70 men joined Battalion last night	
do.	12.		Orderly Room at 2.30 p.m. parades - 8.30 a.m. - 12 noon. Route March under company arrangements from 12 noon to 1 p.m. Weather hot and fine.	
do.	13.		Company parades, and 1 hour's Route March. Baths. Pay. During forenoon Warning Order to move to relieve 52nd Division in the line. Our promised period of rest and training and re-organisation is once again to be denied to 51st (H) Division. Enemy 'planes about every night - so far, no bombs dropped very near us. Weather hot and fine.	
do.	14.		Day spent in re-organisation and preparing for the trenches. Organisation of all Battalions in 16 platoons of 16 sections to be strictly insisted on. In some Battalions/	

(A7092) Wt. W12899/M1293. 75,000. 1/17. D.D. & L., Ltd. Forms/C.2118/14.

3.

Army Form C. 2118.

WAR DIARY
or
INTELLIGENCE SUMMARY.
(Erase heading not required)

Instructions regarding War Diaries and Intelligence Summaries are contained in F. S. Regs., Part II. and the Staff Manual respectively. Title pages will be prepared in manuscript.

Place	Date	Hour	Summary of Events and Information	Remarks and references to Appendices
CAUCOURT	1917 August		Battalions in France, platoons have varied in numbers amazingly. - 9, 11, 12, 14, etc. Commanding officer's conference with Company Commanders at Orderly Room. At 3 p.m., Inspection of Brigade transport, all three Battalions, by Divisional Judges. Result of competition - 6th Seaforth Highlanders 1st, and 6th Gordon Highlanders 2nd, with difference of only 12 points between them. Battalion Orderly Room was occupied most of the day by a Field General Court Martial trying several of our cases. Ration strength - 831. Weather hot and fine.	CDC
"	15.		Informed to-day that we are to move to relieve 52nd and 57th Divisions in the line on the 18th. Parades - 8.30 a.m. to 11 a.m. Battalion Route March - 11 a.m. to 1 p.m. Officers' parade - 2.30 p.m. to 3.30 p.m. The Brigadier-General, W.H.E. SEGRAVE, D.S.O. and the Brigade Major, Captain R. ADAM, dined at Battalion Headquarters. Weather fine. Wind south west.	
"	16.		Commanding Officer attended conference with Inspector General of Training - General MAXSE. Company parades and specialists classes during forenoon. 5th Seaforth Highrs. in next village held sports to-day.	
"	17.		Commanding Officer and Assistant Adjutant (Lieut. J. COLLIER) went up to the line to arrange relief with 8th King's Liverpool Regt. Inspection of all companies and Headquarters Details by 2nd-in-command, 10 a.m. to 12.30 p.m. In afternoon, Battalion Sports held. Very successful gathering. 4.30 p.m. to 7.15 p.m. Races, 5 a side football, transport driving competition, and transport wrestling on horseback - (Grooms v. drivers, won by Grooms). In evening word from Brigade received that we are to relieve a different sector of the line, i.e., one south of the SCARPE instead of NORTH of it: but this gave cancelled — original idea adhered to —	
CAUCOURT/ R. L. H. Line	18.		The Battalion marched from CAUCOURT at 1.50 p.m. and entrained on light railway at ESTREE CAUCHIE, whence it was conveyed to ANZIN. Here there was a halt and the troops had a meal - hot tea and bully. At 7.30 p.m. Battalion marched with 100 yards/	

Army Form C. 2118.

WAR DIARY
or
INTELLIGENCE SUMMARY.
(Erase heading not required.)

Instructions regarding War Diaries and Intelligence Summaries are contained in F.S. Regs., Part II. and the Staff Manual respectively. Title pages will be prepared in manuscript.

Place	Date	Hour	Summary of Events and Information	Remarks and references to Appendices
FAMPOUX in the line	Aug 18		100 yards between platoons, to positions as Battalion in support in Right Brigade Sector of Divisional Front. Division with three Brigades in the line, each 1 Battalion in front line, 1 in reserve support and 1 out in Reserve. 5th Seaforth Highlanders of this Brigade in front line, with their right on River SCARPE at FAMPOUX. This battalion relieved 8th K. Ling's Liverpool Regt. in support, our right on River SCARPE in front of ATHIES. Relief complete at 11.30 p.m. Dispositions :- Headquarters in Railway Embankment at HERVIN FARM. "A" Company - ATHIES. "B" " - Railway Embankment - 2 platoons in TILLOY TRENCH. "C" " - do. - "D" " - do. - 2 platoons in EFFIE SWITCH. Day fair, cloudy.	
St the Loire	19.		Battalion of Liverpool Regt. on right of SCARPE advanced this morning and occupied ICELAND and IONIAN TRENCHES, and MORAY TRENCH beyond, thus clearing face of the hill but leaving enemy on crest. Enemy raid took place on 5th Seaforth Highrs. front, repulsed, leaving 1 officer (died of wounds) in our hands. Rations came up at 9.30 p.m. Commanding officer attended conference with R.Q.C. at 6 p.m. 5th Seaforth Highrs. are to attack enemy trench along sunken road on immediate front, tomorrow morning. This battalion to attack beyond with two companies the following morning. If left at peace, amenities of this place are considerable. Railway Embankment 70 feet high affords complete protection to tiers or terraces of comfortable huts. Also a clean flowing river and several lakes for bathing and even boating. The embankment gives cover to a large area in which free movement by day goes on.	
Do.	20.		5th Seaforth Highlanders attack succeeded at second attempt. Preparations for the attack by two companies of this battalion occupied the day. "B" and "D" companies under Lieutenants C.G. BLACKLAWS and H. GRAY respectively, detailed. These officers with their platoon commanders went up to reconnoitre the ground during the day. During the afternoon enemy made a counter-attack on the sunken road taken by 5th Seaforth Highlanders this morning - repulsed with loss. This road is jumping off	

WAR DIARY
or
INTELLIGENCE SUMMARY
(Erase heading not required.)

Army Form C. 2118.

Place	Date	Hour	Summary of Events and Information	Remarks and references to Appendices

In the field

20 — off point for our two companies in the attack. Night fine. Moon full. Considerable mist over low ground. Lieut. Colonel J.G. THOM, commanding, D.S.O., M.C., Commdg., moved to Battalion Headquarters of 5th Seaforth Highrs. for the operation.

21 — Zero was at 1.30 a.m. and both companies went over at zero plus 10 on left of barrage. This appears to have been very imperfect and over 20 casualties out of 30 were due to our own artillery. Objectives gained, some prisoners captured, and a number of the enemy killed. Three Machine guns captured, positions held throughout the day. Casualties – 1 officer wounded, /2/Lieut. W.T. SMITH) and 26 Other Ranks, wounded. We had two men killed. After dark to-night, "B" and "D" companies were relieved by two companies of the 5th Seaforth Highlanders and came back into CAROLINA TRENCH and CAM VALLEY, remaining as a reserve under the orders of officer commanding, 5th Seaforth Highlanders.
Day extremely hot. Bathing in lakes.

22 — Enquiry to-day into shortness of our artillery barrage. No doubt whatever of its having been short and uneven. Several cases of gas poisoning developed in "B" and "D" companies to-day. The trenches, MORAY, IONIAN, and ICELAND, occupied by Liverpool Regt, on right of River SCARPE were very hot and all troops bathed in lakes during the day.
withdrawn from yesterday, thus opening right flank of this Brigade for 2000 yards along River and giving it a "front" of over 3,000 yards. Enemy, however, does not seem very enterprising.

23 — Cooler. Wind has changed from S.W. to N.W. and N.N.W. Bathing throughout the day. 5th Seaforth Highlanders in our front line had various successful sallies from gas, these not permanent but unfit for a week or more. Low ground in FAMPOUX reported full of gas. Nearly whole of T.M.B. personnel knocked out by the same "Mustard" gas. A platoon of "D" Company, 6th Gordon Highlanders carried out a patrol reconnaissance of 1 and in river south of FAMPOUX in early part of to-night. Heavy gunfire heard all day coming from the south.

24 — Asst. Adj. (Lieut. J. COLLIER) and Medical Officer (Capt. H.H. JAMIESON), left to-day on PARIS leave. Temporary M.O., American Army, came last night, — MALTBY

153rd/

Army Form C. 2118.

WAR DIARY
OF
INTELLIGENCE SUMMARY.
(Erase heading not required.)

Place	Date	Hour	Summary of Events and Information	Remarks and references to Appendices
In the Line	23rd and 24th		153rd Infantry Brigade on our left made an attack last night and captured two trenches - PIPPIN and ZION, bringing their front approximately level with ours and covering out left flank. Enemy sending over a large number of Mustard gas shells and 5th Seaforth Highrs. on our front had many casualties from this cause to-day. This Battalion relieved 5th Seaforth Highrs. in front line to-night, 6th Seaforth Highlanders coming up into our place, in support. Relief completed midnight. Dispositions :- "B" Company - Right front company, holding posts along the R. SCARPE. "D" - Left front company, holding newly captured trenches and quarry, with 153rd Brigade on their left. "A" & "C" Companies - in support, in COSSACK and CAROLINA TRENCHES. Day fine, cooler, Wind N.	
do.	25.		S.O.S. sent up on 153rd Brigade front at 4 a.m. followed by our own barrage and the Bosch coming down on respective front lines. In addition, enemy shelled CAM Avenue - our main C.T. - from 11.30 p.m. to 2 a.m. This was largely with gas shells. The forward trenches are very battered and all the area affected with Mustard Gas. The joint result of last night's and this morning's bombardments with the previous gas shelling, has been that we have had over 100 men sent down to-day suffering from Mustard Gas besides 5 or 6 wounded. The "B" Company posts in SCARPE VALLEY cannot move or be visited by day, being under close enemy observation from the higher ground on south or right bank of the SCARPE. The forward company, "D" Coy. can be reached with care. Day hot and fine. Wind S.E. Thunder and rain to-night. Canadians on south side of the SCARPE are to attack to-morrow and 51st Division in conjunction are to make an advance on North bank. Commanding Officer conferred at Brigade Headquarters at 6.30 p.m. and held conference of company commanders at 7.30 p.m.	
do.	26.		At 3 a.m. our barrage for the Canadians attack on the south side of the river, opened. It sounded tremendous and continued. The Canadians walked behind it and took all their objectives and moved on beyond MONCHY le PREUX. Our attack was launched at 10 a.m. 153rd Brigade on our left had a comparitively light barrage and our two companies had none on right of the attack had none. Our first objective however was gained, i.e. the line of trenches on crest of and far side of MOUNT PLEASANT/	

(A7292) Wt. W14839/M1293 750,000 1/17 D.D. & L., Ltd. Forms/C.2118/14

WAR DIARY
or
INTELLIGENCE-SUMMARY.

(Erase heading not required.)

Army Form C. 2118.

Place	Date	Hour	Summary of Events and Information	Remarks and references to Appendices
In the Line	1917 23rd April		PLEASANT between Railway and River, with capture of three trench mortars. The second objective was not reached, but a great part of the ground towards it was won. The attack was carried out by "D" and "B" Companies and "A" and "C" were moved up into support. Battalion Headquarters were moved up to DINGWALL TRENCH and then to STOKE TRENCH on North side of FAMPOUX. Intelligence of position of our new front line was very long in coming in. 153rd Brigade on our left had reported that they were on East side of GREEN AND HILL while we were actually in touch with their right along way down the Western slope. This led to somewhat acrimonious debate with Brigade who were taking their information of 153rd from Division.	
do.	24.		During the night by means of an officer's patrol, 2/Lieut. R.I. FRAME (Cameron Highrs.) attached to this Battln.), the position of companies and platoons was ascertained. A wire got forward to CRASH TRENCH by the Railway Embankment North and clear of FAMPOUX, to which Battalion Headquarters moved. The battalion, throughout the day, held a line from the River SCARPE to the Railway (inclusive) and were in touch with 7th Gordon Highrs. of 153rd Brigade on left. The enemy, about mid-day, began attacking down the Railway and on front of 7th (Gordon Highrs)., with determination and pushed latter back from WELCOME to CARVE TRENCH, which was occupied by our "C" and "D" Companies. At 2.30 p.m. our artillery barrage came down, and the 6th Seaforth Highrs. passing through, attacked and carried first objective, and part of second, this left "A" and "B" Companies of this Battalion in support; our "C" and "D" Coys. who had formed a covering flank facing south along the Railway during the attack, holding portion of front line in CARVE TRENCH on North side of Railway between 6th Seaforth Highrs. and 7th Gordon Highrs.	
do.	25.		positions were maintained throughout the night and this day. Enemy machine guns, sniping, and artillery, were all active. Canadians on south of River SCARPE made further progress to East and South and are now in possession of JIGSAW WOOD. 6th Gordon Highrs. relieved to-night by 4th Gordon Highrs. of 154 Brigade, who do an attack to-morrow. Relief was carried out without casualties or mishap between 9 p.m. and midnight. The troops marched back 10 miles to BALMORAL CAMP, where they arrived during early hours of the morning. Night was fine and cool.	

Battalion/

Army Form C. 2118.

WAR DIARY
or
INTELLIGENCE SUMMARY.
(Erase heading not required.)

Instructions regarding War Diaries and Intelligence Summaries are contained in F. S. Regs., Part II. and the Staff Manual respectively. Title pages will be prepared in manuscript.

Place	Date	Hour	Summary of Events and Information	Remarks and references to Appendices
BALMORAL CAMP FLANDERS	29/4		Battalion rested and cleaned up. ECURIE WOOD Baths only available for a portion of the Battalion to-day. Total Casualties - 4 Officers & 251 O.Rs. Weather - Fair, cool. Small pay to troops to-day.	
do.	30.	3 p.m.	Battalion rested and refitted. Commanding Officer addressed the Battalion at 3 p.m. Football in afternoon. Men very cheery and looking clean and smart. Theatre in camp and canteen supplies coming in.	
do.	31.		Baths forenoon and afternoon. Companies at disposal of company commanders for inspections and re-organisation. Congratulations received on capture of anti-tank gun discovered to-day in ground this battalion had overrun in attack. "The Times" and "Daily Mail" have both special long accounts of the 51st Division's continual battle service during this year. (Issue of 30th August). The "Balmoral" troupe gave a re-opening performance of "TURNIP TOPS" at 5.30 p.m as good a show as ever. Big house - crowded to the back door. Following distinctions published in orders :- Bar to MILITARY CROSS. Lieut. (A/Capt.) R. RISK, M.C. 2/Lt. (A/Capt.) J.S. RIDDELL, M.C. Adjutant. MILITARY CROSS. 2/Lt. (A/Capt.) H.J. MILNE. 2/Lieut. T.O. MORISON. DISTINGUISHED CONDUCT MEDALS awarded ...3 Bars to MILITARY MEDAL do. ...3 MILITARY MEDALS do. ...12	STRENGTH

Army Form C. 2118.

WAR DIARY
or
INTELLIGENCE-SUMMARY.

(Erase heading not required.)

Instructions regarding War Diaries and Intelligence Summaries are contained in F. S. Regs., Part II. and the Staff Manual respectively. Title pages will be prepared in manuscript.

Place	Date	Hour	Summary of Events and Information	Remarks and references to Appendices

Bohainvent of Guartier Corps	1918 Aug 31		STRENGTH at end of last month ... Officers. Other Ranks. 20 591
			
			INCREASE.
			  Drafts joined ... Officers Other Ranks
			                       15 200
			  Casuals joined ... - 35 15 334
			
			DECREASE.
			  Killed ... - 243
			  Wounded ... 4 6
			  Missing ... 1 1
			  Died of wounds 1 1
			  Evacuated sick 1 37
			  To U.K. sick 1 -
			  Transferred to 152nd - -
			  Infy. Rde. Hdqrs. 1 -
			  To U.K. for duty 1 -
			  To U.K. for commission - 1 44 925
			                                                               7 297
			
			STRENGTH at end of this month ... 37 628
			
			                                       (signed)
			                                       Lieut. Colonel,
			                     Commanding 6th Battln., Gordon Highlanders.
			
			31st August, 1918.	

SECRET.

War Diary

COPY NO. 11

6TH GORDON HIGHLANDERS.

Operation Orders No. 202.

2nd August, 1918.

Reference Map :-
   CHALONS, 1/20,000.

1.   The 6th Gordon Highlanders will proceed by route march to AVIZE during the night 2nd/3rd August, where the Battalion will entrain.

2.   Starting Point   ...   .   -   CROSS ROADS (Half kilometre
                                                S.W. of OIRY).

   Time   ...   .   -
      For Transport   ...   -   12 midnight.
      For H.Q. A C & D Coys. -   1.30 a.m., 3rd instant.

   Route   ...   .   -   Main Road to AVIZE.

   Order of March ...   .   -   H.Q., A, C, & D, Coys.

   Distance   ...   .   -   100 yards between Coys.

   Dress   ...   .   -   Marching Order.

3.   Company areas will be left scrupulously clean and the usual certificates will be rendered.

4.   Administrative Instructions will be issued later.

5.   ACKNOWLEDGE.

                                 a/ R. BISK, Capt. & Adj.,
                                    6th Gordon Highlanders.

Copies to :-

   1   File.
   2   H.Q., 152nd Inf. Bde.
   3 - 6 Companies.
   7   Q.M.
   8   T.O.
   9   Officer i/c H.Q. Details.
   10   H.Q. Mess.
   11   War Diary.

SECRET.   COPY NO. 9

6TH GORDON HIGHLANDERS.

ADMINISTRATIVE INSTRUCTIONS issued in conjunction
with Operation Orders No. 202 of 2nd August, 1918.

1. Company Officers' valises will be returned to Transport by 9 p.m. to-night. Headquarters Officers' valises and Headquarters' and Company Mess Kits will be ready for collection at 10.30 p.m. at respective messes

2. Rations for to-morrow will be carried on the men. One day's train ration will be drawn at Entraining point and will be taken in bulk on the train. Supply Wagons loaded with one day's rations will proceed with Battalion on the train.

3. Breast Ropes for Horse Trucks will be provided by Battalion Transport.

4. A Medical Officer and Motor Ambulance will be at entraining and detraining points. A Veterinary Officer will be at entraining point.

5. Journey is expected to take 28 hours.

6. Lewis Guns and Magazines will be taken with Companies and will be kept ready for instant action. Lewis Gun N.C.Os. will accompany Lewis Gun Limbers and will superintend unloading of Lewis Guns and Magazines at station on arrival of Companies.

7. Sufficient fuel for cooking on day of arrival will be taken on train.

8. Officers Commanding Companies will arrange a hot meal for their men at 9 p.m. to-night.

9. ACKNOWLEDGE.

sd/ R. RISK, Capt. & Adj.,
6th Gordon Highlanders.

2nd August, 1918.

Copies to all recipients of O.O. No. 202.

SECRET.   6th GORDON HIGHLANDERS.   COPY No...11..

Operation Orders No. 23.

16th August 1918.

Reference Map :- TRENCH 1/10,000
                 S.B. M.R. 1/20,000
                 4t.R.   1/4,000

1. The Battalion will relieve the 8th King's Liverpool Regiment on 16th August, 1918 in Brigade Support, Headquarters - M.13.b.9..5.

    A Coy., 6th Gordon Hrs. will take over from A Coy., King's L'pool Regt.
    B   "   "   "   "   "   "   "   " B "   "   "   "
    C   "   "   "   "   "   "   "   " C "   "   "   "
    D   "   "   "   "   "   "   "   " D "   "   "   "

2. The line is held on a one battalion front, 5th Seaforth Highrs. in front, 6th Seaforth Highrs. in reserve. The 170th Brigade is on the Right, and the 153rd Brigade is on the Left.

3. The Battalion will parade at 2.50 p.m. on football field, in close column of companies, facing S.W. and will march to M.3.b., whence it will be conveyed to ARMIN by light Railway. Lewis Guns and Drums will be taken by train. Captain W. McCASH, M.C. will report to Entraining Officer at 2.30p.m.
    The Battalion will move from ARMIN at 7.50 p.m. by platoons at 100 yards interval in the following order :-
    H.Q., A., B., C., D Companies.

4. Guides as follows :- 1 for Battalion H.Q. and 1 per platoon and company H.Q. will meet the Battalion at Railway Bridge, M.14.a.8.3.

5. There will be no movement East of the ARMIN - LENS Railway during progress of relief before 9.30 p.m.

6. Advance party as follows :- 2/Lieut. W. WHIN and 1 N.C.O. from Battalion H.Q., 1 Officer per company and 1 N.C.O. per platoon, Battalion and Company Gas N.C.Os., will proceed by lorry to M.13.b.3.2. where they will be met by guides from the 8th King's Liverpool Regiment.
    All maps, photos and defence schemes, trench stores and work in hand will be taken over on relief.

7. Disposition maps showing posts and location of platoons will be sent to Battalion H.Q. by 5 p.m., 16th August, 1918.

8. Echelon "B" as already detailed will be accommodated at WAVERLEY CAMP and on detraining at ARMIN will come under the orders of Captain E. WIN, M.C.

9. Completion of relief will be reported to Battn. H.Q. by telephone, by code - "N.W. 300 NOTED"

                                    Sd/ E. WIN, Capt. & Adjt.,
Copies to - usual recipients.   6th Gordon Highlanders.

SECRET   6TH A.& S.H. HIGHLANDERS   COPY No......

ADMINISTRATIVE INSTRUCTIONS ISSUED IN CONJUNCTION WITH   O.O. No. 23.

18th August, 1918.

1. ENTRAINING.
    There will be a train of 6 trucks each capable of carrying 3.
for each company, and train of 3 trucks for Headquarters. Journey
will last about 5½ hours. Food will be taken at AMIENS. Company
parties and limbers and one for Headquarters will meet battalion at ARMY
to carry guns etc. forward to Battalion Headquarters in the line.

2. RATIONS.
    Rations for 20th will be drawn from AMIENS on arrival and will be
carried on the men.

3. PACKS.
    Packs will be taken into the line.

4. TRENCH STORES.
    List of trench stores signed both by officer taking over and
officer handing over will be forwarded to Battalion Headquarters by
10 a.m. 19th instant.

5. BILLETS.
    Billets and their surroundings will be left scrupulously clean.
Usual certificate will be rendered before moving off.

                                        sd/ R. KING, Capt. & Adjt.,
                                        6th A.& S.H. Highlanders.

Copies to recipients of Operations Orders No. 23.

A second platoon of B. Coy. will be specially detailed to occupy the Quarry in H.18.a.2.4.

D Coy will detail one platoon to occupy enemy trench running from H.17.d.8.1 to H.17.d.85.50.

6. Artillery. At Zero a barrage will be put down on the objective as shown on Map. This barrage will lift at Zero + 10 minutes and will be laid on the new S.O.S. line as shown on Map where it will stand until Zero + 30. In addition a Howitzer barrage will be placed at Zero on the points marked ⊙ on attached Map where it will remain until Zero + 30.

7. On the Capture of the objective Lewis Gun Posts will be established by B. Coy. at

    N.E.
        edge of Quarry.
At junction of objective with FAMPOUX-PLOUVAIN Road,

and by "D" Company at

    H.17.d.8.7. and H.17.d.8.5
Posts are marked on Map.

8. Dumps. Dumps of S.A.A. and Bombs will be established in the Sunken Road Assembly position at its junction with CAMEL TRENCH and at H.17.d.50.95.

9. Reports on Prisoners to from Battalion H.Q. at H.15.c.3.0.

10. Watches will be synchronised at 8 p.m. at Battalion Headquarters.

11. Zero hour will be 1.30 a.m.

12. Acknowledge.

                              Lieut. & Adj.
                        6th Gordon Highlanders.

20.8.18.

Secret. 6th Gordon Highrs.
Administrative Arrangements for O.O. No. 204.

1. All letters, documents and orders giving an identification of this unit will be left behind.

2. Dress. Battle Order with 170 rounds S.A.A. Lewis Gunners - 50 rounds S.A.A. Bombs - 4 per man in special sandbag carrier.

Tools - 2 men per section will carry picks. Remainder of section shovels.

No. 1 & 2 Lewis Gunners will NOT carry bombs or tools.

~~Iron rations & water~~ Iron ration will be carried. Waterbottles to be filled.

Each Company will carry 5 S.O.S. Rifle Grenades.

Very Pistols 1" and ammunition will be carried by Platoon Commanders and No.1 Lewis Gunners.

Wire Cutters and Wire Breakers will be carried under orders to be given by Company Commanders.

3. Lewis Guns will be carried and all magazines.

4. Times will be as follows:-

Dump Packs and remove identification   8 pm.

Teas to be taken at 8.30 pm.

Report at Battalion HQrs. to draw tools bombs and wire cutters at 9.15 pm.

March off 10 pm.

Forbes
Lieut. /Adjt.
6th Battalion Gordon Highlrs.

20th Augt. 1918.

Secret   6th Gordon Highrs.   Copy No. 8

Addendum to O.O. No. 206 of 25.8.18.

1. On receipt of this order O.C. A Coy. will detail a strong platoon under an officer to be attached to C Coy. and to move forward with that Coy. when it moves into Sunken Road running Northward through H.17.c. Until C Coy. moves forward this platoon will remain in its present accommodation.

2. During the advance of the 153rd Infantry Brigade O.C. 177th Brigade R.F.A will fire on the railway embankment from the bridge at H.18.d.25.15 to I.13.c.40.60 with four 4.5" hows from O to O + 40 and with two hows on the quarry in T.13.a.20.20 from O to O + 40. A proportion of the rounds fired will be smoke. At O + 40 all six hows will be lifted to the High ground West of Station Cross Roads I.12.a.90.30 which they will shell till O+60.

3. The advance of the Brigade on our left will be covered by a barrage which will extend about 50 yards South of CAMEL AVENUE.

4. In the event of a big success the 153rd Brigade are to occupy the Brown line (2nd objective) East of railway and if MOUNT PLEASANT has been taken by B Coy. 6th Gordon Highlanders, B & D Coys. 6th Gor. Hrs. will occupy the Brown line (2nd objective) from B.13.b.4.8 Southward. If B Coy. has failed to take MOUNT PLEASANT in the first operation D Coy. will extend a defensive flank along CAMEL TRENCH to its junction with CALICO keeping in touch with B Coy. which will keep a defensive flank along the railway.

5. Special precautions will be taken in view of possibility of booby traps. Information has been received that enemy has recently put arsenic in wells and all troops will be warned against drinking water that has not been tested.

6. The Canadian Battn. attacking on the right of this Brigade will be the 4th C.M.R. Battn.

7. Acknowledge.

A Risk
Capt. & Adjt.
6th Gordon Highlanders.

26.8.18.

Secret   6th Gordon Highlanders.   Copy No 8

Operation Order No 206.
25th August 1918.

Reference Maps:-
     ROEUX 1/20,000.
     SCARPE VALLEY 1/20,000.

1. The Canadian Corps will attack South of the River SCARPE (with river inclusive to left flank) tomorrow 26th instant at an hour to be notified later.

   First objective (reached Zero + 47) the line of the grid between H.29 and 30.

   Second objective (reached Zero + 103) the line of the grid between H and I.

   On reaching the second objective the attack will be exploited as far as possible according to circumstances.

2. In the event of the attack by the Canadian Corps being successful an attack by the 51st (Highland) Division will be carried out at an hour to be notified later. The boundaries and objectives for this attack are as shown on attached map.
        First objective   Green.
        Second   "   Brown.
        Third   "   Dotted Brown
        Fourth   "   Yellow.

3. The attack by the 153rd and 154th Brigades will be carried out under a barrage. On this attack being launched D Coy. of the 6th Gor: Hrs: will advance by CAMEL AVENUE and CAMEL TRENCH and will capture COOT TRENCH from CAMEL TRENCH to the Railway Embankment. There will be no barrage on our front.

4. At the same time B Coy. 6th Gor: Hrs: will act as follows:-
   (a) 2 platoons will proceed from DINGWALL TRENCH along the road through FAMPOUX to CRASH TRENCH which they will capture.
   (b) 2 platoons will move down DINGWALL TRENCH to the River and from there will proceed along the bank of the River until they reach the Railway Embankment. They will then proceed along the Railway Embankment until touch is found with D Coy. at COOT TRENCH. The whole of B Coy. will then line the Railway facing South.
   (c) On the line of the Railway having been captured B Coy. will then endeavour to push Southwards and capture the first objective where it is shown South of the Railway on the map. If this is found impossible after a determined effort, he will maintain a defensive flank facing South on the line of the Railway.

5. At/

2.

5. At Zero hour C & A Coys. will act as follows:—
No. 12 Platoon C Coy. accompanied by two Vickers Guns of 1st Life Guards M.G. Bn. will (under orders of O.C. B Coy.) move forward and cross the river at H.23.a.95.90 by bridge or pontoon if it is there, whence they will proceed by bridge at H.23.a.9.6 to take up a position on the high ground about H.24.a.3.2 or on Railway Embankment near there. From the position taken up they will assist the advance with Lewis Gun and Machine Gun fire. Remainder of C Coy. will move into Sunken Road running North through H.17.b. and will establish Coy. H.Q. at dugout H.17.b.3.3. A Coy. will move into STONE SUPPORT. C Coy. will keep in close touch with front Coys. and will move forward to reinforce if and when required by them.

6. B. Coy. will leave their present H.Q. tonight and will occupy H.Q. in DINGWALL TRENCH.
   No. 12 Platoon C Coy. will also proceed to DINGWALL TRENCH immediately on arrival of 2 Vickers guns of 1st Life Guards M.G. Battn. at C Coy. H.Q. at 11 p.m. tonight. No. 12 Platoon will then come under orders of O.C. B Coy.

7. To avoid possibility of casualties from barrage for attack by Canadian Corps, O.C. B Coy. will withdraw all his posts to Northern end of DINGWALL TRENCH at 1 A.M. tomorrow 26th The whole Coy. will be in position in DINGWALL TRENCH by 2 A.M.

8. Coys. will intimate tonight by code "H.22 received" when they are in position and are equipped and in readiness in accordance with Administrative Instructions issued herewith.

9. A report centre for Bn. H.Q. will be established at dugout H.17.b.3.3. at Zero hour for 51st (H) Division.

10. Acknowledge.

Capt. Adj.
6th Gordon Highrs.

Copies to:—
1. File
2. H.Q. 152 Brigade.
3–6. Coys.
7. H.Q. Details
8. H.Q. Mess
9. War Diary.

<u>Secret.</u>　　　　6th Gordon Highrs.　　　　Copy No. 8

Administrative Instructions issued in
conjunction with O.O. No. 206 of 25.8.18

Ry. Maps:-
ROEUX 1/20000.
SCARPE VALLEY 1/20,000.

1. Company Commanders will ensure that all waterbottles are filled tonight and kept full until their Coys. are moved off tomorrow.

2. All men except Lewis Gunners will be completed to 170 rds. S.A.A. per man. All Lewis Gun Magazines will be filled tonight. Each man will carry two No. 5 Mills Grenades in his pockets.

3. Company Commdrs. will ensure that all Coy. packs have been dumped together. Company Cooks will be left in charge of their packs and Cooking utensils. Location of dumps to be notified to Bn. H.Q. by 2 a.m. ~~midnight~~. Fighting order will be assumed forthwith.

4. 50% of the men of B, C, & D Coys. will carry shovels. The necessary number will be delivered to B. Coy. tonight. D & C Coys. will equip themselves.

5. Company Commdrs. will ensure that tomorrow's rations are not recklessly consumed and that the unconsumed portion of the ration is carried by each man when Companies move off.

6. A dump of 8 boxes S.A.A. and 20 boxes No 5 Mills Grenades will be established at Quarry H.18.a.1.4. This dump will be formed as far as possible by D Coy. tonight. O.C. D Coy. will report by 9 a.m. tomorrow how many boxes S.A.A. and bombs are required to complete to the numbers laid down. A further dump of S.A.A. and bombs will be established at H.24.a.4.y tomorrow by 6th Seaforth Highrs.

A.A.Risk
Capt. & Adj.
6th Gordon Highrs.

Copies to recipients of O.O. No. 206.

6TH GORDON HIGHLANDERS.

Nominal Roll of Officers by Companies - 30th Augt. 1918.

Headquarters.

Lieut. Colonel	Thom	J.G. D.S.O., M.C.	Commanding Officer.
Major	Cranstoun	C.J.E.	2nd-in-Command.
Captain	Risk	R. M.C.	Adjutant.
Hon. Capt.	Findlay	F.W. M.C.	Quartermaster.
Lieut.	Collier	J.	Asst. Adjutant. Leave.
"	Cowie	C.A.	L.G.O.
"	Raitt	J.L.	R.S.O.
2/Lieut.	Morison	I.O.	B.I.O. On leave.
"	Philip	A.	T.O.
Capt. & Rev.	O'Connor	J.J. (C.F.)	R.C. Chaplain. att.
Capt.	Jamieson	H.H. (A.A.M.C.)	M.O. att. on leave.
Lieut.	Maltby	B. (U.S.Army)	M.O. temp. attached.

"A" Company.

Captain	Fleming	W.J.C.	Company Commander.
Lieut.	Hay	J.L.	
2/Lieut.	Alexander	F.P.W.	Divl. L.G. Course.
"	Brunskill	A.A.J. (A. & S.H.)	
"	Hall	F.	
"	Cheyne	A.I.	
"	Thornton	A.	att. 152nd T.M.B.
"	Thomson	T.D.	

"B" Company.

Rank	Name	Initials	Notes
A/Captain	Mackay	K.	Company Commander.
Lieut.	Blacklaws	C.B.	
"	Paterson	J.R.	Town Major, MARCEUIL.
"	Black	J. (11th R.H.)	
2/Lieut.	Wilson	N.J.	att. 152nd Bde. H.Q.
"	Macdonald	E.C.	
"	Leys	J.M. (A. & S.H.)	

"C" Company.

2/Lieut.	Reid	A.	Company Commander.
"	Henry	R.	Divl. Musketry Course
"	Conlon	G.W.R.	
"	Frame	R.L. (Cameron Hrs.)	

"D" Company.

A/Captain	Gray	H.	Company Commander.
2/Lieut.	Mitchell	R.W.	Divl. Bombing Course.
"	Clapperton	H.	
"	Weir	W.	
"	Hastings	G.G.	
"	Grosert	A.K.	Hospital

-o-o-o-o-o-o-o-o-o-o-o-o-o-o-o-o-o-o-

152/3-1
WI 47

Confidential

War Diary
of
6th Battn. The Gordon Highlanders
for period
1/9/18 to 30/9/18

(Volume 47.)

"Copy" 100/

6th Gordon Highlanders
Operation Orders No. 208
8th September, 1918.

Copy No 10

Reference Map:-
Sheet 51B. N.W. 1/20,000

1. The 6th Gordon High'rs will be relieved in support on the evening of 9th September, 1918, by 6th Seaforth High'rs and, on relief, will move forward and relieve the 5th Seaforth High'rs in the Front Line.

2. Relief by the 6th Seaforth High'rs will be carried out as follows:-
   "A" Coy. 6th Sea. H. will relieve "A" Coy. 6th Gordon H.
   "B"   "   "   "   "   "   "   "B"   "   "   "
   "C"   "   "   "   "   "   "   "C"   "   "   "
   "D"   "   "   "   "   "   "   "D"   "   "   "

3. Guides for 6th Seaforth High'rs will be provided as follows:- 1 per Platoon, 1 per Coy. H.Q., 1 for Batt'n H.Q.
   "A" and "B" Companies' guides will be at Railway Arch, H.18.d.2.1., at 6.30p.m. Guides for the rest of relieving Batt'n will be at foot of CAM VALLEY, H.15.c.9.6. at 6p.m.

4. Relief of 5th Seaforth High'rs will be carried out as follows:-
   (Rt. Front Coy) "A" Coy. 6th G.H. will relieve "D" Coy 5th S.H.
   (Left   "   ") "B"   "   "   "   "   "   "A"   "   "   "
   (Rt. Support Coy) "C" "   "   "   "   "   "B"   "   "   "
   (Left   "   ) "D"   "   "   "   "   "   "C"   "   "   "

5. Advance Party of 6th Gordon High'rs as follows, will report at Batt'n H.Q. of 5th Seaforth High'rs at 2p.m:-
   1 officer and 1 N.C.O. per company.
   1 officer and 1 N.C.O. for Batt'n H.Q.

6. Guides for this Batt'n will be provided by 5th Seaforth High'rs as follows:-
   1 per Platoon; 1 per Company H.Q.
   These guides will rendezvous as follows:-
   For "A" and "B" Coys., 6th Gordon H., at INDIA CAVE, I.19.b.3.6. at 7.30 p.m.
   For "C" and "D" Coys., 6th Gordon H., at RAILWAY ARCH, H.18.d.2.1. at 7.30 p.m.

7. Route for relief of 5th Seaforth High'rs will be as follows:-
   "A" Coy. 6th G.H. by road running through I.19.a. & b.
   "B" "   "   "   COREY AVENUE.
   "C" & "D" Coys., 6th G.H. - ARRAS - FAMPOUX Rd., H.18.d.2.1., road running through I.19.a. & b. and 20.a.
   Batt'n H.Q. 6th G.H. - ARRAS - FAMPOUX Rd., H.18.d.2.1.

   all/

7. All movement by day light will be by Platoons, or equivalent, at 200 yds. interval.

8. All Photographs, Trench Orders and Trench Stores will be handed over on relief. Receipts for Stores handed and taken over will be forwarded to Bn. H.Q by 12 noon on 10th inst.

9. Disposition Maps will be forwarded to Bn. H.Q. by 12 noon on 10th inst.

10. Completion of relief will be notified to Bn. H.Q. by code - "X 89 RECEIVED"

11. ACKNOWLEDGE.

P. Rush
Captain & Adjt.
6th Gordon High'rs

Copies to :-
1 File.
2 H.Q. 152nd Infy. Bde.
3 O.C. 5th Seaforth H'rs.
4 O.C. 6th Seaforth H'rs.
5 - 8 Companies
9 Q.M. and T.O.
10 H.Q. Details
11 War Diary.

Army Form C. 2118.

Confidential.

WAR DIARY
or
INTELLIGENCE-SUMMARY.

(Erase heading not required.)

Instructions regarding War Diaries and Intelligence Summaries are contained in F. S. Regs., Part II. and the Staff Manual respectively. Title pages will be prepared in manuscript.

Place	Date	Hour	Summary of Events and Information	Remarks and references to Appendices
DUFF CAMP.	1/9		Inspection (Adjutant's) of Companies and H.Q. Details - 11.30 a.m. to 1 p.m. and 2 p.m. - 3.30 p.m. No Church Parades - Presbyterian Padre not being available. R.C. Voluntary Service - 9.30 a.m.	
do	2		Battalion on ROCLINCOURT RANGE by Companies - morning and afternoon, and on Bombing Ground, every man throwing at least one live bomb. News from everywhere front is everywhere of advance both North and South. Very high commendation by Canadian Corps Commander of this Division received in letter published to-day, written on the Division leaving his command and going to 22nd Corps. Weather fair - cool or cold. A 14" Naval gun has just come into the valley 800 yards West of us and shells DOUAI, each shot shaking our Camp like an earthquake.	
do TRENCHES.	3		At 10 a.m. received notice that the Corps Commander, Major General GODLEY was coming to present Medals at 12 noon. This presentation accordingly took place, the Battalion being drawn up in three sides of a square on Football Field West of Camp, and marching back past the General in column of route back into Camp after the ceremony. The Battalion moved into the line in Support relieving the 6th Bn., The Seaforth Highlanders in the FAMPOUX Sector. "A" and "B" Companies forward in CORDITE and CORONA Trenches, Headquarters, and "C" and "D" Companies about CAM VALLEY. "A" and "B" taken up "C" and "D" Companies marched to their allotted area. to the forward areas to-night. in 'Buses. Relief complete by 8.30 p.m. Enemy 'planes active - bombed the CAM Valley and the forward areas to-night.	C.O. 20%
do	4		News good - big advances made in North and South. 14,600 prisoners taken since September 1st. 15,700 taken by British forces during August. Our two forward Companies "A" and "B", are under Officer Commanding, 5th Bn., The Seaforth Highlanders (Battalion in front line) for counter-attack purposes if necessary./	

Army Form C. 2118.

WAR DIARY
or
INTELLIGENCE-SUMMARY.
(Erase heading not required.)

Place	Date	Hour	Summary of Events and Information	Remarks and references to Appendices
TRENCHES	1918 Sept. 5.		necessary. They have accommodation in the "caves" of ROEUX. Accommodation of two Supporting Companies is meagre and all Battalion Pioneers plus extra labour engaged in improving it. Strength (Trench) to-day - 336.	J.L.
do.	6.		Work on Huts, Latrines, and Cookhouses continued. Commanding Officer visited the forward Companies in MOUNT PLEASANT Trenches. The "caves" of ROEUX are yielding their secrets - boilers, engines, dynamos, thousands of Bosche bombs, etc. Enemy sending good deal of gas over, both on front system and back among our battery positions. Weather fair.	J.L.
do.	7.		Work proceeded with. Hut accommodation for "C" Company is now provided. Lieut. Colonel J.G. THOM, D.S.O., M.C., left to attend an Army Course of 10 days. Reconnaissance of front line carried out by Company Officers and Battalion Scouts. Weather fair, warmer, some thunder.	J.L.
do.	8.		Enemy gas shells about Battalion H.Q. 6.30 a.m. Work proceeded with. Weather sultry - thunder storms. Exploration of "caves" of ROEUX continues.	J.L.
do.	9.		Quiet day. Weather unsettled and high South West wind. Cold. The B.G.C. dined at Battalion H.Q. this evening. (Brigadier General E. SEGRAVE, D.S.O.).	OO.208.
do.	10.		This battalion relieved 5th Bn., The Seaforth Highlanders in front line being relieved in Support by 6th Bn., The Seaforth Highlanders. Dispositions - "A" Coy. (Capt. W.J.C. FLEMING) - Right Front Company, "B" . (Lieut. C.G. BLACKLAWS) - Left . in CRIBB and CLIFF Trenches with Outpost East side of village of PLOUVAIN, "C" and "D" Companies being Right and Left Support Companies in CANDY and CARROT Trenches at reverse slope foot of the HAUSA - DELBAR Ridge. Relief completed by 10.30 p.m. Patrols out to-night from each of front Coys.. Trench Strength - 339.1	J.L.

Army Form C. 2118.

- 3 -

WAR DIARY
or
INTELLIGENCE SUMMARY.

(Erase heading not required.)

Place	Date	Hour	Summary of Events and Information	Remarks and references to Appendices

TRENCHES	1918 Sep 10		Defence Scheme received last night - require some change in dispositions - carried out after dark to-night. Two platoons of "A" Coy. moved from CRIB in front line to HAUSA - DELBAR Crest where new main line of resistance is partially completed. "B" Coy. takes over from "A" Coy. one Outpost group and holds all the front line from the marshes to the Battalion left boundary.
			   Patrols last night reported no sign of enemy and a later patrol after daylight was sent out to ensure that he was still holding his line (the ROUVROY - FRESNES Line). This drew fire and the patrol returned. At 3 p.m. a daylight patrol of 1 Officer and 2 Other Ranks went out between River and marshes and close to BIACHE, encountered an enemy party of 12 or 15 which when fired on, tried to cut our patrol off. Lieut. T.D. THOMSON however, managed to fight his way back and though seriously wounded (five bullet wounds and some bomb splinters) got back with both his men slightly wounded, having killed 3 or 4 of the enemy and wounded several more.
			   Orders received for a new Post Line to be begun in front of our Outposts. The laying out and execution of this work is left to the Battalions in the front line. In touch with Black Watch (154th Infantry Brigade) on our left and Yorks & Lancs., 11th Division, on our right on South side of SCARPE.
			   B.G.C. visited Battalion to-day, lunching at H.Q.	

do.	11.		Work on new line in front of Outposts begun and went smoothly last night. Line laid out (wavy) by Captain & Adjutant R. RISK, M.C. 145 yards dug 8' wide 1' deep.
			   Some casualties in "B" Coy. at morning "Stand To" - 1 man killed and 6 wounded by one shell landing in the midst of a post in front line.
			   Without warning, a Colonel of 7th W. Yorks and a party of Officers and Other Ranks came up at 1 p.m. to arrange for taking over from us to-morrow night. Dispositions to-night changed to some extent. "A" Coy. back from front to support line. "B" Coy. takes whole Battalion front which is 200 yards shorter owing to 6th Bn.. The Seaforth Highlanders coming into line on our right. "C" Coy. withdrawn drawn after dark from Support line to INDIA Cave. "D" Coy. remains in Support line.
			6th Bn., The Seaforth Highlanders two companies taking over from The/	

do.	12.			

Army Form C. 2118.

WAR DIARY
or
INTELLIGENCE SUMMARY

(Erase heading not required.)

Instructions regarding War Diaries and Intelligence Summaries are contained in F. S. Regs., Part II. and the Staff Manual respectively. Title pages will be prepared in manuscript.

Place	Date	Hour	Summary of Events and Information	Remarks and references to Appendices
TRENCHES	1918 April 11		The 51st Division is to be relieved in the line and to go into Army Reserve about CHATEAU de la HAIE. Weather unsettled – strong S.E. wind.	
do.	12		6th Bn., The Seaforth Highlanders two companies taking over from 6th Bn., Black Watch on our left as well as from our left front company took long time and it was 3 a.m. before new dispositions reported complete. Battalion relieved after dark by 7th W. Yorks and marched down as relieved by platoons to ATHIES where light railway trains waiting which took them to CHATEAU de la HAIE. A meal of hot porridge and hot rum-punch was ready for all in two cookers at the trains.	
CHATEAU de la HAIE.	13.		Last train reached CHATEAU de la HAIE about 7 a.m. Day spent mostly in sleep broken by intervals of feeding.	
do.	14.		Day spent in inspections, cleaning, baths, pay, and rest. Thunder showers have made the Camp which is in the grove round the Chateau very muddy.	
do.	15.		Church Parades in a.m. Day fine and sunny. Conference 4.30 p.m. to 6 p.m. of Battalion C.Os. at 152nd Brigade H.Q. on training and organisation.	
do	16.		First day's training. Platoons weak and work pretty "ragged", yet going with a will and promising rapid improvement. Parade hours 8.30 a.m. – 12.30 p.m. B.G.C. visited Parade Ground. Lieut. Colonel J. G. THOM, D.S.O., M.C.; rejoined the Battalion from 1st Army School and resumed command this evening. Company Commanders Conference on training etc. 2.15 p.m. – 4 p.m.	
do.	17.		Reveille 7 a.m. Parades 8.45 a.m. to 12.30 p.m. Draft of 134 inspected by Commanding Officer 10 a.m. A large proportion are casuals and the general standard good. Work of Companies (section and platoon) going well – very marked advance on yesterday's work.	
do.	18.		Battalion Parade 8.45 a.m. – 9.15 a.m. "Fall In" by drum and march past in column of fours. "A"/	

Army Form C. 2118.

WAR DIARY
or
INTELLIGENCE SUMMARY.
(Erase heading not required.)

Place	Date	Hour	Summary of Events and Information	Remarks and references to Appendices
CHATEAU de la HAIE	1914 JULY 18		"A" Company carried out Musketry on MARQUEFFLES Range. "B", "C", & "D" Coys. at platoon and section training. First practice of the attack. General Cartew - Campbell, Commanding 51st (Highland) Division visited Battln. during parades.	JC
do.	19		Battalion parade and march past 8.45 a.m. - 9.15 a.m. Thereafter inspection of all Companies in turn, H.Q. Details and Band, by Commanding Officer. Other work - Musketry and practice of the attack. Specialists under their instructors as usual. Miniature Range with disappearing targets completed and in use to-day. An officers Competition Shoot.	JC
do.	20.		Warning Order received to-night. 152nd Brigade to be prepared to relieve 49th Division in the line on Sunday 22nd. The Battalion received another draft of 100 other ranks - Inspection of by Commanding Officer in afternoon.	JC
do.	21.		Heavy rain delayed Battalion for an hour and broke up the mornings work. Orderly Room at 2 p.m. Tactical exercise for all officers and full rank N.C.Os. 2.30 p.m. - 4.30 p.m. Scheme - Attack and pursuit. Draft of 97 arrived this p.m. bringing Battalion up nearly to establishment. Orders to-night - 152nd Brigade to move to DUFF CAMP, ECURIE, as Divisional Reserve on 23rd.	JC
do.	22.		Weather stormy and unsettled, much heavy rain. Companies - Baths and pay, weather interfering with work. Map reading lecture and sysseums exercise for officers under Second-in-Command 2.30 p.m. - 4 p.m. 100th Performance of "Turnip Tops" by the "Balmorals" at ECOIVRES - lorries to take a number of Officers and men went from Brigade H.Q. at 4 p.m. Companies had a pay (15 Francs). Church Parades 9.15 a.m. and 11 a.m. Stormy and wet.	JC
DUFF CAMP	23.		152nd Brigade moved by march route to ECURIE. Battalion paraded 9.30 a.m. and moved to its position at head of Brigade Column passing starting point 10.30 a.m. Route - VILLERS AUX BOIS - MONT ST. ELOI - MADAGASCAR CORNER. At 1.45 p.m. the Battalion reached DUFF Camp by ECURIE WOOD, its destination. Transport and Cookers/	O.O. 210

Army Form C. 2118.

WAR DIARY
or
INTELLIGENCE SUMMARY.
(Erase heading not required.)

Instructions regarding War Diaries and Intelligence
Summaries are contained in F. S. Regs, Part II.
and the Staff Manual respectively. Title pages
will be prepared in manuscript.

Place	Date	Hour	Summary of Events and Information	Remarks and references to Appendices
Duff Camp	1918 Sep. 23		Cookers preceded the Battalion and the dinners were ready on arrival of the troops. Some light showers - afternoon and night very fine.	
do.	24.		Battalion parade 8.45 a.m. Fitting of kilts not good enough. This gone into this a.m. and in p.m. All men requiring fitting paraded and necessary alterations to be done by massed tailors to-night in an all night sitting. Companies during morning carried out the attack practice. Very imperfect and a demonstration by one Company to take place to-morrow. In p.m. bombing and rifle bombing carried out by all Companies. Battalion Attack Scheme to take place on 27th. Gro--und gone over by Commanding Officer and Company Commanders this evening. Lieut. J.L. RAITT, Battalion Signalling Officer, gave lecture to all Officers on methods of transmitting intelligence in action 5 p.m. Weather fine.	
do.	25.		Battalion parade 8.45 a.m. followed by well executed demonstration of the attack by "B" Company under Captain P.M. Mackenzie. Thereafter "A", "C" and "D" Coys. carried out the practice. "A" and "B" Companies on Range - 100 yards and 200 yards - in afternoon. "C" and "D" Coys. wiring in afternoon and Box Respirator Drill. Captain & Adjutant R. RISK, M.C., left on Special Leave to U.K.	
do.	26.		Battalion parade 8.45 a.m. and thereafter carried out practice of the Battalion in the attack on a two Company front, "A" and "B" taking first objective, "C" and "D" second, going through "A" and "B". The practice was well carried out on the whole by all Companies. Day fine. News from Eastern front good. In PALESTINE, General ALLENBY'S Forces have defeated and captured the Turkish Armies opposed to them - 40,000 prisoners with guns, transport, etc. On the Bulgarian front the Allies are advancing on about 100 miles and Bulgars in full retreat.	
do.	27.		Battalion Tactical Scheme - for which yesterday's work was a rehearsal. The troops were in position 10 a.m. One section R.A. attached to the Battalion for the exercise. G.O.C. Division, and B.G.C. present. Zero hour 10.30 a.m. 2/Lieut. I.O. MORISON, M.C./	

Army Form C. 2118.

WAR DIARY
or
INTELLIGENCE-SUMMARY.
(Erase heading not required.)

- 7 -

Instructions regarding War Diaries and Intelligence Summaries are contained in F. S. Regs., Part II. and the Staff Manual respectively. Title pages will be prepared in manuscript.

Place	Date 1918	Hour	Summary of Events and Information	Remarks and references to Appendices
DUFF CAMP	Feb. 27		T.O. MORISON, M.C. and H.Q. Details furnished a skeleton enemy. Direction was well kept and formations good. The advance was rather too rapid until close contact was gained when there was too much hesitation by section leaders in tackling Machine gun positions. Signalling from front to rear was very successfully carried out throughout the exercise by visual (lamp) and by loop set (wireless). The exercise was completed by 1 p.m.	
do.	28.		Observed as General Holiday by orders of the Brigadier General Commanding. Men at Baths. Weather very unsettled - windy and rainy. News very good. Major C.J.E. CRANSTOUN proceeded to United Kingdom on special leave. Commanding Officer lectured Company Commanders on Company kit and supervision generally and also with regards care of men's feet to prevent Trench Feet trouble. Football Match played by 6th Bn., The Gordon Highlanders against Royal Berkshire Regiment resulted in a win for The Gordon Highlanders by two goals to nil.	
RAILWAY EMBANKMENT	29.		Battalion relieved the 7th Bn., The Gordon Highlanders and to be in reserve in the LOUVAIN Sector, at about 5 p.m. "C" Coy. in COSSACK TRENCH and CAM AVENUE. "D" Coy. in CAROLINA TRENCH. Headquarters, & "A" & "B" Coys. at RAILWAY EMBANKMENT. Lieut. J.L. RAITT and 1 N.C.O. proceeded as Headquarters Advance Party leaving ECURIE at 12 noon. 1 Officer and 1 N.C.O. paraded and proceeded as Advance Party for Companies. Battalion marched from Starting Point at 2.30 p.m. Route of march - Track to Road Junction H.13.b.5.5. thence by ARRAS - FAMPOUX ROAD. Order of march - "C", "D", Headquarters, "A", "B", at 200 yards interval. Q.M. Stores and Transport remain at ECURIE. Weather, dull, cloudy and showery. News from front lines very good.	O.O. 211.
do.	30.		Weather dull, cloudy and threatening rain during morning. "A" & "B" Coys. at Railway Embankment carrying out Physical Training, Box Respirator Drill, Musketry etc. "C" and "D" Coys. positions visited by Commanding Officer during morning. "C" & "D" Coys. carrying out Box Respirator Drill, Musketry, P.T., and rifle exercises and improving shelters and trenches generally. Instructions were issued by Commdg. Officer to construct several new shelters for men behind trenches - this especially applied to "C" Company. Received news that Bulgaria has given in. Honours/	

Army Form C. 2118.

WAR DIARY
or
INTELLIGENCE SUMMARY.
(Erase heading not required.)

Instructions regarding War Diaries and Intelligence Summaries are contained in F. S. Regs., Part II. and the Staff Manual respectively. Title pages will be prepared in manuscript.

Place	Date	Hour	Summary of Events and Information	Remarks and references to Appendices
RAILWAY EMBANKMENT	1918 Sept 30		Honours during month –	
			MILITARY CROSS – Lieut. C.G. BLACKLAWS.	
			D.C.M. – 1 other rank.	
			M.M. – 5 other ranks.	
			Officers. Other ranks.	
			Strength last month 33 628	
			INCREASE. O.R.	
			Drafts 1 10	
			Casuals 1 32	
			M.M. – 8	
			— 2 —	
			10 50	
			43 1008	
			DECREASE.	
			Killed – 2	
			Wounded – –	
			Evacuated sick – –	
			To Base unfit – –	
			152nd T.M.B. 4 50	
			— 2 —	
			30 940	
			STRENGTH at end of this month 30 940	

30th September, 1918.

[signature]
Lieut. Colonel,
Commanding 6th Battalion, The Gordon Highlanders.

War Diary.

SECRET.   6th BATTN., GORDON HIGHLANDERS.   COPY NO. 10.

Operation Order No. 267.

2nd September, 1918.

Reference Maps:-
    51B   1/40,000.
    51B N.W.1/20,000.

1. RELIEF.

The 6th Bn. Gordon Highlanders will relieve the 5th Bn. Seaforth Highrs. in support in FAMPOUX SECTOR to-morrow, 3rd September 1918. Relief will take place as follows:-

"A" Coy. 6th Gordon Highrs. will relieve "C" Coy 5th Sea. Hrs.
"B"   "   "   "   "   "B" "   "   "   "
These two companies will be in CHARITY and CORONA area and will be under the orders of O.C., 5th Bn. Seaforth Highrs. for counterattack.

"C" Coy. 6th Gordon Highrs. will relieve "A" & "D" Coys.
                                                         5th Bn. Seaforth Highrs.

"D" Coy. 6th Gordon Highrs. will take over accommodation in CAN AVENUE between NEUFS SWITCH and MAXIMS LANE.

2. ADVANCE PARTY.

An Advance party as follows:-
    Lieut. J. L. BATTY and 1 N.C.O. for Headquarters
        and all Pioneers.
    1 Officer and 1 N.C.O. per company.
Will parade at orderly room at 10 a.m. This party (except the officer and N.C.O. from "D" Coy., who will proceed direct to their own area) will then proceed to Headquarters, 5th Bn. Seaforth Highrs. (N.10.c.65.95.) where H.Q. party will take over, and guides for "A", "B" and "C" companies will be provided.

3. ORDER OF MARCH.

The Battalion will march off as follows:-

starting point   ...   ...   A.27.c.9.5.

time   ...   ...   2.30 p.m.

route   ...   ...   Track to Road Junction O.13.b.9.5.
                                thence by ARRAS - FAMPOUX Road to
                                track N.15.c.9.5. where guides will
                                be met.

order of march   ...   ...   A. B. Hq. (saddles), C, D.

distance   ...   ...   200 yards between platoons or
                                equivalent.

dress   ...   ...   Marching Order.

4. GUIDES.

Guides as follows:-
    1 for Battalion Headquarters.
    1 per platoon and 1 per Company stores, for "A", "B" &
        "C" coys. will be at N.15.c.9.5. at 6.30 p.m.
O.C. "D" Company will take over area allotted to him without guides.

5. TRENCH STORES.

All photographs, maps, and trench stores will be taken over. List of trench stores taken over will be forwarded to orderly room by 10 a.m. 4th instant.

6. TRANSPORT.

W.Q. and Company limbers will accompany the Battalion and will be unloaded as follows:-
    "A" and "B" Coys. at N.10.d.7.1.
    H.Q., "C", & "D" coys. at N.15.c.9.5.

7:/

Page 2.

7. **DISPOSITIONS:**
Sketch maps showing location of companies and their battle positions will be forwarded to orderly room by 12 a.m. 4th instant.

8. **COMPLETION OF RELIEF.**
Completion of relief will be notified by code "R.27 received".

9. **ADMINISTRATIVE INSTRUCTIONS:**
Administrative instructions will be issued later.

10. **A C K N O W L E D G E**

sd/ R. RIST, Capt. & Adj.,
6th Bn., Gordon Highlanders.

SECRET.   COPY NO. ......
                         6TH GORDON HIGHLANDERS.
ADMINISTRATIVE INSTRUCTIONS ISSUED IN CONJUNCTION WITH O.O. 207.
                         2nd September, 1918.

Reference Maps:-
    Sheet 51 B. 1/40,000
    Sheet 51 B. N.W. 1/20,000

1. MARCH.
        Two cookers will accompany the battalion to H.13.b.5.5.
where a halt will be made and tea issued.   Cookers will march in
rear of "A" Company.   Battalion will move off H.13.b.5.5. at 6 p.m.
in same order as before.

2. ECHELON "B".
        Echelon "B", as follows, will be left out of the line :-
    Lewis Gun and Musketry Instructors.
    Lewis Gun Class.
    R.S.M's Class.
    1 Cook per Company.

        Lieut. C.A. COWIE will be in command of Echelon "B".   He
will arrange accommodation with Area Commandant at MADAGASCAR.

3. CAMP.
        Lieut. W. WEIR will hand over accommodation in present
camp to Advance party of 6th Seaforth Highlanders who are taking
over the camp.

4. RATIONS ETC.
        Rations for 4th instant will be carried by the men.
Twelve tins of water per company & H.Q. will be taken on Limbers
and carried from unloading point.   Thereafter no water will be
brought up, as there are water points in the line.   Rations will
be brought up daily as follows :-
        H.Q. & "C" and "D" Companies   - To H.15.c.9.5. at 6 p.m. where
                                          Ration parties will meet Limbers.

        "A" & "B" Companies   - To H.18.d.7.1. at 6.30 p.m.
                                          where Ration parties will
                                          meet Limbers.

5. CAMP & SURROUNDINGS.
        This camp will be left scrupulously clean.   The usual
certificates will be rendered by 2.30 p.m.

6. ACKNOWLEDGE.

                                         Sd/ R. RISK, Captain & Adjutant,
                                               6th Gordon Highlanders.

Copies to :-
    All recipients of Operation Orders No. 207.

SECRET. 6TH GORDON HIGHLANDERS COPY NO......

CORRIGENDUM to Operation Orders No. 207 dated 2nd September, 1918.
3rd September, 1918

Reference Maps :-
   Sheet 51B., 1/40,000.
   Sheet 51B N.W., 1/20,000.

1. Reference para. 3 - "A" & "B" Companies and H.Q. Details will move to forward area by 'Bus. Starting time for "C" & "D" Companies will be 3 p.m. and NOT 2.30 p.m. as ordered.

2. There will be 10 'Buses at MADAGASCAR Cross Roads at 6.30 p.m. These are allotted as follows :-
      "A" Company - 4 'Buses.
      "B" Company - 4 "
      H.Q. Details - 2 "

"A" & "B" Companies and H.Q. Details will be told off in parties of 25 for embussing.
Debussing points will be as follows :-
      H.Q. Details - H.15.c.9.5.
      "A" & "B" Coys. - H.17.b.6.8.
Guides as already detailed will be at these points at 7 p.m.

3. Reference para. 6 - Only "C" & "D" Company Limbers will proceed at 3 p.m.
H.Q. and "A" & "B" Company Limbers will NOT be required.
Lewis Guns, water, dixies etc. for them will be taken on 'Buses and carried from debussing point.
Only one cooker will accompany "C" & "D" Companies to H.13.b.5.5. where tea will be issued.

4. ACKNOWLEDGE.

                                  Captain & Adjutant,
                                  6th Gordon Highlanders.

Copies to :-
   All recipients of Operation Orders No. 207.

SECRET.   The Gordon Highlanders   Copy No. 13

OPERATION ORDER No. 216

22nd September, 1918.

Reference Maps:-
    Sheets 44B., 51C., & 51N., 1/40,000.

1. **MOVE.**
    The Battalion will move from CHAPEAU-de-la-HAIE area by march route on 23rd September, 1918 to DUFF CAMP, A.27.a.9.2. to relieve the 6th Duke of Wellington's Regt.

2. **PARADE.**
    The Battalion will form up on Football Ground, WEST of Camp at 9.30 a.m. in mass.   Markers to report to R. S. M. on the ground at 9.20 a.m.
    DRESS: Marching Order.

3. BRIGADE STARTING POINT - Cross Roads, X.19. Central.
    TIME - 10.30 a.m.
    ROUTE - Cross Roads W.30.c.6.4. - Main LE PARCQ, ABBEVILLE, ARRAS Road - Cross Roads G.1.d.6.0.
    ORDER OF MARCH - H.Q., A., B., C., D.
    DISTANCE - 100 yards will be maintained between Companies and between "D" Company and Transport.

3. **ADVANCE PARTY.**
    1 N.C.O. per Company and Corporal FORBES for Battalion Hdqrs, will report to 2/Lieut. I.C. MORRISON, M.C. at Orderly Room at 8 a.m. Party will report to Staff Captain at VILLERS-AU-BOIS Station (1 mile N.W. of VILLERS-AU-BOIS) at 8.30 a.m. to proceed by motor lorry.

4. **HANDING OVER.**
    Billets will be left scrupulously clean. Lieut. J. RECTOR, M.C. will hand over to District Commandant. All Camp stores, etc. and forward receipts for same to Battalion Headquarters by 6 p.m., 23rd instant.
    He will also obtain and forward a certificate that the Camp and Horse-Lines have been left in a clean and sanitary condition.

5. **LOCATION.**
    Q.M. Store and Transport Lines will be at COLLINGWOOD CAMP about A.28.c.1.1. (Ref. Map 51N.)

6. **ACKNOWLEDGE.**

                            (Signed) R. NEW, Captain & Adjutant,
                                6th Bn., The Gordon Highlanders.

Copies to:-
    No. 1 File.
       2 H.Q. 152nd Infantry Brigade.
       3 O.C. 6th Duke of Wellington's Regt.
       4 - 7 Companies.
       8 H.Q. Details.
       9 M.O. & Q.M.
      10 Lieut. J. RECTOR, M.C.
      11 2/Lieut. I. C. MORRISON, M.C.
      12 Headquarters Mess.
      13 War Diary.

SECRET. Copy No. 13

The Gordon Highlanders.

ADMINISTRATIVE INSTRUCTIONS issued in conjunction with O.O. 210.

22nd September, 1918.

1. All Camp Stores in DIFF CAMP will be taken over and lists forwarded by Officers Commanding Companies and 2/Lieut. I.O. MORISON, M.C. to Battalion Headquarters by 7 p.m. 23rd., instant, special attention being paid to checking ammunition, reserve rations, tents, trench shelters and tarpaulins.
   2/Lieut. I. O. MORISON, M.C. will also take over all maps, Defence Schemes and details of work in hand and proposed.

2. Valises will be collected from officers' huts at 8.30 a.m. and Mess Kits and Orderly Room boxes at 9 a.m.

3. Transport Officer will detail a mounted N.C.O. to take over Transport Lines of 6th Duke of Wellington's Regt. at 9.30 a.m.

4. Quartermaster will detail a guide to proceed with Advance Party to VILLERS-AU-BOIS Station to guide back a motor lorry. This lorry may be used for two trips to move Battalion baggage.

(Signed) R. NEW, Captain & Adjutant,
6th Bn., The Gordon Highlanders.

Copies to all recipients of O.O. 210.

6th Battn., THE BLACK HIGHLANDERS.

Amendment to Operation Order No. 211 dated 28th September, 1918.

29th September, 1918.

Para. 3 should be amended to read :-

Distance - 10 yards between Platoons
  instead of
  200 yards between Companies.

Acknowledge

(Signed) J. COIIAR, Lieut. & Adjt.
6th Bn., The Gordon Highlanders.

Copies to :-
All recipients of Operation Order No. 211.

SECRET.   THE GORDON HIGHLANDERS.   COPY NO. 11

OPERATION ORDER NO. 211.

28th September, 1918.

Reference Map:-
    SHEET. 51B.N.W. (1/20,000).

1. RELIEF.
    The 6th Bn., The Gordon Highlanders will relieve the 7th Bn., The
Gordon Highlanders in reserve in the ALBUVILE Sector to-morrow 29th
September, 1918.
    Companies will take over from the same Companies of the 7th
Bn., The Gordon Highlanders as follows:-
    "C" Coy. in COOLEY TRENCH and BAY AVENUE.
    "D" Coy. in CAMELLIA TRENCH.
    Headquarters, "A" & "B" Coys. in Railway Embankment Q.13.d.& c.

2. ADVANCE PARTY.
    An advance party as follows:-
        1 Lieut. J. I. SMITH and Cpl. GILBERT for Headquarters,
        1 Officer and 1 N.C.O. per Company,
will parade at orderly room at 11 a.m.

3. ORDER OF MARCH.
    The Battalion will march off as follows:-

    Starting Point   -   A.27.a.9.5.
    Time   -   2.30 p.m.
    Route   -   Track to Road Junction Q.15.b.5.5. thence
                            by ALBUM - FAMPOUX Road.
    Order of March   -   "C", "D", H.Q., "A", "B".
    Distance   -   200 yards between Companies.
    Dress   -   Marching order.
    Guides   -   None.

4. TRENCH STORES.
    All Maps, Photographs, Programmes of Work, and Trench Stores
will be taken over.
    Lists of Trench Stores taken over will be forwarded to Orderly
Room by 9 p.m. on 29th September, 1918.

5. TRANSPORT.
    Battalion and M.G. limbers will accompany the Battalion.

6. LOCATIONS.
    Sketch Maps showing location of Companies will be forwarded to
Orderly Room by 9 p.m. 29th instant.

7. COMPLETION OF RELIEF.
    Completion of Relief will be notified by the code word
"HOWARD".

8.   ACKNOWLEDGE.

                            sd/. J. COLLIE, Lieut. & A/Adjutant.
                                 6th Bn., The Gordon Highlanders.

Issued at 11 p.m. 28.9.18.

Copies to:-
    No. 1   File.
            and all recipients of S.S. issued herewith.

SECRET.   THE GORDON HIGHLANDERS.   Copy No...11....

ADMINISTRATIVE INSTRUCTIONS issued in conjunction with O.O. No. 21.
==

                    28th September, 1918.
                    - - - - - - - - - -

1. Q.M. STORES & TRANSPORT LINES:
        Q.M. Stores and Transport Lines will remain in present location.

2. PERSONNEL LEFT AT TRANSPORT LINES.
        Above will consist of :-
            3 L.G. Instructors and Lewis Gun Class.
            S.B.'s Class.
            1 Cook per Company.
        Lieut. M. GRAY will be in command of this personnel, which
will be accommodated in BIVOUAC TENTS. Nominal Rolls of personnel
left out to be rendered to Orderly Room by 12 noon, 29th instant.

3. CAMP:
        2/Lieut. L. ROBERTSON, D.C.M., and C/L. TOMBES will hand over
accommodation, stores, etc., in present Camp.
        The Camp will be left scrupulously clean. The usual certificates
will be rendered to Orderly Room by 2.30 p.m.

4. RATIONS.
        Rations will be brought up by limber daily as follows :-
            H.Q., "A" and "B" Coys. to S.15.b.9.9. at 5 p.m.
            "C" and "D" Coys. to COW Valley, S.15.b.1.5. at 5.15 p.m.
        Sandbags sent up with rations will be carefully kept and
returned the following day to Q.M. Stores.
        There are Water Points in the line.

5. BLANKETS:
        Blankets securely rolled by sections and clearly labelled will
be dumped at Q.M. Stores by 11 a.m. to-morrow 29th instant.

                                    sd/. J. DITTON, Lieut. & A/Adjutant,
                                         6th Bn., The Gordon Highlanders.

Copies to :-
        No. 1   File.
            2   H.Q., 152nd Inf. Bde.
            3   C.O., 7th Bn. The Gordon Highrs.
        4 - 7   O. C. Companies.
            8   H.Q. Details.
            9   Q.M.
           10   M.O.
           11   H.Q. Mess.
           12   War Diary.
        13 & 14 Spare.